THE POWER OF GOD

The Power of God

A Jonathan Edwards Commentary on the Book of Romans

EDITED AND COMPILED BY

David S. Lovi &
Benjamin Westerhoff

PICKWICK *Publications* · Eugene, Oregon

THE POWER OF GOD
A Jonathan Edwards Commentary on the Book of Romans

Pickwick Publications
An Imprint of Wipf and Stock Publishers
199 W. 8th Ave., Suite 3
Eugene, OR 97401

www.wipfandstock.com

ISBN 13: 978-1-62032-012-9

Cataloging-in-Publication data:

Lovi, David S.

The power of God : a Jonathan Edwards commentary on the book of Romans / edited by David S. Lovi and Benjamin Westerhoff.

p.; 23 cm—Includes index.

ISBN 13: 978-1-62032-012-9

1. Edwards, Jonathan, 1703–1758. 2. Bible. N.T. Romans—Commentaries. I. Westerhoff, Benjamin. II. Sweeney, Douglas. III. Title.

BX7260.E3 L594 2013

Manufactured in the USA.

For my wife Amy, I cannot express how much you mean to me. You are truly my beloved.

—David

For Maria, you're my wife for life. I love you.
Isaiah, I love you my son. Isaiah 9:6

—Ben

Contents

Foreword

The book you now hold in your hands is a labor of love—love for the biblical book of Romans, love for the preacher Jonathan Edwards (1703–58), love for the teacher John Gerstner (1914–96), and love for the Christian church today.

Paul's epistle to the Romans is one of the most beloved writings in the entire biblical canon, especially for Augustinians and Protestants. It is the subject of thousands of commentaries, many by the most important doctors of the church: Augustine, Aquinas, Luther, Calvin, Hodge, and Barth, to name a few. It offers the doctrines of sin, the gospel, and salvation in a nutshell. It is the basis for the structure of the first Protestant textbook in what later came to be categorized as systematic theology, Philip Melanchthon's *Loci Communes* (1521). It is a frequently-cited sourcebook of the Reformation *solas*, which teach that salvation comes by grace alone through faith alone because of the work of God through Christ alone. It is the site of the "Romans road," a standard tool for sharing the gospel used by myriad evangelists in the evangelical movement. It is a central text of scripture, in short, employed by many readers as a key to the whole Bible.

Jonathan Edwards never published a major commentary on Romans. He did, however, preach about and write about Romans at numerous times throughout his life. Though he is highly regarded today as a great literary artist, natural scientist, philosopher and psychologist of religion, he was chiefly a biblical thinker, a minister of the Word. And inasmuch as he remains one of the most important thought leaders in all of Christian history, it is high time that someone has put together a major collection of his writings on the biblical book of Romans.

John Gerstner once attempted to compile a similar volume. A famous conference speaker and faculty member at Pittsburgh Seminary as well as Trinity Evangelical Divinity School, he was enjoined by Perry Miller to edit a volume of Edwards' sermons on the epistle to the Romans for *The Works of Jonathan Edwards* published by Yale University Press. He never finished this undertaking. But he did spend many summers poring over Edwards' manuscripts. These labors bore fruit in several other publishing projects and, perhaps more importantly, in the pioneering work Gerstner did to promote Edwards among evangelical Christians during the mid-twentieth-century Edwards renaissance.

David Lovi and Ben Westerhoff are two of the evangelicals inspired by Gerstner's work. It is fitting, then, that they are the ones to complete what Gerstner started: a major compilation of Edwards' work in the book of Romans. This is not a volume of sermons. Unlike Gerstner's own project, it contains biblical commentary from many different sources, including sermons, published treatises, and exegetical manuscripts. It is ordered canonically, much as a commentary would be. And it is aimed at Christian preachers and other ministers of the Word. Dr. Gerstner would be proud. In fact, if Edwards was correct about the lives of saints in heaven, Gerstner is looking down in gratitude for the work of Lovi and Westerhoff, joyful for its place in God's eternal plan of redemption.

Whether or not Edwards was right about the lives of those in heaven, I am confident that the saints on earth will profit from this book. May it inspire and inform future ministers of the Word, helping them unlock the treasure chest of scripture for those they serve.

Douglas A. Sweeney
Professor of Church History and the History of Christian Thought;
Director of the Jonathan Edwards Center
Trinity Evangelical Divinity School

Introduction

As the passing of two and a half centuries has shown, the ministry and thought of the greatest American theologian, Jonathan Edwards, not only lives on today, but is still peerless in its depth of insight. That simple fact makes it almost shocking that until now, no one has endeavored to compile and collate his comments on individual books of the Bible.

In fact, the only thing close to a commentary that Edwards ever wrote was a private notebook on the book of Revelation. However, anyone who has delved into Edwards' oeuvre can very quickly deduce that he has commented extensively on the Bible in addition to Revelation. John H. Gerstner, who wrote extensively on the theology of Edwards, had once averred that Edwards probably commented on every verse of the Bible. While that was a slight exaggeration on Gerstner's part, it is not very far off base. The Edwards corpus is extraordinarily massive, and that at a time when paper was a scarce commodity. Edwards' comments on particular Bible verses however, are found in the diaspora of his voluminous writings, spanning sermons, books, miscellaneous comments, private notebooks, letters, a biography, treatises, his "Blank Bible", and various handbooks.

In 2010, the editors decided that it would be helpful to gather everything Jonathan Edwards ever wrote on the book of Romans and organize it into a commentary. So that is what we have done. Readers of this Romans commentary will be pleased to possess almost everything Edwards has ever written, gleaned from his massive corpus concerning the book of Romans, the exception being only a very small amount of un-transcribed material. In addition, we have included the sermon explication portions of all of Edwards' sermons on Romans. Edwards' explications were always given at the beginning of his sermons and they served to unfold the particular passage in which he was engaged. We have found them to be very helpful, both in understanding the progression of Edwards' preaching style (he used far more sermon notes in the first half of his ministry, and less after he encountered George Whitefield), and also his extraordinary depth of insight when it came to expounding a text.

Why Romans and why Edwards? Well, Romans contains core Christian soteriology and biblical theology. A number of theological themes found in Romans have emerged in recent years as points of contention. For example, N. T. Wright and John Piper have written several books in dialogue concerning the true nature of justification. Rob Bell's book *Love Wins* touches on God's wrath (or in his case, lack thereof), who it is directed towards, and how long it will last. We felt that since Romans is such a touch point of contention in our day, it would be good to have a voice from the past speak on it. Other themes such as Israel, predestination, the church, Christian living, faith, the Law, resurrection, sin and other biblical theological motifs are addressed in this epistle as well. So Romans was a logical choice for Edwards to weigh in on.

Why Jonathan Edwards? First of all, Edwards was incredibly prolific. Perry Miller has called him a genius and on par with Melville, Twain, and Emerson (*Jonathan Edwards* Miller, xvi). As one of the greatest minds in American history, and one of America's greatest pastors, we thought that his comments on the book of Romans would be an invaluable resource for pastors, theologians, New Testament scholars, Edwards scholars, church historians, and curious readers of the Bible. We hope that Edwards' commentary on Romans will lay open next to other respected commentaries, as pastors prepare sermons, or as church historians attempt to understand Edwards' view on God's Sovereignty (see his comments on Romans 9). We are certain that the material contained herein will fire up the hearts and minds of students of the Bible and of Jonathan Edwards.

We would like to extend our utmost thanks to the people who have made this book possible: Dr. Doug Sweeney and Dr. Kenneth Minkema, thank you so much for encouraging this project, and for your consistent willingness to lend advice and assistance. It is no exaggeration to say that this book would not have come to fruition without your help. A word of appreciation and thanks must also be given to the late Dr. John H. Gerstner who being dead yet speaketh! Gerstner's lectures on the Theology of Jonathan Edwards were the original impetus for this commentary, and we have been continually blessed by listening to them over and over throughout the years. Thank you so much to our lovely wives, Amy Lovi and Maria Westerhoff. You have put up with our spending long hours in front of the computer screen and on the phone, and you have done so with much grace! May the Lord reward your patience! We would like to also thank Christian Amondson and Robin Parry from Pickwick Publications and Wipf & Stock for offering to publish this book.

A note on the text: We present Edwards to you as John Gerstner liked to say, "warts and all" just as the manuscripts are in the Yale archives. Sometimes Edwards uses words like "don't" where we would use "doesn't," "ben't" for "be not," "mayn't" for "may not" etc. Often modern editions of Edwards' works omit these idiosyncratic spellings, but in order to preserve the language and in keeping with the integrity of the Yale edition of his works (www.http://edwards.yale.edu/), we give you Edwards in his own words.

Soli Deo Gloria!

ROMANS CHAPTER 1

Romans 1:1–3

All the promises which were made to the church of old, of the Messiah as a future Saviour, from that made to our first parents in paradise, to that which was delivered by the prophet Malachi, show it to be impossible that Christ should not have persevered in perfect holiness. The ancient predictions given to God's church, of the Messiah as a Savior, were of the nature of promises; as is evident by the predictions themselves, and the manner of delivering them. But they are expressly, and very often called promises in the New Testament; as in *Luke 1:54–55*, *Luke 1:72–73*; *Acts 13:32–33*; *Romans 1:1–3*; and ch. *15:8*; *Hebrews 6:13*, etc. These promises were often made with great solemnity, and confirmed with an oath; as in *Genesis 22:16–17*, "By myself have I sworn, saith the Lord, that in blessing, I will bless thee, and in multiplying, I will multiply thy seed, as the stars of heaven, and as the sand which is upon the seashore: . . . and in thy seed shall all the nations of the earth be blessed. ***Freedom of the Will (WJE Online Vol. 1)***

Romans 1:3–4

Christ's anointing don't only mark out Christ as being our mediator, but 'tis his anointing that qualifies and fits him for the work of mediator; hence arises the value and efficacy of his sufferings and obedience. If he had not been anointed, they would not have availed; because if it had not been for this anointing with the Holy Ghost, he would not have been united to the divine nature. 'Tis by the Holy Spirit that Christ is the Son of God. *Romans 1:3–4*, "Concerning his Son Jesus Christ, which was made of the seed of David according to the flesh; and declared to be the Son of God with power, according to the Spirit of holiness." Hence arises the value of Christ's sacrifice. *Hebrews 9:14*, "How much more shall the blood of Christ, who through the eternal Spirit offered himself without spot to God, purge your consciences from dead works." It was by virtue of this anointing, his thus having the Spirit, that he was accepted and justified as our mediator. *1 Timothy 3:16*, "Justified in the Spirit." And therefore, the same Holy Ghost by which he was begotten in the womb of the Virgin Mary, was that by which he was begotten again from the dead in the womb of the earth. *1 Peter 3:18*, "Put to death in the flesh, quickened by the Spirit."

Romans 1:4

Hence it is that the Spirit of God, the third person in the Trinity, is so often called the Holy Spirit, as though "Holy" were an epithet some way or other peculiarly belonging to him, which can be no other way than that the holiness of God does consist in him. He is not only infinitely holy as the Father and the Son are, but he is the holiness of God itself in the abstract. The holiness of the Father and the Son does consist in breathing forth this Spirit. Therefore he is not only called the Holy Spirit, but the "Spirit of holiness." *Romans 1:4*, "According to the Spirit of holiness." ***Writings on the Trinity, Grace, and Faith (WJE Online Vol. 21)***

Romans 1:5

See *1 Corinthians 1:1*. "Paul, called to be an apostle of Jesus Christ *through the will of God*." St. Paul, when he calls himself an apostle, does commonly add some such clause, as here, "through the will of God." So *2 Corinthians 1:1*, "Paul, an apostle of Jesus Christ by the will of God"; and the very same words, *Ephesians 1:1*, and *Colossians 1:1*, and *2 Timothy 1:1*. And *1 Timothy 1:1*, "Paul, an apostle of Jesus Christ by the commandment of God our Savior, and Lord Jesus Christ"; and *Romans 1:1*, "Paul, a servant of Jesus Christ, called to be an apostle, separated unto the gospel of God." *Romans 1:5*, "By whom we have received grace and apostleship," which was because he continually carried a deep sense of his unworthiness to be an apostle, who before was so great a sinner; and how it was not owing to anything in him that he was promoted to such dignity, but only to the sovereign will, and pleasure, and free grace of God, that, of a persecutor of the church, made him an apostle in the church. Therefore when he takes the honor of the name of an apostle, he ascribes [it] to God's sovereign pleasure and grace. The cause of it is a sense of what he expresses in *1 Corinthians 15:9–10*. "For I am the least of the apostles, and am not meet to be called an apostle, because I persecuted the church of God. But by the grace of God I am what I am." *Ephesians 3:8*, "Unto me, who am less than the least of all saints, is this grace given, that I should preach among the Gentiles the unsearchable riches of Christ." ***Notes on Scripture (WJE Online Vol. 15)***

Romans 1:5

"By whom we have received grace and apostleship, for obedience to the faith among all nations *for his name*." *Matthew 19:29*, "Everyone that forsaketh houses or brethren, etc. . . . *for my name's sake*, shall receive an hundred fold, and shall inherit everlasting life." *3 John 7*, "Because that *for his name's sake* they went forth, taking nothing of the Gentiles." *Revelation 2:3*, "And hast borne, and hast patience, and *for my name's sake* hast labored, and hast not fainted." ***Ethical Writings (WJE Online Vol. 8)***

"By whom we have received grace and apostleship," which was because he continually carried a deep sense of his unworthiness to be an apostle, who before was so great a sinner; and how it was not owing to anything in him that he was promoted to such dignity, but only to the sovereign will, and pleasure, and free grace of God, that, of a persecutor of the church, made him an apostle in the church. Therefore when he takes the honor of the name of an apostle, he ascribes [it] to God's sovereign pleasure and grace. The cause of it is a sense of what he expresses in *1 Corinthians 15:9–10*. "For I am the least of the apostles, and am not meet to be called an apostle, because I persecuted the church of God. But by the grace of God I am what I am." *Ephesians 3:8*, "Unto me, who am less than the least of all saints, is this grace given, that I should preach among the Gentiles the unsearchable riches of Christ." ***Notes on Scripture (WJE Online Vol. 15)***

Romans 1:6

This is ascribed to Jesus Christ. *Romans 1:6*, "Among whom also ye are the called of Jesus Christ." *1 Corinthians 7:17*, "as the Lord hath called everyone." *John 10:3*, "and he calleth his own sheep by name, and leadeth them out." *John 10:16*, "other sheep have I, which are not of this fold: them also I must bring in, and they shall hear my voice." *Ephesians 1:18*, "that ye may know what is the hope of his calling." ***The "Miscellanies," (Entry Nos. 1153–1360) (WJE Online Vol. 23)***

Romans 1:7

The apostles in the very superscription or direction of their letters to these churches, and in their salutations at the beginning of their epistles, speak of them as gracious persons. For instance, the apostle Peter in the direction of his first letter to all professing Jewish Christians through many countries, says thus [*1 Peter 1:1–2*], "To the strangers scattered through Pontus, etc. elect, according to the foreknowledge of God the Father, through sanctification of the Spirit unto obedience, and sprinkling of the blood of Jesus Christ." And in directing his second epistle to the same persons, he says thus [*2 Peter 1:1*], "Simon Peter a servant and an apostle of Jesus Christ, to them that have obtained like precious faith with us," etc. And the apostle Paul directs his epistle to the Romans thus [*Romans 1:7*], "To them that be at Rome, beloved of God." ***Ecclesiastical Writings (WJE Online Vol. 12)***

The apostles continually in their epistles speak to them and of them as supposing and judging them to be gracious persons. Thus the apostle Paul in his epistle to the church of the Romans, ch. *Romans 1:7*, speaks or the members of that church as "beloved of God." In ch. *Romans 6:17–18*, etc. he "thanks God that they had obeyed from the heart that form of doctrine which had been delivered them, and were made free from sin, and become the servants of righteousness," etc. ***Ecclesiastical Writings (WJE Online Vol. 12)***

So the Apostle, in the beginning of his epistle to the Romans, says that he writes to those at Rome that were "beloved of God, called to be saints" [*Romans 1:7*], and yet he exhorts 'em to be transformed by the renewing of their mind. *Romans 12:1–2*, "I beseech you therefore, by the mercies of God, that ye present your bodies a living sacrifice, holy, acceptable unto God, which is your reasonable service. And be not conformed unto this world: but be ye transformed by the renewing of your mind." ***Sermons and Discourses, 1739–1742 (WJE Online Vol. 22)***

So it was with the church of the ROMANS. The Apostle, in his epistle to the members of that church, calls 'em "beloved of God." *Romans 1:7*, "To all that are at Rome, beloved of God, called to be saints"; i.e. in a judgment of charity, they were such as were beloved of God. So in *Romans 6:17–18*, etc., he says to 'em, "ye were the servants of sin, but ye have obeyed from the heart that form of doctrine which was delivered you," and "being made free from sin, are become the servants of righteousness." ***Sermons and Discourses, 1743–1758 (WJE Online Vol. 25)***

Romans 1:8

Because it is thus profitable to hear of the work of God in other places, therefore the Apostle praises God that the faith of the Christian Romans was spoken of throughout the whole world. *Romans 1:8*, "First, I thank my God through Jesus Christ for you all, that your faith is spoken of throughout the world." ***Sermons and Discourses, 1739–1742 (WJE Online Vol. 22)***

Romans 1:11

So he speaks of his earnest care for others, *2 Corinthians 8:16*, and of his bowels of pity or mercy towards them, *Philippians 2:1*, and of his concern for others, even to anguish of heart, *2 Corinthians 2:4*. "For out of much affliction, and anguish of heart, I wrote unto you, with many tears; not that ye should be grieved; but that ye might know the love which I have more abundantly unto you." He speaks of the great conflict of his soul for them (*Colossians 2:1*). He speaks of great and continual grief that he had in his heart from compassion to the Jews (*Romans 9:2*). He speaks of his mouth's being opened, and his heart enlarged towards Christians, *2 Corinthians 6:11*. "O ye Corinthians, our mouth is open unto you, our heart is enlarged!" He often speaks of his affectionate and longing desires (*1 Thessalonians 2:8, Romans 1:11, Philippians 1:8* and ch. *4:1*, II *Timothy 1:4*). ***Religious Affections (WJE Online Vol. 2)***

Thus saving knowledge is called "spiritual understanding." *Colossians 1:9*, "We desire that ye might be filled with the knowledge of his will in all wisdom and spiritual understanding." So the influences, graces and comforts of God's Spirit are called "spiritual blessings." *Ephesians 1:3*, "Blessed be the God and Father of our Lord Jesus Christ, who hath blessed us with all spiritual blessings in heavenly places in Christ." So the imparting of any gracious benefit is called the imparting of a spiritual gift. *Romans 1:11*, "For I long to see you, that I may impart unto you some spiritual gift." And the fruits of the Spirit which are offered to God are called "spiritual sacrifices." *1 Peter 2:5*, "A spiritual priesthood, to offer up spiritual sacrifices, acceptable to God by Jesus Christ." And a spiritual person signifies the same in Scripture as a gracious person, and sometimes one that is much under the influence of grace. *1 Corinthians 2:15*, "He that is spiritual judgeth all things, yet he himself is judged of no man"; and *1 Corinthians 3:1*, "And I, brethren, could not speak unto you as unto spiritual, but as unto carnal." *Galatians 6:1*, "If a man be overtaken in a fault, ye which are spiritual, restore such an one in the spirit of meekness." And to be graciously minded is called in Scripture a being "spiritually minded." ***Writings on the Trinity, Grace, and Faith (WJE Online Vol. 21)***

Romans 1:16

"I am not ashamed of the gospel of Christ. That I should be ashamed to preach it at Rome, the metropolis and mistress of the world." It is the power of God to salvation to everyone that believeth, to the Jew first, and also to the Greek." *Ques.* How is the gospel "the power of God to salvation to those that believe, to the Jew first?" And so it is said in the Romans 2:10, that God will render "glory, honor, and peace to every man that worketh good, to the Jew first." *Arts.* God was ready to justify all that believed in Christ, and to reward all that work good, but especially the Jews, for the peculiar favor he bore to that nation for their forefathers' sakes, as Romans 11:28, and because they were born in covenant, or were his covenant people by descent. See *Romans 2:25*, "For circumcision verily profiteth," etc. ***The "Blank Bible" (WJE Online Vol. 24)***

Romans 1:16–18

Romans 1:16–18. JUSTIFICATION. CHRIST'S RIGHTEOUSNESS. "For I am not ashamed of the gospel of Christ," etc., "For therein is the righteousness of God revealed from faith to faith; as it is written, The just shall live by faith. For the wrath of God is revealed from heaven against all ungodliness and unrighteousness of men." In these verses I would note two things. First, that here, in the beginning of this discourse of his of the wickedness of the whole world, both Jews and Gentiles, that is continued from this place to the *Romans 3:19*, *Romans 3:20*, and *Romans 3:21* verses of *Romans 3*, as well as in the conclusion in that part of the *Romans 3*, he manifests his design in it all to be to show that all are guilty, and in a state of condemnation, and therefore can't be saved by their own righteousness, that it must be by the righteousness of God through Christ received by faith alone. He here in the *Romans 3:17* asserts that 'tis thus only that men have justification, and then in the *Romans 3:18* enters on the reason why, "For the wrath of God is revealed from heaven against all ungodliness and unrighteousness of men, who hold the truth in unrighteousness"; and so goes on, setting forth the ungodliness and unrighteousness of men through most of those three first chapters, and then at the end, concludes his argument as he began it, that, seeing all are under sin, "Therefore by the deeds of the law shall no flesh living be justified in his sight" [*Romans 3:20*], but that 'tis by "the righteousness of God which is by the faith of Christ" [*Romans 3:22*]. Secondly, I observe that by "the righteousness of God" in this place can't be meant only God's way of justifying a sinner, but hereby is meant the moral, legal righteousness which God had provided for sinners. 'Tis evident by two things. 1. 'Tis the righteousness or justice which those that are justified have, by which they are righteous or just, as is evident by the Apostle's selecting that passage of the Old Testament to cite on this occasion, "The *just* shall live by faith" [*Habakkuk 2:4*]. 2. 'Tis evident by the antithesis, for here 'tis most manifest that the "righteousness of God," by which God's people are just, in one verse, is opposed to the "unrighteousness of men," by which they in themselves are unjust, as is evident by the argument of the Apostle in these verses. 'Tis a righteousness that believers are vested with, as is evident by *Romans 3:22–23*. The same is also manifest by the antithesis in that place; the same is manifest both those ways, by *Philippians 3:9*. ***Notes on Scripture (WJE Online Vol. 15)***

Romans 1:17

By "righteousness" here seems to be meant the way of the justification of sinners by Christ. 'Tis not only meant Christ's active [righteousness]: a great deal more is intended than that. So by the term "righteousness," when it is spoken with respect to the Mediator in Scripture, is almost always thus to be taken. Christ is called "the Lord our righteousness," that is, he is he in whom we have justification. So it is said, in the Lord Jehovah we have righteousness and strength [*Isaiah 12:2*, *Isaiah 26:4*], that is, in him we have acceptance with God as righteous. We read, *Romans 4:11*, that circumcision was the seal of the righteousness of faith, i.e. a seal of the way of justification by faith; and [in the] thirteenth verse, that the promise that Abraham should be heir [of the world] was through the righteousness of faith. So, very evidently, it is to be understood, *Romans 3:21–22* and *Romans 1:17*. It is not to be understood of the holiness of God's nature, or the personal holiness or innocence of Christ, but God's way of justifying man. ***Sermons and Discourses: 1723–1729 (WJE Online Vol. 14)***

And that God in justification has respect, not only to the first act of faith, but also to future persevering acts, in this sense, viz. as expressed in life, seems manifest by *Romans 1:17*, "For therein is the righteousness of God revealed, from faith to faith: As it is written, The just shall live by faith." And *Hebrews 10:38–39*, "Now the just shall live by faith; but if any man draw back, my soul shall have no pleasure in him. But we are not of them who draw back unto perdition, but of them that believe to the saving of the soul." ***Sermons and Discourses, 1734–1738 (WJE Online Vol. 19)***

It seems to be because continuance in faith is necessary to continuance in justification, at least in part, that the Apostle expresses himself as he does, *Romans 1:17*, "For therein the righteousness of God is revealed from faith unto faith: as it is written, The just shall live by faith." Or the righteousness of God is revealed, as we receive it and have the benefit of it, from faith, or by faith, unto faith. For 'tis by faith that we first perceive and know this righteousness, and do at first receive and embrace it, and do at first become interested in it. And being once interested in it, we have the continuance of faith in the future persevering exercises of it made sure to us, which is necessary in order to a suitable continuance [in a] justified state. And, faith continuing, our interest in God's righteousness continues, and we are continued in a justified state, and shall certainly have the future eternal reward of righteousness. ***The "Miscellanies," (Entry Nos. 1153–1360) (WJE Online Vol. 23)***

"[T]he just shall live by faith" [*Romans 1:17*], agreeable to that, *1 Peter 1:5*, "We are kept by the power of God through faith unto salvation"; and agreeable to that, *Hebrews 10:35–39*, "Cast not away therefore your confidence, which hath great recompense of reward. For ye have need of patience, that, after ye have done the will of God, ye might receive the promise. For yet a little while, and he that shall come will come, and will not tarry. Now the just shall live by faith: but if any man draw back, my soul shall have no pleasure in him. But we are not of them who draw back unto perdition; but of them that believe to the saving of the soul"; and *Hebrews 3:6*, *Hebrews 3:14*, *Hebrews 3:18*, *Hebrews 3:19*, and *Hebrews 4:1*, *Hebrews 4:11*; *Hebrews 6:4*, *Hebrews 6:11*, *Hebrews 6:12*; and the former part of the *John 15*, "Abide in me, and I in you. . . . If a man abide not in me, he is cast forth as a branch . . . ; continue ye in my love. If ye keep my commandments, ye shall abide in my love; even as I have kept my Father's commandments, and abide in his love" [*John 15:4–10*]. It was impossible that Christ should not continue in his Father's love. He was entitled to such help and support from him as should be effectual to uphold him in obedience to his Father. And yet it was true that, if Christ had not kept the Father's commandments, he could not have continued in his love. He would have been cast out of favor. ***The "Miscellanies," (Entry Nos. 1153–1360) (WJE Online Vol. 23)***

Beware how you entertain any such doctrine as that there is no essential difference between common and saving faith, and that both consist in a mere assent of the understanding to the doctrines of religion. That this doctrine is false appears by what has been said; and if it be false, it must needs be exceedingly dangerous. Saving faith, as you well know, is abundantly insisted on in the Bible as in a peculiar manner the condition of salvation, being the thing by which we are justified. How much is that doctrine insisted on in the New Testament: we are [said to be] justified by faith, and by faith alone; by faith we are saved, and "This is the work of God, that we believe on him whom he hath sent" [*John 6:29*]; "The just shall live by faith" [*Romans 1:17*]; "We are all the children of God by faith in Jesus Christ" [*Galatians 3:26*]; "He that believeth shall be saved, and he that believeth not shall be damned" [*Mark 16:16*]. Therefore, doubtless saving faith, whatever that be, is the grand condition of an interest in Christ and his great salvation. And if it be so, of what vast importance is it that we should have [a] right notion [of] what it is; for certainly nothing at all—nothing in religion—is of greater importance than that which teaches us how we may be saved. If salvation itself be of infinite importance, then it is of equal importance that we don't mistake the terms of it; and if this be of infinite importance, then that doctrine that teaches that to be the terms that is not so, but very diverse, is infinitely dangerous. What we want a revelation from God for, chiefly, is to teach us the terms of his favor, and the way of salvation. And that which the revelation God has given us in the Bible teaches to be [the] way is faith in Christ; therefore, that doctrine that teaches something else to be saving faith, that is essentially another thing, teaches entirely another way of salvation, and therefore such doctrine does in effect make void the revelation we have in the Bible, as it makes void the special end of it, which is to teach us the true way of salvation. The gospel is the revelation of the way of life by faith in Christ; therefore, he that teaches something else to be that faith which is essentially diverse from what the gospel of Christ teaches, he teaches another gospel, and he does in effect teach another religion than the religion of Christ. For what is religion but that way of exercising our respect to God, which is the term of his favor and acceptance to a title to his eternal rewards? The Scripture teaches this in a special manner to be saving faith in Jesus Christ; therefore, he that teaches another faith instead of that teaches another religion. Therefore, such doctrine as I have opposed must needs be destructive and damnable, i.e. directly tending to man's damnation, leading such as embrace it to rest in something essentially different from the grand condition of salvation. ***Sermons and Discourses, 1743–1758 (WJE Online Vol. 25)***

Romans 1:18

Though there be a principle of atheism in the heart of all ungodly men, yet there is also a natural faculty of reason, and the atheistical principle never can so far prevail against the principle of reason as so far to hinder its exercise or wholly to put out the light of nature in this particular. God hath showed to every man his own existence by the light of nature; *Romans 1:19–20*, "Because that which may be known of God is manifest in them; for God hath showed it unto them. For the invisible things of him from the creation of the world are clearly seen, being understood by the things that are made" (*Romans 1:18*). So that the heathen held the truth in unrighteousness; *Romans 1:18*, "For the wrath of God is revealed from heaven against all ungodliness and unrighteousness of men, who hold the truth in unrighteousness." ***Sermons and Discourses, 1730–1733 (WJE Online Vol. 17)***

It seems to be a mistake of many that the Apostle, in what he says of men's wickedness in the *Romans 1*, has respect only to the Gentiles, and that in what he says in the *Romans 2*, he has respect only to the Jews. 'Tis true that in the *Romans 1* he evidently has his eye chiefly on the wickedness that prevailed [in the Gentile] world. But that is not his professed design in it, only to describe the sin of the pagan world, but the wickedness of the world of mankind. 'Tis all unrighteousness and ungodliness of men that hold the truth in unrighteousness. And in the *Romans 2* he has his eye chiefly on the Jews, but it is not his professed design to speak only of them, as appears by his beginning in the *Romans 2:1*, the universal terms that he uses in it. "Therefore thou art inexcusable, O MAN (not O Jew). WHOSOEVER thou art (*of mankind*, whether Jew or Gentile) that judgest," etc. In the *Romans 1:32*, the Apostle speaks of the wickedness of mankind in general, and shows how they "hold the truth in unrighteousness," as he had said before (*Romans 1:18*). And the special design of that verse is to set forth how they are all alike, and all agreed in wickedness, and in the same kind of wickedness. Though they all have that light that is sufficient to teach them that those that commit such things deserve the condemnation and wrath of God, and so death and destruction, which they are very ready to acknowledge and declare in the case of others when they see their wickedness, their unrighteousness, covetousness, maliciousness, envy, murder, debate, deceit, malignity, etc.: I say, though when they see others guilty of such things, they can easily see that they are worthy of death, and are forward to express it, yet they do the very same things, and not only so, but they show plainly that they have just such hearts. They show a full practical consent to all the wickedness of others that they are forward to condemn and to declare worthy of death. Thus unreasonable are they, and inconsistent with themselves. Thus the beginning of the *Romans 2* comes in. "Therefore thou art inexcusable, O man, whosoever thou art that judgest." Thou that art forward to condemn others as worthy of death, "for wherein thou judgest another, thou condemnest thyself." Thou art very unreasonable and exceeding inconsistent with thyself, "for thou that judgest dost the same things," and showest that thou hast pleasure in their practice. There is at the same time that you judge them, a full practical consent to and good liking of the very same practices. So God of old condemned the Jews for that in their practice they had justified Samaria and Sodom, and were a comfort to 'em, and yet had judged them (*Ezekiel 16:51–52, Ezekiel 16:54*). ***The "Blank Bible" (WJE Online Vol. 24)***

Romans 1:19–20

Doubtless it is the supreme God which is here spoken [of]. And what Godhead of the supreme God—that which is clearly to be seen by the creation of the world—but his supreme Godhead? And what can that invisible glory and power of this God here spoken of be but that by which he is distinguished from other beings and may be known to be what he is? 'Tis said, that which may be known of God is clearly manifest by this work. But doubtless one thing, and infinitely the most important thing, that may be known of God is his supreme dignity and glory, that glory of his which he has as supreme God. But if the creation of the world ben't a work peculiar to him, how are these things so clearly manifested by this work? ***The "Miscellanies," (Entry Nos. 1153–1360) (WJE Online Vol. 23)***

Romans 1:19

The whole creation of God preaches to us; its creatures declare to us his majesty, his wisdom and power, and mercy: *Psalms 19:1–2*, [*Psalms 19:4*],

"The heavens declare the glory of God; and the firmament showeth his handiwork. Day unto day uttereth speech, and night unto night showeth knowledge. Their line is gone out through all the earth, and their words to the end of the world." *Job 12:7–8*, "But ask now the beasts, and they shall teach thee; and the fowls of the air, and they shall tell thee: or speak to the earth, and it shall teach thee: and the fishes of the sea shall declare unto thee." [See also] *Romans 1:19–20*. If we look to the heavens or the earth; or birds, beasts, or fishes; or plants and trees: if we do but take notice of it, they all declare to us that we ought to worship, to fear, to love and obey, the God that made all these things. The workmanship of God in our own bodies and souls proclaims aloud the same: all the creatures do declare the same thing. ***Sermons and Discourses 1720–1723 (WJE Online Vol. 10)***

Romans 1:20

If any object against what has been maintained, that it tends to atheism; I know not on what grounds such an objection can be raised, unless it be that some atheists have held a doctrine of necessity which they suppose to be like this. But if it be so, I am persuaded the Arminians would not look upon it just, that their notion of freedom and contingence should be charged with a tendency to all the errors that ever any embraced, who have held such opinions. The Stoic philosophers, whom the Calvinists are charged with agreeing with, were no atheists, but the greatest theists, and nearest akin to Christians in their opinions concerning the unity and the perfections of the Godhead, of all the heathen philosophers. And Epicurus, that chief father of atheism, maintained no such doctrine of necessity, but was the greatest maintainer of contingence. The doctrine of necessity, which supposes a necessary connection of all events, on some antecedent ground and reason of their existence, is the only medium we have to prove the being of God. And the contrary doctrine of contingence, even as maintained by Arminians (which certainly implies or infers, that events may come into existence, or begin to be, without dependence on anything foregoing, as their cause, ground or reason) takes away all proof of the being of God; which proof is summarily expressed by the Apostle, in *Romans 1:20*. And this is a tendency to atheism with a witness. So that indeed it is the doctrine of Arminians, and not of the Calvinists, that is justly charged with a tendency to atheism; it being built on a foundation that is the utter subversion of every demonstrative argument for the proof of a deity. ***Freedom of the Will (WJE Online Vol. 1)***

Romans 1:21

"Glorified him not as God, neither were thankful." The respect we owe to God consists in two things, viz. a supreme regard to God for what he is in himself as his divine glory, and that respect we owe him for his goodness to us. Both are here mentioned. ***The "Blank Bible" (WJE Online Vol. 24)***

Romans 1:22

Their foolish heart was darkened, as the Apostle says (*Romans 1:22*). Being without revelation, notwithstanding all the light of natural reason, they sunk into brutish ignorance and into such vain, absurd, and ridiculous conceptions of things, that we that have been taught better by divine revelation, can scarce conceive how it was possible for rational creatures to have such thoughts. There was not one nation in the whole world, but that of the Jews, that retained the knowledge of the true God. Instead of worshipping him, they worshipped the sun, moon, and stars, and their dead ancestors and kings. They made images of gold, silver, and brass, and worshipped them as gods. These images they made some in the shape of man; some in the form of calves and oxen; [some in the form of] serpents; some in monstrous shapes, as half human and half of a beast or fish. Some worshipped the fire, and some worshipped devils that used to appear in bodily shapes to them. Some worshipped beasts themselves, such as bulls and serpents. Some worshipped the growth of their fields and gardens. Some made gods of certain mortal diseases, and worshipped them, because they were afraid of them. And the manner of their worshipping their gods showed the gross darkness they were in, which was with innumerable ridiculous and monstrous rites and ceremonies. We read in Scripture of their cutting themselves, till the blood gushed out upon them. Some of their gods they worshipped with most obscene rites. They worshipped the god Bacchus by drunken revels to his honor, which they thought pleasing to him, because he was the god of wine. Others they worshipped with most obscene rites, acts of fornication, and other horridly obscene actions, and unnatural impurities, as not to be mentioned; and thought they did what was well pleasing to their gods. And the images of the gods that they thus worshipped were exhibited naked in a most obscene manner. So it seems to have been with the god of the Moabites that is called Baalpeor, which is a word that signifies one that publicly and boastingly shows his nakedness. And the Moabites used to worship him by acts of uncleanness.

Hence the children of Israel, when they offered "in the matter of Peor," committed whoredom, as we are told, with the daughters of Moab, [in the] twenty-fifth of Numbers, of which Zimri and Cozbi were an instance. It was a common thing through the heathen world for 'em to offer human sacrifices to their idols, sometimes adult persons and sometimes children. So they worshipped the god Moloch. They were wont to offer their children to be cruelly tormented to death in the fire to that idol, burning them to death in burning brass. ***Sermons and Discourses, 1734–1738 (WJE Online Vol. 19)***

Romans 1:24

Dr. Whitby asserts freedom, not only from coaction, but necessity, to be essential to anything deserving the name of "sin," and to an action's being culpable: in these words (*Discourse on Five Points*, ed. 3, p. 348), "If they be thus necessitated, then neither their sins of omission or commission could deserve that name; it being essential to the nature of sin, according to St. Austin's definition, that it be an action, *a quo liberum est abstinere*. Three things seem plainly necessary to make an action or omission culpable: 1. That it be in our power to perform or forbear it: for, as Origen, and all the fathers say, no man is blameworthy for not doing what he could not do. And elsewhere the Doctor insists, that when any do evil of necessity, what they do is no vice, that they are guilty of no fault, are worthy of no blame, dispraise, or dishonor, but are unblamable. If these things are true, in Dr. Whitby's sense of necessity, they will prove all such to be blameless, who are given up of God to sin, in what they commit after they are thus given up. That there is such a thing as men's being judicially given up to sin, is certain, if the Scripture rightly informs us; such a thing being often there spoken of: as in *Psalms 81:12*, "So I gave them up to their own hearts' lust, and they walked in their own counsels." *Acts 7:42*, "Then God turned, and gave them up to worship the host of heaven." *Romans 1:24*, "Wherefore, God also gave them up to uncleanness, through the lusts of their own hearts, to dishonor their own bodies between themselves." V. *26*, "For this cause God gave them up to vile affections." V. *28*, "And even as they did not like to retain God in their knowledge, God gave them over to a reprobate mind, to do those things that are not convenient." ***Freedom of the Will (WJE Online Vol. 1)***

Some have been finally given up to sin that never have sinned so much as you, nor against so many means; some that never have had so much wickedness, nor shown so much obstinacy, as particularly those mentioned. *Romans 1:24*, "Wherefore God also gave them up to uncleanness through the lusts of their own hearts, to dishonor their own bodies between themselves." They were heathen that the Apostle there speaks of, that never heard of the way of salvation, never enjoyed the ordinances of the gospel, their sin and wickedness never comparable to yours. For that is what we are often taught in Scripture, that the heathen that live in darkness don't provoke God ever so much as sinners under the light of the gospel. And they here mentioned never showed themselves a tenth part so obstinate as you. For though the Apostle observes in the *Romans 1:19–20*, that they had means used with them, yet the means used with them were nothing in comparison of yours. They had only the light of nature, but [you had the light of the gospel]. And if some have sinned more, and under greater means before [they were] given up, [that is] no argument [that] you are not in danger. For God han't limited himself to such a degree of wickedness and obstinacy in inflicting this judgment, but uses his own sovereign [pleasure]. All that continue obstinate in [wickedness], when God is using means [to reclaim them], deserve it; and he lengthens out his forbearance according to his own sovereign pleasure. ***Sermons and Discourses, 1734–1738 (WJE Online Vol. 19)***

Romans 1:25

We may observe its continuance signified here by two expressions: forever and from generation to generation. The latter seems to be exegetical or explanatory of the former. The phrase forever is variously used in Scripture. Sometimes thereby is meant as long as a man lives; so is it said the servant that has his ear bored through with an awl to the door of his master should be his servant forever. Sometimes thereby is meant during the continuance of the Jewish state; so of many of the ceremonial and judicial laws, it is said that they should be statutes forever. Sometimes ‹thereby is meant› as long as the world stands or to the end of the generations of men; so it is said *Ecclesiastes 1:4*, "One generation passeth away and another comes but [the earth abideth for ever]." Sometimes thereby is meant to all eternity; so it is said God is "blessed forevermore," *Romans 1:25*, and so it is said *John 6:51*, he that may "eat of this bread, he shall live forever." ***A History of the Work of Redemption (WJE Online Vol. 9)***

Romans 1:27

Taylor's commentary on the Apostle's discussion of men lusting after men cites Cicero who, "without any Mark of Disapprobation," refers to a man of high rank who practiced "this worse than beastly Vice," and also notes that other men and philosophers were "Admirers of young men." This Taylor called a "most detestable Vice" (*Paraphrase with Notes on the Epistle to the Romans*, 3:20–21). ***The "Blank Bible" (WJE Online Vol. 24)***

Romans 1:28

That men should forsake the true God for idols, is an evidence of the most astonishing folly and stupidity, by God's own testimony. *Jeremiah 2:12–13*, "Be astonished, O ye heavens, at this, and be ye horribly afraid, be ye very desolate, saith the Lord: for my people have committed two evils; they have forsaken me the fountain of living waters, and have hewed out to themselves cisterns, broken cisterns, that can hold no water." And that mankind in general did thus, so soon after the flood, was from the evil propensity of their hearts, and because they did not like to retain God in their knowledge; as is evident by *Romans 1:28*. ***Original Sin (WJE Online Vol. 3)***

Romans 1:30

To "glory" is for a person to express his high esteem of his own advantages of excellency, honor or happiness above others. The word in the text in the original signifies to show forth one's own praise, or to exalt oneself with one's own praises. Therefore boasting or glorying is generally taken in an ill sense, as an expression of a haughty disposition. Thus when the Apostle, when he is setting forth the exceeding great wickedness of the heathen, he mentions this, amongst other things, that they were "boasters" (*Romans 1:30*). Self-praise is spoken of, as by the wise man, as a foolish thing. *Proverbs 27:2*, "Let another praise thee, and not thine own mouth; a stranger, and not thine own lips. ***Sermons and Discourses: 1723–1729 (WJE Online Vol. 14)***

Romans 1:31

"Without natural affection." ἄστοργη may include the absence both of parental and filial affection. The custom of exposing newborn infants, which prevailed so generally in the heathen world, and that among polite nations and persons in other respects not destitute of humanity, is a most striking instance of the truth of this assertion, as that of killing their aged parents also was of the counterpart. ***The "Blank Bible" (WJE Online Vol. 24)***

Gratitude being thus a natural principle, it renders ingratitude so much the more vile and heinous; because it shows a dreadful prevalence of wickedness when it even overbears, and suppresses the better principles of human nature: as it is mentioned as an evidence of the high degree of the wickedness of many of the heathen, that they were without natural affection (*Romans 1:31*). But that the want of gratitude, or natural affection, are evidences of an high degree of vice, is no argument that all gratitude and natural affection, has the nature of virtue, or saving grace. ***Religious Affections (WJE Online Vol. 2)***

Romans 1:32—2:1

It seems to be a mistake of many that the Apostle, in what he says of men's wickedness in the *Romans 1*, has respect only to the Gentiles, and that in what he says in the *Romans 2*, he has respect only to the Jews. 'Tis true that in the *Romans 1* he evidently has his eye chiefly on the wickedness that prevailed [in the Gentile] world. But that is not his professed design in it, only to describe the sin of the pagan world, but the wickedness of the world of mankind. 'Tis all unrighteousness and ungodliness of men that hold the truth in unrighteousness. And in the *Romans 2* he has his eye chiefly on the Jews, but it is not his professed design to speak only of them, as appears by his beginning in the *Romans 2:1*, the universal terms that he uses in it. "Therefore thou art inexcusable, O MAN (not O Jew). WHOSOEVER thou art (*of mankind*, whether Jew or Gentile) that judgest," etc. In the *Romans 1:32*, the Apostle speaks of the wickedness of mankind in general, and shows how they "hold the truth in unrighteousness," as he had said before (*Romans 1:18*). And the special design of that verse is to set forth how they are all alike, and all agreed in wickedness, and in the same kind of wickedness. Though they all have that light that is sufficient to teach them that those that commit such things deserve the condemnation and wrath of God, and so death and destruction, which they are very ready to acknowledge and declare in the case of others when they see their wickedness, their unrighteousness, covetousness, maliciousness, envy, murder, debate, deceit, malignity, etc.: I say, though when they see others guilty of such things, they can easily see that they are worthy of death, and are forward to express it, yet they do the very same things, and not only so, but they show plainly that they have just such hearts. They show a full practical consent to all the wickedness of others that they are forward to condemn and to declare worthy of death. Thus unreasonable are they, and inconsistent with themselves. Thus the beginning of the *Romans 2* comes in. "Therefore thou art inexcusable, O man, whosoever thou art that judgest." Thou that art forward to condemn others as worthy of death, "for wherein thou judgest another, thou condemnest thyself." Thou art very unreasonable and exceeding inconsistent with thyself, "for thou that judgest dost the same things," and showest that thou hast pleasure in their practice. There is at the same time that you judge them, a full practical consent to and good liking of the very same practices. So God of old condemned the Jews for that in their practice they had justified Samaria and Sodom, and were a comfort to 'em, and yet had judged them (Ezekiel 16:51–52, *Ezekiel 16:54*). ***The "Blank Bible" (WJE Online Vol. 24)***

ROMANS CHAPTER 2

Romans 2:1

If men were humbly sensible of their own failings they would not be very forward or pleased in judging others; for "as in water face answereth to face, so the heart of man to man," *Proverbs 27:19*. There are the same heads of corruption in one man's heart as another; and if those men who are most busy in censuring others would but look inward, and seriously examine their own hearts and lives, they might generally see the same dispositions, and the same things, the same kind of behavior at some time or other, for which they judge others, or at least things very much like them. And an aptness to judge and condemn shows an arrogant, proud disposition. It has a show of persons' setting up themselves above others, as though they were fit to be the lords and judges of their fellow servants, as if it were fit that they should stand or fall at their sentence. ***Ethical Writings (WJE Online Vol. 8)***

As Moses put a veil over his face [*Exodus 34:33*], so he hid the covenant in an ark. The ark itself was hidden by the veil of the temple, and the book of the covenant was hid by the cover of the ark; i.e. they were as it were hidden under Christ's flesh. The carnal typical ordinances of the Old Testament are in Scripture represented as Christ's flesh (*Romans 2:1–4; Colossians 2:14*). The veil signified the flesh of Christ (*Hebrews 10:20*), and so doth the cover of the ark, or the ark considered as distinct from what was contained in it. The covenant of grace was, and the glorious things of the gospel were, contained in that book that was laid up in the ark; but it was as it were shut up in a cabinet, hid under types and dark dispensations. Christ rent the veil from the top to the bottom; so he opened the cabinet of the ark. ***Notes on Scripture (WJE Online Vol. 15)***

[T]he Apostle in this *Romans 2*, directs himself especially to those that had a high conceit of their own holiness, made their boast of God, and were confident of their own discerning, and that they knew God's will, and approved the things that were more excellent, "*or tried the things that differ*," as it is in the margin (*Romans 2:18*), and were confident that they were guides of the blind, a light of them which are in darkness, instructors of the foolish, teachers of babes, and so took upon them to judge others. See *Romans 2:1*, and *Romans 2:17–20*. These things show that for any to take upon [themselves], by only a little occasional conversation with others that are professors of godliness, [to judge them] as hypocrites, unexperienced and unconverted men, is a great error. ***Notes on Scripture (WJE Online Vol. 15)***

When men are full of zeal and indignation against the sins of others and at the same time have but little to do at home, find little to employ their zealous opposition against them; and while they seem strenuous in speech and behavior to oppose others' iniquities and all the while indulge themselves in the same things as others as bad, and are careless and quiet in their own wickedness: their zeal will serve to no other purpose but their condemnation. Their great Judge shall condemn them as those that are self-condemned, *Romans 2:1–3*, "Therefore thou art inexcusable, O man, whosoever thou art that judgest: for wherein thou judgest another, thou condemnest thyself; for thou that judgest doest the same things. But we are sure that the judgment of God is according to truth against them which commit such things. And thinkest thou this, O man, that judgest them which do such things, and doest the same, that thou shalt escape the judgment of God?" And v. *Romans 2:21*. ***Sermons and Discourses, 1739–1742 (WJE Online Vol. 22)***

[*Ezekiel 16:51–52*.] See *Romans 1:32* and *Romans 2:1* notes. ***The "Blank Bible" (WJE Online Vol. 24)***

It seems to be a mistake of many that the Apostle, in what he says of men's wickedness in the *Romans 1*, has respect only to the Gentiles, and that in what he says in the *Romans 2*, he has respect only to the Jews. 'Tis true that in the *Romans 1* he evidently has his eye chiefly on the wickedness that prevailed [in the Gentile] world. But that is not his professed design in it, only to describe the sin of the pagan world, but the wickedness of the world of mankind. 'Tis all unrighteousness and ungodliness of men that hold the truth in unrighteousness. And in the *Romans 2* he has his eye chiefly on the Jews, but it is not his professed design to speak only of them, as appears by his beginning in the *Romans 2:1*, the universal terms that he uses in it. ***The "Blank Bible" (WJE Online Vol. 24)***

["O man."] This is spoken emphatically, a poor, weak, fallible, sinful man, in opposition to God, mentioned in the next verse. [*Romans 2:1–2 ff.*] The Apostle has a special eye to the Jews when he speaks of them that judge others, for it was very much their manner of that day to trust in themselves that they were righteous, and to condemn others. See note on *Matthew 7:1*. ***The "Blank Bible" (WJE Online Vol. 24)***

Second Inf. Hence we may learn that there are none in these days have a gift of discerning and certainly knowing who are true Christians. It is evident that this can't be known by men certainly any other way than by immediate revelation, because God only knows of [it] himself by his own discerning. Nothing is more plain than that the knowing [of] the gracious sincerity, or the insincerity, of professors of godliness is spoken of in Scripture as the divine prerogative . . . *Romans 2:29*, "He is a Jew who is one inwardly; and circumcision is that of the heart, in the spirit, and not in the letter; whose praise is not of men, but of God." The Apostle is speaking with regard to those self-conceited [persons in] *Romans 2:1*, "Therefore thou art inexcusable, O man, whosoever thou art that judgest: for wherein thou judgest another, thou condemnest thyself; for thou that judgest doest the same things." [And in *Romans 2:17–20*,] "Behold, thou art called a Jew, and restest in the law, and makest thy boast of God, and knowest his will, and approvest the things that are more excellent, being instructed out of the law; and art confident that thou thyself art a guide of the blind, a light of them which are in darkness, an instructor of the foolish, a teacher of babes, which hast the form of knowledge and of the truth in the law." It further appears that 'tis not God's manner thus immediately to make known [the workings of the Holy Spirit] because he has directed us to judge by other means: fruits, [for the] tree is known by its fruit. Some would argue from hence that persons may certainly know [the state of others], but the Word don't imply certain knowledge: but only that we shall know and distinguish by this rule, so as shall ordinarily be sufficient for our own safety. [This does] not always mean certainty. *1 Samuel 23:17*, "Thou shalt be king . . . that also Saul my father knoweth." *2 Samuel 17:10*, "All Israel knoweth thy father is valiant man." 'Tis God's prerogative to judge infallibly according to men's works. But then these persons don't pretend to know this way, but either by their sheep's clothing or by immediate revelation. ***Sermons and Discourses, 1743–1758 (WJE Online Vol. 25)***

Romans 2:2

The Apostle's words here do doubtless imply that he was sure that their punishment would be terrible, in that it would be "according to truth," i.e. would be such a punishment as their crime deserves, which implies that if the sin was not punished according to its desert, God's judgment would not be according to truth. Otherwise what does the Apostle build his confidence and sureness upon, that they shall be punished, if God's judgment may be according to truth and justice, and yet not punish them as they deserve, or if God be under no necessity in honor to his truth or justice to punish sin according to its desert? Why was the Apostle so sure, from the truth or justice of God, that sin would be punished as it deserves? This text shows plainly that God is obliged to punish sin as it deserves.

When it is said, "the judgment of God is according to truth," the meaning is that God's judgment will be a true judgment; he will judge things as they be, or that his judgment will be conformed to the nature of things. Now the act of judging with regard to any crime is twofold, viz. declaring the guilt, and sentencing to punishment. God shall do these according to truth. His declaration of guilt shall be as the case is indeed, and his sentence to punishment shall be that which shall be agreeable thereto. His declaration of guilt and his sentence to punishment shall both have the same language, and the language of both shall be true. They shall both speak true, or as the thing is. The Apostle has evidently respect to both these, not only declaration of guilt, but sentencing to punishment, as is evident by the context. Hence it follows that if God did not sentence to that punishment that sin deserves, his judgment would not be according to truth; and therefore God is obliged to punish sin as it deserves. ***The "Blank Bible" (WJE Online Vol. 24)***

Romans 2:3

So we may argue from *Romans 2:3–12*, *Romans 2:16*, where the Apostle speaks of men's treasuring up "wrath against the day of wrath and revelation of the righteous judgment of God" by their abusing the day wherein God exercises towards them the riches of his goodness, forbearance and long-suffering, which should lead 'em to repentance, plainly intimating, *Romans 2:6*, that the Judge in that day would "render every one according to his deeds: to them who by patient continuance in well doing," etc., "eternal life. But to them who are contentious," etc., "tribulation and wrath," etc. And that "as many as sinned without law" should "perish without law," and that "as many as have sinned in the law" should "be judged by the law," which plainly shows that they are to be judged according to their deeds during this life, wherein alone there is this distinction of some sinning without the law and some sinning in the law. ***The "Miscellanies," (Entry Nos. 1153–1360) (WJE Online Vol. 23)***

Consider how God has threatened that if we are forward censoriously to condemn others we shall be condemned ourselves. *Matthew 7* at the beginning: "Judge not, that ye be not judged. For with what judgment ye judge, ye shall be judged: and with what measure ye mete, it shall be measured to you again." And *Romans 2:3*, " And thinkest thou this, O man, that judgest them which do such things, and doest the same, that thou shalt escape the judgment of God?" These are awful threatenings, threatenings of that being who is to be our Judge, and by whom it infinitely concerns us to be acquitted when we come to be judged by him, and from whom a sentence of condemnation will be infinitely dreadful. Therefore, as we would not receive condemnation for ourselves, let us not mete this measure to others. ***Ethical Writings (WJE Online Vol. 8)***

Romans 2:4

The long-suffering of God is very wonderful. He bears innumerable injuries from men, and those which are very great. If we consider the wickedness there is in the world, and then consider how God continues the world, does not destroy it, but is continually blessing it with innumerable streams of good, and supplying and supporting the world, how rich his daily bounties are to it, how he causes the sun to rise and shed forth his beams on the evil and on the good, and sendeth rain on the just and on the unjust. And if we consider the goodness of God to some particular populous cities, how vast the quantity of the fruits of God's goodness is which is daily spent upon them, and consumed by them, and then consider what wickedness [there was in these very cities, it will show us how amazingly great is his long-suffering. And if we consider the same long-suffering has been manifest to very many particular persons, in all ages of the world. He is long-suffering to the sinners that he spares, and to whom he offers his mercy, even while they are rebelling against him.] And especially if we consider God's long-suffering towards his elect, many of whom live long in sin, and are great sinners, and God bears with them, yea, bears to the end, and finally is pleased to forgive, and never punishes the, but makes them the vessels of mercy and glory, and shows mercy to them even while enemies, as the apostle Paul takes notice it was with himself. *1 Timothy 1:13–16*, "Who was before a blasphemer, and a persecutor, and injurious: but I obtained mercy, because I did it ignorantly in unbelief. And the grace of our Lord was exceeding abundant with faith and love which is in Christ Jesus. This is a faithful saying, and worthy of all acceptation, that Christ Jesus came into the world to save sinners; of whom I am chief. Howbeit for this cause I obtained mercy, that in me first Jesus Christ might show forth all long-suffering for a pattern, to them which should hereafter believe on him to life everlasting." Now it is the nature of love, or at least love to a superior as such, even to incline and dispose to imitation. A child's love to his father disposes him to imitate his father, and especially does the love of God's children dispose them to imitate their Heavenly Father. ***Ethical Writings (WJE Online Vol. 8)***

"And account that the longsuffering of our Lord is salvation, even as our beloved brother Paul also, according to the wisdom given unto him, hath written unto you." Dr. Doddridge supposes that this epistle was written both to Christian Jews and Gentiles, as well as the former epistle, and that "the passage referred to is in his epistle to the Romans (*Romans 2:4*), where he testifies "that the goodness of God leadeth to repentance." ***The "Blank Bible" (WJE Online Vol. 24)***

That professing Christians are said to be sanctified, washed, etc., does not argue that all professing Christians are so indeed: for Taylor himself says, it should be carefully observed, that "'tis very common, in the sacred writings, to express, not only our Christian privileges, but also the duty to which they oblige, in the present, or preterperfect tense: or, to speak of that as done, which only ought to be done, and which, in fact, may possibly never be done." *Matthew 5:13*, "Ye are the salt of the earth," i.e. "ye ought to be"; *Romans 2:4*, "the goodness of God leadeth thee to repentance," i.e. "ought to lead thee"; ch. *Romans 6:2, 11*, ch. *Romans 8:9*, *Colossians 3:3*, *1 Peter 1:6*, "Wherein ye greatly rejoice," i.e. "ought to rejoice"; *2 Corinthians 3:18*, "we all, with open face beholding as in a glass the glory of the Lord, are changed into the same image from glory to glory"; *1 Corinthians 5:7*, "ye are unleavened," i.e. "obliged by the Christian profession to be"; *Hebrews 13:14*, "we seek a city to come"; *1 John 2:12–15*, *1 John 3:9*, *vv. 4, 18*, and in other places. See Taylor's *Key*, p. 139, no. 244, and p. 141, no. 246.13 This overthrows all his supposed proofs, that those which he calls "antecedent blessings," do really belong to all professing Christians. ***"Controversies" Notebook (WJE Online Vol. 27)***

Romans 2:5

'Tis an evidence that true religion, or holiness of heart, lies very much in the affection of the heart, that the Scriptures place the sin of the heart very much in hardness of heart. Thus the Scriptures do everywhere. It was hardness of heart, which excited grief and displeasure in Christ towards the Jews, *Mark 3:5*. "He looked round about on them with anger, being grieved for the hardness of their hearts." It is from men's having such a heart as this, that they treasure up wrath for themselves. *Romans 2:5*, "After thy hardness and impenitent heart, treasurest up unto thy self wrath, against the day of wrath, and revelation of the righteous judgment of God." The reason given why the house of Israel would not obey God, was that they were hard-hearted. *Ezekiel 3:7*, "But the house of Israel will not hearken unto thee; for they will not hearken unto me: for all the house of Israel are impudent and hard-hearted." ***Religious Affections (WJE Online Vol. 2)***

For God's future judging of men, in order to their eternal retribution, will not be his trying, and finding out, and passing a judgment upon the state of men's hearts, in his own mind; but it will be a declarative judgment: and the end of it will be, not God's forming a judgment within himself, but the manifestation of his judgment, and the righteousness of it, to men's own consciences, and to the world. And therefore the Day of Judgment is called the day of the revelation of the righteous judgment of God (*Romans 2:5*). And the end of God's future trial and judgment of men, as to the part that each one in particular is to have in the judgment, will be especially the clear manifestation of God's righteous judgment, with respect to him, to his conscience . . . ***Religious Affections (WJE Online Vol. 2)***

It [God's perfection] is spoken of as the end of the Day of Judgment, that grand consummation of God's moral government of the world, and the day for the bringing all things to their designed ultimate issue. It is called "the day of the revelation of the righteous judgment of God," *Romans 2:5*. ***Ethical Writings (WJE Online Vol. 8)***

A wicked man is a servant of sin: his powers and faculties are all employed in the service of sin, and in fitting [them] for hell. And all his possessions are so used by him as to be subservient to the same purpose. Some men spend their time in "treasuring up wrath against the day of wrath" (*Romans 2:5*). Thus do all unclean persons, that live in lascivious practices in secret. Thus do all malicious persons. Thus do all profane persons, that neglect duties of religion. Thus do all unjust persons, and those that are fraudulent or oppressive in their dealings. Thus do all backbiters and revilers. Thus do all covetous persons, that set their hearts chiefly on the riches of this world. Thus do tavern-haunters, and frequenters of evil company; and many other kinds of persons that might be mentioned. ***Sermons and Discourses, 1730–1733 (WJE Online Vol. 17)***

God in his dealings with men with relation to their eternal state, has a great respect to that, viz. that his justice be made manifest, and especially to the conviction of men's own consciences. For this end a day of judgment is appointed, wherein God, though he needs it not, being omniscient, will yet judge men in a formal manner to make his justice manifest to the world and to men's own consciences. Therefore that day is called the day of the "revelation of the righteous judgment of God" (*Romans 2:5*). And hence, God in judging men will make so much of works, though works are not that by which they are primarily entitled to justification, but being visible evidences of that which is so to the world and to their own consciences. Hence, everyone shall be judged according to his works. ***The "Miscellanies," (Entry Nos. 501–832) (WJE Online Vol. 18)***

God himself when he acts towards men as judge, in order to a declarative judgment, makes use of evidences, and so judges men by their works. And therefore at the day of judgment, God will judge men according to their works: for though God will stand in no need of evidence to inform him what is right, yet 'tis to be considered that he will then sit in judgment; not as earthly judges do, to find out what is right in a cause, but to declare and manifest what is right; and therefore that day is called by the Apostle, "the day of the revelation of the righteous judgment of God" (*Romans 2:5*). ***Sermons and Discourses, 1734–1738 (WJE Online Vol. 19)***

Thus justice shall be administered at the great day to ministers and their people: and to that end they shall meet together, that they may not only receive justice to themselves, but see justice done to the other party: for this is the end of that great day, to reveal, or declare "the righteous judgment of God" (*Romans 2:5*). Ministers shall have justice done them, and they shall see justice done to their people: and the people shall receive justice themselves from their Judge, and shall see justice done to their minister. And so all things will be adjusted and settled forever between them; everyone being sentenced and recompensed according to his works; either in receiving and wearing a crown of eternal joy and glory, or in suffering everlasting shame and pain. ***Sermons and Discourses, 1743–1758 (WJE Online Vol. 25)***

[T]he end of the day of judgment, is not to find out what is just, as it is with human judgments, but 'tis to manifest what is just; to make known God's justice in the judgment which he will execute, to men's own consciences, and to the world. And therefore, that day is called "the day of wrath, and revelation of the righteous judgment of God" (*Romans 2:5*). Now sinners often cavil against the justice of God's dispensations, and particularly, the justice of the punishment, which God threatens for their sins; excusing themselves, and condemning God: but when God comes to manifest their wickedness in the light of that day, and to call them to an account, they will be speechless; *Matthew 22:11–12*, "And when the king came to see the guests, he saw there, a man which had not on a wedding garment. And he saith unto him, Friend, how camest thou in hither, not having a wedding garment? And he was speechless." When the King of heaven and earth comes to judgment, their consciences will be so perfectly enlightened and convinced, by the all-searching light, they shall then stand in; that their mouths will be effectually stopped, as to all excuses for themselves, all pleading of their own righteousness, to excuse or justify them; and all objections against the justice of their Judge; that their conscience will condemn them only, and not God. ***Sermons and Discourses, 1743–1758 (WJE Online Vol. 25)***

Romans 2:5, "revelation of the righteous judgment of God." ***"Controversies" Notebook (WJE Online Vol. 27)***

Romans 2:6

So men's practice is the only evidence, that Christ represents the future judgment as regulated by, in that most particular description of the Day of Judgment, which we have in the holy Bible, *Matthew 25*, at the latter end. See also *Romans 2:6–13*, *Jeremiah 17:10*, *Job 34:11*, *Proverbs 24:12*, *Jeremiah 32:19*, *Revelation 22:12*, *Matthew 16:27*, *Revelation 2:23*, *Ezekiel 33:20*, *1 Peter 1:17*. ***Religious Affections (WJE Online Vol. 2)***

By the following texts it seems plain that the sum of the happiness of the saints, and not only certain additaments, are given in reward for the saints' inherent holiness and their good works . . . *Romans 2:6–7*, *Romans 2:10*, "Who will *render to* every man according to his deeds: to them who by patient continuance in well doing seek for glory, honor and immortality, eternal life . . . glory, honor and peace to every man that worketh good." *Revelation 22:12*, "Behold, I come quickly; and my reward is with me, to give every man according as his work shall be." *Matthew 16:27*, "For the Son of man shall come in the glory of his Father with his angels; and then shall he REWARD every man according to his works." ***The "Miscellanies," (Entry Nos. 501–832) (WJE Online Vol. 18)***

So we may argue from *Romans 2:3–12*, *Romans 2:16*, where the Apostle speaks of men's treasuring up "wrath against the day of wrath and revelation of the righteous judgment of God" by their abusing the day wherein God exercises towards them the riches of his goodness, forbearance and long-suffering, which should lead 'em to repentance, plainly intimating, *Romans 2:6*, that the Judge in that day would "render every one according to his deeds: to them who by patient continuance in well doing," etc., "eternal life. But to them who are contentious," etc., "tribulation and wrath," etc. And that "as many as sinned without law" should "perish without law," and that "as many as have sinned in the law" should "be judged by the law," which plainly shows that they are to be judged according to their deeds during this life, wherein alone there is this distinction of some sinning without the law and some sinning in the law. ***The "Miscellanies," (Entry Nos. 1153–1360) (WJE Online Vol. 23)***

Romans 2:7

True saints may be guilty of some kinds and degrees of backsliding, and may be foiled by particular temptations, and may fall into sin, yea great sins: but they can never fall away so, as to grow weary of religion, and the service of God, and habitually to dislike it and neglect it; either on its own account, or on account of the difficulties that attend it: as is evident by *Galatians 6:9, Romans 2:7, Hebrews 10:36, Isaiah 43:22, Malachi 1:13*. They can never backslide, so as to continue no longer in a *way* of universal obedience; or so, that it shall cease to be their *manner* to observe all the rules of Christianity, and do all duties required, even the most difficult, and in the most difficult circumstances. ***Religious Affections (WJE Online Vol. 2)***

God gives men their choice. They may have their inheritance where they choose it, and may obtain heaven if they will seek it by patient continuance in well-doing, *Romans 2:7*. We are all of us, as it were, set here in this world as in a large wilderness with divers countries about it, with several ways or paths leading to those different countries, and we are left to our choice what course we will take. If we heartily choose heaven, and set our hearts chiefly on that blessed Canaan, that land of love, and love the path which leads to it, we may walk in it; and if we continue so to do, it will certainly lead us to heaven at last. Let what we have heard of the land of love excite us all to turn our faces towards that land, and bend our course thitherward. Is not what we have heard of the happy state of that country and the many delights which are in it enough to make us thirst after it, and to cause us with the greatest earnestness and steadfastness of resolution to press towards, and to spend our whole lives in traveling in the way which leads thither? What joyful news might it well be to us when we hear of such a world of perfect peace and holy love, to hear that there is an opportunity for us to come, that we may spend an eternity in such a world. ***Ethical Writings (WJE Online Vol. 8)***

Ch. Romans 8:18, "The sufferings of this present time are not worthy to be compared with the glory which shall be revealed in us." See also *ch. Romans 2:7*, *Romans 2:10* and *Romans 3:23* and *Romans 9:23*. ***Ethical Writings (WJE Online Vol. 8)***

Obj. 1. We frequently find promises of eternal life and salvation, and sometimes of justification itself, made to our own virtue and obedience. Eternal life is promised to obedience, in *Romans 2:7*, "To them who by patient continuance in well doing, seek for glory, honor and immortality, eternal life." And the like in innumerable other places. And justification itself is promised to that virtue of a forgiving spirit or temper in us, *Matthew 6:14–15*, "For if ye forgive men their trespasses, your heavenly Father will also forgive you; but if ye forgive not men their trespasses, neither will your Father forgive your trespasses." All allow that justification in great part consists in the forgiveness of sins. To this I answer, (1) These things being promised to our virtue and obedience, argues no more, than that there is a connection between them and evangelical obedience; which I have already observed is not the thing in dispute. All that can be proved by obedience and salvation being connected in the promise, is that obedience and salvation are connected in fact; which nobody denies, and whether it be owned or denied, is as has been shown, nothing to the purpose. There is no need that an admission to a title to salvation, should be given on the account of our obedience, in order to the promises being true. If we find such a promise, that he that obeys shall he saved, or he that is holy shall be justified, all that is needful in order to such promises being true, is that it be really so, that he that obeys shall be saved, and that holiness and justification shall indeed go together: that proposition may be a truth, that he that obeys shall be saved, because obedience and salvation are connected together in fact; and yet an acceptance to a title to salvation not be granted upon the account of any of our own virtue or obedience. What is a promise, but only a declaration of future truth, for the comfort and encouragement of the person to whom it is declared? Promises are conditional propositions; and as has been already observed, it is not the thing in dispute, whether other things besides faith mayn't have the place of the condition in such propositions wherein pardon and salvation are the consequent. ***Sermons and Discourses, 1734–1738 (WJE Online Vol. 19)***

A godly man ordinarily lives an holy life, which implies not only negative, but positive religion. The condition of the reward is not only to avoid wicked practices, but to continue and persevere "in well doing" (*Romans 2:7*). *Galatians 6:9*, "Be not weary in well doing: in due time ye shall reap, if ye faint not"; implying that if they fainted, or ceased from well doing, they were not like to reap. ***Sermons and Discourses, 1734–1738 (WJE Online Vol. 19)***

And so we are encouraged to seek glory, honor, and immortality by the promise of eternal life as the reward for it (*Romans 2:7*). And glory, honor, and peace is promised to them that work good (*Romans 2:10*). And hence Christ so often promises a crown and kingdom, and the honor of sitting with him on his throne, and judging the world, or even judging angels. Such great honor is set forth for us to seek after; and we never find any blamed for seeking such honor too much, or too much of such honor. ***Sermons and Discourses, 1734–1738 (WJE Online Vol. 19)***

From *Romans 2:7*, where he supposes "the Apostle is rather representing the terms of the covenant of works, than the terms of the covenant of grace. God will render 'indignation and wrath, [tribulation and anguish,] upon every soul of man that doth evil' [*Romans 2:8–9*]; but eternal life, with glory, honor and peace 'to them who, by patient continuance in well doing, seek for glory, honor and immortality' [*Romans 2:7*], and *Romans 2:10*, 'glory, honor and peace to every man that worketh good.'" Dr. Watts supposes it to be agreeable to the design of the Apostle in these three first chapters of the Romans here to represent the terms of the covenant of works, and show how all men are brought under condemnation by the law. ***The "Miscellanies," 833–1152 (WJE Online Vol. 20)***

John 8:31, "Ye continue in my word, then are ye my disciples indeed." *Romans 2:7*, "To them who by patient continuance in well doing seek for glory and honor and immortality, eternal life." *Romans 11:22*, "Behold therefore the goodness and severity of God: on them which fell, severity; but towards thee, goodness, if thou continue in his goodness: otherwise thou also shalt be cut off." *Colossians 1:21–23*, "You [. . .] hath he reconciled [. . .], to present you holy and unblameable and unreproveable in his sight: if ye continue in the faith grounded and settled, and be not moved away from the hope of the gospel." *Galatians 6:9*, "We shall reap, if we faint not." **Writings on the Trinity, Grace, and Faith (WJE Online Vol. 21)**

Romans 2:8

By that iniquity which is here mentioned is meant all sin or wickedness of life and conversation; and by the truth all holiness of life, as is confirmed by that place in *Romans 2:8* where the same Apostle mentions "the truth" and "unrighteousness" together, as here he mentions "the truth" and "iniquity." And there it is evident by the truth he means walking in holy practice, or well-doing; and by iniquity, wickedness in men's deeds or practice. ***Ethical Writings (WJE Online Vol. 8)***

["But unto them that are contentious."] The Apostle in this word has respect to the perverse spirit of the Jews' quarreling with the gospel that revealed justification by faith alone, and abolished their ceremonial law, and admitted the Gentiles to equal privileges with themselves, etc. ***The "Blank Bible" (WJE Online Vol. 24)***

Romans 2:9

In the *Romans 1*, he showed how the Gentiles were under sin; in the *Romans 2*, he shows how the Jews are under sin; in the beginning of this chapter, he answers an objection; and in the *Romans 2:9*, he sums up the matter: "What then? are we better than they? No, in no wise: for we have before proved both Jews and Gentiles, that they are all under sin"; and then proves what he had insisted on out of the Old Testament: "As it is written, There is none righteous, no, not one: there is none that understandeth, there is none that seeketh after God. They are all gone out of the way, they are together become unprofitable; there is none that doth good, no, not one." ***The "Blank Bible" (WJE Online Vol. 24)***

Romans 2:12, "As many as have sinned without law shall *perish*" (or be *destroyed*, as the word signifies) "without law." What that perishing is, is there described in the context: "*indignation and wrath, tribulation and anguish*" *Romans 2:8–9*. ***"Controversies" Notebook (WJE Online Vol. 27)***

[*Romans 2:8–9*. "Indignation and wrath, tribulation and anguish."] Here seems to be a reference to these words, *Psalms 78:49*, when speaking of the Egyptians, it is said, "He cast upon them the fierceness of his anger, wrath, indignation, and trouble." ***The "Blank Bible" (WJE Online Vol. 24)***

I would observe one thing further under this head, viz. that ungodly men which live under the gospel, notwithstanding any moral sincerity they may have, are worse, and more provoking enemies to God, than the very heathen, who never sinned against gospel light and mercy. This is very manifest by the Scriptures, particularly *Matthew 10:13–14*; *Amos 3:2*; *Romans 2:9*; *2 Peter 2:21*; *Revelation 3:15–16*. ***Ecclesiastical Writings (WJE Online Vol. 12)***

In the *Romans 1*, he showed how the Gentiles were under sin; in the *Romans 2*, he shows how the Jews are under sin; in the beginning of this chapter, he answers an objection; and in the *Romans 2:9*, he sums up the matter: "What then? are we better than they? No, in no wise: for we have before proved both Jews and Gentiles, that they are all under sin"; and then proves what he had insisted on out of the Old Testament: "As it is written, There is none righteous, no, not one: there is none that understandeth, there is none that seeketh after God. They are all gone out of the way, they are together become unprofitable; there is none that doth good, no, not one." ***Sermons and Discourses, 1734–1738 (WJE Online Vol. 19)***

Romans 2:10

["To the Jew first, and also to the Gentile."] See *Romans 1:16*. *Mark 4:25*. "For he that hath, to him shall be given; and he that hath not, from him shall be taken away, even that which he hath." Spiritual and heavenly gifts are not given only in proportion to a person's improvement of what he has; so that he that has but little, if he improves it as well in proportion to what he has, shall receive as great a reward as he that has a great deal. For then the additional talent should with equal reason be given to him, who at first received the two talents, as to him who received five (*Matthew 25:28*); but it was not, and the reason is given in the *Matthew 25:29*. "For to everyone that hath shall be given, and he shall have abundance; but from him that hath not shall be taken away, even that which he hath." It is so with respect to advantages and privileges too: he that improves great advantages well shall receive a greater reward than he that improves small ones; otherwise there could be no advantage. Therefore "glory, honor, and peace is given to every man that worketh good, but to the Jew first" (*Romans 2:10*). ***Notes on Scripture (WJE Online Vol. 15)***

And so we are encouraged to seek glory, honor, and immortality by the promise of eternal life as the reward for it (*Romans 2:7*). And glory, honor, and peace is promised to them that work good (*Romans 2:10*). And hence Christ so often promises a crown and kingdom, and the honor of sitting with him on his throne, and judging the world, or even judging angels. Such great honor is set forth for us to seek after; and we never find any blamed for seeking such honor too much, or too much of such honor. ***Sermons and Discourses, 1734–1738 (WJE Online Vol. 19)***

Ques. How is the gospel "the power of God to salvation to those that believe, to the Jew first?" And so it is said in the *Romans 2:10*, that God will render "glory, honor, and peace to every man that worketh good, to the Jew first." *Arts.* God was ready to justify all that believed in Christ, and to reward all that work good, but especially the Jews, for the peculiar favor he bore to that nation for their forefathers' sakes, as *Romans 11:28*, and because they were born in covenant, or were his covenant people by descent. See *Romans 2:25*, "For circumcision verily profiteth," etc. ***The "Blank Bible" (WJE Online Vol. 24)***

Romans 2:12

"As many as have sinned without law shall perish" (or be destroyed, as the word signifies) "without law." What that perishing is, is there described in the context: "indignation and wrath, tribulation and anguish" *Romans 2:8–9*. ***"Controversies" Notebook (WJE Online Vol. 27)***

Secondly, to suppose that there is no law in being, by which men are exposed to death for *personal sins*, where or when the revealed law of God in or after Moses' time is not in being, is contrary to this Apostle's own doctrine in this epistle. *Romans 2:12, 14–15*, "For as many as have sinned without law" (i.e. revealed law) "shall perish without law." But how they can be exposed to die and perish, who have not the law of Moses, nor any revealed law, the Apostle shews us in the fourteenth and fifteenth verses; viz. in that they have the law of nature, by which they fall under sentence to this punishment. ***Original Sin (WJE Online Vol. 3)***

The Apostle, in all the preceding part of this epistle, wherever he has the phrase, "the law," evidently intends the moral law principally: as in the *Romans 2:12*. "For as many as have sinned without law, shall also perish without law." ***Sermons and Discourses, 1734–1738 (WJE Online Vol. 19)***

By those that are "under the law," is meant the Jews, and the Gentiles by those that are without law; as appears by the *Romans 2:12*. There is special reason to understand the law, as speaking to and of them, to whom it was immediately given. And therefore the Jews would be unreasonable in exempting themselves. And if we examine the places of the Old Testament, whence these passages are taken, we shall see plainly that special respect is had to the wickedness of the people of that nation, in every one of them. So that the law shuts all up in universal and desperate wickedness, "that every mouth may be stopped." The mouths of the Jews, as well as of the Gentiles; notwithstanding all those privileges by which they were distinguished from the Gentiles. ***Sermons and Discourses, 1734–1738 (WJE Online Vol. 19)***

For the Apostle here resumes the argument he was upon in the foregoing chapter, that the Jews and circumcision, as well as Gentiles, are exposed to [the] wrath and curse of God. By those that are "without [the] law" is meant the Gentiles, and those that are "under the law," the Jews, as appears by the *Romans 2:12*. It is to be noted that in each of these places in the Old Testament quoted in the foregoing verses, special respect is had to those that were of the nation of Israel; and they are spoken more especially and immediately of them. ***The "Blank Bible" (WJE Online Vol. 24)***

Romans 2:13

["For not the hearers," etc.] By this verse it appears that the apostle Paul and the apostle James were of the same mind in the matter of justification, however their expressions seem to be opposite. Here the apostle Paul says the same thing that the apostle James means, when he says a man is justified by works, and not by faith only. It is doubtless the same thing that the apostle James meant, if we would explain him by himself, for he expresses himself elsewhere almost in the same words that Paul does here (*James 1:22–23, James 1:25*). ***The "Blank Bible" (WJE Online Vol. 24)***

The law of works then in short, is that law which requires perfect obedience, without any remission or abatement; so that by that law a man cannot be just, or justified, without an exact performance of every tittle. Such a perfect obedience in the New Testament is termed δικαιοσύνη which we translate *righteousness*. In which last passage 'tis also to be noted, that Mr. Locke by the law of works don't understand the ceremonial law, but the covenant of works: as he more fully expresses himself in the next Paragraph but one: Where this law of works was to be found, the New Testament tells us, viz. in the law delivered by Moses. *John 1:17*, "The law was given by Moses, but grace and truth came by Jesus Christ." *John 7:19*, "Did not Moses give you the law," says our Savior, "and yet none of you keep the law." And this is the law which he speaks of, *Luke 10:28*, "This do and thou shalt live." This is that which St. Paul so often styles the law without any other distinction. *Romans 2:13*, "Not the hearers of the law are just before God, but the doers of the law are justified." 'Tis needless to quote any more places, his epistles are all full of it, especially this to the Romans. ***Sermons and Discourses, 1734–1738 (WJE Online Vol. 19)***

Luke 2:25, "Simeon, a just man." *Luke 23:50*, "Joseph, a counselor, a just man." *Matthew 13:41*, "shall sever the wicked from among the just." [*Mark 6:20*,] "knowing that he was a just man and a holy." *Matthew 27:19*, "Have nothing to do with that just man." *Matthew 27:24*, "I am free from the blood of this just person." *Luke 1:17*, "the disobedient to the wisdom of the just." *Luke 14:14*, "at the resurrection of the just." *Luke 15:7*, "than over ninety and nine just persons." *Luke 20:20*, "that should feign themselves just persons." *John 5:30*, "yet my judgment is just." *Acts 10:22*, "Cornelius was a just man." *Acts 24:15*, "there shall be a resurrection, both of the just and the unjust." *Romans 2:13*, "not the hearers of the law are just, but the doers of the law shall be justified." *Romans 7:12*, "the commandment is holy, and just." *Colossians 4:1*, "Masters, give your servants that which is just." *Titus 1:7–8*, "a bishop must be just." *Hebrews 12:23*, "the spirits of just men made perfect." *James 5:6*, "Ye have condemned and killed the just." *1 Peter 3:18*, "the just for the unjust." [*2 Peter 2:7*,] "And delivered just Lot." *Revelation 15:3*, "just and true are thy ways." *Acts 3:14*, "ye denied the Holy One and the Just." *Acts 7:52*, "showed before the coming of the Just One." *Acts 22:14*, "know his will, and see that Just One." ***Writings on the Trinity, Grace, and Faith (WJE Online Vol. 21)***

There are many things make it exceeding plain that the Apostle don't, by the terms righteousness and justification, intend merely God's mercy and grant of favor and deliverance from a great calamity, and bringing into a state of great privilege. The Apostle in these places sets righteousness expressly in opposition to condemnation, sin, disobedience. He speaks of the justification of *sinners*, and with regard to works of righteousness. How plain is the meaning of the expression in that place, *Romans 2:13*, "not the hearers of the law are just before God, but the doers of the law shall be justified," where it plainly appears that to be justified is to be reputed and accepted as just before God. So *Isaiah 53:11*, "by his knowledge shall my righteous servant justify many." *Jatzik Tzaddik*: the union and relation of these two terms plainly show their meaning. *Romans 5:19*, "by the obedience of one many shall be made righteous." *Romans 8:4*, "That the righteousness of the law might be fulfilled in us, who walk not after the flesh, but after the Spirit." *1 John 2:1*, "if any man sin, we have an advocate with Father, Jesus Christ the righteous." *Romans 5:18*, "by the righteousness of one the free gift came upon all men to justification of life." ***Writings on the Trinity, Grace, and Faith (WJE Online Vol. 21)***

Romans 2:14

The Apostle, having spoken of the lusts of the mind, and of the flesh, in the words before, his meaning here is, that these are natural unto men, they are the very inclination of their minds, the natural frame of their hearts. . . . And though he only saith, we are "children of wrath by nature," yet this wrath must be for something; for God is not angry with us for what is not sin: therefore it implies, that our natural disposition, all those lusts which he had mentioned, and that flesh which is the mother of these lusts, is that which is man›s nature. . . . "By nature," is that which a man doth being left to nature; as *Romans 2:14*, "The Gentiles . . . do by nature the things of the law," from the natural principles that are in them. ***"Controversies" Notebook (WJE Online Vol. 27)***

Romans 2:14–15

There is certainly such a thing as a conscience in the mind of every man; there never was a man yet but what has experienced it: man brings it into the world with him. Heathens and atheists have it as well as other men; see what the Apostle saith of the heathen, *Romans 2:14–15*: "For when the Gentiles, which have not the law, do by nature the things contained in the law, these, having not the law, are a law unto themselves: which show the work of the law written in their hearts, their conscience also bearing witness, and their thoughts the meanwhile accusing or else excusing one another." Little children show that they have a conscience in them before ever they [hear] anything of the Word of God. Now this conscience that God has implanted in us naturally makes men afraid when they have committed any secret sins. Though no man in the world sees them, yet if they are not very much hardened they [are] naturally apprehensive of punishment, and I believe every one here present has experienced this first or last. So also when we have done any virtuous act, any good action, we naturally expect that it will be the better with us for it. ***Sermons and Discourses 1720–1723 (WJE Online Vol. 10)***

A natural man has no sense of the beauty and amiableness of virtue and the turpitude and odiousness of vice, but yet every man has that naturally within that testifies to him that some things are right and others wrong. Thus if a man steals or commits murder, there is something within that tells him that he has done wrong. He knows that he has not done well; *Romans 2:14–15*, "For when the Gentiles, which have not the law, do by nature the things contained in the law, these, having not the law, are a law unto themselves: which show the work of the law written in their hearts, their conscience also bearing witness, and their thoughts the meanwhile accusing or else excusing one another." ***Sermons and Discourses, 1730–1733 (WJE Online Vol. 17)***

The Apostle says, *Romans 2:14–15*, that "the Gentiles, which have not the law, do by nature the things contained in the law; these, having not the law, are a law unto themselves: which show the work of the law written in their hearts, their conscience also bearing witness." In order to men's having the law of God made known to them by the light of nature, two things are necessary. The light of nature must not [only] discover to them that these and those things are their duty, i.e. that they are right, that there is a justice and equality in them, and the contrary unjust; but it must discover to 'em also, that 'tis the will of God that they should be done, and that they shall incur his displeasure by the contrary. For a law is a signification of the will of a lawgiver, with the danger of the effects of his displeasure, in case of the breach of that law. ***The "Miscellanies," (Entry Nos. 501–832) (WJE Online Vol. 18)***

I would inquire whether the law of nature, i.e. the nature and fitness of things, requires perfect virtue. If not, then what is virtue? The very definition of it, the nature of it, even according to the most noted and, for ought I know, all Arminian divines, is overthrown, viz. that virtue is an agreeableness to the nature, truth, reason and fitness of things. If so, then the law of nature must require everything that the nature, truth, reason and fitness of things requires: for to say that the fitness of things don't require all that is agreeable to the fitness of thing, is a plain contradiction. But if so—that is, it requires all that is agreeable to fitness in every point—then it requires perfect virtue and holiness. Now I would inquire whether or no all mankind ben't under the obligations of the law of nature If any says no, Christians who are under the gospel are released from that law and are under a milder law; then I would inquire whether the heathen that never heard of the gospel, and the heathen that lived before Christ and the apostles preached the gospel abroad in the world, were not under the law of nature. I trust this will not be denied. The Apostle plainly teaches it, *Romans 2:14–15*, and Arminian writers generally allow and assert it. And then, lastly, I would ask whether Christians that are under the gospel have less of duty, less holiness, required of 'em than those that live in the grossest heathenish darkness, are not obliged to such perfection from high degrees of virtue as they. ***"Controversies" Notebook (WJE Online Vol. 27)***

Romans 2:15

The godly have experience, and therefore know what it is: they know what the several graces of the Spirit are, they know what faith is, they know what divine love is, they know what repentance is and what spiritual joy is. And therefore when they read or hear of these things, they understand the Word. And therefore it is said that the godly have God's law "written in their hearts" [*Romans 2:15*], because they have these things in their hearts which the law recommends; and therefore when they read or hear, they find an agreement as there is between an original [and] an exact copy. ***Sermons and Discourses: 1723–1729 (WJE Online Vol. 14)***

That he would clearly make known his will to them, that they need not be at much pains to find it out, as in *Deuteronomy 30:11*, *Deuteronomy 30:14*, and *Romans 10:8–9* and *Romans 2:15*. Hence the effect of [it] here is said to be, "They shall all know me, from the least to the greatest" [*Jeremiah 31:34*]. So *Hebrews 8:13*. ***Writings on the Trinity, Grace, and Faith (WJE Online Vol. 21)***

'Tis true it is the heart that God looks at; godliness lies in the disposition of the heart, but godliness consists not in an *heart* to purpose to fulfill God's commandments, but in an *heart* actually to do it. The children of Israel had an heart to purpose to keep all God's commands. They say, "All that the Lord hath said, we will hear, and do." But God says, "O that there were such a heart in them, that they would fear me, and keep all my commandments always" commandments must needs be the proper evidence whether they have a heart actually to do God's commandments, and not only a heart to purpose and intend to do them. To the like purpose is that representation of sincere godliness of *God's law's being written on the heart* [*Romans 2:15, 2 Corinthians 3:2–3*], which signifies that true godliness consists in an heart to do God's commands, or perform God's law. ***Writings on the Trinity, Grace, and Faith (WJE Online Vol. 21)***

Romans 2:16

A secondary rule of judgment will be the gospel, wherein it is said, "He that believeth shall be saved; and he that believeth not [shall be damned]"

[*Mark 16:16*]. *Romans 2:16*, "In the day when God shall judge the secrets of men by Jesus Christ according to my gospel." It will be by the gospel, or covenant of grace, that believers shall have eternal blessedness adjudged to them. When it is found that the Law hinders not, that the curse and condemnation of the Law stands not against them, they shall have the reward of eternal life given them according to the glorious gospel of Jesus Christ: which gospel will be found, as well as the Law, to condemn the ungodly. They, being found not to have believed on the name of the Lord Jesus Christ, shall be condemned according to the tenor of that gospel. ***Sermons and Discourses: 1723–1729 (WJE Online Vol. 14)***

And then in *Romans 2:16* the Apostle repeatedly tells us when these things shall be, that men shall thus receive their retribution according to their deeds and circumstances in their state wherein there are these distinctions: "In the day," says he, "when God shall judge the secrets of men according to my gospel," which shows that this life is the only state of trial, and that all men shall be judged at the end of this world according to their behavior in this life, and not according to their behavior in another state of trial between this life and that day; which, with respect to most, will be so vastly longer than this life, and when they (as is supposed) will be under more powerful means to bring 'em to repentance. ***The "Miscellanies," (Entry Nos. 1153–1360) (WJE Online Vol. 23)***

Romans 2:17

The many texts against judging. *Proverbs 26:12*, "Seest thou a man wise in his own conceit? There is more hope of a fool than of him." *Isaiah 5:21*, "Woe to them that are wise in their own eyes, and prudent in their own sight." *Isaiah 65:5*, "Which say, Stand by thyself; come not near to me. For I am holier than thou." [*Luke 18:9*, *Luke 18:11*], the Pharisees "trusted in themselves that they were righteous, and despised others; they thanked God that they were "not as other men." *Romans 2:17–20*, "Thou makest thy boast of God, and knowest his will, and approvest the things that are more excellent, and art confident that thou thyself art a guide of the blind, a light of them which are in darkness, an instructor of the foolish, a teacher of babes." ***The "Miscellanies," 833–1152 (WJE Online Vol. 20)***

Romans 2:18

'Tis the moral law, and not the ceremonial that is written in the hearts of those who are destitute of divine revelation. And so in the *Romans 2:18* "Thou approvest the things that are more excellent, being instructed out of the law." 'Tis the moral law, that shows us the nature of things, and teaches us what is excellent. ***Sermons and Discourses, 1734–1738 (WJE Online Vol. 19)***

Romans 2:19

The first thing is this; he that is under the prevalence of this distemper, is apt to think highly of his attainments in religion, as comparing himself with others. 'Tis natural for him to fall into that thought of himself, that he is an eminent saint, that he is very high amongst the saints, and has distinguishably good and great experiences. That is the secret language of his heart, *Luke 18:11*, "God, I thank thee, that I am not as other men." And *Isaiah 65:5*, "I am holier than thou." Hence such are apt to put themselves forward among God's people, and as it were to take a high seat among them, as if there was no doubt of it but it belonged to them. They, as it were, naturally do that which Christ condemns (*Luke 14:7*, etc.), take the highest room. This they do, by being forward to take upon 'em the place and business of the chief: to guide, teach, direct and manage; they are confident that they are guides to the blind, a light of them which are in darkness, instructors of the foolish, teachers of babes (*Romans 2:19–20*). 'Tis natural for them to take it for granted, that it belongs to them to do the part of dictators and masters in matters of religion; and so they implicitly affect to be called of men "Rabbi," which is by interpretation "Master," as the Pharisees did (*Matthew 23:6–7*), i.e. they are apt to expect that others should regard 'em, and yield to 'em, as masters, in matters of religion. ***Religious Affections (WJE Online Vol. 2)***

Romans 2:20

The Apostle seems to make a distinction between mere speculative knowledge of the things of religion, and spiritual knowledge, in calling that "the form of knowledge, and of the truth"; *Romans 2:20*, "which has the form of knowledge, and of the truth in the law." The latter is often represented by relishing, smelling, or tasting; *2 Corinthians 2:14*, "Now thanks be to God, which always causeth us to triumph in Christ Jesus, and maketh manifest the savor of his knowledge, in every place." *Matthew 16:23*, "Thou savorest not the things that be of God, but those things that be of man." *1 Peter 2:2–3*, "As newborn babes, desire the sincere milk of the word, that ye may grow thereby; if so be ye have tasted that the Lord is gracious." *Canticles 1:3*, "Because of the savor of thy good ointment, thy name is as ointment poured forth; therefore do the virgins love thee"; compared with, *1 John 2:20*, "But ye have an unction from the holy One, and ye know all things." ***Religious Affections (WJE Online Vol. 2)***

'Tis the moral law, that shows us the nature of things, and teaches us what is excellent. *Romans 2:20*, "Thou hast a form of knowledge, and truth in the law." 'Tis the moral law, as is evident by what follows, *Romans 2:22* ... ***Sermons and Discourses, 1734–1738 (WJE Online Vol. 19)***

Romans 2:21

Thus it was [with] the Jews, especially with their teachers, the priests, and scribes, and Pharisees. Thus they saw many things, and observed not; and opened the ears, and yet heard not themselves, as it follows in *Romans 2:21*. "Thou therefore which teachest another, teachest thou not thyself?" *Isaiah 43:3*. ***The "Blank Bible" (WJE Online Vol. 24)***

Romans 2:21–22

The Apostle in these verses seems to allude to those words in *Psalms 50:16–18*. "Thou that preachest a man should not steal, dost thou steal? Thou that sayst a man should not commit adultery, dost thou commit adultery? Thou that abhorrest idols, dost thou commit sacrilege?" "Grotius on this text proves from Josephus, that some of the Jewish priests lived by rapine, depriving others of their share of the tithes, and even suffering them to perish for want; that others were guilty of gross uncleanness. And as for sacrilegiously robbing God and his altar, it had been complained of as early as Malachi's days (*Malachi 1:8*, *Malachi 1:12–13*). So that the instances here are given with great propriety." ***The "Blank Bible" (WJE Online Vol. 24)***

Romans 2:22

["Thou that abhorrest idols, dost thou commit sacrilege?"] Sacrilege was violating the temple of God, and to a high degree profaning it, especially robbing God of the sacred things. But one of the visible professing people of God was to regard his own body and soul as the temple, and all within him as God's property devoted sacred to him. And therefore by such an one's living in wickedness, God's temple was defiled and altogether violated, and God robbed of all its sacred treasures, vessels, and utensils, which are wickedly taken from him, and devoted to idols, and used in their service. What the sin here intended by the Apostle is we may learn by *1 Corinthians 6:15–20*, and *1 Corinthians 3:16–17*; *Ezekiel 16:15–19*; *Ezekiel 20:39*. There is a sacrilege in the wicked lives of the professors of religion far more aggravated than the idolatry of the heathen. ***The "Blank Bible" (WJE Online Vol. 24)***

Romans 2:23

There is a sacrilege in the wicked lives of the professors of religion far more aggravated than the idolatry of the heathen. Thou that gloriest in the law as thine honor, art thou so inconsistent with thyself as at the same time, by breaking the law, to dishonor the lawgiver? Dost thou expose the God to contempt that thou gloriest in? ***The "Blank Bible" (WJE Online Vol. 24)***

To stop them from boasting of their righteousness, as Jews were wont to do; as the Apostle observes in the *Romans 2:23*. That the Apostle has respect to stopping their mouths in this respect, appears by the *Romans 2:27* of the context, "Where is boasting then? It is excluded." The law stops our mouths from making any plea for life, the favor of God, or any positive good, from our own righteousness. ***Sermons and Discourses, 1734–1738 (WJE Online Vol. 19)***

Romans 2:25

["For circumcision verily profiteth, if thou keep the law."] A profession or visibility of religion profiteth, if we live according to our profession; otherwise it only aggravates our condemnation. See note on *Romans 1:16*. ***The "Blank Bible" (WJE Online Vol. 24)***

God was ready to justify all that believed in Christ, and to reward all that work good, but especially the Jews, for the peculiar favor he bore to that nation for their forefathers' sakes, as *Romans 11:28*, and because they were born in covenant, or were his covenant people by descent. See *Romans 2:25*, "For circumcision verily profiteth," etc. ***The "Blank Bible" (WJE Online Vol. 24)***

Romans 2:26

[*Romans 4:5*. Abraham's "faith is counted for righteousness."] There is no need to understand the Apostle that his faith, though in itself an imperfect righteousness, is accepted instead of a perfect righteousness, as that God had respect to any goodness or righteousness at all in faith; but only that God, by reason of his faith in God, accepted of him and dealt with him as though he had been righteous in himself. So the Apostle uses the phrase, *Romans 2:26*, "If the uncircumcision keep the law, shall not his uncircumcision be counted for circumcision," εἰς περιτομὴν λογισθήσεται? Not that his uncircumcision in itself shall be esteemed as of any value at all, but only that he shall fare no worse than if he were circumcised. ***The "Blank Bible" (WJE Online Vol. 24)***

Romans 2:27

Adultery, idolatry, and sacrilege, surely are the breaking of the moral, and not the ceremonial law. So in the *Romans 2:27*, "And shall not uncircumcision which is by nature, if it fulfill the law, judge thee, who by the letter and circumcision dost transgress the law," i.e. the Gentiles, that you despise because uncircumcised, if they live moral and holy lives, in obedience to the moral law, shall condemn you though circumcised. And so there is not one place in all the preceding part of the epistle, where the Apostle speaks of the law, but that he most apparently intends principally the moral law: and yet when the Apostle, in continuance of the same discourse, comes to tell us that we can't be justified by the works of the law, then they will needs have it, that he means only the ceremonial law; yea though all this discourse about the moral law, showing how the Jews as well as Gentiles have violated it, is evidently preparatory, and introductory to that doctrine, *Romans 3:20*, that "no flesh," that is none of mankind, neither Jews nor Gentiles, can be justified by the works of the law. ***Sermons and Discourses, 1734–1738 (WJE Online Vol. 19)***

To stop them from boasting of their righteousness, as Jews were wont to do; as the Apostle observes in the *Romans 2:23*. That the Apostle has respect to stopping their mouths in this respect, appears by the *Romans 2:27* of the context, "Where is boasting then? It is excluded." The law stops our mouths from making any plea for life, the favor of God, or any positive good, from our own righteousness. ***Sermons and Discourses, 1734–1738 (WJE Online Vol. 19)***

"By nature" imports . . . that his birth is a cause some way or other, or a foundation of his being thus corrupt. . . . As in *Romans 2:27*, the Gentiles are called "the uncircumcision by nature," i.e. by birth; not in respect of their natural constitution, but in respect of a privilege that the Jews had by birth, which the Gentiles had not. . . . So in *Galatians 2:15*, in opposition thereunto, saith he, "We who are Jews by nature"; that is, who have the privilege of Jews by birth. ***"Controversies" Notebook (WJE Online Vol. 27).***

Romans 2:28

"But peace shall be upon Israel." *Romans 9:6* and *Romans 2:28*. ***The "Blank Bible" (WJE Online Vol. 24)***

The Scriptures lay the main weight on the religion of the heart. We are often told here that God looks at the heart; and that "he is not a Jew," that is "one outwardly" [*Romans 2:28*]; and that those tokens that are "highly esteemed among men is abomination in the sight of God" [*Luke 16:15*]; and tells us that this is the first and greatest commandment: "thou shalt love the Lord thy God with all thy heart, and with all thy soul, and with all thy mind, and with all thy strength" [*Mark 12:30*]. But next to the religion of the heart towards God, the Scripture lays the greatest weight on duties of righteousness and love towards men, and prefers those much before external acts of worship. ***Sermons and Discourses, 1739–1742 (WJE Online Vol. 22)***

Romans 2:28–29

Regeneration is that whereby men come to have the character of true Christians; as is evident, and as is confessed; and so is circumcision of heart: for by this men become Jews inwardly, or Jews in the spiritual and Christian sense (and that is the same as being true Christians), as of old proselytes were made Jews by circumcision of the flesh. *Romans 2:28–29*, "For he is not a Jew, which is one outwardly; neither is that circumcision, which is outward of the flesh: but he is a Jew, which is one inwardly; and *circumcision* is that of the *heart*, in the spirit and not in the letter, whose praise is not of men, but of God." ***Original Sin (WJE Online Vol. 3)***

Thus "ten men shall take hold, out of all languages of the nations, of the skirt of him that is a Jew" (in the sense of the Apostle, *Romans 2:28–29*), "saying, We will go with you; for we have heard, that God is with you" [*Zechariah 8:23*]. And thus that shall be fulfilled, *Psalms 65:2*, "O thou that hearest prayer, unto thee shall all flesh come." ***Apocalyptic Writings (WJE Online Vol. 5)***

The Apostle speaks, in like manner, of the members of the church of Philippi as spiritually circumcised (i.e. in profession and visibility) and tells wherein this circumcision appeared. *Philippians 3:3*, "For we are the circumcision, which worship God in the Spirit, and rejoice in Christ Jesus, and have no confidence in the flesh." And in *Romans 2:28–29* the Apostle speaks of this Christian circumcision and Jewish circumcision together, calling the former the circumcision of the heart. "But he is not a Jew which is one outwardly, neither is that circumcision which is outward in the *flesh*; but he is a Jew, which is one inwardly, and circumcision is that of the *heart*; in the spirit, not in the letter; whose praise is not of men, but of God." And whereas in this prophecy of Ezekiel it is foretold, that none should enter into the Christian sanctuary or church, but such as are circumcised in heart and circumcised in flesh; thereby I suppose is intended, that none should be admitted but such as were visibly regenerated, and also baptized with outward baptism. ***Ecclesiastical Writings (WJE Online Vol. 12)***

Romans 2:29

And it is against the doctrines of Scripture, which do plainly teach us that the state of others' souls towards God, cannot be known by us, as in *Revelation 2:17*. "To him that overcometh, will I give to eat of the hidden manna; and I will give him a white stone, and in the stone a new name written, which no man knoweth, saving he that receiveth it." And *Romans 2:29*, "He is a Jew, which is one inwardly; and circumcision is that of the heart; in the spirit, and not in the letter; whose praise is not of men, but of God." That by this last expression, "whose praise is not of men, but of God," the Apostle has respect to the insufficiency of men to judge concerning him, whether he be inwardly a Jew or no (as they could easily see by outward marks, whether men were outwardly Jews) and would signify, that it belongs to God alone to give a determining voice in this matter, is confirmed by the same Apostle's use of the phrase, in *1 Corinthians 4:5*,

"Therefore judge nothing before the time, until the Lord come; who both will bring to light the hidden things of darkness, and will make manifest the counsels of the hearts"; and then shall every man have praise to God. ***Religious Affections (WJE Online Vol. 2)***

Their life is said to be "hidden," *Colossians 3:3–4*. Their food is the "hidden manna" [*Revelation 2:17*]; they have meat to eat that others know not of [*John 4:32*]; a stranger intermeddles not with their joys [*Proverbs 14:10*]: the heart in which they possess their divine distinguishing ornaments is the hidden man, and in the sight of God only, *1 Peter 3:4*. Their new name, that Christ has given them, "no man knows but he that receives it," *Revelation 2:17*. The praise of the true Israelites, whose "circumcision is that of the heart," is not of men but of God, *Romans 2:29*; that is, they can be certainly known and discerned to be Israelites, so as to have the honor that belongs to such, only of God; as appears by the use of the like expression by the same apostle, *1 Corinthians 4:5*. Speaking there of its being God's prerogative to judge who are upright Christians, and that which he will do at the Day of Judgment, he adds, "and then shall every man have praise of God." ***The Great Awakening (WJE Online Vol. 4)***

"But he is a Jew, which is one inwardly; and circumcision is that of the heart, in the spirit, and not in the letter; *whose praise is not of men, but of God*." That by this last expression, "whose praise is not of men, but of God," the Apostle has respect to the insufficiency of men to judge concerning him, whether he be inwardly a Jew, or no, and would signify that it belongs to God alone to give a voice in that matter, is confirmed by the same Apostle's use of the like phrase in *1 Corinthians 4:5*. "Therefore judge nothing before the time, until the Lord come, who both will bring to light the hidden things of darkness, and will make manifest the counsels of the hearts: *and then shall every man have praise of God*." The Apostle in the two foregoing verses says, "But with me it is a very small thing that I should be judged of you, or of man's judgment; yea, I judge not mine own self. For I know nothing of myself; yet am I not hereby justified, but he that judgeth me is the Lord" [*1 Corinthians 4:3–4*]. And again, it is further confirmed, because the Apostle in this *Romans 2*, directs himself especially to those that had a high conceit of their own holiness, made their boast of God, and were confident of their own discerning, and that they knew God's will, and approved the things that were more excellent, "*or tried the things that differ*," as it is in the margin (*Romans 2:18*), and were confident that they were guides of the blind, a light of them which are in darkness, instructors of the foolish, teachers of babes, and so took upon them to judge others. ***Notes on Scripture (WJE Online Vol. 15)***

Now the Apostle could not mean that merely the being circumcised would render Christ of no profit or effect to a person, for we read that Paul himself took Timothy and circumcised him because of the Jews (*Acts 16:3*). Therefore, 'tis a being circumcised under some particular apprehension, or notion, or with some certain view, that must be the thing that is fatal; and the Apostle must mean that Christ shall profit them nothing if they are circumcised under that notion or with that view that those Jews were, that were zealous for it and urged the necessity of it to them. But they were zealous of it as a thing that gave them great dignity, and on the account of which they were highly esteemed of God as something to be boasted of or gloried in, as *Galatians 6:12–14* and *Galatians 5:26* and *Galatians 6:3*; that which they sought praise by (*Romans 2:29*). ***The "Miscellanies," (Entry Nos. 501–832) (WJE Online Vol. 18)***

Ezekiel 36:26–27, "A new heart also will I give you, and a new spirit will I put within you: and I will take away the stony heart out of your flesh, and I will give you an heart of flesh. And I will put my spirit within you, and cause you to walk in my statutes, and ye shall keep my judgments, and do them." *Romans 2:29*, "But he is a Jew, that is one inwardly; and circumcision is that of the heart, in the spirit, and not in the letter." *Philippians 3:2–3*, "Beware of the concision. For we are the circumcision, which worship God in the spirit, and rejoice in Christ Jesus, and have no confidence in the flesh"; i.e. have no confidence in such external things as the Jewish circumcision, as being that worship that is acceptable to God, because 'tis not in the Spirit. ***Writings on the Trinity, Grace, and Faith (WJE Online Vol. 21)***

Romans 2:29, "He is a Jew who is one inwardly; and circumcision is that of the heart, in the spirit, and not in the letter; whose praise is not of men, but of God." The Apostle is speaking with regard to those self-conceited [persons in] *Romans 2:1*, "Therefore thou art inexcusable, O man, whosoever thou art that judgest: for wherein thou judgest another, thou condemnest thyself; for thou that judgest doest the same things." [And in *Romans 2:17–20*,] "Behold, thou art called a Jew, and restest in the law, and makest thy boast of God, and knowest his will, and approvest the things that are more excellent, being instructed out of the law; and art confident that thou thyself art a guide of the blind, a light of them which are in darkness, an instructor of the foolish, a teacher of babes, which hast the form of knowledge and of the truth in the law." It further appears that 'tis not God's manner thus immediately to make known [the workings of the Holy Spirit] because he has directed us to judge by other means: fruits, [for the] tree is known by its fruit. Some would argue from hence that persons may certainly know [the state of others], but the Word don't imply certain knowledge: but only that we shall know and distinguish by this rule, so as shall ordinarily be sufficient for our own safety. ***Sermons and Discourses, 1743–1758 (WJE Online Vol. 25)***

ROMANS CHAPTER 3

Romans 3:1

["What profit is there of circumcision?"] This inquiry has reference to what the Apostle had said before, *Romans 2:25*. ***The "Blank Bible" (WJE Online Vol. 24)***

Romans 3:2–4 ff.

"Chiefly, because unto them were committed the oracles of God." They had greater advantage for faith, because they had the ground of faith more fully and clearly set before them, viz. the word or truth of God. This ground of faith he, in the next verse, calls "the faith of God." This can be a just ground of faith, as it relies on the faithfulness of God whose word or truth it is. 'Tis this strength of the ground of faith that makes it an advantage to have this ground. The unbelief of some don't argue that the ground is vain and insufficient so as that it's no advantage to have it. If "the oracles of God" ben't true, then it's no advantage to have 'em committed to us; but the unbelief of some don't argue that for the word of God or oracles of God to be without effect, or vain, or no advantage, is for 'em not to be true, or not to be a good ground for faith. But the unbelief of some, that have had the abundant enjoyment of these oracles, don't argue that τά λόγια, or "the oracles of God," which the Apostle speaks of, especially intends the promises and prophecies of Christ and his salvation that he made to Abraham and others. ***The "Blank Bible" (WJE Online Vol. 24)***

Romans 3:4.

["God forbid," etc.] So far from that, that man's unbelief shall be made to commend the faith of God. God's truth will shine the brighter for men's opposition to it. The Romans 3:5 and Romans 3:7 refer to this. ***The "Blank Bible" (WJE Online Vol. 24)***

Romans 3:5

["I speak as a man."] Men will be ready to make such objections. ***The "Blank Bible" (WJE Online Vol. 24)***

By the word "righteousness" in the New Testament is not meant salvation and deliverance. *Matthew 3:15*, "thus it becomest us to fulfill all righteousness." *Matthew 21:32*, "John came in the way of righteousness." *Matthew 5:6*, "Blessed are they that hunger and thirst after righteousness." *Matthew 5:20*, "except your righteousness exceed the righteousness of the scribes and Pharisees, ye shall in no case enter into the kingdom of heaven." *Acts 10:35*, "he that feareth God and worketh righteousness." *Acts 24:25*, "Paul reasoned of temperance, righteousness." *Romans 2:26*, "if the uncircumcised keep the righteousness of the law." *Romans 3:5*, "Now if our unrighteousness commend the righteousness of God." *Romans 4:6*, "to whom God imputeth righteousness without works." *Romans 4:11*, "That righteousness might be imputed to them." *Romans 4:18*, "as by the offense of one judgment came upon all men to condemnation; so by the righteousness of one the free gift came upon all men to justification of life." *Romans 6:18*, "Being made free from sin, ye become the servants of righteousness." *Romans 6:13*, "instruments of righteousness unto holiness." *Romans 6:19*, "yield your members servants to righteousness." *Romans 6:20*, "ye were free from righteousness." *Romans 8:4*, "That the righteousness of the law might be fulfilled in us." *Romans 8:10*, "the body is dead because of sin; but the Spirit is life because of righteousness." *Romans 14:17*, "the kingdom of God is righteousness, peace." *1 Corinthians 1:30*, "who of God is made to us wisdom, righteousness, sanctification, and redemption." *1 Corinthians 15:34*, "Awake to righteousness." *2 Corinthians 6:7*, "armor of righteousness." *2 Corinthians 6:14*, "what fellowship hath righteousness with unrighteousness?" *2 Corinthians 9:10*, "increase the fruits of your righteousness." *2 Corinthians 11:15*, "as the ministers of righteousness." *Ephesians 6:14*, "having on the breastplate of righteousness." *Philippians 3:6*, "touching the righteousness of the law, blameless." *1 Timothy*

6:11, "follow after righteousness." *2 Timothy 2:22*, "follow righteousness." *Titus 3:5*, "Not by works of righteousness." *Hebrews 11:33*, "through faith wrought righteousness." *James 1:20*, "the wrath of man worketh not the righteousness of God." *James 3:18*, "the fruit of righteousness is sown in peace." *2 Peter 2:5*, "Noah, a preacher of righteousness." *1 John 2:29*, "every one that doth righteousness is born of God." *1 John 3:7*, "every one that doth righteousness is righteous, even as he is righteous." *1 John 3:10*, "doth not righteousness is not of God." *Revelation 19:8*, "The fine linen is the righteousness of saints." ***Writings on the Trinity, Grace, and Faith (WJE Online Vol. 21)***

"Mr. Locke has offered another exposition of these words, and by the 'righteousness' here spoken of, understands the righteousness of God, in keeping his word with the nation of the Jews, notwithstanding their provocations; or, as he explains it more fully in his notes on *Romans 3:5* to which he refers, God's 'faithfulness' in keeping his promise of saving believers, Gentiles as well as Jews, by righteousness through faith in Jesus Christ. But this seems to be as ill supported as that of Grotius. For I cannot find one single passage in the whole New Testament, where *δικαιοσυνης θεο* is used in that sense. Most certainly it is used in a very different sense in this context, *Romans 3:21*, *Romans 3:23*, and throughout this epistle, where it always signifies, either the righteousness by which we are justified, or that perfection of God which makes such righteousness necessary to our justification. In the former sense it is used, *Romans 9:30–31*, and *Romans 10:4*. And both these senses seem to have place, *Romans 10:3*, where the word is used twice in one verse. And as to the sense which it bears in the *Romans 3:5*, which is the only passage Mr. Locke refers to in support of his opinion, 'tis evidently to be understood there of the justice of God, that perfection which is manifested and displayed in punishing the sin and unrighteousness of men; the sense it likewise bears in the text under consideration. Not to add, that the Apostle speaks here of the 'remission' of the sins of particular persons, even of all that died in faith under the dispensation of the Old Testament, and not of the remission of the sins of the Jews nationally considered, as Mr. Locke is obliged to understand it consistently with the sense of the text. Compare *Hebrews 9:15*." Rawlin on *Justification*, pp. 94–95. ***The "Miscellanies," (Entry Nos. 1153–1360) (WJE Online Vol. 23)***

Romans 3:7

That the ultimate end of moral goodness or righteousness is answered in God's glory being attained, is supposed in the objection which the Apostle makes or supposes some will make, in *Romans 3:7*, "For if the truth of God hath more abounded through my lie unto his glory, why am I judged as a sinner?" I.e., seeing the great end of righteousness is answered by my sin, in God's being glorified, why is my sin condemned and punished: and why is not my vice equivalent to virtue? ***Ethical Writings (WJE Online Vol. 8)***

Romans 3:9

["Now we know that whatsoever," etc.] By the law here is meant the Old Testament. Respect is here had to the words in the foregoing verses, quoted out of the Old Testament, as being part of what the law saith. Those whom the Apostle has a special respect to, speaking of those that "are under the law," are the Jews. He argues that these things he had quoted out of the law, describing men's wickedness, are spoken to and so of the Jews, "that every mouth may be stopped," that the Jews might be stopped as well as the Gentiles, that the Jews might become guilty and appear sinners, as well as other nations, agreeably to *Romans 3:9*. "Are we no better than they? No, in no wise. Both Jews and Gentiles are all under sin." For the Apostle here resumes the argument he was upon in the foregoing chapter, that the Jews and circumcision, as well as Gentiles, are exposed to [the] wrath and curse of God. By those that are "without [the] law" is meant the Gentiles, and those that are "under the law," the Jews, as appears by the *Romans 2:12*. It is to be noted that in each of these places in the Old Testament quoted in the foregoing verses, special respect is had to those that were of the nation of Israel; and they are spoken more especially and immediately of them. ***The "Blank Bible" (WJE Online Vol. 24)***

["What then?"] This has reference to what is said in the *Romans 3:2*. ***The "Blank Bible" (WJE Online Vol. 24)***

The main subject of the doctrinal part of this epistle, is the free grace of God, in the salvation of men by Jesus Christ; especially as it appears in the doctrine of justification by faith alone. And the more clearly to evince this doctrine, and show the reason of it, the Apostle, in the first place, establishes that point, that no flesh living can be justified by the deeds of the law. And to prove it, he is very large and particular in showing, that all mankind, not only the Gentiles, but Jews, are under sin, and so under the condemnation to the law; which is what he insists upon from the beginning of the epistle to this place. He first begins with the Gentiles; and in the *Romans 1*, shows that they are under sin, by setting forth the exceeding corruptions and horrid wickedness, that overspread the Gentile world: and then through the *Romans 2–3*, to the text and following verse, he shows the same of the Jews, that they also are in the same circumstances with the Gentiles, in this regard. They had an high thought of themselves, because they were God's covenant people, and circumcised, and the children of Abraham. They despised the Gentiles, as polluted, condemned, and accursed; but looked on themselves, on account of their external privileges, and ceremonial and moral righteousness, as a pure and holy people, and the children of God; as the Apostle observes in the *Romans 2*. It was therefore strange doctrine to them, that they also were unclean and guilty in God's sight, and under the condemnation and curse of the law. The Apostle does therefore, on account of their strong prejudices against such doctrine, the more particularly insist upon it, and shows that they are no better than the Gentiles; as in the *Romans 3:9*, "What then? Are we better than they? No, in no wise: for we have before proved both Jews and Gentiles, that they are all under sin." And to convince them of it, he then produces certain passages out of their own law, or the Old Testament (whose authority they pretended a great regard to), from the *Romans 3:9*. And it may be observed, that the Apostle first, cites certain passages to prove that mankind are all corrupt, in the *Romans 3:10–12*; "As it is written, There is none righteous, no not one: there is none that understandeth: there is none that seeketh after God: they are all gone out of the way: they are together become unprofitable: there is none that doeth good; no not one." Secondly the passages he cites next, are to prove that not only are all corrupt, but each one wholly corrupt, as it were all over unclean, from the crown of his head, to the soles of his feet; and therefore several particular parts of the body are mentioned, as the throat, the tongue, the lips, the mouth, the feet. *Romans 3:13–15*, "Their throat is an open sepulcher, with their tongues they have used deceit, the poison of asps is under their lips; whose mouth is full of cursing and bitterness, their feet are swift to shed blood." And, thirdly, he quotes other passages to show, that each one is not only all over corrupt, but corrupt to a desperate degree, in the *Romans 3:16–18*; in which the exceeding degree of their corruption is shown, both by affirming and denying: by affirmatively expressing the most pernicious nature and tendency of their wickedness, in the *Romans 3:16*, "Destruction and misery are in their ways." And then by denying all good, or godliness, in them, in the *Romans 3:17–18*, "And the way of peace have they not known: there is no fear of God before their eyes." And then, lest the Jews should think these passages of their law don't concern them, and that only the Gentiles are intended in them, the Apostle shows in the verse of the text, not only that they are not exempt, but that they especially must be understood, "Now we know, that whatsoever things the law saith, it saith to them that are under the law." By those that are "under the law," is meant the Jews, and the Gentiles by those that are without law; as appears by the *Romans 2:12*. There is special reason to understand the law, as speaking to and of them, to whom it was immediately given. And therefore the Jews would be unreasonable in exempting themselves. And if we examine the places of the Old Testament, whence these passages are taken, we shall see plainly that special respect is had to the wickedness of the people of that nation, in every one of them. So that the law shuts all up in universal and desperate wickedness, "that every mouth may be stopped." The mouths of the Jews, as well as of the Gentiles; notwithstanding all those privileges by which they were distinguished from the Gentiles. ***Sermons and Discourses, 1734–1738 (WJE Online Vol. 19)***

Romans 3:10

[And following verses.] The passages here quoted out of the Old Testament are to prove three things. 1. That mankind are universally sinful; that everyone is corrupt. That is what is aimed at in the *Romans 3:10–12*. 2. That everyone is not only corrupt, but everyone totally corrupt in every part. That is aimed at by the quotations in the *Romans 3:13–15*, where the several parts of the body are mentioned. And 3. That everyone is not only corrupt in every part, but corrupt throughout in an exceeding degree, in the *Romans 3:16–18*. ***The "Blank Bible" (WJE Online Vol. 24)***

Romans 3:10–12

Original depravity may well be argued from wickedness being often spoken of in Scripture as a thing *belonging to the race of mankind, and as if it were a property of the species*. So in *Psalms 14:2–3*, "The Lord looked down from heaven upon the children of men, to see if there were any that did understand, and seek God. They are all gone aside; they are altogether become filthy: there is none that doth good; no, not one." The like we have again, *Psalms 53:2–3*. Dr. Taylor says, "The Holy Spirit don't mean this of every individual; because in the very same Psalm, he speaks of some that were righteous. *Psalms 14:5*, 'God is in the generation of the righteous.'" But how little is this observation to the purpose? For who ever supposed, that no unrighteous men were ever changed by divine grace, and afterwards made righteous? The Psalmist is speaking of what men are as they are the CHILDREN OF MEN, born of the corrupt human race; and not as born of God, whereby they come to be the children of God, and of the *generation of the righteous.* The apostle Paul cites this place in *Romans 3:10–12*, to prove the universal corruption of mankind; but yet in the same chapter he supposes, these same persons here spoken of as wicked, may become righteous, through the righteousness and grace of God. ***Original Sin (WJE Online Vol. 3)***

Original depravity may well be argued from wickedness being often spoken of in Scripture as a thing *belonging to the race of mankind, and as if it were a property of the species.* So in *Psalms 14:2–3*, "The Lord looked down from heaven upon the children of men, to see if there were any that did understand, and seek God. They are all gone aside; they are altogether become filthy: there is none that doth good; no, not one." The like we have again, *Psalms 53:2–3*. Dr. Taylor says, "The Holy Spirit don't mean this of every individual; because in the very same Psalm, he speaks of some that were righteous. *Psalms 14:5*, 'God is in the generation of the righteous.'" But how little is this observation to the purpose? For whoever supposed, that no unrighteous men were ever changed by divine grace, and afterwards made righteous? The Psalmist is speaking of what men are as they are the CHILDREN OF MEN, born of the corrupt human race; and not as born of God, whereby they come to be the children of God, and of the *generation of the righteous.* The apostle Paul cites this place in *Romans 3:10–12*, to prove the universal corruption of mankind; but yet in the same chapter he supposes, these same persons here spoken of as wicked, may become righteous, through the righteousness and grace of God. ***Original Sin (WJE Online Vol. 3)***

According to this, the universality of the terms that are found in these places, which the Apostle cites from the Old Testament, to prove that *all the world, both Jews and gentiles, are under sin*, is nothing to his purpose. The Apostle uses universal terms in his proposition, and in his conclusion, that ALL are under sin, that EVERY MOUTH is stopped, ALL THE WORLD guilty, that by the deeds of the law NO FLESH can be justified. And he chooses out a number of universal sayings or clauses out of the Old Testament, to confirm this universality; as, "There is none righteous;

no, not one; they are all gone out of the way; there is none that understandeth," etc. [*Romans 3:10–11*]. But yet the universality of these expressions is nothing to his purpose; because the universal terms found in 'em have indeed no reference to any such universality as this the Apostle speaks of, nor anything akin to it; they mean no universality, either in the collective sense, or personal sense; no universality of the nations of the world, or of particular persons in those nations, or in any one nation in the world: "But only of those of whom they are true." That is, "There is none of them righteous, of whom it is true, that they are not righteous, no, not one: there is none that understand, of whom it is true, that they understand not: they are all gone out of the way, of whom it is true, that they are gone out of the way," etc. Or these expressions are to be understood concerning that strong party in Israel, in David's and Solomon's days and in the prophets' days: they are to be understood of them universally. And what is that to the Apostle's purpose? How does such an universality of wickedness, as this—that all were wicked in Israel, who were wicked, or that there was a particular evil party, all of which were wicked—confirm that universality which the Apostle would prove, viz. that all Jews and Gentiles, and the whole world were wicked, and every mouth stopped, and that no flesh could be justified by their own righteousness. ***Original Sin (WJE Online Vol. 3)***

Romans 3:10–18

Adam's fall has framed all men's hearts alike in this matter. Hence the Apostle, *Romans 3:10–18*, proves the corruption of natures, hearts and lives of men, from what the Psalmist says of the wicked in his day, *Psalms 14:1–3*, *Psalms 5:9*, *Psalms 140:3*, *Psalms 10:7*, *Psalms 36:1*; and from what Jeremiah saith of the wicked in his day, *Jeremiah 9:3*; and from what Isaiah said of those that lived in his time, *Isaiah 57:7–8*; and concludes with that, v. 19, "Now we know that what things soever the law saith, it saith to them that are under the law: that every mouth may be stopped, and that all the world may become guilty before God." ***"Controversies" Notebook (WJE Online Vol. 27)***

Romans 3:13 ff

Those places of the Old Testament that are quoted in the *Romans 3:13* and following verses 4 seem to be chosen out by the Apostle because they express the utter and total corruption and depravity of these of whom they are spoken. The Apostle would show the universality of the corruption, and therefore chooses these texts that mention the several parts of the body: the throat, the tongue, the lips, the mouth, the feet. The *Romans 3:15–16* are part of the same quotation with the seventeenth. And this is added, because they express the utter corruption of the wicked by both affirming and denying, by affirming depravity and perverseness of 'em in the *Romans 3:16*, and denying righteousness of 'em in the *Romans 3:17*. The quotation of the *Psalms 36:1* denies all godliness or fear of God of them [*Romans 3:18*]. ***The "Blank Bible"***

Some of the most poisonous sorts of serpents have their tongue for their weapon, wherewith they mortally sting others, and serpents commonly threaten with their tongues, to represent the venomous nature of the tongues of wicked men, and how much the corruption of the heart flows out by that member, and in how venomous and deadly a manner it is put forth thereby. And therefore & tis said of wicked men that the poison of asps is under their tongues [*Romans 3:13*], and the apostle James says the tongue is "full of deadly poison" (*James 9.8*), and that it is "a fire, a world of iniquity" and sets together "on fire the course of nature; and is set on fire of hell. For every kind of beasts and of birds, and of serpents, and of things in the sea, is tamed, and hath been tamed of mankind: But the tongue can no man tame; it is an unruly evil, full of deadly poison" [*James 3:6–8*]. And *Psalms 140:3*, "They have sharpened their tongues like a serpent." ***Typological Writings (WJE Online Vol. 11)***

Those places of the Old Testament that are quoted in the *Romans 3:13* and following verses seem to be chosen out by the Apostle because they express the utter and total corruption and depravity of these of whom they are spoken. The Apostle would show the universality of the corruption, and therefore chooses these texts that mention the several parts of the body: the throat, the tongue, the lips, the mouth, the feet. The *Romans 3:15–16* are part of the same quotation with the seventeenth. And this is added, because they express the utter corruption of the wicked by both affirming and denying, by affirming depravity and perverseness of 'em in the *Romans 3:16*, and denying righteousness of 'em in the *Romans 3:17*. The quotation of the *Psalms 36:1* denies all godliness or fear of God of them [*Romans 3:18*]. ***The "Blank Bible" (WJE Online Vol. 24)***

Romans 3:14

Here nothing can be said to abate the nonsense, but this, that the Apostle would convince the Jews, that they were capable of being wicked as well as other nations; and to prove it, he mentions some texts, which show that there was a wicked party in Israel, a thousand years ago: and that as to the universal terms which happened to be in these texts, the Apostle had no respect to these; but his reciting them is as it were accidental, they happened to be in some texts which speak of an evil party in Israel, and the Apostle cites 'em as they are, not because they are any more to his purpose for the universal terms, which happen to be in them. But let the reader look on the words of the Apostle, and observe the violence of such a supposition. Particularly let the words of the *ninth and tenth* verses, and their connection, be observed. "All are under sin: as it is written, there is none righteous; no, not one." How plain it is, that the Apostle cites that latter universal clause out of the *Romans 3:14*, to confirm the preceding universal words of his own proposition? And yet it will follow from the things which Dr. Taylor supposes, that the universality of the terms in the last words, "There is none righteous; no, not one," have no relation at all to that universality he speaks of in the preceding clause, to which they are joined, "All are under sin"; and is no more a confirmation of it, than if the words were thus: "There are *some*, or there are *many* in Israel, that are not righteous." ***Original Sin (WJE Online Vol. 3)***

Romans 3:15

In Proverbs 1:16 'tis said of sinners, "Their feet run to evil, and make haste to shed blood." This the Apostle in *Romans 3:15* cites as belonging to the description of all natural men. So in the description of the wicked (*Proverbs 4:14–19*), 'tis said, that "they sleep not unless they have done mischief," that "they drink the wine of violence," etc. and yet by "the wicked" there is meant the same with the graceless man; as appears by the antithesis, there made [*Proverbs 4:18*] between him and the just or "righteous whose path is as the shining light which shineth more and more to the perfect day." ***Ecclesiastical Writings (WJE Online Vol. 12)***

Romans 3:17

First, that here, in the beginning of this discourse of his of the wickedness of the whole world, both Jews and Gentiles, that is continued from this place to the *Romans 3:19*, *Romans 3:20*, and *Romans 3:21* verses of *Romans 3*, as well as in the conclusion in that part of the *Romans 3*, he manifests his design in it all to be to show that all are guilty, and in a state of condemnation, and therefore can't be saved by their own righteousness, that it must be by the righteousness of God through Christ received by faith alone. He here in the *Romans 3:17* asserts that 'tis thus only that men have justification, and then in the *Romans 3:18* enters on the reason why, "For the wrath of God is revealed from heaven against all ungodliness and unrighteousness of men, who hold the truth in unrighteousness"; and so goes on, setting forth the ungodliness and unrighteousness of men through most of those three first chapters, and then at the end, concludes his argument as he began it, that, seeing all are under sin, "Therefore by the deeds of the law shall no flesh living be justified in his sight" [*Romans 3:20*], but that 'tis by "the righteousness of God which is by the faith of Christ" [*Romans 3:22*]. ***Notes on Scripture (WJE Online Vol. 15)***

Romans 3:19

["Now we know that whatsoever," etc.] By the law here is meant the Old Testament. Respect is here had to the words in the foregoing verses, quoted out of the Old Testament, as being part of what the law saith. Those whom the Apostle has a special respect to, speaking of those that "are under the law," are the Jews. He argues that these things he had quoted out of the law, describing men's wickedness, are spoken to and so of the Jews, "that every mouth may be stopped," that the Jews might be stopped as well as the Gentiles, that the Jews might become guilty and appear sinners, as well as other nations, agreeably to *Romans 3:9*. "Are we no better than they? No, in no wise. Both Jews and Gentiles are all under sin." For the Apostle here resumes the argument he was upon in the foregoing chapter, that the Jews and circumcision, as well as Gentiles, are exposed to [the] wrath and curse of God. By those that are "without [the] law" is meant the Gentiles, and those that are "under the law," the Jews, as appears by the *Romans 2:12*. It is to be noted that in each of these places in the Old Testament quoted in the foregoing verses, special respect is had to those that were of the nation of Israel; and they are spoken more especially and immediately of them. ***The "Blank Bible" (WJE Online Vol. 24)***

When sinners are the subjects of great convictions of conscience, and a remarkable work of the law; 'tis only a transacting the business of the day of judgment, in the conscience beforehand: God sits enthroned in the conscience, as at the last day, he will sit enthroned in the clouds of heaven; the sinner is arraigned, as it were, at God's bar; and God appears in his awful greatness, as a just and holy, sin–hating and sin–revenging God, as he will then. The sinner's iniquities are brought to light; his sins set in order before him; the hidden things of darkness, and the counsels of the heart are made manifest; as it will be then: many witnesses do, as it were, rise up against the sinner under convictions of conscience; as they will against the wicked, at the day of judgment: and the books are opened, particularly the book of God's strict and holy law, is opened in the conscience, and its rules applied for the condemnation of the sinner; which is the book that will be opened at the day of judgment, as the grand rule of judgment, to all such wicked men as have lived under it: and the sentence of the law is pronounced against the sinner; and the justice of the sentence made manifest; as it will be at the day of judgment. The conviction of a sinner at the day of judgment, will be a work of the law, as well as the conviction of conscience in this world: and the work of the law (if the work be *merely legal*) be sure, is never carried further in the consciences of sinners now, than it will be at that day, when its work will be perfect, in thoroughly stopping the sinner's mouth. *Romans 3:19*, "Now we know, that what things soever the law saith, it saith to them that are under the law; that every mouth may be stopped, and all the world may become guilty before God." Every mouth shall be stopped by the law, either now or hereafter; and all the world shall become sensibly guilty before God; guilty of death, deserving of damnation. And therefore, if sinners have been the subjects of a great work of the law, and have thus become guilty, and their mouths have been stopped; it is no certain sign that ever they have been converted. ***Sermons and Discourses, 1743–1758 (WJE Online Vol. 25)***

And whatever minister has a like occasion to deal with souls, in a flock under such circumstances, as this was in the last year, I can't but think he will soon find himself under a necessity greatly to insist upon it with them, that God is under no manner of obligation to shew mercy to any natural man, whose heart is not turned to God: and that a man can challenge nothing, either in absolute justice or by free promise, from anything he does before he has believed on Jesus Christ or has true repentance begun in him. It appears to me, that if I had taught those that came to me under trouble any other doctrine, I should have taken a most direct course utterly to have undone them; I should have directly crossed what was plainly the drift of the Spirit of God in his influences upon them; for if they had believed what I said, it would either have promoted self-flattery and carelessness, and so put an end to their awakenings; or cherished and established their contention and strife with God, concerning his dealings with them and others, and blocked up their way to that humiliation before the sovereign disposer of life and death, whereby God is wont to prepare them for his consolations. And yet those that have been under awakenings have oftentimes plainly stood in need of being encouraged, by being told of the infinite and all-sufficient mercy of God in Christ; and that 'tis God's manner to succeed diligence and to bless his own means, that so awakenings and encouragements, fear and hope may be duly mixed and proportioned to preserve their minds in a just medium between the two extremes of self-flattery and despondence, both which tend to slackness and negligence, and in the end to security. I think I have found that no discourses have been more remarkably blessed, than those in which the doctrine of God's absolute sovereignty with regard to the salvation of sinners, and his just liberty with regard to answering the prayers, or succeeding the pains of natural men, continuing such, have been insisted on. I never found so much immediate saving fruit, in any measure, of any discourses I have offered to my congregation, as some from those words, *Romans 3:19*, "That every mouth may be stopped"; endeavoring to shew from thence that it would be just with God forever to reject and cast off mere natural men. ***The Great Awakening (WJE Online Vol. 4)***

Romans 3:19–20

That every one of mankind, at least of them that are capable of acting as moral agents, are guilty of sin (not now taking it for granted that they come guilty into the world) is a thing most clearly and abundantly evident from the holy Scriptures. *1 Kings 8:46*, "If any man sin against thee, for there is no man that sinneth not." *Ecclesiastes 7:20*, "There is not a just man upon earth that doth good, and sinneth not." *Job 9:2–3*, "I know it is so of a truth" (i.e. as Bildad had just before said, that God would not cast away a perfect man, etc.), "but how should man be just with God? If he will contend with him, he cannot answer him one of a thousand." To the like purpose, *Psalms 143:2*, "Enter not into judgment with thy servant; for in thy sight shall no man living be justified." So the words of the Apostle (in which he has apparent reference to those words of the Psalmist), *Romans 3:19–20*, "That every mouth may be stopped, and all the world become guilty before God. Therefore by the deeds of the law there shall no flesh be justified in his sight: for by the law is the knowledge of sin." So *Galatians 2:16, 1 John 1:7–10*, "If we walk in the light, the blood of Christ cleanseth us from all sin. If we say that we have no sin, we deceive ourselves, and the truth is not in us. If we confess our sins, he is faithful and just to forgive us our sins, and to cleanse us from all unrighteousness. If we say that we have not sinned, we make him a liar, and his word is not in us." As in this place, so in innumerable other places, confession and repentance of sin are spoken of as duties proper for all; as also prayer to God for pardon of sin; and forgiveness of those that injure us, from that motive, that we hope to be forgiven of God. Universal guilt of sin might also be demonstrated from the appointment, and the declared use and end, of the ancient sacrifices; and also from the ransom, which everyone that was numbered in Israel, was directed to pay, to make atonement for his soul (*Exodus 30:11–16*). All are represented, not only as being sinful, but as having great and manifold iniquity (*Job 9:2–3*; *James 3:1–12*). ***Original Sin (WJE Online Vol. 3)***

Very commonly when men first are made sensible of their dangers, their mouths are open against God and his dealings; that is, their hearts are full of murmurings. But 'tis God's manner, before he comforts and reveals his mercy and love to them, to stop their mouths and make 'em to own their guilt, and so to acknowledge their guilt as that they shall acknowledge their desert of the threatened punishment; *Romans 3:19–20*, "Now we know that what things soever the law saith, it saith to them that are under the law: that every mouth may be stopped, and all the world may become guilty before God. Therefore by the deeds of the law there shall no flesh be justified in his sight: for by the law is the knowledge of sin." ***Sermons and Discourses, 1730–1733 (WJE Online Vol. 17)***

Romans 3:19.

["Now we know that whatsoever," etc.] By the law here is meant the Old Testament. Respect is here had to the words in the foregoing verses, quoted out of the Old Testament, as being part of what the law saith. Those whom the Apostle has a special respect to, speaking of those that "are under the law," are the Jews. He argues that these things he had quoted out of the law, describing men's wickedness, are spoken to and so of the Jews, "that every mouth may be stopped," that the Jews might be stopped as well as the Gentiles, that the Jews might become guilty and appear sinners, as well as other nations, agreeably to *Romans 3:9*. "Are we no better than they? No, in no wise. Both Jews and Gentiles are all under sin." For the Apostle here resumes the argument he was upon in the foregoing chapter, that the Jews and circumcision, as well as Gentiles, are exposed to [the] wrath and curse of God. By those that are "without [the] law" is meant the Gentiles, and those that are "under the law," the Jews, as appears by the *Romans 2:12*. It is to be noted that in each of these places in the Old Testament quoted in the foregoing verses, special respect is had to those that were of the nation of Israel; and they are spoken more especially and immediately of them. ***The "Blank Bible" (WJE Online Vol. 24)***

Romans 3:23

In the *Romans 3*, our having been guilty of breaches of the moral law, is an argument that the Apostle uses why we cannot be justified by the works of the law; beginning with the *Romans 3:9* there he proves out of the Old Testament, that all are under sin; "there is none righteous no, not one": "their throat is an open sepulcher: with their tongues have they used deceit": "their mouth is full of cursing and bitterness"; and "their feet swift to shed blood." And so he goes on mentioning only those things that are breaches of the moral law, and then when he has done, his conclusion is, in the *Romans 3:19–20*, "Now we know that whatsoever things the law saith, it saith to them that are under the law, that every mouth may be stopped, and all the world may become guilty before God. Therefore by the deeds of the law, shall no flesh be justified in his sight." This is most evidently his argument, because all had sinned (as it was said in the *Romans 3:9*) and been guilty of those breaches of the moral law, that he had mentioned (and it is repeated over again, afterward *Romans 3:23*). "For all have sinned and come short of the glory of God." Therefore none at all can be justified by the deeds of the law: now if the Apostle meant only that we are not justified by the deeds of the ceremonial law, what kind of arguing would that be, "Their mouth is full of cursing and bitterness, their feet are swift to shed blood," therefore, they can't be justified by the deeds of the Mosaic administration? They are guilty of the breaches of the moral law, and therefore they can't be justified by the deeds of the ceremonial law? Doubtless the Apostle's argument is, that the very same law they have broken and sinned against, can never justify 'em as observers of it, because every law don't justify, but necessarily condemns its violators: and therefore our breaches of the moral law, argue no more, than that we can't be justified by that law that we have broken. ***Sermons and Discourses, 1734–1738 (WJE Online Vol. 19)***

Romans 3:24

If there were no other text in the Bible about justification but this, this would clearly and invincibly prove that we are not justified by any of our own goodness, virtue, or righteousness or for the excellency or righteousness of anything that we have done in religion; because 'tis here so fully and strongly asserted: but this text does abundantly confirm other texts of the Apostle, where he denies justification by works of the law: there is no doubt can be rationally made but that, when the Apostle here shows that God saves us according to his mercy, in that he don't save us by "works of righteousness that we have done" (*Titus 3:5*), and that so we are "justified by grace" (*Titus 3:7*), herein opposing salvation by works, and salvation by grace, he means the same works as he does in other places, where he in like manner opposes works and grace, the same works as in *Romans 11:6*, "And if by grace then is it no more of works; otherwise grace is no more grace: but if it be of works, then it is no more grace; otherwise work is no more work." And the same works as in *Romans 4:4*, "Now to him that worketh, is the reward not reckoned of grace but of debt." And the same works that are spoken of in the context of the *Romans 3:24* of the foregoing chapter, which the Apostle there calls works of the law "being justified freely by his grace . . ." And of the *Romans 4:16*, "Therefore 'tis of faith, that it might be by grace." Where in the context, the righteousness of faith, is opposed to the righteousness of the law: for here God's saving us according to his mercy, and justifying us by grace, is opposed to saving us by works of righteousness that we have done, in the same manner as in those places justifying us by his grace, is opposed to justifying us by works of the law. ***Sermons and Discourses, 1734–1738 (WJE Online Vol. 19)***

The following passages from Dr. Guise, in the *Berry Street Sermons*, Sermon 21, illustrate this point. "The Apostle states the notion of grace in justification, saying, 'If by grace, then it is no more of the works: otherwise grace is no more grace. But if it be of works, then it is no more grace: otherwise, work is no more work' (*Romans 11:6*). But lest we should take the term *grace* in some laxer sense, as it is concerned in our justification, it is further said to be 'freely by his grace' (*Romans 3:24*) to exclude all conceit, as though there were anything in us, for which this favor of God is extended to us. And in the following chapter, the Apostle excludes all our works from having any share in our title to this blessing, 'that the reward may be reckoned to be of grace, not of debt,' and speaks of God's 'justifying the ungodly,' to show what their character was, till he justified them (*Romans 4:4–5*). And what but grace could move him to justify persons of that character? Accordingly, in the next chapter, he seems to strain the powers of language to set out the freeness and riches of this grace, calling it 'the grace of God,' and 'the gift by grace, which had abounded unto many,' and 'the free gift' in delivering from 'many offenses unto justification' (*Romans 5:15–16*)." ***The "Miscellanies," 833–1152 (WJE Online Vol. 20)***

Romans 3:9–24

[COMMENT: This is an extended section from Jonathan Edwards' Observations on *Romans 3:9–24*]

If the Scriptures represent all mankind as wicked in their first state, before they are made partakers of the benefits of Christ's redemption, then they are wicked by nature: for doubtless men's first state is their native state, or the state they come into the world in. But the Scriptures do thus represent all mankind.

Before I mention particular texts to this purpose, I would observe, that it alters not the case as to the argument in hand, whether we suppose these texts speak directly of infants, or only of such as are capable of some understanding, so as to understand something of their own duty and state. For if it be so with all mankind, that as soon as ever they are capable of reflecting and knowing their own moral state, they find themselves wicked, this proves that they are wicked by nature, either born wicked, or born with an infallible disposition to be wicked as soon as possible, if there be any difference between these; and either of 'em will prove men to be born exceedingly depraved. I have before proved, that a native propensity to sin certainly follows from many things said in the Scripture, of mankind; but what I intend now, is something more direct, to prove by direct Scripture-testimony, that all mankind in their first state are really of a wicked character.

To this purpose is exceeding full, express and abundant that passage of the Apostle, in *Romans 3* beginning with the *ninth verse to the end of the twenty-fourth*; which I shall set down at large, distinguishing the universal terms which are here so often repeated, by a distinct character. The

Apostle having in the first chapter, vv. 16–17, laid down his proposition, that none can be saved in any other way than through the righteousness of God, by faith in Jesus Christ, he proceeds to prove this point, by showing particularly that all are in themselves wicked, and without any righteousness of their own. First, he insists on the wickedness of the gentiles, in the first chapter; and next, on the wickedness of the Jews, in the second chapter. And then in this place, he comes to sum up the matter, and draw the conclusion in the words following: "What then, are we better than they? No, in no wise; for we have before proved both Jews and gentiles, that they are all under sin; as it is written, there is NONE righteous, NO, NOT ONE; there is NONE that understandeth; there is NONE that seeketh after God; they are ALL gone out of the way; they are TOGETHER become unprofitable; there is NONE that doth good, NO, NOT ONE. Their throat is an open sepulchre; with their tongues they have used deceit; the poison of asps is under their lips; whose mouth is full of cursing and bitterness; their feet are swift to shed blood–destruction and misery are in their ways, and the way of peace they have not known; there is no fear of God before their eyes. Now we know, that whatsoever things the law saith, it saith to them that are under the law, that EVERY mouth may be stopped, and ALL THE WORLD may become guilty before God. Therefore by the deeds of the law, there shall NO FLESH be justified in his sight; for by the law is the knowledge of sin. But now the righteousness of God without the law is manifest, being witnessed by the law and the prophets; even the righteousness of God, which is by faith of Jesus Christ, unto ALL, and upon ALL them that believe; for there is NO DIFFERENCE. For ALL have sinned, and come short of the glory of God, being justified freely by his grace, through the redemption which is in Jesus Christ."

Here the thing which I would prove, viz. that mankind in their first state, before they are interested in the benefits of Christ's redemption, are universally wicked, is declared with the utmost possible fullness and precision. So that if here this matter ben't set forth plainly, expressly and fully, it must be because no words can do it, and it is not in the power of language or any manner of terms and phrases, however contrived and heaped up one upon another, determinately to signify any such thing.

Dr. Taylor to take off the force of the whole, would have us to understand (pp. 104–107) that these passages, quoted from the Psalms, and other parts of the Old Testament, don't speak of all mankind, nor of all the Jews; but only of them of whom they were true. He observes, there were many that were innocent and righteous; though there were also many, a strong party, that were wicked, corrupt, etc. of whom these texts were to be understood. Concerning which I would observe the following things.

1. According to this, the universality of the terms that are found in these places, which the Apostle cites from the Old Testament, to prove that *all the world, both Jews and gentiles, are under sin*, is nothing to his purpose. The Apostle uses universal terms in his proposition, and in his conclusion, that ALL are under sin, that EVERY MOUTH is stopped, ALL THE WORLD guilty, that by the deeds of the law NO FLESH can be justified. And he chooses out a number of universal sayings or clauses out of the Old Testament, to confirm this universality; as, "There is none righteous; no, not one; they are all gone out of the way; there is none that understandeth," etc. [*Romans 3:10–11*]. But yet the universality of these expressions is nothing to his purpose; because the universal terms found in 'em have indeed no reference to any such universality as this the Apostle speaks of, nor anything akin to it; they mean no universality, either in the collective sense, or personal sense; no universality of the nations of the world, or of particular persons in those nations, or in any one nation in the world: "But only of those of whom they are true." That is, "There is none of them righteous, of whom it is true, that they are not righteous, no, not one: there is none that understand, of whom it is true, that they understand not: they are all gone out of the way, of whom it is true, that they are gone out of the way," etc. Or these expressions are to be understood concerning that strong party in Israel, in David's and Solomon's days and in the prophets' days: they are to be understood of them universally. And what is that to the Apostle's purpose? How does such an universality of wickedness, as this—that all were wicked in Israel, who were wicked, or that there was a particular evil party, all of which were wicked—confirm that universality which the Apostle would prove, viz. that all Jews and Gentiles, and the whole world were wicked, and every mouth stopped, and that no flesh could be justified by their own righteousness.

Here nothing can be said to abate the nonsense, but this, that the Apostle would convince the Jews, that they were capable of being wicked as well as other nations; and to prove it, he mentions some texts, which show that there was a wicked party in Israel, a thousand years ago: and that as to the universal terms which happened to be in these texts, the Apostle had no respect to these; but his reciting them is as it were accidental, they happened to be in some texts which speak of an evil party in Israel, and the Apostle cites 'em as they are, not because they are any more to his purpose for the universal terms, which happen to be in them. But let the reader look on the words of the Apostle, and observe the violence of such a supposition. Particularly let the words of the *ninth and tenth* verses, and their connection, be observed. "All are under sin: as it is written, there is none righteous; no, not one." How plain it is, that the Apostle cites that latter universal clause out of the *Romans 3:14*, to confirm the preceding universal words of his own proposition? And yet it will follow from the things which Dr. Taylor supposes, that the universality of the terms in the last words, "There is none righteous; no, not one," have no relation at all to that universality he speaks of in the preceding clause, to which they are joined, "All are under sin"; and is no more a confirmation of it, than if the words were thus: "There are *some*, or there are *many* in Israel, that are not righteous."

2. To suppose, the Apostle's design in citing these passages, was only to prove to the Jews, that of old there was a considerable number of their nation that were wicked men, is to suppose him to have gone about to prove what none of the Jews denied, or made the least doubt of. Even the Pharisees, the most self-righteous sect of them, who went furthest in glorying in the distinction of their nation from other nations, as a holy people, knew it, and owned it: they openly confessed that their "forefathers killed the prophets" (*Matthew 23:29–31*). And if the Apostle's design had been only to refresh their memories, to put 'em in mind of the ancient wickedness of their nation, to lead to reflection on themselves as guilty of the like wickedness (as Stephen does, *Acts 7*), what need had the Apostle to go so far about to prove this; gathering up many sentences here and there, which prove that their Scriptures did speak of some as wicked men; and then, in the next place, to prove that the wicked men spoken of must be of the nation of the Jews, by this argument that "What things soever the law saith, it saith to them that are under the law," or that whatsoever the books of the Old Testament said, it must be understood of that people that had the Old Testament? What need had the Apostle of such an ambages or fetch as this,to prove to the Jews, that there had been many of their nation in some of the ancient ages, which were wicked men; when the Old Testament was full of passages that asserted this expressly, not only of a strong party, but of the nation in general? How much more would it have been to

such a purpose, to have put 'em in mind of the wickedness of the people in general, in worshipping the golden calf, and the unbelief, murmuring and perverseness of the whole congregation in the wilderness, for forty years, as Stephen does? Which things he had no need to prove to be spoken of their nation, by any such indirect argument as that, "Whatsoever things the law saith, it saith to them that are under the law."

3. It would have been impertinent to the Apostle's purpose, even as our author understands his purpose, for him to have gone about to convince the Jews, that there had been a strong party of bad men in David's and Solomon's and the prophets' times. For Dr. Taylor supposes, the Apostle's aim is to prove the great corruption of both Jews and Gentiles at that day, when Christ came into the world.

In order the more fully to evade the clear and abundant testimonies to the doctrine of original sin, contained in this part of the holy Scripture, our author says, the Apostle is here speaking of bodies of people, of Jews and Gentiles in a collective sense, as two great bodies into which mankind are divided; speaking of them in their collective capacity, and not with respect to particular persons; that the Apostle's design is to prove, neither of these two great collective bodies, in their collective sense, can be justified by law, because both were corrupt; and so, that no more is implied, than that the generality of both were wicked. On this I observe,

(1) That this supposed sense disagrees extremely with the terms and language which the Apostle here makes use of. For according to this, we must understand, either

First, that the Apostle means no universality at all, but only the far greater part. But if the words which the Apostle uses, don't most fully and determinately signify an universality, no words ever used in the Bible are sufficient to do it. I might challenge any man to produce any one paragraph in the Scripture, from the beginning to the end, where there is such a repetition and accumulation of terms, so strongly and emphatically and carefully to express the most perfect and absolute universality; or any place to be compared to it. What instance is there in the Scripture, or indeed any other writing, when the meaning is only the much greater part, where this meaning is signified in such a manner, by repeating such expressions, "They are all . . . they are all . . . they are all . . . together . . . every one . . . all the world," joined to multiplied negative terms, to show the universality to be without exception; saying, "There is no flesh . . . there is none . . . there is none . . . there is none," four times over; besides the addition of "no, not one . . . no, not one," once and again!

Or secondly, if any universality at all be allowed, it is only of the collective bodies spoken of; and these collective bodies but two, as Dr. Taylor reckons them, viz. the Jewish nation, and the gentile world; supposing the Apostle is here representing each of these parts of mankind as being wicked. But is this the way of men's using language, when speaking of but two things, to express themselves in universal terms, of such a sort, and in such a manner, and when they mean no more than that the thing affirmed is predicated of both of them? If a man speaking of his two feet as both lame should say, "All my feet are lame. They are all lame. All together are become weak; none of my feet are strong, none of them are sound; no, not one," would not he be thought to be lame in his understanding as well as his feet? When the Apostle says, "That every mouth may be stopped," must we suppose that he speaks only of those two great collective bodies, figuratively ascribing to each of them a mouth, and mean that those two mouths are stopped!

And besides, according to our author's own interpretation, the universal terms used in these texts cited from the Old Testament, have no respect to those two great collective bodies, nor indeed to either of them; but to some in Israel, a particular disaffected party in that one nation, which was made up of wicked men. So that his interpretation is every way absurd and inconsistent.

(2) If the Apostle is speaking only of the wickedness or guilt of great collective bodies, then it will follow, that also the justification he here treats of, is no other than the justification of such collective bodies. For they are the same he speaks of as guilty and wicked, that he argues cannot be justified by the works of the law, by reason of their being wicked. Otherwise his argument is wholly disannulled. If the guilt he speaks of be only of collective bodies, then what he argues from that guilt, must be only, that collective bodies cannot be justified by the works of the law, having no respect to the justification of particular persons. And indeed this is Dr. Taylor's declared opinion. He supposes, the Apostle here, and in other parts or this epistle, is speaking of men's justification considered only as in their collective capacity. But the contrary is most manifest. The twenty-sixth and twenty-eighth verses of this third chapter can't, without the utmost violence, be understood otherwise than of the justification of particular persons. "That he might be just, and the justifier of HIM that believeth in Jesus. . . . Therefore we conclude that A MAN is justified by faith, without the deeds of the law." So *ch. 4:5*, "But to HIM that worketh not, but believeth on him that justifieth the ungodly, HIS faith is counted

for righteousness." And what the Apostle cites in the sixth, seventh, and eighth verses from the book of Psalms, evidently shows, that he is speaking of the justification of particular persons. "Even as David also describeth the blessedness of THE MAN unto whom God imputeth righteousness without works, saying, blessed are they whose iniquities are forgiven and whose sins are covered." David says these things in the *Psalms 32*, with a special respect to his own particular case; there expressing the great distress he was in, while under a sense of the guilt of his personal sin, and the great joy he had when God forgave him, as in *Psalms 32:3*, *Psalms 32:4*.

And then, it is very plain in that paragraph of the third chapter, which we have been upon, that it is the justification of particular persons that the Apostle speaks of, by that place in the Old Testament, which he refers to in v. 20. "Therefore by the deeds of the law, there shall no flesh be justified in his sight." He refers to that in *Psalms 143*: "Enter not into judgment with thy servant; for in thy sight shall NO MAN LIVING be justified." Here the Psalmist is not speaking of the justification of a nation, as a collective body, or of one of the two parts of the world, but of a particular man. And 'tis further manifest, that the Apostle is here speaking of personal justification, inasmuch as this place is evidently parallel with that, *Galatians 3:10–11*. "For as many as are of the works of the law, are under the curse: for it is written, cursed is EVERYONE that continueth not in all things that are written in the book of the law to do them. But that NO MAN is justified by the works of the law, is evident; for the just shall live by faith." It is plain, that this place is parallel with that in the *Romans 3*, not only as the thing asserted is the same, and the argument by which it is proved here, is the same as there, viz. that all are guilty, and exposed to he condemned by the law; but the same saying of the Old Testament is cited here in the beginning of this discourse in Galatians (*ch. 1:16*). And many other things demonstrate, that the Apostle is speaking of the same justification in both places, which I omit for brevity's sake.

And besides all these things, our author's interpretation makes the Apostle's argument wholly void another way. The Apostle is speaking of a certain subject, which cannot be justified by the works of the law; and his argument is, that that same subject is guilty, and is condemned by the law. If he means, that one subject, suppose a collective body or bodies, can't be justified by the law, because another subject, another collective body, is condemned by the law, 'tis plain, the argument would be quite vain and impertinent. Yet thus the argument must stand according to Dr. Taylor's interpretation. The collective bodies, which he supposes are spoken of as wicked and condemned by the law, considered as in their collective capacity, are those two, the Jewish nation, and the heathen world: but the collective body which he supposes the Apostle speaks of as justified without the deeds of the law, is neither of these, but the Christian church, or body of believers; which is a new collective body, a new creature, and a new man (according to our author's understanding of such phrases), which never had any existence before it was justified, and therefore never was wicked or condemned unless it was with regard to the individuals of which it was constituted: and it does not appear, according to our author's scheme, that these individuals had before been generally wicked. For according to him there was a number both among the Jews and gentiles, that were righteous before. And how does it appear, but that the comparatively few Jews and gentiles, of which this new-created collective body was constituted, were chiefly of the best of each?

So that in every view this author's way of explaining this passage in the third of Romans, appears vain and absurd. And so clearly and fully has the Apostle expressed himself, that 'tis doubtless impossible to invent any other sense to put upon his words, than that which will imply that all mankind, even every individual of the whole race but their Redeemer himself, are in their first original state corrupt and wicked.

Before I leave this passage of the Apostle, it may be proper to observe, that it not only is a most clear, and full testimony to the native depravity of mankind, but also plainly declares that natural depravity to be total and exceeding great. 'Tis the Apostle's manifest design in these citations from the Old Testament, to shew these three things: 1. That *all mankind* are by nature *corrupt*. 2. That everyone is *altogether corrupt*, and as it were, depraved in every part. 3. That they are in every part *corrupt in an exceeding degree*. With respect to the second of these, that everyone is wholly, an as it were in every part corrupt, 'tis plain, the Apostle chooses out, and puts together those particular passages of the Old Testament, wherein most of those members of the body are mentioned, that are the soul's chief instruments or organs of external action. The hands (implicitly) in those expressions, "They are together become unprofitable, there is none that doeth good." The throat, tongue, lips, and mouth, the organs of speech; in those words, "Their throat is an open sepulchre: with their tongues they have used deceit: the poison of asps is under their lips; whose mouth is full of cursing and bitterness." The feet, in those words (*v. 15*), "Their feet are swift to shed blood." These things together signify, that man is as it were all over corrupt, in every part. And not only is the total corruption thus intimated, by enumerating the several parts, but by denying of all good; any true understanding or spiritual knowledge, any virtuous action, or so much as truly virtuous desire, or seeking after God. "There is none that understandeth; there is none that seeketh after God: there is none that doth good; the way of peace have they not known." And in general, by denying all true piety or religion in men, in their first state. V. *18*, "There is no fear of God before their eyes." The expressions also are evidently chosen to denote a most extreme and desperate wickedness of heart. And exceeding depravity is ascribed to every part: to the throat, the scent of an open sepulchre; to the tongue and lips, deceit and the poison of asps; to the mouth, cursing and bitterness; of their feet it is said, they are swift to shed blood: and with regard to the whole man, 'tis said, destruction and misery are in their ways. The representation is very strong, of each of these things, viz. that all mankind are corrupt; that everyone is wholly, and altogether corrupt; and also extremely and desperately corrupt. And it is plain, 'tis not accidental, that we have here such a collection of such strong expressions, so emphatically signifying these things; but that they are chosen of the Apostle on design, as being directly and fully to his purpose; which purpose appears in all his discourse in the whole of this chapter, and indeed from the beginning of the epistle. ***Original Sin (WJE Online Vol. 3)***

Romans 3:25

We find that Christ himself is called *ιλαστηριον* in *Romans 3:25*. This signified that whatever was done with the sacrifices at the altar in the court of the temple, and whatever was done in the holy place at the altar of incense, it was by virtue of what was there in the Holy of Holies, over the covering of the ark, that the sacrifices were of any avail, and that atonement was truly made. And our translation of it, "a mercy seat," suggests a wrong idea to us, as though God was represented as having his seat there in the temple over the ark, as accepting the sacrifices and forgiving sins. Whereas this is not agreeable to Scripture representations. The propitiatory is rather represented as the place where atonement was made, and the sacrifice effectually offered, than the place where it was accepted and favor granted. Heaven is constantly represented as being [the] throne of God, and where he sat to hear the prayers and accept the offerings that were made. Thus how often is this repeated by Solomon in *1 Kings 8*, when he prays that God would hear, accept and forgive those that should pray towards the temple where God had placed his name: "then hear thou in heaven, thy dwelling place," says he (*1 Kings 8:30*, *1 Kings 8:32*, *1 Kings 8:34*, *1 Kings 8:36*, *1 Kings 8:39*, *1 Kings 8:43*, *1 Kings 8:45*, *1 Kings 8:49*). He don't say, "hear thou on the propitiatory," or "hear thou between the cherubims." ***Writings on the Trinity, Grace, and Faith (WJE Online Vol. 21)***

Romans 3:25–26

And that Christ justifies persons by his own righteousness and obedience to God as his servant, or his righteousness that he performed by being a servant that thoroughly obeyed him, that he was subject to, is implied in *Isaiah 53:11*, "By his knowledge shall my righteous servant justify many." To what purpose is he here mentioned in the character of a righteous servant, when God speaks of his making others righteous, or bringing others to a title to the same character, but that they are made or set forth as righteous by partaking of his righteousness. The manner of expression in the Hebrew shows plainly that there is a designed relation between the character of *righteous* in the Messiah, and the effect, *justifying* many: קידצי קידצ ידבצ. "Justificabit justus servus meus": my servant that is RIGHTEOUS shall make RIGHTEOUS. The same seems evidently to be intended by the Apostle, *Romans 3:25–26*, "Whom God hath set forth to be a propitiation, through faith in his blood, to declare his righteousness." God's righteousness, that he here speaks of, is that which Christians receive by faith, and which the Apostle often calls the righteousness of God, and sets in opposition to our righteousness; this is plain by the context. And then it follows in the next verse, "To declare, I say, at this time his righteousness: that he may *be just*" (i.e. in the person of Jesus), "and the *justifier* of him that believes in Jesus," intimating that God justifies by his justice, or makes righteous by his righteousness, in justifying him that is in Christ. ***The "Miscellanies," 833–1152 (WJE Online Vol. 20)***

Romans 3:26.

["Sins that are past."] I.e. that were committed in past ages before Christ died, as *Hebrews 9:15*. And therefore it follows in the *Romans 3:26*, "To declare, I say, at this time his righteousness," that is, this time of Christ's appearing. Before, the Apostle was speaking of past ages. The righteousness of God in pardoning those sins then committed was not fully declared then in the time, but now it is at this time.

Although they also have been great sinners and have deserved eternal death, yet it won't be against justice or the law for 'em to be thus justified, as they are in Christ. But the acquitting of them will be an act of justice; it will be but giving the reward merited by Christ's righteousness. *Romans 3:26*, "That God may be just, and the justifier of him that believeth in Jesus." He gives everyone their due proportion. ***Sermons and Discourses: 1723–1729 (WJE Online Vol. 14)***

Justification, washing from sin, delivering from guilt, forgiving sin, admitting to favor and to the glorious benefits of righteousness in the sight of God, are often spoken as belonging peculiarly to God. *Romans 3:26*, "To declare, I say, at this time his righteousness: that he might be just, and the justifier," etc. *Romans 3:30*, "Seeing it is one God" that justifieth, etc. *Romans 8:30*, when he called he also justified. *Romans 8:33*, "It is God that justifieth." *Isaiah 43:25*, "I [. . .] am he that blotteth out thy transgressions for mine own sake." *Psalms 51:2*, *Psalms 51:4*, "Wash me thoroughly from mine iniquity, and cleanse me from my sin. . . . Against thee, thee only, have I sinned." Therefore the Jews said, *Luke 5:21*, "Who can forgive sins, but God only?" ***The "Miscellanies," (Entry Nos. 1153–1360) (WJE Online Vol. 23)***

Romans 3:27

Christ's acts of righteousness may be distributed with respect [to] the legal laws Christ obeyed in that righteousness he performed. But here it must be observed in general that all the precepts that Christ obeyed may [be] reduced to one law, and that is that which the Apostle calls "the law of works," *Romans 3:27*. Every command that Christ obeyed may be reduced to that great and everlasting law of God that is contained in the covenant of works, that eternal rule of righteousness that God had established between himself and mankind. ***A History of the Work of Redemption (WJE Online Vol. 9)***

Every command that Christ, when he was in his state of humiliation, obeyed may be reduced to one law, and that is that which the Apostle calls the law of works, to which indeed all laws of God properly so called may be reduced (*Romans 3:27*). But the commands that Christ obeyed may be distributed into three particular laws, viz. the law that he was subject to merely as man, which was (1) the moral law; and the law that he was subject to as a Jew, which includes (2) the ceremonial law, and all the positive precepts that were peculiar to that nation. (3) The mediatorial law, which contained those commands of God that he was subject to purely as he was mediator, to which belong all those commands that the Father gave him to work such miracles, and teach such doctrines, and so to labor in the works of his public ministry, and to yield himself to such sufferings: for as he often tells us, he did all those things agreeable to the Father's direction, and in obedience to his Father's commandments. ***The "Miscellanies," (Entry Nos. 501–832) (WJE Online Vol. 18)***

Again, in the Apostle's account, a benefit being of our works gives occasion for boasting, and that therefore God has contrived that our salvation shall not be [of] our works but of mere grace (*Romans 3:27*, *Ephesians 2:9*); and that both the salvation and condition of it, neither of them be of our works, but that with regard to all we are God's workmanship and his creation antecedent to our works; and his grace and power in producing this workmanship, and his determination or purpose with regard to 'em, are all prior to our works, and the cause of 'em. See also *Romans 11:4–6*. ***Writings on the Trinity, Grace, and Faith (WJE Online Vol. 21)***

Romans 3:28

And again, we often find the works of the law set by this Apostle in opposition to the free grace of God, and therefore thereby must be intended our own excellency. For wherein does grace appear, but in being bestowed on them that are no more excellent, that are so unworthy, so far from deserving anything? *Romans 3:20*, *Romans 3:24*, *Romans 3:27*, *Romans 3:28*; and *Titus 3:5*, where, instead of works of law, the Apostle says works of righteousness; *Romans 11:6* and *Romans 4:4*; *Galatians 5:4*; *Ephesians 2:8*, *Ephesians 2:9*. ***The "Miscellanies," (Entry Nos. 501–832) (WJE Online Vol. 18)***

Romans 3:30

Justification, washing from sin, delivering from guilt, forgiving sin, admitting to favor and to the glorious benefits of righteousness in the sight of God, are often spoken as belonging peculiarly to God. *Romans 3:26*, "To declare, I say, at this time his righteousness: that he might be just, and the justifier," etc. *Romans 3:30*, "Seeing it is one God" that justifieth, etc. *Romans 8:30*, when he called he also justified. *Romans 8:33*, "It is God that justifieth." *Isaiah 43:25*, "I [. . .] am he that blotteth out thy transgressions for mine own sake." *Psalms 51:2*, *Psalms 51:4*, "Wash me thoroughly from mine iniquity, and cleanse me from my sin. . . . Against thee, thee only, have I sinned." Therefore the Jews said, *Luke 5:21*, "Who can forgive sins, but God only?" ***The "Miscellanies," (Entry Nos. 1153–1360) (WJE Online Vol. 23)***

ROMANS CHAPTER 4

[*Romans 4.*] This chapter much confirms me in it, that the epistle to the Hebrews is of Paul's writing. The method, manner, and way of arguing is exceedingly like, as also it is throughout this epistle to the Romans. ***The "Blank Bible" (WJE Online Vol. 24)***

Romans 4:1–2

The Apostle informs us that the design of the gospel is to cut off all glorying, not only before God, but also before men (*Romans 4:1–2*). Some pretend to great humiliation, that is very haughty, audacious and assuming in their external appearance and behavior . . . ***Religious Affections (WJE Online Vol. 2)***

Romans 4:2

[*Romans 4:2*] This way of man's seeking his own salvation is fatal to man, doubtless because of that in it by which it is contrary to God's way, or to his aim in the way that he has contrived; which is that salvation should be wholly for Christ's sake, and that free grace alone should be exalted, and boasting be excluded, and all glory should belong to God and none to us (*Romans 3:27*, *Ephesians 2:19*, *Romans 4:2*, *1 Corinthians 1:29–31*). Doubtless, therefore, seeking justification by the works of the law is fatal upon the account of the boasting that is included in it. ***The "Miscellanies," (Entry Nos. 501–832) (WJE Online Vol. 18)***

This is plainly what our divines intend when they say that faith don't justify as a work, or a righteousness, viz. that it don't justify as a part of our moral goodness or excellency, or that it don't justify as a work, in the sense that man was to have been justified by his works by the covenant of works, which was to have a title to eternal life, given him of God in testimony of his pleasedness with his works, or his regard to the inherent excellency and beauty of his obedience. And this is certainly what the apostle Paul means, when he so much insists upon it that we are not justified by works, viz. that we are not justified by them as good works, or by any goodness, value, or excellency of our works. For the proof of this I shall at present mention but one thing (being like to have occasion to say what shall make it more abundantly manifest afterwards), and that is, the Apostle, from time to time, speaking of our not being justified by works, as the thing that excludes all boasting (*Ephesians 2:9*; *Romans 3:27* and *Romans 4:2*). ***Sermons and Discourses, 1734–1738 (WJE Online Vol. 19)***

Romans 4:3

The Scripture speaks of after-acts of faith in both Abraham and Noah, as giving a title to the righteousness which is the matter of justification. See *Romans 4:3*, *Hebrews 11:7*. ***The "Miscellanies," (Entry Nos. 501–832) (WJE Online Vol. 18)***

It was impossible that Christ should not continue in his Father's love. He was entitled to such help and support from him as should be effectual to uphold him in obedience to his Father. And yet it was true that, if Christ had not kept the Father's commandments, he could not have continued in his love. He would have been cast out of favor. See *Romans 11:22*, *Colossians 1:21–23*, *1 Timothy 2:15*, *2 Timothy 4:7–8*, *Romans 4:3* compared with *Genesis 15:6*, *1 John 2:24–28*. ***The "Miscellanies," (Entry Nos. 501–832) (WJE Online Vol. 18)***

[*Romans 4:3*, 5. "His faith is counted for righteousness."] "It is not said, His faith is accounted or imputed instead of righteousness, which would have required the word ὑπέρ or ἀτί, but it is εἰς δικαιοσύνην, that is, faith is imputed or reckoned to our account, as an important or necessary thing, in order to our having a justifying righteousness." Dr. Watts, *Works*, vol. 2, p. 550. ***The "Blank Bible" (WJE Online Vol. 24)***

Romans 4:3–4

Romans 4:3–4. "What saith the scripture? Abraham believed God, and it was counted to him for righteousness." The Apostle lays stress upon the word "counted," or "imputed." If he had had a righteousness of his own, upon the account of which the reward was of proper debt, it would not have been expressed in this manner, as he evidently argues in the following verses. Abraham's believing God was not righteousness, but was only counted for it. It was of God's grace looked upon as supplying the room of righteousness. ***Notes on Scripture (WJE Online Vol. 15)***

Romans 4:4

God might very justly leave all men universally to perish in sin. And if so, it can't be unjust in him to leave some of them to perish. God, because he saves some, is not at all the more under obligations to save others, if he is under no obligation to save any at all. Those that are saved, are saved from mere grace; and if so, it follows that those that perish, perish from mere justice: for if justice was obliged to save one from perishing, it would be no grace to save him. Grace and debt are inconsistent (*Romans 4:4*). Men are all sinners, and therefore all of 'em deserve eternal misery; and them that are appointed to eternal misery, are justly and righteously appointed to it. And if you say that God appointed that you should be sinners, and therefore it necessarily came to pass, we have already shown that God deals most justly and reasonably in so doing; and therefore no fault can justly be found with God's dealing in this matter from the beginning to the end. ***Sermons and Discourses: 1723–1729 (WJE Online Vol. 14)***

For righteousness, or an exact obedience to the law, seems by the Scripture to have a claim of right to eternal life. *Romans 4:4*, "To him that worketh," i.e. does the works of the law, "is the reward not reckoned of grace, but of debt." On the other side it seems the unalterable purpose of the divine justice, that no unrighteous person, no one that is guilty of any breach of the law, should be in Paradise; but that the wages of sin should be to every man, as it was to Adam, an exclusion of him out of that happy state of immortality, and bring death upon him. ***Sermons and Discourses, 1734–1738 (WJE Online Vol. 19)***

Taylor insists upon it, that our full and final justification is of works and not only of grace, and yet he allows that this final justification is spoken of in Scripture as being of grace, *2 Timothy 1:18* and *Jude 21* (Taylor's *Key*, p. 176). But how does this consist with what the Apostle says, *Romans 4:4*, "Now to him that worketh the reward is not reckoned of grace, but of debt"; and *Romans 11:6*, "And if by grace, then it is no more of works: otherwise grace is no more grace. But if it be of works, then it is no more grace: otherwise work is no more work"? ***Writings on the Trinity, Grace, and Faith (WJE Online Vol. 21)***

[*Romans 4:4*. "The reward not reckoned of grace," etc.] "Raphelius has shown that μισθόν don't only signify a reward of debt, but also a gift of favor, and that the phrase μισθόν δωρεάν occurs in Herodotus; so that a reward of grace or favor is a classical as well as theological expression." Doddridge, *in loc.* ***The "Blank Bible" (WJE Online Vol. 24)***

Romans 4:4–5

And in the following chapter, the Apostle excludes all our works from having any share in our title to this blessing, "that the reward may be reckoned to be of grace, not of debt," and speaks of God's "justifying the ungodly," to show what their character was, till he justified them (*Romans 4:4–5*). And what but grace could move him to justify persons of that character? Accordingly, in the next chapter, he seems to strain the powers of language to set out the freeness and riches of this grace, calling it "the grace of God," and "the gift by grace, which had abounded unto many," and "the free gift" in delivering from "many offenses unto justification" (*Romans 5:15–16*). ***The "Miscellanies," 833–1152 (WJE Online Vol. 20)***

Romans 4:5

Goodness or loveliness is not prior in the order of nature to justification, or is not to be considered as prior in the order and method of God's proceeding in this affair. There is indeed something in man that is really and spiritually good, that is prior in the order of nature to justification, viz. faith. But there is nothing that is accepted as goodness till after justification. Though a respect to the natural suitableness between such a qualification and such a state be prior in the order of nature to justification, yet the acceptance even of faith, as any goodness or loveliness in the believer in the order of nature, follows justification. The goodness is justly looked upon as nothing till the man is justified; and therefore, the man is respected in justification as ungodly and altogether hateful in himself (*Romans 4:5*). ***The "Miscellanies," (Entry Nos. 501–832) (WJE Online Vol. 18)***

'Tis plain, in order to this, the holiness must be perfect, because if there be any sin, this is an infinite evil, brings an infinite odiousness and demerit on the person, that all the holiness he can have can in no measure be any balance for; so but that still the person, on the whole, must be looked upon as without any moral value or amiableness, yea, on the contrary, as being infinitely odious. But in the way of gospel grace, the use and influence of the inherent qualification is quite diverse. It is not at all to recommend to any benefit as a moral value of the subject in the sight of

God, but only a natural fitness or proper and suitable capacity for it, which may be as [God] has constituted things in Christ without any moral value or preciousness of the subject; and although the person, taken as he is, all things in him being estimated together, is wholly odious and ill-deserving, ungodly and guilty in the sight of God. And thus God justifies the ungodly (*Romans 4:5*). ***Writings on the Trinity, Grace, and Faith (WJE Online Vol. 21)***

[*Romans 4:5*. "His faith is counted for righteousness."] There is no need to understand the Apostle that his faith, though in itself an imperfect righteousness, is accepted instead of a perfect righteousness, as that God had respect to any goodness or righteousness at all in faith; but only that God, by reason of his faith in God, accepted of him and dealt with him as though he had been righteous in himself. So the Apostle uses the phrase, *Romans 2:26*, "If the uncircumcision keep the law, shall not his uncircumcision be counted for circumcision," εἰς περιτομὴν λογισθήσεται? Not that his uncircumcision in itself shall be esteemed as of any value at all, but only that he shall fare no worse than if he were circumcised. ***The "Blank Bible" (WJE Online Vol. 24)***

Romans 4:6

'Tis plain that this is the force of the expression in the preceding verses: in the last verse but one, 'tis manifest the Apostle lays the stress of his argument for the free grace of God, from that text he cites out of text of the Old Testament about Abraham, on the word *counted* or *imputed*, and that this is the thing that he supposed God to show his grace in, viz. in his counting something for righteousness, in his consequential dealings with Abraham, that was no righteousness in itself. And in the next verse which immediately precedes the text, "Now to him that worketh is the reward not reckoned of grace, but of debt"; the word there translated *reckoned*, is the same that in the other verses is rendered *imputed*, and *counted:* and 'tis as much as if the Apostle had said, "As to him that works, there is no need of any gracious reckoning, or counting it for righteousness, and causing the reward to follow as if it were a righteousness; for if he has works he has that which is a righteousness in itself, to which the reward properly belongs." This is further evident by the words that follow, *Romans 4:6*, "Even as David also described the blessedness of the man unto whom God imputeth righteousness without works"; what can here be meant by imputing righteousness without works, but imputing righteousness to him that has none of his own? ***Sermons and Discourses, 1734–1738 (WJE Online Vol. 19)***

The Apostle don't only say, that we are not justified by the works of the law, but that we are not justified by works, using a general term . . . *Romans 4:6*, "God imputeth righteousness without works." ***Sermons and Discourses, 1734–1738 (WJE Online Vol. 19)***

Romans 4:6. I would explain what we mean by the imputation of Christ's righteousness. Sometimes the expression is taken by our divines in a larger sense, for the imputation of all that Christ did and suffered for our redemption, whereby we are free from guilt, and stand righteous in the sight of God; and so implies the imputation both of Christ's satisfaction, and obedience. But here I intend it in a stricter sense, for the imputation of that righteousness, or moral goodness, that consists in the obedience of Christ. And by that righteousness being imputed to us, is meant no other than this, that that righteousness of Christ is accepted for us, and admitted instead of that perfect inherent righteousness that ought to be in ourselves: Christ's perfect obedience shall be reckoned to our account, so that we shall have the benefit of it, as though we had performed it ourselves: and so we suppose that a title to eternal life is given us as the reward of this righteousness. The Scripture uses the word *impute* in this sense, viz. for reckoning anything belonging to any person, to another person's account: as Philem. *Philemon 18*, "If he have wronged thee, or oweth thee ought put that on mine account." In the original it is τούτο ἐμοί ἐλλόγα: *impute that to me*. 'Tis a word of the same root with that which is translated *impute. Romans 4:6*, "To whom God imputeth righteousness without works." ***Sermons and Discourses, 1734–1738 (WJE Online Vol. 19)***

By the word "righteousness" in the New Testament is not meant salvation and deliverance . . . ***Writings on the Trinity, Grace, and Faith (WJE Online Vol. 21)***

The Apostle speaks of imputing righteousness without works [*Romans 4:6*]—how absurd is the expression "imputeth salvation," "reckoneth deliverance" and *Romans 4:11*, "that righteousness might be imputed to him also." ***Writings on the Trinity, Grace, and Faith (WJE Online Vol. 21)***

Romans 4:9

Romans 4:9, "we say that faith was reckoned to Abraham for righteousness." "I think nothing can be easier than to understand how this may be said in full consistence with our being justified by the imputation of the righteousness of Christ, that is, our being treated by God as righteous for the sake of what he has done and suffered: for though this be the meritorious cause of our acceptance with God, yet faith may be said to be imputed to us, *εις δικαιοσυνην*, 'in order to our being justified' or becoming righteous; that is, . . . as we are charged as debtors in the book of God's account, what Christ has done in fulfilling righteousness for us is charged as the grand balance of the account; but that it may appear that we are, according to the tenor of the gospel, entitled to the benefit of this, it is also entered in the book of God's remembrance 'that we are believers'; and this appearing, we are graciously discharged, yea and rewarded, as if we ourselves had been perfectly innocent and obedient." Doddridge, *Family Expositor* (1836 ed.), "A Paraphrase and Notes on the Epistle to the Romans," §8, p. 508, n.e. ***Writings on the Trinity, Grace, and Faith (WJE Online Vol. 21)***

Romans 4:11

[*Romans 4:11*. "That he might be the father of all them that believe."] Circumcision was a seal that he should be the father of all that believe. ***The "Miscellanies," (Entry Nos. 501–832) (WJE Online Vol. 18)***

Circumcision was a seal of the covenant of grace as appears by the first institution, as we have an account of it in the *Genesis 17*. It there appears to be a seal of that covenant by which God promised to make him the father of many nations, as appears by the *Genesis 17:5* compared with the *Genesis 17:9–10*. And we are expressly taught that it was a seal of the righteousness of faith, *Romans 4:11*; speaking of Abraham, the Apostle says he received "the sign of circumcision a seal of the righteousness of faith." ***A History of the Work of Redemption (WJE Online Vol. 9)***

By "righteousness" here seems to be meant the way of the justification of sinners by Christ. 'Tis not only meant Christ's active [righteousness]: a great deal more is intended than that. So by the term "righteousness," when it is spoken with respect to the Mediator in Scripture, is almost always thus to be taken. Christ is called "the Lord our righteousness," that is, he is he in whom we have justification. So it is said, in the Lord Jehovah we have righteousness and strength [*Isaiah 12:2*; *26:4*], that is, in him we have acceptance with God as righteous. We read, *Romans 4:11*, that circumcision was the seal of the righteousness of faith, i.e. a seal of the way of justification by faith; and [in the] thirteenth verse, that the promise that Abraham should be heir [of the world] was through the righteousness of faith. So, very evidently, it is to be understood, *Romans 3:21–22* and *Romans 1:17*.

It is not to be understood of the holiness of God's nature, or the personal holiness or innocence of Christ, but God's way of justifying man. ***Sermons and Discourses: 1723–1729 (WJE Online Vol. 14)***

Abraham might well represent Christ, for Christ is Abraham's seed; and he might well represent the church, for he was the father of the church, the father of all that believe, as the Apostle testifies [*Romans 4:11*]. And besides, Abraham and his household was then as it were God's visible church, God had separated Abraham from the rest of the world to that end, that his church might be continued in his family. ***Notes on Scripture (WJE Online Vol. 15)***

"The motions of sins, which were by the law." "τὰ διὰ τοῦ νόμου might properly have been rendered, 'under the law,' or 'notwithstanding the law.' So *Romans 4:11*, 'That he might be the father of all them that believe,' δί ἀκροβυστίᾳ, 'under uncircumcision,' or 'notwithstanding they be not circumcised.' And *1 Timothy 2:15*, σωθήσεται δὲ διὰ τῆς τεκνογονίας, 'She shall be saved under,' or 'in the state of,' or 'notwithstanding childbearing.'" See Taylor, *Original Sin*, p. 211d–e. ***The "Blank Bible" (WJE Online Vol. 24)***

And the Apostle plainly tells us what was the design of it (circumcision), in *Romans 4:11*: "he received the sign of circumcision, a seal of the righteousness of the faith which he had [yet] being uncircumcised." Mind the expression. The Apostle don't say only it was "a seal of the righteousness of faith," but "a seal of the righteousness of faith which he had" first, before he was circumcised—the righteousness of faith in him. That was the previous qualification for his receiving this seal of the covenant of grace. He first complied with the condition of the covenant of grace, viz. faith, justifying faith, before he was circumcised; and circumcision was a seal of it, as being now in him. The Apostle don't say that it was a seal of that moral sincerity that he had, but a seal of the righteousness of the faith which he had. And this the Apostle says as declaring the nature and design of the institution when first given. For he is here speaking of God's establishing the covenant of grace with Abraham, as the common father of the church of God that should be in all succeeding ages, the father of all God's covenant people, the pattern of all that should be circumcised afterwards; as appears by the following words: "And he received the sign of circumcision, a seal of the righteousness of the faith which he had yet being uncircumcised: that he might be the father of all them that believe, though they be not circumcised; that it might be imputed to them also: and the father of circumcision to them who are not of the circumcision only, but also walk in the steps of that faith of our father Abraham, which he had being yet uncircumcised." By this it is evident that in this matter of the covenant and the seals of the covenant, he was the grand pattern [of] all his seed that should be to the end of the world. ***Sermons and Discourses, 1743–1758 (WJE Online Vol. 25)***

Romans 4:12

Romans 4:12. "And the father of circumcision to them who are not of the circumcision only, but also walk in the steps of that faith of our father Abraham," etc. In the foregoing verse it is set forth how Abraham is the father of those that are *uncircumcised*, if they have the faith of Abraham. In this verse the Apostle declares that he also is the father of the *circumcised*, who han't only, or barely, circumcision, but also walk in the steps of the faith of their father Abraham. So that, put both verses together, this is what the Apostle declares: that Abraham received circumcision, a seal of the righteousness of faith, which he had being yet uncircumcised, whereby God sealed to him the promise he made to him, that he should be the father of all such as should believe as he had done, and only to such, whether they were circumcised or not, that he should be the father of the uncircumcised Gentiles that should believe as he had done, and the father of no more of the circumcised Jews than should believe as he had done. ***Notes on Scripture (WJE Online Vol. 15)***

"[S]eeing the Apostle's whole Argument turns upon this Point, That all Men die, not thro' their *own* Sins, but thro' the one Offence of *Adam*, who can doubt but the Words, *for that all have sinned* [*Romans 4:12*], must be understood in a like Sense to those, *all are made Sinners*, however the particular manner of expression be accounted for?" Taylor, *Paraphrase*, p. 393: "This demonstrates, that no Man, in this World, is under Law, the Covenant of Works, or the broken Law of Works. For if we were *now*, at any Time, under the broken Law of Works, then should we be in a State of final and eternal Damnation, without Hope, or Remedy: Because there now remains *NO MORE* Sacrifice for Sins, *Hebrews 10:26*. But it is one first and grand Principle of the Gospel, that we are not under *Law*, but under Grace, *Romans 6:14*." ***"Original Sin" Notebook (WJE Online Vol. 34)***

Called "the father of circumcision," because his circumcision was a seal of that promise that he should be the father of all those that walked in the steps of his faith. Circumcision sealed him the father of many nations, of all that were as he was, that is, believers. The expression of "father of circumcision" imports no more than, he that was by circumcision the father, or by circumcision sealed the father, or the father sealed such by circumcision, which agrees well with the foregoing verse. Or when it is said that he was "the father of circumcision," the meaning is that he was the circumcised father of all that should believe, for it was after he was circumcised that he begat Isaac, from whom came Jesus Christ. ***The "Blank Bible" (WJE Online Vol. 24)***

Romans 4:13

Abraham conquered the chief nations and princes of the world, which was a seal of what God promised him, "that he should be the heir of the world" (*Romans 4:13*). He conquered them, not with an hired army, but only with the armed soldiers of his own household; so the armies that go forth with Christ unto battle to subdue the world (*Revelation 19:14*), they are his church, which is his household. Abraham conquers the kings of the earth and their armies, united and joining all their force together; and therein his victory was a type of Christ's victory. ***Notes on Scripture (WJE Online Vol. 15)***

It is natural and reasonable to suppose, that the whole world should finally be given to Christ, as one whose right it is to reign, as the proper heir of him, who is originally the king of all nations, and the possessor of heaven and earth: and the Scripture teaches us, that God the Father hath constituted his Son, as God-man, and in his kingdom of grace, or mediatorial kingdom, to be "the heir of the world," that he might in this kingdom have "the heathen for his inheritance, and the utmost ends of the earth for his possession" (*Hebrews 1:2* and *Hebrews 2:8*; *Psalms 2:6–8*). Thus Abraham is said to be "the heir of the world," not in himself, but in his seed, which is Christ (*Romans 4:13*). ***Apocalyptic Writings (WJE Online Vol. 5)***

"For when God made promise to Abraham, because he could swear by no greater, he sware by himself, saying, Surely blessing I will bless thee, and multiplying I will multiply thee." This promise is chiefly fulfilled in the great increase of the church of God by the Messiah, and particularly in the calling of the Gentiles, pursuant to the promise made to Abraham that in his seed all the families of the earth should be blessed (*Romans 4:11*, *Romans 4:13*, *Romans 4:16–17*; *Hebrews 11:12*). ***The "Miscellanies," (Entry Nos. 1153–1360) (WJE Online Vol. 23)***

Romans 4:14

Romans 4:14. The children of Israel were in no danger of being led by this expression (if they duly considered it) to trust in their own righteousness to the prejudice of free grace, for its being in such a manner promised, as it here is, that it should be accepted as their righteousness, plainly shows that in itself it is not a righteousness, and is so only as God is pleased of his grace to promise to accept it, and impute it to 'em as such. If it were in its own nature a righteousness, and could in reason challenge to be accepted of God as such, what need of making such a particular promise, that "it shall be our righteousness," as though it was our righteousness, because God would make it to be so, or would by his grace put the value of a righteousness upon it? *Galatians 3:18*, "For if the inheritance be of the law, it is no more of promise; but [God] gave it to Abraham by promise." Also *Romans 4:14*. ***The "Blank Bible" (WJE Online Vol. 24)***

To the like purpose is that, *Romans 4:14*, and also *II Corinthians 3:6–9*, where the law is called "the letter that kills, the ministration of death, and the ministration of condemnation." The wrath, condemnation and death which is threatened in the law to all its transgressors, is final perdition, the second death, eternal ruin; as is very plain, and confessed. And this punishment which the law threatens for every sin, is a just punishment; being what every sin truly deserves; God's law being a righteous law, and the sentence of it a righteous sentence. ***Original Sin (WJE Online Vol. 3)***

Romans 4:15

'Tis its agreement or disagreement with its proper rule. Whenever anything is said to be in any respect right or wrong, it is with respect to some rule. If there were no rule that things were to be regulated by, nothing could be denominated either right or wrong; because in such a case nothing could be said to be either agreeable or disagreeable to rule. *Romans 4:15*, "Where no law is, there is no transgression." ***Sermons and Discourses, 1734–1738 (WJE Online Vol. 19)***

But how they can be exposed to die and perish, who have not the law of Moses, nor any revealed law, the Apostle shews us in the fourteenth and fifteenth verses; viz. in that they have the law of nature, by which they fall under sentence to this punishment. "For when the Gentiles which have not the law, do by nature the things contained in the law, these having not the law, are a law to themselves; which shew the work of the law written in their hearts; their conscience also bearing witness." Their conscience not only bore witness to the duty prescribed by this law, but also to the punishment before spoken of, as that which they who sinned without law, were liable to suffer, viz. that they should perish. In which the Apostle is yet more express (ch. 1:32), speaking more especially of the heathen "who knowing the judgment of God, that they which commit such things are worthy of death." Dr. Taylor often calls the law the *rule of right*: and this rule of right sentenced those sinners to death, who were not under the law of Moses, according to this author's own paraphrase of this verse, in these words, "The heathen were not ignorant of the rule of right, which God has implanted in the human nature; and which shews that they which commit such things, are deserving of death." And he himself supposes Abraham, who lived between Adam and Moses, to be under law, by which he would have been exposed to punishment without hope, were it not for the promise of grace, in his *Paraphrase* on *Romans 4:15*. ***Original Sin (WJE Online Vol. 3)***

To show that by the works of the law, which the Apostle says we are not justified by, is not meant only the outward obedience to the law. Answer that objection, that that place seems to favor it, as "touching the righteousness which is of the law, blameless" [*Philippians 3:6*]; i.e. as the Pharisees and the Jews in general from [old] understood the law. As in the foregoing verse, the Apostle says that, "touching the law, a Pharisee"; i.e. he interpreted the law in the manner that the Pharisees did. And now he adds that, according to that interpretation, he was blameless touching the righteousness of the law. He can't mean otherwise, for elsewhere [he] observes that the law, rightly understood, condemns all as it is says, "Cursed is every one that continueth not in all things which are written in the book of the law to do them" [*Galatians 3:10*]; and that by it is "the knowledge of sin" [*Romans 3:20*]; and that he was "alive without the law once; but when the commandment came, sin revived, and I died" [*Romans 7:9*]; and that "the law worketh wrath" [*Romans 4:15*], and many other things of the like nature. ***Writings on the Trinity, Grace, and Faith (WJE Online Vol. 21)***

And he himself in his Paraphrase on *Romans 4:15*, supposes that Abraham (who lived between Adam & Moses) to be yet under Law by which he would have been exposed to Punishmt (sic) without Hope. ***"Original Sin" Notebook (WJE Online Vol. 34)***

Romans 4:16

Lastly, this is contrary to God's design of glorifying his free grace by Jesus Christ. That is the design which God has had upon his heart from all eternity, and which he early manifested, and for which indeed he made this world and in subordination to which he orders and disposes all things. In this way, God always intended to glorify himself and his Son. They therefore that think to be saved by their own righteousness, they what in them lies do [to] overthrow this whole design. *Romans 4:16*, "Therefore it is of faith, that it might be by grace." *1 Corinthians 1:29*, "That no flesh should glory in his presence." ***Sermons and Discourses: 1723–1729 (WJE Online Vol. 14)***

If there were no other text in the Bible about justification but this, this would clearly and invincibly prove that we are not justified by any of our own goodness, virtue, or righteousness or for the excellency or righteousness of anything that we have done in religion; because 'tis here so fully and strongly asserted: but this text does abundantly confirm other texts of the Apostle, where he denies justification by works of the law: there is no doubt can be rationally made but that, when the Apostle here shows that God saves us according to his mercy, in that he don't save us by "works of righteousness that we have done" (*Titus 3:5*), and that so we are "justified by grace" (*Titus 3:7*), herein opposing salvation by works, and salvation by grace, he means the same works as he does in other places, where he in like manner opposes works and grace, the same works as in *Romans 11:6*, "And if by grace then is it no more of works; otherwise grace is no more grace: but if it be of works, then it is no more grace; otherwise work is no more work." And the same works as in *Romans 4:4*, "Now to him that worketh, is the reward not reckoned of grace but of debt." And the same works that are spoken of in the context of the *Romans 3:24* of the foregoing chapter, which the Apostle there calls works of the law "being justified freely by his grace . . ." And of the *Romans 4:16*, "Therefore 'tis of faith, that it might be by grace." Where in the context, the righteousness of faith, is opposed to the righteousness of the law: for here God's saving us according to his mercy, and justifying us by grace, is opposed to saving us by works of righteousness that we have done, in the same manner as in those places justifying us by his grace, is opposed to justifying us by works of the law. ***Sermons and Discourses, 1734–1738 (WJE Online Vol. 19)***

That scheme of justification that manifestly takes from, or diminishes the grace of God, is undoubtedly to be rejected; for 'tis the declared design of God in the gospel to exalt the freedom and riches of his grace, in that method of justification of sinners, and way of admitting them to his favor, and the blessed fruits of it, which it declares. The Scripture teaches that the way of justification that is appointed in the gospel covenant, is appointed, as it is, for that end, that free grace might be expressed and glorified; Romans 4:16, "Therefore it is of faith, that it might be by grace." The exercising, and magnifying the free grace of God in the gospel contrivance for the justification and salvation of sinners, is evidently the chief design of it; and this freedom and riches of grace of the gospel is everywhere spoken of in Scripture as the chief glory of it. Therefore that doctrine that derogates from the free grace of God in justifying sinners, as it is most opposite to God's design, so it must be exceeding offensive to him. ***Sermons and Discourses, 1734–1738 (WJE Online Vol. 19)***

But the great and most distinguishing difference between that covenant and the covenant of grace is, that by the covenant or grace we are not thus justified by our own works, but only by faith in Jesus Christ. 'Tis on this account chiefly that the new covenant deserves the name of a covenant of grace, as is evident by *Romans 4:16*, "Therefore it is of faith, that it might be by grace." And *Romans 3:20*, *Romans 3:24*, "Therefore by the deeds of the law there shall no flesh be justified in his sight; . . . being justified freely by his grace, trough the redemption that is in Jesus Christ." ***Sermons and Discourses, 1734–1738 (WJE Online Vol. 19)***

Another distinguishing Scripture note of saving faith is that it is the faith of Abraham; *Romans 4:16*, "Therefore it is of faith, that it might be by grace; to the end the promise might be sure to all the seed; not to that only which is of the law, but to that also which is of the faith of Abraham; who is the father of us all." Now, "the faith of Abraham" can't be faith of the degree of that Abraham's was, for undoubtedly multitudes are in a state of salvation that han't that eminency [of faith]; therefore, nothing can be meant by the faith of Abraham but faith of the same nature and kind. ***Sermons and Discourses, 1743–1758 (WJE Online Vol. 25)***

[*Romans 4:16–17*. "Before him whom he believed, even God, who quickeneth the dead, and calleth those things which be not as though they were."] Abraham believed in him "who quickeneth the dead," and so was able to make him the father of many nations, notwithstanding all the difficulties that were in the way, and particularly notwithstanding the deadness of his body and of Sarah's womb. He believed in him who "calleth those things that be not as though they were," as God did when he said to Abraham, "I have made thee the father of many nations" [*Genesis 17:5*], as though it were already done, for it was as certain it would be, seeing God promised it, as if it were done already, and that notwithstanding all the difficulties that were in the way. "And calleth those things that are not as though they were." "That this is to be understood of summoning them, as it were to rise into being, and appear before him, Eisner has well proved on this place." ***The "Blank Bible" (WJE Online Vol. 24)***

Romans 4:18

"Who against hope believed in hope, that he might become the father of many nations." Dr. Doddridge translates it thus: "Who against hope, believed with hope that he should become the father of many nations." ***The "Blank Bible" (WJE Online Vol. 24)***

Romans 4:19

Romans 4:19. "His own body now dead." *Objection*. But he had many children afterwards by Keturah. *Ans*. God miraculously restored to him the ability or gift of begetting children after he had lost it, so that it continued long afterwards, which is agreeable to God's manner of working. When he bestows a benefit by a miracle, 'tis commonly a durable thing, and not vanishing as a shadow. See Poole's *Synopsis, in loc*., p. 94, place marked in the margin. ***The "Blank Bible" (WJE Online Vol. 24)***

Romans 4:25

And it may be looked upon as part of the success of Christ's purchase if it be considered that Christ did not rise as a private person but as the head of all the elect church; so that they did, as it were, all rise in him. Christ was justified in his resurrection, i.e. God acquitted and discharged him hereby as having done and suffered enough for the sins of all the elect, *Romans 4:25*. ***A History of the Work of Redemption (WJE Online Vol. 9)***

Romans 4:25, "He was delivered for our offenses, and raised again for our justification." That is, delivered for our offenses, and raised again that he might see to the application of his sufferings to our justification, and that he might plead them for our justifying. ***The "Miscellanies": (Entry Nos. a–z, aa–zz, 1–500) (WJE Online Vol. 13)***

Had not Christ perfectly satisfied for the sins of men, and so done away all his imputed guilt, he could not have appeared a second time without sin, but must always have remained under the tokens of God's curse for sin. But at the day of judgment he will appear infinitely far from that. The glory he will appear in at the day of judgment will be the greatest and brightest evidence of all, of his having fully satisfied for sin. His resurrection is a glorious evidence of, and therefore is called, his "justification" [*Romans 4:25*]. ***Notes on Scripture (WJE Online Vol. 15)***

And indeed the justification of a believer is no other than his being admitted to communion in, or participation of the justification of this head and surety of all believers; for as Christ suffered the punishment of sin, not as a private person but as our surety, so when after this suffering he was raised from the dead, he was therein justified, not as a private person, but as the surety and representative of all that should believe in him; so that he was raised again not only for his own, but also for our justification, according to the Apostle. *Romans 4:25*, "Who was delivered for our offenses, and raised again for our justification." ***Sermons and Discourses, 1734–1738 (WJE Online Vol. 19)***

When Christ had once undertaken with God, to stand for us, and put himself under our law, by that law he was obliged to suffer, and by the same law he was obliged to obey: by the same law, after he had taken man's guilt upon him, he himself being our surety, could not be acquitted, till he had suffered, nor rewarded till he had obeyed: but he was not acquitted as a private person, but as our head, and believers are acquitted in his acquittance; nor was he accepted to a reward for his obedience as a private person, but as our head, and we are accepted to a reward in his acceptance. The Scripture teaches us, that when Christ was raised from the dead, he was justified; which justification as I have already shown, implies, both his acquittance from our guilt, and his acceptance to the exaltation and glory that was the reward of his obedience: but believers, as soon as they believe are admitted to partake with Christ in this his justification: hence we are told that he was "raised again for our justification" (*Romans 4:25*). ***Sermons and Discourses, 1734–1738 (WJE Online Vol. 19)***

To show the abundant ground God has given us for our hope, whereby we may be assured that 'tis "hope that makes not ashamed." The Apostle is here speaking of an hope of glory as the fruit of our justification and peace with God that we have by Christ's blood, as is evident by the *Romans 4:25*, together with the first and second of this, and is here showing what sure and abundant evidence it is that we shall obtain what we hope for, that we are already justified, and have peace with God by such means, viz. by the blood of Christ, as in [the] *Romans 4:25*. ***The "Blank Bible" (WJE Online Vol. 24)***

ROMANS CHAPTER 5

Romans 5:1–2

That a believer's justification implies not only deliverance from the wrath of God, but a title to glory, is evident by *Romans 5:1–2*, where the Apostle mentions both these as joint benefits implied in justification. "Therefore being justified by faith, we *have peace with God* through our Lord Jesus Christ: by whom also we have access into this grace wherein we stand, and *rejoice in hope of the glory of God*." So remission of sins, and inheritance among them that are sanctified, are mentioned together as what are jointly obtained by faith in Christ. *Acts 26:18*, "That they may receive forgiveness of sins, and inheritance among them that are sanctified through faith that is in me." Both these are without any doubt implied in that passing from death to life, which Christ speaks of as the fruit of faith, and which he opposes to condemnation. *John 5:24*, "Verily, I say unto you, He that heareth my word, and believeth on him that sent me, hath everlasting life, and shall not come into condemnation; but is passed from death to life."

There is a threefold benefit of justification mentioned in these two verses. 1. Peace with God, which consists in deliverance from God's displeasure and wrath. 2. The present free and rich bounty of God that we are admitted to, those spiritual enjoyments, and that spiritual good and blessedness, which is bestowed upon us in this life, as in the beginning of the next verse, "By whom also we have access by faith to this grace wherein we stand." 3. Our hope of future blessedness, or those fruits of God's grace that are to be given hereafter, in these words, "And rejoice in hope of the glory of God." ***The "Blank Bible" (WJE Online Vol. 24)***

Romans 5:2

["By whom we have access by faith into this grace wherein we stand."] "By whom we have been introduced into this grace, etc., τὴν προσαγωγὴν ἐσχήκαμεν. Raphelius has shown from Herodotus, that προσαγωγή is often used as a sacerdotal phrase, and signifies 'being with great solemnity introduced, as into the more immediate presence of a deity in his temple, so as by a supposed interpreter, from thence called προσαγωγεύς, the Introducer, to have a kind of conference with the deity.'" ***The "Blank Bible" (WJE Online Vol. 24)***

All that were in good standing in all those churches are saints, as the Apostle expresses charity for. And they are such as had hope of themselves. The Apostle speaks of the members of the church of the Romans, *Romans 5:2*, of their "rejoicing in hope of the glory of God," and so of the Christian Hebrews as having that hope which was an anchor [*Hebrews 6:19*]. Such passages we find all over the epistles. ***Sermons and Discourses, 1743–1758 (WJE Online Vol. 25)***

Romans 5:3

The Apostle teaches us in *Romans 5:3* that Christians who suffer for Christ's sake have reason to glory in tribulations. And the Apostle tells us of himself, and the sufferings he underwent for Christ, *2 Corinthians 6:10*, that though he was sorrowful, yet he was always rejoicing. And the Apostle commends the Christian Hebrews, chapter *Hebrews 10:34*, that they took joyfully the spoiling of their goods, knowing in themselves that they had in heaven a better and an enduring substance. ***Ethical Writings (WJE Online Vol. 8)***

"And hope maketh not ashamed." I.e. in Scripture language, our hope don't bring us into disappointment, "because the love of God is shed abroad in our hearts by the Holy Ghost which is given to us." The argument of the Apostle in these words is this: Our hope of the glory of God is not an hope that only occasions the grief of disappointment, but meets with success, and has already obtained the thing hoped for in some degree in the earnests of it, in the earnests of the Spirit that are given in our hearts (*Ephesians 1:13–14, 2 Corinthians 5:5–6, 2 Corinthians 1:20–22, Ephesians 4:30, Romans 8:23*), which we feel in that holy, sweet, and divine love that "is shed abroad" in us, which is the breathing, and the proper and natural act of the Holy Ghost. Thus we are enabled to "glory in tribulations" [*Romans 5:3.*]. ***The "Blank Bible" (WJE Online Vol. 24)***

Romans 5:3–4

"I am persuaded, as Calvin is, that all the several trials of men, are to show them to themselves, and to the world, that they be but counterfeits; and to make saints known to themselves, the better. . . . *Romans 5:3–4*, 'Tribulation works trial, and that hope.' *Proverbs 17:3*. If you will know whether it will hold weight, the trial will tell you."

Thus when God is said to prove Israel by the difficulties they met with in the wilderness, and by the difficulties they met with from their enemies in Canaan, to know what was in their hearts, whether they would keep his commandments or no; it must be understood that it was to discover them to themselves, that they might know what was in their own hearts. So when God tempted or tried Abraham with that difficult command of offering up his son, it was not for his satisfaction, whether he feared God or no, but for Abraham's own greater satisfaction and comfort, and the more clear manifestation of the favor of God to him. When Abraham had proved faithful under this trial, God says to him, "Now I know that thou fearest God, seeing thou hast not withheld thy son, thine only son from me" [*Genesis 22:12*]. ***Religious Affections (WJE Online Vol. 2)***

Romans 5:4

["Patience, experience."] The word translated "experience" is *δοκιμή*, trial or proof. The best proof of the fruits of grace is the experience of its exercise under trials, and this therefore works hope. ***The "Blank Bible" (WJE Online Vol. 24)***

Romans 5:5

["Because the love of God is shed abroad in our hearts by the Holy Ghost which is given unto us."] By this expression 'tis evident that love to God is something else besides a mere act of judgment, or merely a judicious determination of the mind as to its choice and the course of life. But there is a divine, sweet, holy, and powerful affection that is as it were diffused in the soul. "And hope maketh not ashamed." I.e. in Scripture language, our hope don't bring us into disappointment, "because the love of God is shed abroad in our hearts by the Holy Ghost which is given to us." The argument of the Apostle in these words is this: Our hope of the glory of God is not an hope that only occasions the grief of disappointment, but meets with success, and has already obtained the thing hoped for in some degree in the earnests of it, in the earnests of the Spirit that are given in our hearts (*Ephesians 1:13–14*, *2 Corinthians 5:5–6*, *2 Corinthians 1:20–22*, *Ephesians 4:30*, *Romans 8:23*), which we feel in that holy, sweet, and divine love that "is shed abroad" in us, which is the breathing, and the proper and natural act of the Holy Ghost. Thus we are enabled to "glory in tribulations" [*Romans 5:3*].

By "the love of God shed abroad in our hearts," the Apostle probably intends so as to include a sense of God's love to us (manifested in giving Christ, as in the following verses), as well our love to God, for 'tis said, "the love *of* God," not "love *to* God." In short, the term "the love of God," as used by the Apostle, when applied to something infused into our hearts and diffused there, is a term of larger signification than as it is commonly understood by us. It includes the whole of that divinely sweet sensation that is in the soul of a Christian when the Holy Ghost is given him as a seal, and earnest, and future glory, exciting as it were in the soul, an inward soul-ravishing sense of mutual love between God and us.

For when we, through hope of the reward, bear "tribulation" with "patience" in waiting for the reward, our patience issues in this joyful "experience" of the earnest of the reward even here in this life. And this does further confirm hope, as in the two foregoing verses, so that we ben't frustrated and left in confusion when we through hope "patiently" bear "tribulation," and under "tribulation patiently" wait for the reward. For when we thus bear and wait, God gives us our reward in the earnest of it, by causing us to feel the earnest of the Spirit in our heart in the sweet exercises of divine love and holy joy, mentioned *Romans 5:11*, so that we do even glory in tribulation. Hence an argument may be drawn that the Holy Ghost is only divine love, or the essence of God flowing out in love and joy, viz. that the Apostle mentions the love of God and joy in God that we feel in our hearts as that by which especially we are sensible of the earnest of the Spirit in our hearts, which is because the nature of the Spirit consists in love and joy.

2. If we compare this with the following verses, we shall find that the Apostle mentions God's communicating to us love to him as the same thing as his giving us and as it were filling our hearts with his love to us.

By "the love of God," the Apostle seems to intend the love of God to us as well as our love to God, as if we felt the love of God in this extensive sense "shed abroad in our hearts," which is because God's love to us and our love to him are in their fountain the same. The Holy Ghost is given to us, and that is in the very nature of it divine love. 'Tis the infinite fountain. And God's love to us is only that fountain's flowing out to us, and our love to God is only something communicated from that fountain to our hearts. And therefore God, in shedding abroad his love in our hearts, does as it were give us possession of that love that was manifested to us in giving Christ to die for us, as spoken of in the following verses.

When persons experience a right belief of the truth of the gospel, such a belief is accompanied with love. They love him whom they believe to be the Christ, the Son of the living God. When the truth of the glorious doctrines and promises of the gospel is seen, those doctrines and those promises are like so many bands, which take hold of the heart to draw it in love to God and Christ. When persons experience a true trust and reliance in Christ, they rely upon him with love, and so do it with delight and sincere acquiescence of soul. The spouse set under Christ's shadow with great delight, rested sweetly under the shadow of his protection because she loved him [*Canticles 2:3*]. When persons experience true comfort and spiritual joy, they draw the heart forth in love. Their joy is the joy of faith and love. They do not rejoice in themselves, but God is their exceeding joy.[1] When persons experience a true hope, their hope is accompanied with the shedding abroad of the love of God in the heart, and so has the evidence of a hope that is true and maketh not ashamed. *Romans 5:5*, "And hope maketh not ashamed, because the love of God is shed abroad in our hearts by the Holy Ghost, which is given unto us." ***Ethical Writings (WJE Online Vol. 8)***

It is a frequent thing for the Apostle to mention suffering in the cause of Christ as a fruit of love; and therefore it is not probable that he would omit so great a fruit of love in this place, where he is professedly reckoning up the various fruits of love or charity. It is common for the Apostle elsewhere to mention suffering in the cause of religion as a fruit of love or charity. So he does in *2 Corinthians 5:14*. There he had been in the foregoing chapter, and in that chapter from the beginning, speaking of the sufferings which he underwent in the cause of Christ, insomuch that others were ready to look upon him as beside himself, so to expose himself. But he gives this reason for it; that the love of Christ constrained him. So in *Romans 5:3–5*, he gives as a reason why they gloried in tribulations, and bare them with patience and hope, and without shame, viz. that the love of

God was shed abroad in their hearts by the Holy Ghost given unto them [*Romans 5:5*]. And again, *Romans 8:35–37*, the Apostle speaks of the love of Christ, that tribulation, distress, persecution, famine, nakedness, peril nor sword could overcome [*Romans 8:35*]. Now suffering in the cause of Christ being so great a fruit of charity, and that which the Apostle elsewhere often speaks of as a fruit of charity, it does not appear likely that he would omit it in this place where he professedly treats of the various fruits of charity. ***Ethical Writings (WJE Online Vol. 8)***

That the Holy Ghost is love. *2 Corinthians 6:6*, "By kindness, by the Holy Ghost, by love unfeigned." *Romans 15:30*, "Now I beseech you, brethren, for the Lord Jesus Christ's sake, and for the love of the Spirit." *Philippians 2:1–2*, "If there be therefore any consolation in Christ, [if] any comfort of love, if any fellowship of the Spirit, if any bowels and mercies, fulfill ye my joy, that ye be likeminded, having the same love, being of one accord, of one mind." *Romans 5:5*, "Having the love of God shed abroad in our hearts by the Holy Ghost which is given to us." *Galatians 5:22–23*, "But the fruit of the Spirit is love, joy, peace, longsuffering, gentleness, goodness, faith, meekness, temperance." *Ephesians 5:9*, "For the Spirit is in all goodness and righteousness and truth." *Colossians 1:8*, "Who declared unto us your love in the Spirit." *1 Thessalonians 1:6*, "Having received the word in much affliction, with joy of the Holy Ghost." *Romans 14:17*, "The kingdom of God is righteousness, and peace, and joy in the Holy Ghost." ***The "Miscellanies": (Entry Nos. a–z, aa–zz, 1–500) (WJE Online Vol. 13)***

The Scripture seems in many places to speak of love in Christians as if it were the same with the Spirit of God in them, or at least as the prime and most natural breathing and acting of the Spirit in the soul. *Philippians 2:1*, "If there be therefore any consolation in Christ, any comfort of love, any fellowship of the Spirit, any bowels and mercies, fulfill ye my joy, that ye be like-minded, having the same love, being of one accord, of one mind." *2 Corinthians 6:6*, "By kindness, by the Holy Ghost, by love unfeigned." *Romans 15:30*, "Now I beseech you, brethren, for the Lord Jesus Christ's sake, and for the love of the Spirit." *Colossians 1:8*, "Who declared unto us your love in the Spirit." *Romans 5:5*, having "the love of God shed abroad in our hearts by the Holy Ghost which is given to us" (see notes on this text). *Galatians 5:13–16*, "Use not liberty for an occasion to the flesh, but by love serve one another. For all the law is fulfilled in one word, even in this: Thou shalt love thy neighbor as thyself. But if ye bite and devour one another, take heed that ye be not consumed one of another. This I say then, Walk in the Spirit, and ye shall not fulfill the lust of the flesh." The Apostle argues that Christian liberty don't make way for fulfilling the lusts of the flesh, in biting and devouring one another and the like, because a principle of love, which was the fulfilling of the law, would prevent it; and in the *Galatians 5:16* he asserts the same thing in other words: "This I say then, Walk in the Spirit, and ye shall not fulfill the lust of the flesh." ***Writings on the Trinity, Grace, and Faith (WJE Online Vol. 21)***

Again, the Scripture seems in many places to speak of love in Christians as if it were the same with the Spirit of God in them, or at least as the prime and most natural breathing and acting of the Spirit in the soul. So *Romans 5:5*, "Because the love of God is shed abroad in our hearts by the Holy Ghost which is given unto us." *Colossians 1:8*, "Who also declared unto us your love in the Spirit." *2 Corinthians 6:6*, "By kindness, by the Holy Ghost, by love unfeigned." *Philippians 2:1*, "If there be therefore any consolation in Christ, if any comfort of love, if any fellowship of the Spirit, if any bowels and mercies, fulfill ye my joy, that ye be like-minded, having the same love, being of one accord, of one mind." ***Writings on the Trinity, Grace, and Faith (WJE Online Vol. 21)***

And in this work it is that the heart is put in tune, and it is put into a capacity and disposition truly and sincerely to praise God and to make that heavenly melody, which is made in singing this new song, by exercising these divine principles of divine love and divine joy. "The love of God is shed abroad" in the heart by the Holy Ghost (*Romans 5:5*). And spiritual rejoicing is called "joy in the Holy Ghost" [*Romans 14:17*]. This saving work of God in the heart is redemption by power, as the other is redemption by purchase. And seeing it is thus—that this knowledge of the things to be sung, and the ability to make the melody of the song, is imparted no other way than by the saving work of the Spirit, whereby the soul is redeemed by power—hence we may see another reason why no man can learn that song but they that are redeemed. Other men are dumb and dead as to any such heavenly exercise as this. They can exalt their idols, but they can't exalt God. They can rejoice in the objects of their lusts, in their worldliness and in their carnal pleasures, but they can't rejoice in Christ Jesus. They can howl, but they can't sing the new song. ***Sermons and Discourses, 1739–1742 (WJE Online Vol. 22)***

Romans 5:7

"By "a good man" and "a righteous man" here is meant the same things. The terms seem to be synonymous. ***The "Blank Bible" (WJE Online Vol. 24)***

Romans 5:9

The death of Christ and the blood of [Christ] are very often spoken of in Scripture as saving, as a righteousness, or as meritorious, and as sweet and acceptable to God's holiness, perhaps not less frequently than as a propitiation. So in the *Isaiah 53*, it is spoken of as a propitiation for sin in the former part, but in *Isaiah 53:12* 'tis spoken of as positively meritorious: "Therefore will I divide him a portion with the great, and he shall divide the spoil with the strong, because he hath poured out his soul unto death." So *John 10:17–18*, "Therefore doth my Father love me, because I lay down my life that I might take it up again. No man taketh it from me, but I lay it down of myself: I have power to lay it down, and I have power to take it again. This commandment received I of my Father." If the Father loves Christ because he laid down his life, he doubtless also loves those that are his, on the same account. *Acts 20:28*—there God is said to have purchased the church with his own blood, but this certainly signifies something more than being set at liberty from hell; it signifies also their being brought into a relation to God as his, into a covenant relation, whereby he is their God and they are his people, as appears by the scope of the place: "Take heed, feed the church of God, which he has purchased with his own blood." So in the *Romans 5:9*, we are said to be "justified by his blood." In the *Ephesians 2:13*, we are said to be "made nigh by the blood of Christ." And *Ephesians 5:2*, Christ is there said to "have given himself for us, an offering and a sacrifice to God for a sweet smelling savor," something positively pleasing, amiable and delightful to God, and therefore a price to purchase positive good from God. Hence the typical sacrifices are so very often said to be a sweet savor to God; the places are too many to be mentioned. Christ's dying is spoken of as what he did as a servant doing God's will, with delight and cheerfulness obeying his command, *Hebrews 10:5–7*, *Psalms 40:6–8*. Christ's body broken and his bloodshed don't only deliver us from eternal misery, but procures for us eternal life, as is very manifest by *John 6:51–55*. So the blood of Christ is drink that don't only assuage our disease and torment, but refreshes and makes glad the heart of man like wine. So Christ says, "My blood is drink indeed" [*John 6:55*], and in another place, "I will not henceforth drink of the fruit of the vine, until I drink it new with you in my Father's kingdom" [*Matthew 26:29*]. Believers ben't only delivered from hell, but they enter into heaven by his blood; for Christ himself, as their head, entered into heaven by his own blood, *Hebrews 6:20*, and so we enter into the holiest also by the blood of Christ, *Hebrews 10:19–20*. And hence we read of Christ's entering into the holiest with his own blood to appear before God for us, and not a word of his entering in there with his righteousness or obedience, any otherwise than as it appeared in his blood that he shed. Though the redemption of Christ does consist in his positive righteousness as much as his propitiation, he entered into the holiest of all with his whole ransom, or price of redemption; but half of this consisted in his obedience. But upon this supposition, the reason is plain: the blood of Christ did as much show his righteousness as his propitiation, and appeared as mainly in his blood as his propitiation did. So of old, in all the sacrifices, those great types of Christ, what they had that was to be offered to God was their blood; and other parts of their bodies, wherein life consisted, they had nothing to offer to God but what was offered in the fire. The fat of the innards, which signified the love and obedience of the heart (that was by the Holy Spirit signified by oil and fat), was offered in the fire, and the incense itself was offered in the fire. All which shows that the main of what Christ offered to God as a price for the redemption of man, both to assuage his wrath and positively to procure his favor, was offered up in his sufferings, and especially his last passion. *The "Miscellanies," 833–1152 (WJE Online Vol. 20)*

Romans 5:10

It shows the infallible perseverance of true Christians, that the spiritual life that they have is as partaking with Christ in his resurrection life, or the life that he has received as risen from the dead; and not as partaking of that life that he lived before his death. For they live by Christ living in them (*Galatians 2:20*); this is by the life that he has received since his resurrection, and by communicating to them that fullness that he received when he rose from the dead. When he rose he received the promise of the Father, the Spirit of life without measure, and [he] sheds it forth on believers. The oil poured on the risen head goes down the skirts of the garments [*Psalms 133:2*]. And thus Christ lives in believers by his Spirit's dwelling in them. Believers in their conversion are said to be risen with Christ. *Colossians 2:12–13*, "Ye are risen with him through the faith of the operation of God, who hath raised him from the dead. And you, being dead in your sins and the uncircumcision of your flesh, hath he quickened together with him"; and *Colossians 3:1*, "If ye then be risen with Christ, seek those things which are above, where Christ sitteth on the right hand of God"; and *Ephesians 2:5–6*, "Even when we were dead in sins, hath quickened us together with Christ, and hath raised us up together." *Romans 5:10*, "For if, when we were enemies, we were reconciled to God by the death of his Son, much more, being reconciled, we shall be saved by his life."*Philippians 3:10*, "That I may know him and the power of his resurrection." *Romans 6:4–5*, "Therefore we are buried by him by baptism unto death: that like as Christ was raised up from the dead by the glory of the Father, even so we also should walk in newness [of life]"; and so on throughout that chapter. ***The "Miscellanies," (Entry Nos. 501–832) (WJE Online Vol. 18)***

He never in any act gave so great a manifestation of love to God, and yet never so manifested his love to those that were enemies to God, as in that act. Christ never did anything whereby his love to the Father was so eminently manifested, as in his laying down his life, under such inexpressible sufferings, in obedience to his command, and for the vindication of the honor of his authority and majesty; nor did ever any mere creature give such a testimony of love to God as that was: and yet this was the greatest expression of all, of his love to sinful men, that were enemies to God. *Romans 5:10*, "While we were enemies, we were reconciled to God, by the death of his Son." The greatness of Christ's love to such, appears in nothing so much, as in its being dying love. That blood of Christ that was sweat out, and fell in great drops to the ground, in his agony, was shed from love to God's enemies, and his own. That shame and spitting, that torment of body, and that exceeding sorrow, even unto death, that he endured in his soul, was what he underwent from love to rebels against God, to save them from hell, and to purchase for them eternal glory. Never did Christ so eminently show his regard to God's honor, as in offering up himself a victim to revenging justice, to vindicate God's honor: and yet in this above all, he manifested his love to them that dishonored God, so as to bring such guilt on themselves, that nothing less than his blood could atone for it. ***Sermons and Discourses, 1734–1738 (WJE Online Vol. 19)***

Romans 5:6–10

What the Apostle says in these verses seems to be for two ends, viz. 1. To show the ground of that "love of God that is shed abroad in our hearts," mentioned in the *Romans 5:5*, viz. the wonderful love of God to us in giving Christ to die for us, for as the apostle John says, *1 John 4:10*, "Herein is love, not that we loved," etc., [and *1 John 4:19*, "We love him, because he first loved us."] This is principally the end of what is said in the *Romans 5:6–8*. 2. To show the abundant ground God has given us for our hope, whereby we may be assured that 'tis "hope that makes not ashamed." The

Apostle is here speaking of an hope of glory as the fruit of our justification and peace with God that we have by Christ's blood, as is evident by the *Romans 4:25*, together with the first and second of this, and is here showing what sure and abundant evidence it is that we shall obtain what we hope for, that we are already justified, and have peace with God by such means, viz. by the blood of Christ, as in [the] *Romans 4:25*. ***The "Blank Bible" (WJE Online Vol. 24)***

Romans 5:11

["And not only so," etc.] This verse is to be connected with *Romans 5:5*. There was mentioned one thing wherein that earnest of our future glory, the Spirit of God, was felt, whereby we found our hope not to be a hope that would make us ashamed. He now mentions another, viz. joy. See notes on *Romans 5:5*.

For when we, through hope of the reward, bear "tribulation" with "patience" in waiting for the reward, our patience issues in this joyful "experience" of the earnest of the reward even here in this life. And this does further confirm hope, as in the two foregoing verses, so that we ben't frustrated and left in confusion when we through hope "patiently" bear "tribulation," and under "tribulation patiently" wait for the reward. For when we thus bear and wait, God gives us our reward in the earnest of it, by causing us to feel the earnest of the Spirit in our heart in the sweet exercises of divine love and holy joy, mentioned *Romans 5:11*, so that we do even glory in tribulation. Hence an argument may be drawn that the Holy Ghost is only divine love, or the essence of God flowing out in love and joy, viz. that the Apostle mentions the love of God and joy in God that we feel in our hearts as that by which especially we are sensible of the earnest of the Spirit in our hearts, which is because the nature of the Spirit consists in love and joy. ***The "Blank Bible" (WJE Online Vol. 24)***

["And not only so," etc.] This verse is to be connected with *Romans 5:5*. There was mentioned one thing wherein that earnest of our future glory, the Spirit of God, was felt, whereby we found our hope not to be a hope that would make us ashamed. He now mentions another, viz. joy. See notes on *Romans 5:5*. ***The "Blank Bible" (WJE Online Vol. 24)***

Romans 5:12

Now, by way of reflection on the whole, I would observe, that though there are two or three expressions in this paragraph (*Romans 5:12*, etc.), the design of which is attended with some difficulty and obscurity, as particularly in the thirteenth and fourteenth verses; yet the scope and sense of the discourse in general is not obscure, but on the contrary very clear and manifest; and so is the particular doctrine mainly taught in it. The Apostle sets himself with great care and pains to make it plain, and precisely to fix and settle the point he is upon. And the discourse is so framed, that one part of it does greatly clear and fix the meaning of other parts; and the whole is determined by the clear connection it stands in with other parts of the epistle, and by the manifest drift of all the preceding part of it. ***Original Sin (WJE Online Vol. 3)***

["Wherefore, as by one man sin entered into the world," etc.] The Apostle here resumes the subject he had been upon in the *Romans 1–4*, viz. that all, both Jews and Gentiles, are under sin and condemnation, and that justification is only by Christ, and equally to all mankind, both Jews and Gentiles. These things are, from hence to the end of this chapter, illustrated by the Apostle by observing that all, both Jews and Gentiles, are the posterity of one first father, and all fell in him, and came under condemnation alike by Adam's transgression. And so in it, all are alike saved by Christ, and equally partake of the benefit of the righteousness of the Second Adam. ***The "Blank Bible" (WJE Online Vol. 24)***

The doctrine of original sin is not only here taught, but most plainly, explicitly and abundantly taught. This doctrine is asserted, expressly or implicitly, in almost every verse; and in some of the verses several times. 'Tis fully implied in that first expression in the *Romans 5:12*, "By one man sin entered into the world." Which implies, that sin became *universal* in the world; as the Apostle had before largely shewn it was; and not merely (which would be a trifling insignificant observation) that one man, who was made first, sinned first, before other men sinned; or, that it did not so happen that many men began to sin just together at the same moment. The latter part of the verse, "And death by sin, and so death passed upon all men, for that" (or, if you will, "unto which") "all have sinned," shews, that in the eye of the Judge of the world, in Adam's first sin, *all* sinned; not only in *some sort*, but all sinned so as to be exposed to that death, and final destruction, which is the proper wages of sin. The same doctrine is taught again twice over in the *fourteenth verse*. It is there observed, as a proof of this doctrine, that "death reigned over them which had not sinned after the similitude of Adam's transgression," i.e. by their personal act; and therefore could be exposed to death, only by deriving guilt and pollution from Adam, in consequence of his sin. And 'tis taught again, in those words, "Who is the figure of him that was to come." The resemblance lies very much in this circumstance, viz. our deriving sin, guilt and punishment by Adam's sin, as we do righteousness, justification, and the reward of life by Christ's obedience; for so the Apostle explains himself. The same doctrine is expressly taught again, *v. 15*, "Through the offense of one many be dead." And again twice in the *sixteenth verse*, "It was by one that sinned," i.e. it was by Adam that guilt and punishment (before spoken of) came on mankind: and in these words, "Judgment was by one to condemnation." It is again plainly and fully laid down in the *seventeenth verse*. "By one man's offense, death reigned by one." So again in the eighteenth verse, *"By the offense of one, judgment came upon all men to condemnation." Again, very plainly in the nineteenth verse, "By one man's disobedience, many were made sinners."* ***Original Sin (WJE Online Vol. 3)***

But we have something that is more sure, whereunto we do well if we give heed: *Romans 5:12*, "Wherefore, as by one man sin entered into the world, [and] death by sin; so death passed upon all men, for that all have sinned"; which is as much as if the Apostle had expressly said, "All men have sinned in one man." *Romans 5:15*, "For if through the offence of one many be dead"; in *Romans 5:16*, "for the judgment was by one to condemnation"; *Romans 5:17*, "for if by one man's offence death reigned by one"; *Romans 5:18*, "therefore as by the offence of one judgment came upon all men to condemnation"; and *Romans 5:19*, "for as by one man's disobedience many were made sinners." Also, *1 Corinthians 15:21–22*, "For since by Adam came death, by man also came the resurrection of the dead, for as in Adam all die, so in Christ shall all be made alive." ***Sermons and Discourses 1720–1723 (WJE Online Vol. 10)***

If it be so that God deals most reasonably with us when he holds us guilty for the transgression of our first parents, let everyone see and own his necessity of a Savior, in that every one of the children of Adam have sinned in him and do justly deserve death, yea, eternal death, for that sin. *Romans 5:12*, "Wherefore, as by one man sin entered into the world, and death by sin; and so death passed upon all men, for that all have sinned." If it were for nothing but this, that we have sinned and rebelled in Adam, it would be enough forever to render vain and good for nothing all our own righteousness. If we could weep an ocean of tears, it would [not] be sufficient to satisfy only for that sin. And if we could perform perfect obedience—as perfect as that that the first covenant required, or as the holy angels in heaven perform—it would in no measure satisfy the justice of God for that sin; and we should nevertheless stand in necessity of a Savior. ***Sermons and Discourses: 1723–1729 (WJE Online Vol. 14)***

Hereby the Apostle prepares the way for the second thing he would prove in these words, which he had asserted before (*Romans 5:12*), and which he mainly aims at the proof, viz. that all mankind sinned and fell in Adam. This is evident by Adam's being the legal head of mankind, which is the first thing insinuated. For if God, when he spake to Adam in the singular number, giving him a precept, spake to him as representing his posterity, so it will follow that he spake to him as representing his posterity in the threatening. And this is further evident by this, that death did not only reign from Adam to Moses, but also reigned over them that had not violated Adam's law themselves by their actual personal transgression, as Adam had done. ***The "Blank Bible" (WJE Online Vol. 24)***

"Therefore as by the offense of one," etc. "'Therefore' here is not used as an illative, introducing an inference from the immediately preceding verses, but is the same 'therefore' (or wherefore) which begun *Romans 5:12*, repeated here again with part of the inference that was there begun and left incomplete, the continuation of it being interrupted by the intervention of the proofs of the first part of it. The particle 'as' immediately following 'wherefore' (*Romans 5:12*), is a convincing proof of this, having there or in the following verses nothing to answer it, and so leaves the sense imperfect and suspended, till you come to this verse where the same reasoning is taken again, and the same protasis or first part of the comparison repeated. And then the apodosis or latter part is added to it, and the whole sentence made complete, which to take right one must read thus: v. 12, '*Therefore* as by one man sin entered into the world, and death by sin, and so death passed upon all men,' etc.; *Romans 5:18*, 'I say, *therefore* as by the offense of one, judgment came upon all men to condemnation, even so by the righteousness of one, the free gift came upon all men to justification of life.' A like interruption of what he began to say may be seen, *2 Corinthians 12:14*, and the same discourse, after the interposition of eight verses, began again (*2 Corinthians 13:1*), not to mention others which I think may be found in Paul's epistles." Locke, *in loc.* ***The "Blank Bible" (WJE Online Vol. 24)***

Romans 5:13

I would explain what we mean by the imputation of Christ's righteousness. Sometimes the expression is taken by our divines in a larger sense, for the imputation of all that Christ did and suffered for our redemption, whereby we are free from guilt, and stand righteous in the sight of God; and so implies the imputation both of Christ's satisfaction, and obedience. But here I intend it in a stricter sense, for the imputation of that righteousness, or moral goodness, that consists in the obedience of Christ. And by that righteousness being imputed to us, is meant no other than this, that that righteousness of Christ is accepted for us, and admitted instead of that perfect inherent righteousness that ought to be in ourselves: Christ's perfect obedience shall be reckoned to our account, so that we shall have the benefit of it, as though we had performed it ourselves: and so we suppose that a title to eternal life is given us as the reward of this righteousness. The Scripture uses the word *impute* in this sense, viz. for reckoning anything belonging to any person, to another person's account: as Philem. *Philemon 18*, "If he have wronged thee, or oweth thee ought put that on mine account." In the original it is τούτο έμοί έλλόγα: *impute that to me*. 'Tis a word of the same root with that which is translated *impute. Romans 4:6*, "To whom God imputeth righteousness without works." And 'tis the very same word that is used, *Romans 5:13*, that is translated *impute:* "Sin is not imputed, where there is no law." ***Sermons and Discourses, 1734–1738 (WJE Online Vol. 19)***

Romans 5:13–14

["For until the law sin was in the world, but sin is not imputed when there is no law. Nevertheless, death reigned from Adam to Moses, even over them that had not sinned after the similitude of Adam's transgression."] There are two things the Apostle would prove in these words, one of which establishes the other. First, he would prove that all mankind were under the law God gave to Adam that revealed death to be the wages of sin. This is evident because that sin, as bringing death, was in the world before there was any other legislation or solemn giving of law to mankind besides what was to Adam, viz. in that space of time that was from Adam to Moses. There being sin therefore in the world as bringing death, in that space of time before the giving of the law by Moses, shows that there was a law given of God before that time, threatening death, that they were under, but this could be no other than the law God gave to Adam. This proves that Adam was the legal head of mankind, that mankind were under the law given to him, wherein God threatened death for transgression, and that God in that law given to Adam, saying, "When thou sinnest, thou shalt die," did not only speak to him, though he spake in the singular number, but in him spake to his posterity also.

Hereby the Apostle prepares the way for the second thing he would prove in these words, which he had asserted before (*Romans 5:12*), and which he mainly aims at the proof, viz. that all mankind sinned and fell in Adam. This is evident by Adam's being the legal head of mankind, which is the first thing insinuated. For if God, when he spake to Adam in the singular number, giving him a precept, spake to him as representing his posterity, so it will follow that he spake to him as representing his posterity in the threatening. And this is further evident by this, that death did not only reign from Adam to Moses, but also reigned over them that had not violated Adam's law themselves by their actual personal transgression, as Adam had done. ***The "Blank Bible" (WJE Online Vol. 24)***

Romans 5:14.

"Who is the figure of him that was to come." By this it appears that things before the fall were types of things pertaining to Christ's redemption, as I suppose the creation of man to be of his redemption, and the tree of life a type of Christ. See "Miscellanies," no. 702, fourteenth paragraph. The Apostle here argues that all were guilty of sin even before the law inasmuch as death, the fruit of sin, reigned over all before the law. Therefore by just the same reasoning may infants be proved guilty of sin, in that death reigns over them. The Apostle's reasoning is void, if death ben't an evidence of sin in that person that is the subject of it.

The theory and terminology of Christian typology hark back to the earliest days of the church, when it was used as a way of interpreting passages of Scripture. In part, the conception of typological interpretation derives from certain passages in the New Testament in which particular persons, institutions, and events mentioned in the Old Testament are viewed as figures, types, or foreshadowings of Christ. In *Romans 5:14*, for example, the apostle Paul states that Adam was the "figure of him that was to come," or Christ. These passages gave Christians a way to interpret the Old Testament in light of the New. Events mentioned or described in the former as belonging to the history of the Jews had a significance beyond their actual and historical reality. They were ordained by God to stand as prophetic representations of what was to come, namely, God's full revelation of himself in the person of Christ. ***Typological Writings (WJE Online Vol. 11)***

The Apostle expected of Christians in his time, though that was the infant state of the church, that they should be filled with all knowledge. *Romans 5:14*, "And I myself also am persuaded of you, my brethren, that ye are full of goodness, filled with all knowledge, able to admonish one another." He commends the Corinthians that they abound in knowledge. *2 Corinthians 8:7*, "Therefore, as ye abound in everything, in faith, in utterance, in knowledge." We are commanded to add to virtue, knowledge (*2 Peter 1:5*). ***Sermons and Discourses: 1723–1729 (WJE Online Vol. 14)***

The gift abounds more than the offense, for if it abounded only in an equality, then it would only just remove that death and misery that the offense brought, and restore man to the state he was in before; but it doth much more than so. "But not as the offense, so also is the free gift." The conjunction "but" refers to the last words in the preceding verse, "who is the figure of him that was to come," as much as to say, "But yet though Adam were the figure of Christ, yet the gift or benefit received by Christ is not exactly conformed or confined to the dimensions of the damage received by Adam's fall." ***Sermons and Discourses: 1723–1729 (WJE Online Vol. 14)***

Adam in his creation, or in the state wherein he was created, was a remarkable type of Christ. *Romans 5:14*, "After the similitude of Adam's transgression, who was the figure of him that was to come." He was so in various respects. He was the first man that was formed of the dust of the earth; so Christ was the first begotten from the dead, or first raised out of the grave or dust. So he was the first that was raised out [of] those mean and low circumstances, from weakness, from disgrace and misery that were the fruits of man's sin. He was the first made of all mankind; so Christ was the first born of every creature. As he was he out of whom the woman was taken, even from near his heart, bone of his bone, and flesh of his flesh, by his deep sleep; so Christ was he out of whom the church is, as it were, taken, from his transcendent love and by the deep sleep of his death. As Adam was the natural father of all mankind; so is Christ the spiritual father of all in the new creation. Adam was made the federal head of all his seed; so Christ is the federal head of all his seed. That blessedness that Adam would have obtained if he had stood for himself and his posterity was but a type of the blessedness that Christ obtained for himself and his seed by his obedience; and therefore, that tree of life he should have eat of as a seal of that blessedness, was but a type of that blessedness that the church is brought to eat of by Christ's obedience (*Revelation 2:7*). "Adam was the son of God" (*Luke 3:38*). As Christ was formed immediately out of the womb of a virgin, by the Spirit of God, without the seed of man; so Adam was immediately formed out of the bowels of his mother earth, which is in Scripture made use [of] to represent the formation of the body in the womb (*Psalms 139:15*); and it was from the womb of the earth while yet as it were a virgin, while in its pure and undefiled state. And this was by the Spirit, as the formation of Christ in the womb of the virgin, for it was that which breathed into him the breath of life. Adam, though made of the mean vile dust of the earth, yet was made in the image of God; as is particularly observed, *Genesis 1:27*, "God created man *in his own image, in the image of God* created he him." By which four things are typified: (1) Christ, the antitype of Adam, his being the brightness of God's glory, and the express image of his person. (2) The man Christ Jesus being made in union with the divine nature, so as to be in the divine person. He was made in that person that was the essential image of God; and so had in a sense the Godhead communicated to him. (3) Christ's having the image of God as God–man; as such, representing the person of God the Father as his vicegerent in governing and judging the world. (4) The transcendent advancement of men in their union with God, whereby they partake of the beauty, life, honor and joy of the eternal Son of God; and so are made as gods by communion of his Spirit, whereby they are made partakers of the divine nature. ***The "Miscellanies," (Entry Nos. 501–832) (WJE Online Vol. 18)***

All men are declared to suffer, to be condemned, and to die for the sake of Adam's sin. "Death," says the Apostle, *Romans 5:14*, "reigned from Adam to Moses, even over them that had not sinned after the similitude of Adam's transgression"; that is, not actually as infants, or not against a law given to them in their own persons, with the penalty of death annexed, as was the case for the most part with mankind before the law of Moses. And how it received its dominion, both then and ever since, over all men; viz. not from the absolute pleasure of God, but from sin, and from what sin; he had in part showed before, and more fully expresses in the following verses. It is "through the offense of one that many be dead," v. 15. "The judgment was by one to condemnation," v. 16. And that "upon all men," v. 18. "By one man's offense death reigned by one," v. 17. The death of all men is plainly here derived as a penal effect by virtue of a judicial sentence, and not in the way of merely natural consequence, from the first transgression. *"Controversies" Notebook (WJE Online Vol. 27)*

Romans 5:15

The gift abounds more than the offense, for if it abounded only in an equality, then it would only just remove that death and misery that the offense brought, and restore man to the state he was in before; but it doth much more than so. *The "Blank Bible" (WJE Online Vol. 24)*

Romans 5:16

I.e. we receive much more benefit by the grace of God in Christ than we did mischief by the sin of Adam, in this respect, that that brought the guilt but of one sin upon us, but Christ's satisfaction and the grace of God through that, removes the guilt of many sins from us. *The "Blank Bible" (WJE Online Vol. 24)*

Romans 5:17–19

We are plainly taught it in Scripture. *Romans 5:17–19*, "For if by one man's offense death reigned by one; much more they which receive abundance of grace and of the gift of righteousness shall reign in life by one, Jesus Christ. Therefore as by the offense of one judgment came upon all men to condemnation; even so by the righteousness of one the free gift came upon all men unto justification of life. For as by one man's disobedience many were made sinners, so by the obedience of one shall many be made righteous." Which plainly shows that as what Adam did brought death, as it had the nature of disobedience, so what Christ did brought life, not only as a sacrifice, but as it had the nature of meriting obedience. ["Miscellanies" nos. 381 and 399 discuss the nature of Adam's and Christ's obedience (*Works, 13*, 450–51, 464–65). Though the "positive precepts" each had to heed were different, JE maintains in these entries, the law was nonetheless the same.] *Sermons and Discourses: 1723–1729 (WJE Online Vol. 14)*

Romans 5:18

"Therefore as by the offense of one," etc. "'Therefore' here is not used as an illative, introducing an inference from the immediately preceding verses, but is the same 'therefore' (or wherefore) which begun *Romans 5:12*, repeated here again with part of the inference that was there begun and left incomplete, the continuation of it being interrupted by the intervention of the proofs of the first part of it. The particle 'as' immediately following 'wherefore' (*Romans 5:12*), is a convincing proof of this, having there or in the following verses nothing to answer it, and so leaves the sense imperfect and suspended, till you come to this verse where the same reasoning is taken again, and the same protasis or first part of the comparison repeated. And then the apodosis or latter part is added to it, and the whole sentence made complete, which to take right one must read thus: v. 12, '*Therefore* as by one man sin entered into the world, and death by sin, and so death passed upon all men,' etc.; *Romans 5:18*, 'I say, *therefore* as by the offense of one, judgment came upon all men to condemnation, even so by the righteousness of one, the free gift came upon all men to justification of life.' A like interruption of what he began to say may be seen, *2 Corinthians 12:14*, and the same discourse, after the interposition of eight verses, began again (*2 Corinthians 13:1*), not to mention others which I think may be found in Paul's epistles."

As by the offense of one natural head, condemnation came upon all his natural offspring, so by the righteousness of our spiritual head (or Adam, *1 Corinthians 15:46*) justification came upon all his spiritual offspring. As Adam's sin descends to all that are of him, or that belong to him, so Christ's righteousness goes to all that are of him.

Or when the Apostle says, "the free gift came upon all," he may mean "is preached and offered to all," and is come upon all that will, without exception, Jews and Gentiles. ***The "Blank Bible" (WJE Online Vol. 24)***

There are many things make it exceeding plain that the Apostle don't, by the terms righteousness and justification, intend merely God's mercy and grant of favor and deliverance from a great calamity, and bringing into a state of great privilege. The Apostle in these places sets righteousness expressly in opposition to condemnation, sin, disobedience. He speaks of the justification of *sinners*, and with regard to works of righteousness. How plain is the meaning of the expression in that place, *Romans 2:13*, "not the hearers of the law are just before God, but the doers of the law shall be justified," where it plainly appears that to be justified is to be reputed and accepted as just before God. So *Isaiah 53:11*, "by his knowledge shall my righteous servant justify *many*." The union and relation of these two terms plainly show their meaning. *Romans 5:19*, "by the obedience of one many shall be made righteous." *Romans 8:4*, "That the righteousness of the law might be fulfilled in us, who walk not after the flesh, but after the Spirit." *1 John 2:1*, "if any man sin, we have an advocate with Father, Jesus Christ the righteous." *Romans 5:18*, "by the righteousness of one the free gift came upon all men to justification of life." ***Writings on the Trinity, Grace, and Faith (WJE Online Vol. 21)***

Romans 5:19

There are many things make it exceeding plain that the Apostle don't, by the terms righteousness and justification, intend merely God's mercy and grant of favor and deliverance from a great calamity, and bringing into a state of great privilege. The Apostle in these places sets righteousness expressly in opposition to condemnation, sin, disobedience. He speaks of the justification of *sinners*, and with regard to works of righteousness. How plain is the meaning of the expression in that place, *Romans 2:13*, "not the hearers of the law are just before God, but the doers of the law shall be justified," where it plainly appears that to be justified is to be reputed and accepted as just before God. So *Isaiah 53:11*, "by his knowledge shall my righteous servant justify *many*." *Romans 5:19*, "by the obedience of one many shall be made righteous." *Romans 8:4*, "That the righteousness of the law might be fulfilled in us, who walk not after the flesh, but after the Spirit." *1 John 2:1*, "if any man sin, we have an advocate with Father, Jesus Christ the righteous." *Romans 5:18*, "by the righteousness of one the free gift came upon all men to justification of life." ***Writings on the Trinity, Grace, and Faith (WJE Online Vol. 21)***

Romans 5:20

He [Dr. Taylor] says, that the law of God requires perfect obedience. "God can never require imperfect obedience, or by his holy law allow us to be guilty of any one sin, how small soever. And if the law as a rule of duty were in any respect abolished, then we might in some respects transgress the law, and yet not be guilty of sin. The moral law, or law of nature, is the truth, everlasting, unchangeable; and therefore, as such, can never be abrogated. On the contrary, our Lord Jesus Christ has promulgated it anew under the gospel, fuller and clearer than it was in the Mosaical constitution, or anywhere else; . . . having added to its precepts the sanction of his own divine authority." And many things which he says imply that all mankind do in some degree transgress the law. In p. 228, speaking of what may be gathered from *Romans 7* and *8*, he says, "We are very apt, in a world full of temptation, to be deceived, and drawn into sin by bodily appetites, etc. And the case of those who are under a law threatening death to every sin, must be quite deplorable, if they have no relief from the mercy of the lawgiver." But this is very fully declared in what he says in his *Note on Romans 5:20*, pp. 378–79. His words are as follows: "Indeed, as a rule of action prescribing our duty, it (the law) always was, and always must be a rule ordained for obtaining life; but not as a rule of justification, not as it subjects to death for every transgression. For if it could in its utmost rigor have given us life, then, as the Apostle argues, it would have been against the promise of God. For if there had been a law, in the strict and rigorous sense of law, *which could have made us live*, verily justification should have been by the law." But he supposes, no such law was ever given: and therefore there is need and room enough for the promises of grace; or as he argues (*Galatians 2:21*), it would have frustrated, or rendered useless the grace of God. For if justification came by the law, then truly Christ is dead in vain, then he died to accomplish what was, or *might have been effected* by law it self, without his death. Certainly the law was not brought in among the Jews to be a rule of justification, or to recover 'em out of a state of death, and to procure life by their sinless obedience to it: for in this, as well as in another respect, it was *weak*; not in itself, but through the *weakness* of our flesh (*Romans 8:3*). The law, I conceive, is not a dispensation suitable to the infirmity of the human nature in our present state; or it doth not seem congruous to the goodness of God to afford us no other way of salvation, but by *law*: *which if we once transgress, we are ruined forever*. ***Original Sin (WJE Online Vol. 3)***

And however great the guilt of God's people has been, and how much soever they have offended and provoked God, and deserved his displeasure; that shall be no hindrance to God's bestowing any good that they desire, how excellent soever. For that also is one way in which God designed to magnify the exceeding riches of his grace, even in bestowing it on those that were so unworthy. *Romans 5:20*, "Where sin abounded, grace did much more abound." ***Sermons and Discourses, 1734–1738 (WJE Online Vol. 19)***

ROMANS CHAPTER 6

Romans 6:1

Romans 6:1. By not continuing in sin, but walking in newness of life, and not serving sin; yielding obedience to God and being servants of righteousness; and bringing forth the fruits of righteousness. The Apostle in *Romans 6* has a special respect to external works that are performed, because he particularly explains it by sin's not reigning in our mortal bodies; and yielding our members as "instruments of righteousness unto God"; and yielding our members as "servants of righteousness unto holiness" (see *Romans 6:1*). ***Writings on the Trinity, Grace, and Faith (WJE Online Vol. 21)***

Romans 6:2

Therefore, the true Christian, before he lives to Christ, dies unto sin. Of this sort of death the Apostle speaks in *Romans 6:2*, "How shall we that are dead to sin live any longer therein?" and *1 Peter 2:24*, "Who his own self bore our sins in his own body on the tree, that we, being dead unto sin, should live unto righteousness; by whose stripes ye were healed." This dying unto sin is a true and godly repentance, and hatred of it. By repentance sin receives his deadly wound, such a wound as is never cured, but increases until it has quite deprived the body of sin of all its life. True repentance may very properly be called a dying unto sin, because in that sorrow and contrition, and turning of the heart, the power and activity of sin dies: the sinner's inclination to sin, his love of it, his relish and taste, and the false pleasure he used to experience in it, vanishes and dies; and he relishes sin no more than a dead man relishes food, and so may be said to be dead to sin. Life consists in activity, and the life of sin consists in the activity of it, but by repentance and godly sorrow sin—that is, sinful inclinations are no more active as before—but lies as that that is dead, as there are some remaining motions of sin, but 'tis only like the struggles of one that is dying, and not as the activeness of him that has his life whole in him. ***Sermons and Discourses 1720–1723 (WJE Online Vol. 10)***

You must die unto sin. Of this sort of death the Apostle, in *Romans 6:2*, "How shall we, that are dead to sin, live any longer therein?" and *1 Peter 2:24*, "Who his own self bore our sins in his own body on the tree, that we being dead to sin, should live unto righteousness." Dying unto sin is the mortification of the habit, power, and activity of sin, of the sinner's inclination to it and his love of it. His relish and taste and the false pleasure he used to experience in it vanishes and dies: as a dead man relishes no food, so the regenerate man is dead to sin. ***Sermons and Discourses 1720–1723 (WJE Online Vol. 10)***

Romans 6:3

In whom also ye are Circumcised with the Circumcision made without Hands—Buried with him in Baptism wherein also ye are risen with him—And you being dead in your sins & the uncircumcision of your Flesh hath he quicken'd together with Him having forgiven you all Trepasses the same appears by *Romans 6:3–4*. Know ye not that so many of us as were baptized into Jesus Christ were baptized into his death therefore we are buried with him by Baptism unto death that like as Christ was raised up from the dead by the Glory of the Father even so we also should walk in newness of Life &c—***"Original Sin" Notebook (WJE Online Vol. 34)***

Romans 6:4

In a word, it appears, that man's nature, as in his native state, is a body of sin, which must be destroyed, must die, be buried, and never rise more. For thus the OLD MAN is represented, which is crucified, when men are the subjects of a spiritual resurrection (*Romans 6:4–6*). ***Original Sin (WJE Online Vol. 3)***

That baptism, by which the primitive converts were admitted into the church, was used as an exhibition and token of their being visibly regenerated, dead to sin, alive to God, having the old man crucified, being delivered from the reigning power of sin, being made free from sin, and become the servants of righteousness, those servants of God that have their fruit unto that holiness whose end is everlasting life; as is evident by

Romans 6 throughout. In the former part of the chapter [*Romans 6:4–6*], he speaks of the Christian Romans as "dead to sin," being "buried with Christ in baptism," having their old man crucified with Christ, etc. ***Ecclesiastical Writings (WJE Online Vol. 12)***

Kings 6:6. "And he cut down a stick, and cast [it] in thither; and the iron did swim." The iron that sank in the water [2 Kings 6:5] represents the soul of man that is like iron, exceeding heavy with sin and guilt, and prone to sink down into destruction, and be overwhelmed with misery, which is often compared to deep waters. The stick of wood that was cast in represents Christ, that was of a contrary nature, light, tended not to sink, but to ascend in the water and swim; as Christ, being of a divine and perfectly holy nature, though he might be plunged into affliction, and misery, and death, yet he naturally tended to ascend out of it. It was impossible he should be holden of it. Christ was plunged into our woe, and misery, and the death that we had deserved for ourselves, to bring us out of it. The stick, when that rose, brought up the iron with it; so Christ, when he rose, he brings up believers with him. They are risen with Christ, that they may walk in newness of life [*Romans 6:4*]. "Christ is the first fruits; afterwards those that are Christ's" [*1 Corinthians 15:23*]. He rose again for our justification, and hath thereby begotten us again to a living hope [*1 Peter 1:3*]. ***Notes on Scripture (WJE Online Vol. 15)***

Exodus 2:5 ff. Add this to No. 159. Pharaoh's daughter came to wash herself in the same river into which Moses was cast. So if we would find Christ, and be the spiritual mothers of Christ, we must die with Christ, be "made conformable to his death" [*Philippians 3:10*], be "buried with him by baptism" [*Romans 6:4*], must die to sin, must be crucified to the work [*Galatians 6:14*], and die to the law, and be willing to suffer affliction and persecution with him. By such mortification and humiliation is the soul washed in the river into which Christ was cast. ***Notes on Scripture (WJE Online Vol. 15)***

The resurrection of Christ, which was the beginning of the new creation, was especially from the Father. This was as it were a new birth of Christ, wherein he received a new life. And as by his first birth, wherein he was begotten in the womb of a virgin and born of her, he was begotten, and so that holy thing that was born of her was called the Son of God, so by his second birth, whereby he was born of the womb of the earth (that is often in Scripture represented as our mother), he was also begotten of God. Thus God the Father says to Christ, with respect to his resurrection, "Thou art my Son; this day have I begotten thee" [*Psalms 2:7*], as is evident by *Acts 13:33*, with the context, and *Hebrews 5:5*. Christ glorified not himself to be made a high priest, but he that said unto him, "Thou art my Son; this day have I begotten thee." Christ is said to be raised up by the glory of the Father, *Romans 6:4*. ***The "Miscellanies," 833–1152 (WJE Online Vol. 20)***

"Buried with him by baptism into death." The Anabaptists from thence argue that persons in baptism ought to [be] plunged into and covered with water. But the deceit lies in the English word "buried," which signifies not only putting into a tomb or sepulcher, but is commonly used to signify the same as "covered over." But the word in the original only relates to the funeral of a dead body; it signifies entombed, or put into a sepulcher. A being covered over is "buried" in English, but not in Greek, as if the word be used that is in this verse. But if it be so that the Apostle the rather used this word because of their custom then of immerging persons into the water, and because of some sort of resemblance between plunging and burying, it don't follow that plunging is necessary. For baptism, with washing only, without plunging, does represent that which is often compared to a dying or being buried with Christ, viz. our being cleansed from sin, or as it is expressed in the foregoing verse, a being "dead to sin." ***The "Blank Bible" (WJE Online Vol. 24)***

Romans 6:5

Those that Christ comes down upon in the saving and comforting influences of his Spirit on their souls are cut down by humiliation and mortification. They that are made partakers of the saving benefits of Christ and live through him, they must be the subject of a kind of death. They must be as it were killed before they are made alive. They must die with Christ that they may live with him. *Romans 6:5* "For if we have been planted together in the likeness of his death, we shall be also in the likeness of his resurrection." ***Sermons and Discourses, 1739–1742 (WJE Online Vol. 22)***

Romans 6:6

And 'tis most apparent, that spiritual circumcision, and spiritual baptism, and the spiritual resurrection, are all the same with putting off the old man, and putting on the new man. Here it is manifest, that the spiritual circumcision, baptism, and resurrection, all signify that change, wherein men put off the body of the sins of the flesh: but that is the same thing, in this Apostle's language, as "putting off the old man"; as appears by *Romans 6:6*, "Our OLD MAN is crucified, that the BODY OF SIN may be destroyed." And that putting off the old man is the same with putting off the body of sins, appears further by *Ephesians 4:22–24*, and *Colossians 3:8–10*. ***Original Sin (WJE Online Vol. 3)***

And so far as we are worthy to be credited one by another, in what we say (and persons of good understanding and sound mind, and known and experienced probity, have a right to be believed by their neighbors, when they speak of things that fall under their observation and experience), multitudes in New England have lately been brought to a new and great conviction of the truth and certainty of the things of the Gospel; to a firm persuasion that Christ Jesus is the Son of God, and the great and only Saviour of the world; and that the great doctrines of the Gospel touching reconciliation by his blood, and acceptance in his righteousness, and eternal life and salvation through him, are matters of undoubted truth; together with a most affecting sense of the excellency and sufficiency of this Saviour, and the glorious wisdom and grace of God shining in this way of salvation; and of the wonders of Christ's dying love, and the sincerity of Christ in the invitations of the Gospel, and a consequent affiance and sweet rest of soul in Christ, as a glorious Saviour, a strong rock and high tower, accompanied with an admiring and exalting apprehension of the glory of the divine perfections, God's majesty, holiness, sovereign grace, etc.; with a sensible, strong and sweet love to God, and delight in him, far surpassing all temporal delights, or earthly pleasures; and a rest of soul in him as a portion and the fountain of all good, attended with an abhorrence of sin, and self-loathing for it, and earnest longings of soul after more holiness and conformity to God, with a sense of the great need of God's help in order to holiness of life; together with a most dear love to all that are supposed to be the children of God, and a love to mankind in general, and a most sensible and tender compassion for the souls of sinners, and earnest desires of the advancement of Christ's kingdom in the world. And these things have appeared to be in many of them abiding now for many months, yea, more than a year and [a] half; with an abiding concern to live an holy life, and great complaints of remaining corruption, longing to be more free from the body of sin and death [cf. *Romans 6:6*, *Romans 7:24*, *Romans 8:2*]. ***The Great Awakening (WJE Online Vol. 4)***

Romans 6:6–8

As ‘tis broken for sin. A sacrifice, before it can be offered, must be wounded and slain. The heart of a true Christian is first wounded by a sense of sin, of the great evil and danger of it, and is slain with godly sorrow and true repentance. When the heart truly repents, it dies unto sin. Repentance is compared unto a death in the Word of God; *Romans 6:6–8*, “Knowing this, that our old man is crucified with him. For he that is dead is freed from sin. Now, if we be dead with Christ, we believe that we shall also live with him”; *Romans 6:11*, “Likewise ye also reckon yourselves to be dead indeed unto sin, but alive unto God through Jesus our Lord”; and *Galatians 2:20*. As Christ, when he was offered, he was offered broken upon the cross, so there is some likeness to this when a soul is converted. The heart is offered to God slain and broken; *Psalms 51:17*, “The sacrifices of God are a broken heart: a broken and a contrite spirit.” ***Sermons and Discourses, 1730–1733 (WJE Online Vol. 17)***

Romans 6:8–9

These two verses with the context seem irrefragably to prove perseverance. ***Notes on Scripture (WJE Online Vol. 15)***

Romans 6:9

(6) The Scripture teaches that the believer has grace and spiritual life as partaking of the life of Christ’s resurrection, which is immortal, everlasting life. The Scripture teaches this, *Colossians 2:12*, “Ye are risen with him.” Ver. *Colossians 2:13*, “You hath he quickened together with him.” *Ephesians 2:5–6*, “Even when we were dead in sins, hath quickened us together with Christ; and hath raised us up together.” *Galatians 2:20*, “I live, yet not I, but Christ liveth in me.” Which shows that the believer’s spiritual life cannot fail. For *Revelation 1:18*, “I am he, that liveth and was dead; and behold, I am alive forevermore.” *Romans 6:9*, “Knowing that Christ being raised from the dead dieth no more; death hath no more dominion over him.” ***Ethical Writings (WJE Online Vol. 8)***

For when Christ rose from the dead, that was the beginning of eternal life in him. His life before his death mortal life, a temporal life, but his life after his resurrection was an eternal and immortal life, *Romans 6:9*, “Knowing that Christ being raised from the dead dieth no more; death [hath no more, dominion over him]," *Revelation 1:18*, "I am he that liveth, [and was dead; and, behold I am alive for evermore, Amen]." But he was put in possession of this eternal life as the head of the body, and took possession of it not only to enjoy himself but to bestow [it] on all that believe in him; so that the whole church, as it were, rises in him. And now he that lately suffered so much, after this is to suffer no more forever, but to [have] eternal glory. God the Father neither expects nor desires any more suffering. ***A History of the Work of Redemption (WJE Online Vol. 9)***

Hence it follows that the saints shall surely persevere in their spiritual life and their justified state. The Apostle hence argues in the *Romans 6* that believers are finally freed from sin, and shall live forever with Christ, and that sin shall no more have dominion over them: *Romans 6:9*, "Knowing that Christ being raised from the dead dieth no more; death hath no more dominion over him" ***The "Miscellanies," (Entry Nos. 501–832) (WJE Online Vol. 18)***

Romans 6:11

A sacrifice, before it can be offered, must be wounded and slain. The heart of a true Christian is first wounded by a sense of sin, of the great evil and danger of it, and is slain with godly sorrow and true repentance. When the heart truly repents, it dies unto sin. Repentance is compared unto a death in the Word of God. . . . *Romans 6:11*, "Likewise ye also reckon yourselves to be dead indeed unto sin, but alive unto God through Jesus our Lord." . . . As Christ, when he was offered, he was offered broken upon the cross, so there is some likeness to this when a soul is converted. The heart is offered to God slain and broken; *Psalms 51:17*, "The sacrifices of God are a broken heart: a broken and a contrite spirit." ***Sermons and Discourses, 1730–1733 (WJE Online Vol. 17)***

Romans 6:13

Christians offer up their own hearts to God in sacrifice. They dedicate themselves to God; *Romans 6:13*, "Yield yourselves to God, as those that are alive from the dead." The Christian gives himself to God freely as of mere choice. He doth it heartily; he desires to be God's and to belong to no other. He gives all the faculties of his soul to God. He gives God his heart, and 'tis offered to God as a sacrifice . . ." ***Sermons and Discourses, 1730–1733 (WJE Online Vol. 17)***

"As many of us as have been baptized into Christ, have been baptized into his death." Here he speaks of *all* that have been baptized; and in the continuation of the discourse [*Romans 6:11–18*], explaining what is here said he speaks of their being dead to sin; no longer "under the law, but under grace"; having obeyed the "form of doctrine" from the heart being "made free from sin" and become "the servants of righteousness," etc. *Romans 14:7–8*, "None of us liveth to himself, and no man dieth to himself" (taken together with the context). *2 Corinthians 3:18*, "We all with open face beholding as in a glass," etc. And *Galatians 3:26*, "Ye are all the children of God by faith." ***Ecclesiastical Writings (WJE Online Vol. 12)***

Romans 6:14

That baptism, by which the primitive converts were admitted into the church, was used as an exhibition and token of their being visibly regenerated, dead to sin, alive to God, having the old man crucified, being delivered from the reigning power of sin, being made free from sin, and become the servants of righteousness, those servants of God that have their fruit unto that holiness whose end is everlasting life; as is evident by *Romans 6* throughout. In the former part of the chapter [*Romans 6:4–6*], he speaks of the Christian Romans as "dead to sin," being "buried with Christ in baptism," having their old man crucified with Christ, etc. He don't mean, only, that their baptism laid 'em under special obligations to these things, and was a mark and token of their engagement to be thus hereafter; but was designed as a mark, token and exhibition of their being visibly thus already. As is most manifest by the Apostle's prosecution of his argument in the following part of the chapter. V. *Romans 6:14*: "For sin shall not have dominion over you, for ye are not under the law but under grace." Vv. *Romans 6:17–18*: "God be thanked, ye were the servants of sin, but ye have obeyed from the heart that form of doctrine which was delivered you. Being then made free from sin, ye became the servants of righteousness." V. *Romans 6:22*: "But now being made free from sin, and become servants to God, ye have your fruit unto holiness, and the end everlasting life." ***Ecclesiastical Writings (WJE Online Vol. 12)***

"For sin shall not have dominion over you, for ye are not under the law, but under grace." The law, or covenant of works is not a proper means to bring the fallen creature to the service of God It was a very proper means to be used with man in a state of innocency but it has no tendency to answer this end in our present weak and sinful state; but on the contrary, to have been kept under the law would have had a tendency to hinder it, and would have been a bar in the way of it, and that upon two accounts. 1. It would have tended to discourage persons from any attempts to serve God, because under such a constitution it must necessarily have been looked upon as impossible to please him or serve him to his acceptance; and one in despair of this would have been in no capacity to yield a cheerful service to God, but would rather have been far from any manner of endeavors to serve him at all, but to have abandoned himself to wickedness. By such a despair the dominion of sin would have been dreadfully established, and all yielded up to it, as in the damned in hell. 2. God must necessarily have been looked on as an enemy, which would have tended to drive from him and stir up enmity against him. A fallen creature held under the covenant of works can't look on God as a father and friend, but must necessarily look on him as an enemy, for the least failure of obedience by that constitution, whether past or future, renders him so. But this would greatly establish the dominion of sin or enmity against God in the heart. And indeed, it is the law only that makes wicked men hate God. They hate him no otherwise than as they look upon [him] as acting, either as the giver or judge of the law, and so by the law opposing their sins, and the law tending to establish the hatred of God. Hence 'tis necessary to be brought from under the dominion of it, in order to a willing serving of God. ***Notes on Scripture (WJE Online Vol. 15)***

Romans 6:16

By not continuing in sin, but walking in newness of life, and not serving sin; yielding obedience to God and being servants of righteousness; and bringing forth the fruits of righteousness. The Apostle in Romans 6 has a special respect to external works that are performed, because he particularly explains it by sin's not reigning in our mortal bodies; and yielding our members as "instruments of righteousness unto God"; and yielding our members as "servants of righteousness unto holiness" (see *Romans 6:1, Romans 6:3, Romans 6:6, Romans 6:12, Romans 6:13, Romans 6:16*). ***Writings on the Trinity, Grace, and Faith (WJE Online Vol. 21)***

Romans 6:17

Dr. Owen, on the Spirit, p. 199, speaking of a common work of the Spirit, says, "The effects of this work on the mind, which is the first subject affected with it, proceeds not so far, as to give it delight, complacency and satisfaction in the lovely spiritual nature and excellencies of the things revealed unto it. The true nature of saving illumination consists in this, that it give the mind such a direct intuitive insight and prospect into spiritual things, as that in their own spiritual nature they suit, please, and satisfy it; so that it is transformed into them, cast into the mold of them, and rests in them; *Romans 6:17, Romans 12:2, I Corinthians 2:13–14, II Corinthians 3:18, II Corinthians 4:6.*" ***Religious Affections (WJE Online Vol. 2)***

The heart acquiesces in it. It sees that in this way that it needs nor desires no other way. There is a sweet harmony now between the soul and the gospel; it doth in a lively manner accord and consent to it, and cleave to it. Thus we read of receiving the truth in the love of it, or receiving the love of the truth (*2 Thessalonians 2:10*), and obeying the truth from the heart (*Romans 6:17*). This is that gladly receiving the gospel spoken of, *Acts 2:41*. By this, we may understand what is meant (*Acts 2:41*) when it is said, God opened the heart of Lyddia, that she attended to those things which were spoken by Paul. ***Sermons and Discourses: 1723–1729 (WJE Online Vol. 14)***

Matthew 11:25–26. "At that time Jesus answered and said, I thank thee, O Father, Lord of heaven and earth, that thou hast hid these things from the wise and prudent, and hast revealed them unto babes. Even so, Father, for so it seemed good in thy sight." Christ don't only *praise* God, as God may be praised or glorified for his majesty and greatness, sovereignty or justice, or any perfection or glorious work of his, but he *thanks* him as one interested, as though it were a work of God, whereby he had received a benefit. And so it was; these persons to whom his Father had revealed these things were his before God had revealed them to them, for they were given him from eternity, and he had set his love upon them before the foundation of the world, and for their sakes he came into the world, and he knew them all by name. Their names were written on his heart, and he looked upon them as himself. And therefore he thanks the Father for revealing those things to these that were his, that he so loved and was so greatly concerned for, though they were but poor, weak, helpless, and despicable creatures, when he had passed by others more noble, more wise, and prudent; as a loving father, if he had a number of poor children in themselves very mean and contemptible, might well be the more affected with the goodness of God, and justly have his heart more enlarged with thankfulness, if God should look on his poor children, bestowing infinite blessings upon them, when he saw that the rich and noble, potent and learned, were generally passed by. Persons themselves, that see themselves very weak and distinguishingly contemptible, have the more cause to thank God for saving mercy to them, when they consider how they are distinguished from many far greater and more considerable than they. And so Christ looked upon it that he had like cause of thankfulness on this account, because they being from eternity given to him, he looked on them as himself, and on himself as they. Christ, the head of the elect church, here thanks the Father, with rejoicing in spirit, as Luke tells us [*Luke 10:21*], for that which will be the matter of the most exalted thanksgivings of the church itself to all eternity. Christ thankfully acknowledges God's kindness herein, because he did it of his own will. "Even so, Father, for so it seemed good in thy sight," that is, without regard to their meanness, or others' greatness. Compare this text with *Romans 6:17*. ***Notes on Scripture (WJE Online Vol. 15)***

7. Faith is a receiving of Christ (*John 1:12*; *Hebrews 11:19*; *Colossians 2:5–7*). See no. [100].

8. It is a receiving Christ into the heart (*Romans 10:6–10*).

9. 'Tis accepting of the gospel (*1 Timothy 1:14–15*; *2 Corinthians 11:4*). A true faith includes more than a mere belief of it; it includes all acceptation (*1 Timothy 1:15*).

10. 'Tis something more than merely the assent of the understanding, because 'tis called an "obeying the gospel" (*Romans 10:16*; see no. [104]; *1 Peter 4:17*; *Romans 15:18*; *1 Peter 2:7–8*; *1 Peter 3:1*. 'Tis obeying the form of doctrine from the heart, *Romans 6:17*). This expression of obeying the gospel seems to denote the heart's yielding to the gospel in what it proposes to us in its calls. ***Writings on the Trinity, Grace, and Faith (WJE Online Vol. 21)***

["Which was delivered to you."] In the Greek (as in the margin), "whereto ye were delivered." "No harsh, but an elegant expression, if we observe that St. Paul here speaks of sin and the gospel, as of two masters, and that those he writes to were taken out of the hands of the one, and delivered over to the other, which they, having from their hearts obeyed, were no longer the slaves of sin, he whom they obeyed being by the rule of the foregoing verse truly their master." Mr. Locke, *in loc.* ***The "Blank Bible" (WJE Online Vol. 24)***

Romans 6:17–18

(8) That baptism, by which the primitive converts were admitted into the church, was used as an exhibition and token of their being visibly regenerated, dead to sin, alive to God, having the old man crucified, being delivered from the reigning power of sin, being made free from sin, and become the servants of righteousness, those servants of God that have their fruit unto that holiness whose end is everlasting life; as is evident by *Romans 6* throughout. In the former part of the chapter [*Romans 6:4–6*], he speaks of the Christian Romans as "dead to sin," being "buried with Christ in baptism," having their old man crucified with Christ, etc. He don't mean, only, that their baptism laid 'em under special obligations to these things, and was a mark and token of their engagement to be thus hereafter; but was designed as a mark, token and exhibition of their being visibly thus already. As is most manifest by the Apostle's prosecution of his argument in the following part of the chapter. V. *Romans 6:14*: "For sin shall not have dominion over you, for ye are not under the law but under grace." Vv. *Romans 6:17–18*: "God be thanked, ye were the servants of sin, but ye have obeyed from the heart that form of doctrine which was delivered you. Being then made free from sin, ye became the servants of righteousness." V. *Romans 6:22*: "But now being made free from sin, and become servants to God, ye have your fruit unto holiness, and the end everlasting life." ***Ecclesiastical Writings (WJE Online Vol. 12)***

The word "believe," in the New Testament, answers to the word "trust" in the Old; and therefore the phrase used by Philip, of believing with all the heart, is parallel to that in *Proverbs 3*: "Trust in the Lord with all thine heart." And believing with the heart is a phrase used in the New Testament to signify saving faith. *Romans 10:9–10*, "If thou shalt believe in thine heart, that God hath raised him from the dead, thou shalt be saved; for with the heart man believeth unto righteousness." The same is signified by obeying the form of doctrine from the heart, *Romans 6:17–18*, "But God be thanked, that ye were the servants of sin, but ye have obeyed from the heart that form of doctrine which was delivered you; being then made free from sin, ye became the servants of righteousness." Here it is manifest, that saving faith is intended by obeying the form of doctrine from the heart. ***Ecclesiastical Writings (WJE Online Vol. 12)***

The apostles continually in their epistles speak to them and of them as supposing and judging them to be gracious persons. Thus the apostle Paul in his epistle to the church of the Romans, *Romans 1:7*, speaks or the members of that church as "beloved of God." In ch. *Romans 6:17–18*, etc.

he "thanks God that they had obeyed from the heart that form of doctrine which had been delivered them, and were made free from sin, and become the servants of righteousness," etc. The Apostle in giving thanks to God for this, must not only have a kind of negative charity for them, as not knowing but that they were gracious persons, and so charitably hoping (as we say) that it was so; but he seems to have formed a positive judgment that they were such: his thanksgiving must at least be founded on rational probability; since it would be but mocking of God, to give him thanks for bestowing a mercy which at the same time he did not see reason positively to believe was bestowed. ***Ecclesiastical Writings (WJE Online Vol. 12)***

Romans 6:18

As the children of Israel were redeemed out of Egypt that they might serve God, so are We redeemed by Jesus Christ; not that we might be at liberty to sin, but that we might be at liberty from sin, that so we might serve God. They were delivered from serving their old masters, the Egyptians, that so they might serve God. So we are redeemed from the service of sin, that we might henceforth serve God; being "made free from sin," we are become "the servants of righteousness" *Romans 6:18*, as *Romans 6* throughout. ***The "Blank Bible" (WJE Online Vol. 24)***

By not continuing in sin, but walking in newness of life, and not serving sin; yielding obedience to God and being servants of righteousness; and bringing forth the fruits of righteousness. The Apostle in *Romans 6* has a special respect to external works that are performed, because he particularly explains it by sin's not reigning in our mortal bodies; and yielding our members as "instruments of righteousness unto God"; and yielding our members as "servants of righteousness unto holiness" (see *Romans 6:1*, *Romans 6:3*, *Romans 6:6*, *Romans 6:12*, *Romans 6:13*, *Romans 6:16*, *Romans 6:18*, *Romans 6:19*). So the Apostle in *Romans 12:1* insists upon it. By good works and keeping God's commandments and bringing forth fruit, when spoken of as signs of sincerity, are chiefly intended properly voluntary behavior; because the same is expressed by walking before God and being perfect, walking before him in truth and with a perfect heart, running a race, fighting a good fight. ***Writings on the Trinity, Grace, and Faith (WJE Online Vol. 21)***

Romans 6:19

The body of a wicked man is also enslaved to sin. Whenever the wicked man exercises his body, it is in the service of sin. *Proverbs 21:4*, "And the plowing of the wicked is sin." The hands, feet, tongue, eyes, ears and all are about the devil's work. *Romans 6:19*, "For as ye have yielded your members servants to uncleanness, to iniquity unto iniquity . . ." Thus sin governs the whole man, both soul and body, and all the actions of both. ***Sermons and Discourses 1720–1723 (WJE Online Vol. 10)***

["I speak after the manner of men because of the infirmity of your flesh."] I.e. "I make use of this metaphor of passing of slaves from one master to another, well known to you Romans, the better to let my meaning into your understandings that are yet weak in these matters, being more accustomed to fleshly than spiritual things." Mr. Locke, *in loc*. ***The "Blank Bible" (WJE Online Vol. 24)***

Romans 6:23

["For the wages of sin is death."] The "wages of sin" does not signify here the wages that are paid for sinning, but the wages that sin pays. This is evident not only by the opposition that is put here in this verse between the "wages of sin" and the "gift of God," but it further appears by the whole tenor of St. Paul's discourse, wherein he speaks of sin as a person and a master who hath servants, and is served and obeyed. And so the "wages of sin," being the wages of a person, here must be what it pays. ***The "Blank Bible" (WJE Online Vol. 24)***

But now, let us consider what that death is, which the Scripture ever speaks of as the proper wages of the sin of mankind, and is spoken of as such by God's saints in all ages of the church, from the first beginning of a written revelation, to the conclusion of it. I'll begin with the New Testament. When the apostle Paul says (*Romans 6:23*), "The wages of sin is death," Dr. Taylor tells us (p. 396) that "this means eternal death, the second death, a death widely different from the death we now die." The same Apostle speaks of death as the proper punishment due for sin (in *Romans 7:5* and *8:13*, *II Corinthians 3:7*, *I Corinthians 15:56*). In all which places, Dr. Taylor himself supposes the Apostle to intend eternal death.1 And when the apostle James speaks of death, as the proper reward, fruit and end of sin (*James 1:15*), "Sin, when it is finished, bringeth forth death," 'tis manifest, that our author supposes eternal destruction to be meant. ***Original Sin (WJE Online Vol. 3)***

Consider what poor wages you will have for your services. Death, eternal death, is all the wages that ever you will receive for your service: *Romans 6:23*, "For the wages of sin is death"—after all your pains to please the devil, after all your hard labor, after all those difficulties you undergo in obeying sin's commands; after you have given up your reason, understanding and innocency, and made yourself a beast and a fool that you may serve this, your abject master.

After you have spent your life and your soul in this slavery, after you have been vexed by the fears of death and been scorched by your conscience, and have rotted in sin's prison and Satan's chains, all the wages you shall have for your pains is nothing but one of the chiefest—that is, one of the deepest and hottest—places in the lake of fire and brimstone.

This is the wages due to you for your hard service and cruel servitude. Satan is willing enough you should have it—he'll not begrutch it you—nor God is not so unjust as not to pay it: the harder you labor, and the more work you do for sin, the greater will be your wages. You shall have a larger cup of vengeance and a hotter place than others who have sinned but little in comparison of you. God will deal justly with everyone, will do with all according to their works, and they that do most work for sin will have a reward accordingly, and a proportionable retribution. ***Sermons and Discourses 1720–1723 (WJE Online Vol. 10)***

From the deserts of wicked men, I argue thus: the least sin deserves eternal destruction. Both according to the law of God and according to the reason and nature of things, the law fixes death as the wages of every sin. "In the day that thou eatest thou shalt [surely die]" [*Genesis 2:17*]. Which does not only refer to that one particular sin, but to every other thing that God has forbidden. *Romans 6:23*, "The wages of sin is death." But by death is meant no other than the utter eternal destruction of the creature: not only the death of the body, but the death of the soul; not only transient death, but continuing eternal death. Again, it is written, *Deuteronomy 27:26*, "Cursed be every one that confirmeth not all things written in the book of the law to do them." So that if a man commits but one sin, does but in one article disobey God, he deserves to be cursed of God; which is no other than to be devoted to eternal destruction. **Sermons and Discourses: *1723–1729 (WJE Online Vol. 14)***

We are told, *Romans 6:23*, that "the wages of sin is death," and, *Ezekiel 18:20*, [that] "the soul that sinneth, it shall die," by which is undoubtedly meant eternal destruction. The Scripture has sufficiently explained itself in that matter. When it is said, 'tis its wages, the meaning of it is that it is the recompense it deserves, and the recompense that is appointed or stated. And [that] 'tis not only intended that this is the wages of a wicked life or sinful course, but of one sin, of any one thing that is a sin or a breach of the divine law, is evident by these texts: *Genesis 2:17*, "In the day that thou eatest thereof, thou shalt surely die"; *James 2:10*, "He that offends in one point, is guilty of all"; *Galatians 3:10*, "Cursed is every one that continueth not in all things which are written in the book of the law to do them." ***The "Miscellanies," (Entry Nos. 501–832) (WJE Online Vol. 18)***

Without doubt, that death that was threatened to man at first, in case he sinned, was that same death, if any such there be, that the Scripture declares to be the proper and the threatened punishment of sin, or the wages of sin, by which we can understand nothing else, but the proper and appointed recompense of sin; but this wages is called death. *Romans 6:23*, "The wages of sin is death; but the gift of God is eternal life through Jesus Christ our Lord." Now in order to know what the proper and appointed wages of sin is, we must look and see what is the wages appointed and given, when judgment comes to be passed by the proper judge, and in the proper time of judgment. When he comes thus to reckon with the servants, he will doubtless assign everyone his proper wages; when he comes to call all to an account, he will doubtless give everyone their proper and appointed recompense. But we have seen what this is under the preceding particular. And we may also judge by the death that Christ suffered, who not only suffered the dissolution of the frame of his body, but extreme agonies in his soul, which made him say, "My soul is exceeding sorrowful, even unto death" [*Matthew 26:38*]. 'Tis also manifest that this death that is the wages of sin, is not the death of the body: for doubtless this is the same death that Christ has respect to when he says, that he that believes on him shall not die, but shall live forever (*John 6:49–51*, *John 6:58*). ***The "Miscellanies," (Entry Nos. 501–832) (WJE Online Vol. 18)***

And what is said of the tree of life, seems to show that there was a promise of life, on obedience [*Genesis 3:22*]; and that there was a promise of a glorious life to obedience, is further evident from *Romans 3:23*, "For all have sinned, and come short of the glory of God," which implies that there was a glory that God offered, in case he had not sinned. *Matthew 19:17*, *Leviticus 18:5*, *Ezekiel 20:11*, *Romans 6:23*. And doubtless that, which this promise was made to, was the condition of the covenant. This is as evident as it is that the promise of life was made; and therefore, if the implicit promise of life was not made on that sole condition, his forbearing to eat of the forbidden tree, then it follows that that is not the whole condition of the covenant. ***The "Miscellanies," 833–1152 (WJE Online Vol. 20)***

Here it is in vain for any to say that that was an extraordinary state of things, and the bigger part of members of churches at that day might happen to be truly godly in a judgment of charity. But that is no argument that it ought [not] to be so in an ordinary state of things. For the apostles don't only speak of the bigger part of them as such, but of their all universally being admitted under that notion; and that all that got in that were otherwise, it was unawares, or by a false profession, and that they did not belong there. The Apostles use universal terms. *Galatians 3:26–27*, "ye [are] all the children of God by faith in Jesus Christ. For as many of you as have been baptized [have put on Christ]." He speaks of all as visibly belonging to heaven. *Galatians 4:26*, "Jerusalem which is above [. . .], is the mother of us all." So [also] to the members of the church of Philippi. *Philippians 1:6*, "Being confident of this very thing, that he which hath begun a good work in you will perform it until the day of Jesus Christ: even as it is meet for me to think this of you all." *Romans 6:23*, "as many of us as have been baptized into Christ have been baptized into his death." ***Sermons and Discourses, 1743–1758 (WJE Online Vol. 25)***

It is answered that, however, God cannot, consistent with his justice, inflict the least degree of punishment on a creature who is in all respects guiltless, or any evil or misery that is of a penal nature. But 'tis certain that death is an evil or calamity that must be considered as penal; it is revealed to be so. We are taught that it comes on mankind in way of punishment; as such it was at first denounced as a part of the curse consequent on Adam's sin. And the Apostle says the wages of sin is death *Romans 6:23*, and he elsewhere speaks of all men's dying in Adam; and consequently, as it comes on him as a penal evil, so it doth on the rest of men. It was only as a punishment, and by a judicial proceeding or by force of justice in way of punishing, that it ever came into the world at all; as the Apostle observes, "death by sin; and death passed on all men, for that all have sinned" *Romans 5:12*. And therefore 'tis no virtue in the world, but by virtue of punishing justice; it passes on no man any other way. ***"Controversies" Notebook (WJE Online Vol. 27)***

ROMANS CHAPTER 7

Romans 7:1

"Throughout your generations, ye shall keep it a feast by an ordinance forever." This and such like expressions may be explained by *Romans 7:1.* "Know ye not, brethren (for I speak to them that know the law), how that the law hath dominion over a man as long as he liveth?" The old testament church died in Christ when his body died, and the ordinances of that dispensation were nailed to his cross. ***The "Blank Bible" (WJE Online Vol. 24)***

Romans 7:1–4

"The law hath dominion over a man so long as he liveth," or in commands that respect another man, so long as that other "liveth," for this expression of the Apostle's, "so long as he liveth," is thus to be understood. For in the Apostle's way of speaking, when another is dead, to whom before a man stood related and obliged, the man lives no longer as to that person, but is dead to him. In such manner the Apostle speaks in the *Romans 7:4*. We are said to be "dead to the law," our former husband; i.e. the law, our husband, is dead, as the Apostle explains himself in the *Romans 7:6*, "That being dead wherein," etc., so that we are at liberty to marry another.

Thus we may understand the connection between this and the following verse. The law has dominion over a woman so long as she liveth, and in those commands that relate to her husband, so long as her husband liveth. For when her husband is dead, she is dead to him with respect to that part of the law that respects the relation between her and her husband. She is dead, for her living, with respect to those precepts, consists in the living of the relation between them. The woman is freed from that part of the law that related to her husband, not by any abrogating or disannulling of the law, but because she is in that matter dead, and the law don't any longer reach her. So is the law as a covenant of works dead with respect to us, and we are dead to it by Christ's body, i.e. by the dying of his body, whereby the law was satisfied and fulfilled. The law did as it were die as a covenant of works with respect to the people of Christ when Christ's body died. Note Dr. Doddridge and Taylor translate it, "So long as it liveth," i.e. the Law. ***The "Blank Bible" (WJE Online Vol. 24)***

Romans 7:4

"Thy belly is like a heap of wheat set about with lilies." I.e. thy womb is very fruitful. The good fruit brought forth by thee may, for abundance, be compared to the multitude of grains of corn in an heap of wheat; and the fruits of thy womb are as food to thy husband, as wheat, and are pleasant and delightful like beautiful lilies. *Romans 7:4*, "Wherefore, my brethren, ye are become dead to the law by the body of Christ; that ye should be married unto another, even to him who is raised from the dead, that ye should bring forth fruit unto God." Here the Apostle evidently compares the good fruits Christians bring forth by their spiritual marriage to Christ, to the fruit of the womb that is brought forth by a woman's marriage to an husband. ***Notes on Scripture (WJE Online Vol. 15)***

That there is NO GOOD WORK BEFORE CONVERSION, and actual union with Christ, is manifest from that, *Romans 7:4*, "Wherefore, my brethren, ye also are become dead to the law by the body of Christ; that ye should be married unto another, even to him who is raised from the dead, that we should bring forth fruit unto God." Hence we may argue that there is no lawful child brought forth before that marriage. Seeming virtues and good works before, are not so indeed; they are a spurious brood, being bastards and not children. ESSENTIAL DIFFERENCE BETWEEN COMMON AND SAVING GRACE. ***The "Miscellanies," (Entry Nos. 501–832) (WJE Online Vol. 18)***

"The law hath dominion over a man so long as he liveth," or in commands that respect another man, so long as that other "liveth," for this expression of the Apostle's, "so long as he liveth," is thus to be understood. For in the Apostle's way of speaking, when another is dead, to whom before a man stood related and obliged, the man lives no longer as to that person, but is dead to him. In such manner the Apostle speaks in the *Romans 7:4*. We are said to be "dead to the law," our former husband; i.e. the law, our husband, is dead, as the Apostle explains himself. ***The "Blank Bible" (WJE Online Vol. 24)***

The church is here represented as being married to two husbands, one before Christ's death, and another since his resurrection. The one is Christ in his earthly state, and with his animal body before his death; the other is Christ in his heavenly state, and with his spiritual body. Christ is here represented as two. The law was as it were the body of Christ, or Christ in his earthly state. When Christ died, she was freed from this husband that she might be married to another, even to him that is raised from the dead, that of this husband she might conceive and bring forth fruit unto God. See notes on *Ephesians 2:15* and *Colossians 2:20*. ***The "Blank Bible" (WJE Online Vol. 24)***

["Wherefore my brethren," etc.] The church is here represented as being married to two husbands, one before Christ's death, and another since his resurrection. The one is Christ in his earthly state, and with his animal body before his death; the other is Christ in his heavenly state, and with his spiritual body. Christ is here represented as two. The law was as it were the body of Christ, or Christ in his earthly state. When Christ died, she was freed from this husband that she might be married to another, even to him that is raised from the dead, that of this husband she might conceive and bring forth fruit unto God. See notes on *Ephesians 2:15* and *Colossians 2:20*.

"Ye are become dead to the law." "A metathesis for the law is become dead to you. This is one instance of St. Paul's address. To have said, The law is dead, would have shocked a Jew; therefore he wisely chooseth to say, 'You are dead to the law.' Which is, in effect, the same thing, for the relation is dissolved, which soever of the parties dieth." Taylor, on *Original Sin*. He shows plainly, in the *Romans 7:6* following, that he means that the law is dead, though he don't name it expressly, but by a periphrasis. ***The "Blank Bible" (WJE Online Vol. 24)***

Romans 7:5

'Tis that last clause of the Romans 7:4, "that we should bring forth fruit unto God," that is principally introductory to what is said in this and the following verses. "The motions of sins, which were by the law." "τὰ διὰ τοῦ νόμου might properly have been rendered, 'under the law,' or 'notwithstanding the law.' So *Romans 4:11*, 'That he might be the father of all them that believe,' δί ἀκροβυστίᾳ, 'under uncircumcision,' or 'notwithstanding they be not circumcised.' And *1 Timothy 2:15*, σωθήσεται δὲ διὰ τῆς τεκνογονίας, 'She shall be saved under,' or 'in the state of,' or 'notwithstanding childbearing.'" ***The "Blank Bible" (WJE Online Vol. 24)***

But now, let us consider what that death is, which the Scripture ever speaks of as the proper wages of the sin of mankind, and is spoken of as such by God's saints in all ages of the church, from the first beginning of a written revelation, to the conclusion of it. I'll begin with the New Testament. When the apostle Paul says (*Romans 6:23*), "The wages of sin is death," Dr. Taylor tells us (p. 396) that "this means eternal death, the second death, a death widely different from the death we now die." The same Apostle speaks of death as the proper punishment due for sin (in *Romans 7:5* and *8:13*, *2 Corinthians 3:7*, *1 Corinthians 15:56*). In all which places, Dr. Taylor himself supposes the Apostle to intend eternal death. And when the apostle James speaks of death, as the proper reward, fruit and end of sin (*James 1:15*), "Sin, when it is finished, bringeth forth death," 'tis manifest, that our author supposes eternal destruction to be meant. And the apostle John, agreeable to Dr. Taylor's sense, speaks of the second death, as that which sin unrepented of will bring all men to at last (*Revelation 20:6, 14* and *21:8* and *2:11*). In the same sense the apostle John uses the word in his first epistle (*1 John 3:14*), "We know, that we have passed from death to life, because we love the brethren: he that hateth his brother, abideth in death." In the same manner Christ used the word from time to time, when he was on earth, and spake concerning the punishment and issue of sin. *John 5:24*, "He that heareth my word, and believeth . . . hath everlasting life; and shall not come into condemnation: but is passed from death unto life." Where, according to Dr. Taylor's own way of arguing, it can't be the death which we now die, that Christ speaks of, but eternal death, because it is set in opposition to everlasting life. *John 6:50*, "This is the bread which cometh down from heaven, that a man may eat thereof, and not die." *Ch. 8:51*, "Verily, verily, I say unto you, if a man keep my saying, he shall never see death." *Ch. 11:26*, "And whosoever liveth and believeth in me, shall never die." In which places 'tis plain, Christ don't mean that believers shall never see temporal death. (See also *Matthew 10:29* and *Luke 10:28*.) In like manner, the word was commonly used by the prophets of old, when they spake of death as the proper end and recompense of sin. So, abundantly by the prophet Ezekiel (*Ezekiel 3:18*), "When I say the wicked man, thou shalt surely die." In the original, "dying thou shalt die"—the same form of expression, which God used in the threatening to Adam. We have the same words again (*ch. 33:18*). In *ch. 18:4* it is said, "The soul that sinneth, it shall die." To the like purpose are *ch. 3:19–20* and *18:4–5, 10, 14, 17–21, 24, 26, 28*; ch. *33:8–9, 12–14, 19–20*. And that temporal death is not meant in these places, is plain, because it is promised most absolutely that the righteous shall not die the death spoken of. *Ch. 17:21*, "He shall surely live, he shall not die." (So, *vv. 9, 17, 19* and *22* and *ch. 3:21*.) And 'tis evident, the prophet Jeremiah uses the word in the same sense. *Jeremiah 31:30*, "Every one shall die for his own iniquity." And the same death is spoken of by the prophet Isaiah. *Isaiah 11:4*, "With the breath of his lips shall he slay the wicked." (See also *ch. 66:16* with *v. 24*.) Solomon, who we must suppose was thoroughly acquainted with the sense in which the word was used by the wise, and by the ancients, continually speaks of death as the proper fruit, issue and recompense of sin, using the word only in this sense. *Proverbs 11:19*, "As righteousness tendeth to life, so he that pursueth evil, pursueth it to his own death." (So *ch. 18:32* "be written with the righteous." And thus we find the word "death" used in the Pentateuch, or books of Moses: in which part of the Scripture it is, that we have the account of the threatening of death to Adam. When death, in these books, is spoken of as the proper fruit and appointed reward of sin, it is to be understood of eternal death. So, *Deuteronomy 30:15*, "See, I have set before thee this day, life and good, and death and evil." V. *19*, "I call heaven and earth to record this day against you, that I have set before you life and death, blessing and cursing." The life that is spoken of here, is doubtless the same that is spoken of in *Leviticus 18:5*, "Ye shall therefore keep my statutes and my judgments, which if a man do, he shall live in them." This the Apostle understands of eternal life; as is plain by *Romans 10:5* and *Galatians 3:12*—but that the death threatened for sin in the law of Moses meant eternal death, is what Dr. Taylor abundantly declares. So in his *Note on Romans 5:20*, "Such a constitution the law of Moses was, subjecting those who were under it to death for every transgression; meaning by death ETERNAL DEATH." These are his words. The like he asserts in many other places. When it is said, in the place now mentioned, "I have set before thee life and death, blessing and cursing," without doubt, the same blessing and cursing is meant which God had already set before them with such solemnity, in *Deuteronomy 27* and *28*; where we have the sum of the curses in those last words of the *27th chapter*, "Cursed is everyone, which confirmeth not all the words of this law to do them." Which the Apostle speaks of as a threatening of eternal death; and with him Dr. Taylor himself. 3 In this sense also Job and his friends, spake of death, as the wages and end of sin, who lived before any written revelation, and had their religion and their phraseology about the things of religion from the ancients. ***The "Blank Bible" (WJE Online Vol. 24)***

Romans 7:6

If a man does perform an external service while under the bondage of the law, 'tis no real service; 'tis merely forced by threats and terrors. 'Tis not performed freely and heartily, but is a dead, lifeless obedience. But a being delivered from the law and brought under grace tends to win men to serve God from love, and with the whole heart. *Romans 7:6*, "But now we are delivered from the law, that being dead wherein we were held, that we should serve in newness of the spirit, and not in the oldness of the letter." ***Notes on Scripture (WJE Online Vol. 15)***

Romans 7:7

'Tis evident that when the Apostle says, we can't be justified by the works of the law, he means the moral as well as ceremonial law, by his giving this reason for it, that "by the law is the knowledge of sin," as *Romans 3:20*. "By the deeds of the law shall no flesh be justified in his sight, for by the law is the knowledge of sin." Now that law by which we come to the knowledge of sin, is the moral law chiefly and primarily. If this argument of the Apostle be good, that we can't be justified by the deeds of the law, because it is by the law that we come to the knowledge of sin, then it proves that we can't be justified by the deeds of the moral law, nor by the precepts of Christianity; for by them is the knowledge of sin. If the reason be good, then where the reason holds, the truth holds. 'Tis a miserable shift, and a violent force put upon the words, to say that the meaning is, that by the law of circumcision is the knowledge of sin, because circumcision signifying the taking way of sin, puts men in mind of sin. The plain meaning of the Apostle is that as the law most strictly forbids sin, it tends to convince us of sin, and bring our own consciences to condemn us, instead of justifying of us; that the use of it is to declare to us our own guilt and unworthiness, which is the reverse of justifying and approving of us as virtuous or worthy. This is the Apostle's meaning, if we will allow him to be his own expositor; for he himself in this very epistle explains to us how it is that by the law we have the knowledge of sin, and that 'tis by the law's forbidding sin. *Romans 7:7*, "I had not known sin, but by the law, for I had not known lust, except the law had said, Thou shalt not covet." There the Apostle determines two things, first, that, the way in which, "by the law is the knowledge of sin," is by the law's forbidding sin: and secondly, which is more directly till to the purpose; he determines that 'tis the moral law by which we cone to the knowledge of sin; for says he, "I had not known lust, except the law had said, Thou shalt not covet": now 'tis the moral, and not the ceremonial law, that says thou shalt not covet: therefore when the Apostle argues that by the deeds of the law no flesh living shall be justified, because the law is the knowledge of sin, his argument proves (unless he was mistaken as to the force of his argument), that we can't be justified by the deeds of the moral law. ***Sermons and Discourses, 1734–1738 (WJE Online Vol. 19)***

Romans 7:8

[The] reason why man has the more strong inclination to moral evil when forbidden, is because obedience is submission and subjection, and the commandment is obligation. But natural corruption is against submission and obligation, but loves the lowest kind of liberty as one of those apparent goods that it seeks; and when he disobeys, he looks upon it that he has broke the obligation. When he thinks of the perpetration of such a lust, and thinks how he is strictly upon pain of damnation forbidden, tied by such strict bonds from it, it makes him exceeding uneasy, the consideration is so against corrupt nature; which uneasiness takes away all liberty of thought, and makes the mind dwell upon nothing but the contrary and supposed good, the liberty, causes [him] to meditate upon the pleasantness of the act, and makes it appear much greater than otherwise it would do. ***The "Miscellanies": (Entry Nos. a–z, aa–zz, 1–500) (WJE Online Vol. 13)***

Not only natural sin, but the CORRUPTION of nature is properly sin. "The Apostle calls the depraved bent of the soul, the corruption of our nature, sin, when he says, "But *sin*, taking occasion by the commandment, wrought in me all manner of concupiscence. For without the law *sin* was dead. . . . *Sin*, taking occasion by the commandment, deceived me, and by it slew me. . . . But *sin*, that it might appear sin, working death in me . . . ; *sin* dwelleth in me" *Romans 7:8, 11, 13, 17*. This in other places he calls the flesh, the law of the members, the law of sin, the body of sin, the body of death. "It is no more I, but *sin* then dwelleth in me" *Romans 7:17, 20*. *Catechism Rescued*, pp. 34–35. ***"Controversies" Notebook (WJE Online Vol. 27)***

Romans 7:9

Sin, as it were, lies hid while sinners are unconvinced. They take no notice of it, but God makes the law effectual to bring man's own sins of heart and life to be reflected on and observed; *Romans 7:9*, "I was alive without the law once: but when the commandment came, sin revived." Then sin appeared, came to light, which was not observed before. Joseph's revealing himself to his brethren is probably typical of Christ revealing himself to the soul of a sinner, a making known himself in his love and in his near relation of a brother and redeemer of his soul; but they, before Joseph revealed himself to 'em, were made to reflect upon themselves and say, "We are verily guilty" [*Genesis 42:21*]. ***Sermons and Discourses, 1730–1733 (WJE Online Vol. 17)***

["Sin revived, and I died."] The Apostle by dying, here don't mean a sensibleness of his own death and misery, or a despair of life through his own righteousness, as some have carried it. ***The "Blank Bible" (WJE Online Vol. 24)***

Romans 7:10

He [i.e., Dr. Taylor] observes that "'tis the covenant of works, with the terms of it, as expressed in the books of Moses, which is cited by St. Paul, *Galatians 3:12*, 'The man that doth the commands shall live in or by them'; and *Romans 10:5*. This is called 'the righteousness of the law,' i.e. that which entitles a man to the promise of life. And *Romans 7:10*, 'The commandment of the law which was ordained to life,' shows that life and immortality would have been the reward of obedience to it." ***The "Miscellanies," 833–1152 (WJE Online Vol. 20)***

Romans 7:12

Luke 2:25, "Simeon, a just man." *Luke 23:50*, "Joseph, a counselor, a just man." *Matthew 13:41*, "shall sever the wicked from among the just." [*Mark 6:20*,] "knowing that he was a just man and a holy." *Matthew 27:19*, "Have nothing to do with that just man." *Matthew 27:24*, "I am free from the blood of this just person." *Luke 1:17*, "the disobedient to the wisdom of the just." *Luke 14:14*, "at the resurrection of the just." *Luke 15:7*, "than over ninety and nine just persons." *Luke 20:20*, "that should feign themselves just persons." *John 5:30*, "yet my judgment is just." *Acts 10:22*, "Cornelius was a just man." *Acts 24:15*, "there shall be a resurrection, both of the just and the unjust." *Romans 2:13*, "not the hearers of the law are just, but the doers of the law shall be justified." *Romans 7:12*, "the commandment is holy, and just." *Colossians 4:1*, "Masters, give your servants that which is just." *Titus 1:7–8*, "a bishop must be just." *Hebrews 12:23*, "the spirits of just men made perfect." *James 5:6*, "Ye have condemned and killed the just." *1 Peter 3:18*, "the just for the unjust." [*2 Peter 2:7*,] "And delivered just Lot." *Revelation 15:3*, "just and true are thy ways." *Acts 3:14*, "ye denied the Holy One and the Just." *Acts 7:52*, "showed before the coming of the Just One." *Acts 22:14*, "know his will, and see that Just One." ***Writings on the Trinity, Grace, and Faith (WJE Online Vol. 21)***

Romans 7:13

["Made death unto me."] This is to be connected with the *Romans 7:11* with these words, "and by it" (i.e. by the law) "slew me"; and so with the *Romans 7:10*, "I found the law to be unto death"; and that with the ninth, "when the commandment came, sin revived, and I died"; and that with the fifth, "the motions of sins, which were by the law, did work in our members to bring forth fruit unto death." ***The "Blank Bible" (WJE Online Vol. 24)***

He [i.e., Dr. Taylor] also supposes, that this sentence of the law, thus subjecting men for every, even the *least sin*, and every minutest branch, and *latent principle of sin*, to so dreadful a punishment, is just and righteous, *agreeable to truth and the nature of things*, or to the natural and *proper demerits of sin*. This he is very full in. Thus in p. 21 "It was sin," says he, "which subjected to death by the law, justly threatening sin with death. Which law was given us, that sin might appear; might be set forth in its proper colours; when we saw it subjected us to death by a law perfectly holy, just, and good; that sin by the commandment, by the law, might be represented what it really is, an exceeding great and deadly evil." So in *Note on Romans 5:20*, p. 380. "The law or ministration of death, as it subjects to death for every transgression, is still of use to show the natural and proper demerit of sin." Ibid., pp. 371–72, "The language of the law, dying thou shalt die, is to be understood of the demerit of the transgression, that which it deserves." Ibid., p. 379, the law "was added, saith Mr. Locke on the place, because the Israelites, the posterity of Abraham, were transgressors, as well as other men, to show them their sins, and the punishment and death, which in strict justice they incurred by them. And this appears to be a true comment on *Romans 7:13*. . . . Sin, by virtue of the law, subjected you to death for this end that sin, working death in us by that which is holy, just and good," perfectly consonant to everlasting truth and righteousness. . . . Consequently every sin is in strict justice deserving of wrath and punishment; and the law in its rigor was given to the Jews, to set home this awful truth upon their consciences, to show them the evil and pernicious nature of sin; and that being conscious they had broke the law of God, this might convince them of the great need they had of the favor of the lawgiver, and oblige them, by faith in his goodness, to fly to his mercy for pardon and salvation. ***Original Sin (WJE Online Vol. 3)***

'Tis evident that the Apostle don't mean only the ceremonial law, because he gives this reason why we have righteousness, and a title to the privilege of Gods children, not by the law, but by faith, "that the law worketh wrath." *Romans 4:13–16*, "For the promise that he should be the heir of the world, was not to Abraham, or to his seed through the law, but through the righteousness of faith: for if they which are of the law be heirs, faith is made void, and he promise made of none effect: because the law worketh wrath; for where no law is there is no transgression. Therefore it is of faith that it might be by grace." Now the way in which the law works wrath, by the Apostle' shown account, in the reason he himself annexes, is by forbidding sin, and aggravating the guilt of the transgression; "for," says he, "where no law in here is no transgression": and so, *Romans 7:13*, "That sin by the commandment might become exceeding sinful." If therefore this reason of the Apostle be good, it is much stronger against justification by the moral law, than the ceremonial law; for 'tis by transgressions of the moral law chiefly that there comes wrath; for they are most strictly forbidden, and met terribly threatened. ***Sermons and Discourses, 1734–1738 (WJE Online Vol. 19)***

Romans 7:14

God finds them in a very miserable condition in that he finds 'em under the dominion of sin. They have lost all holiness which was their beauty and glory. They are become sordid and loathsome with the rags and filth of sin. They have lost their liberty and are become slaves to sin and Satan; they are "sold under sin" [*Romans 7:14*]. They are sick of a most foul and mortal disease, with which they are blind and deaf and halt and maimed. ***Sermons and Discourses, 1730–1733 (WJE Online Vol. 17)***

Observe how that, *Romans 7:14*, "I am carnal, sold under sin," etc., even in the sense in which Taylor understands it, will prove original sin or the corruption of nature. ***"Controversies" Notebook (WJE Online Vol. 27)***

Romans 7:14–15ff.

["But I am carnal, sold under sin. For that which I do, I allow not," etc.] The Apostle here and to the end of the chapter speaks in the name of the church of God or of the saints, under the disadvantages that the church was under while under the Mosaic dispensation that was so legal, and the church was treated as a servant, and had not so clear a revelation of gospel grace, and did not enjoy so much of gospel liberty, and being much in bondage under the law had more occasion to prove the weakness of the law and its insufficiency to deliver from the power, either its power of influence over the heart and practice, or its power to condemn the person. For this is the argument that the Apostle had been upon from the *Romans 7:4*, and is what the Apostle speaks of again in the *Romans 8:2–4*. And as these things, which the Apostle here says of himself, represent the circumstances of the Jewish saints before the clear revelation of gospel, and therefore had not so much to lead 'em to their true remedy, so it also represents the state of the saints in all ages in a legal frame, and when they too much forget gospel grace, and fight and strive against sin too much in their own strength and not in an entire reliance on Christ, through whom and through whom alone is deliverance, agreeable to *Romans 7:24*. See note on *Romans 7:20*, and also on *Romans 7:25*. "I am carnal, sold under sin." Ahab sold himself "to work evil" (*1 Kings 21:20*). He did it of choice. He was a willing slave to sin, voluntarily submitted, and gave up himself to the dominion of this master. But the apostle Paul was "sold under sin" as a poor captive against his will, as the context obliges us to understand him.

"But I am carnal, sold under sin." "This is often urged as an argument, that the Apostle here speaks in the person of a wicked man, and is represented as a phrase parallel to *1 Kings 21:20*, *2 Kings 17:17*, where some of the worst of men are described, as having sold themselves to do evil. But the diversity of the expression is obvious. And yet, had this person been represented as lamenting that he had sold himself to sin, it might have been understood as the language of penitent remorse for past guilt, and so very consistent with a good man's character. And the many instances in which very excellent persons, in the distress of their hearts for the remainder of imperfection in their character, adopt this very phrase, plainly show with what propriety Paul might put it into the mouth of one whom he did not consider as an abandoned sinner, and destitute of every principle of true piety." ***The "Blank Bible" (WJE Online Vol. 24)***

Romans 7:15

["That which I do, I *allow* not."] In the original, it is οὐ γινώσκω, "I know not," which confirms that the Apostle here speaks in the name of a true saint, and not in the name of a wicked man. For surely a wicked man "knows" his sins, in the common use of such an expression in Scripture for "approve," "own" as what is near to him and belongs to him. But the Apostle here speaks of his not knowing sin in this sense; he disowns and renounces it. He don't approve of it as that which have any relation to it; and accordingly it is not in the sight of God accounted as what belongs to him. That this is the sense is confirmed by *Romans 7:17* and *Romans 7:20*. See note on *Romans 7:25*. ***The "Blank Bible" (WJE Online Vol. 24)***

Romans 7:18

If by "flesh" and "spirit" when spoken of in the New Testament, and opposed to each other, in discourses on the necessary qualifications for salvation, we are to understand what has been now supposed, it will not only follow, that men by nature are corrupt, but *wholly corrupt*, without any good thing. If by "flesh" is meant man's nature, as he receives it in his first birth, then "therein dwelleth no good thing"; as appears by *Romans 7:18*. 'Tis wholly opposite to God, and to subjection to his law, as appears by *Romans 8:7–8*. 'Tis directly contrary to true holiness, and wholly opposes it, and holiness is opposite to that; as appears by *Galatians 5:17*. So long as men are in their natural state, they not only have no good thing, but it is impossible they should have, or do any good thing; as appears by *Romans 8:8*. There is nothing in their nature, as they have it by the first birth, whence should arise any true subjection to God; as appears by *Romans 8:7*. If there were anything truly good in the flesh, or in man's nature, or natural disposition, under a moral view, then it should only be amended; but the Scripture represents as though we were to be enemies to it, and were to seek nothing short of its entire destruction, as has been observed. And elsewhere the Apostle directs not to the amending of the old man, but putting it off, and putting on the new man; and seeks not to have the body of death made better, but to be delivered from it; and says [*2 Corinthians*

5:17], that "if any man be in Christ, he is a new creature" (which doubtless means the same as a man new-born): "old things are" (not amended) "but passed away, and ALL things are become new." ***Original Sin (WJE Online Vol. 3)***

If by "flesh" is meant man's nature, as he receives it in his first birth, then "therein dwelleth no good thing"; as appears by *Romans 7:18*. 'Tis wholly opposite to God, and to subjection to his law, as appears by *Romans 8:7–8*. 'Tis directly contrary to true holiness, and wholly opposes it, and holiness is opposite to that; as appears by *Galatians 5:17*. So long as men are in their natural state, they not only have no good thing, but it is impossible they should have, or do any good thing; as appears by *Romans 8:8*. There is nothing in their nature, as they have it by the first birth, whence should arise any true subjection to God; as appears by *Romans 8:7*. If there were anything truly good in the flesh, or in man's nature, or natural disposition, under a moral view, then it should only be amended; but the Scripture represents as though we were to be enemies to it, and were to seek nothing short of its entire destruction, as has been observed. And elsewhere the Apostle directs not to the amending of the old man, but putting it off, and putting on the new man; and seeks not to have the body of death made better, but to be delivered from it; and says [2 *Corinthians 5:17*], that "if any man be in Christ, he is a new creature" (which doubtless means the same as a man new-born): "old things are" (not amended) "but passed away, and ALL things are become new." ***Original Sin (WJE Online Vol. 3)***

There is all manner of wickedness. There are the seeds of the greatest and blackest crimes. There are principles of all sorts of wickedness against men; and there is all wickedness against God. There is pride; there is enmity; there is contempt; there is quarrelling; there is atheism; there is blasphemy. There are these things in exceeding strength; the heart is under the power of them, is sold under sin, and is a perfect slave to it. There is hard-heartedness, hardness greater than that of a rock, or an adamant stone. There is obstinacy and perverseness, incorrigibleness and inflexibleness in sin, that won't be overcome by threatenings or promises, by awakenings or encouragements, by judgments or mercies, neither by that which is terrifying, nor that which is winning: the very blood of God won't win the heart of a wicked man. ***Sermons and Discourses, 1734–1738 (WJE Online Vol. 19)***

Romans 7:19

["For the good that I would, I do not; but the evil which I would not, that I do."] "If the meaning of such expressions as these were, that upon the whole, the person using them went on in a prevailing course of habitual wickedness against the convictions and dictates of his own conscience, one would have imagined Paul would have rebuked such an one with great severity, and answered these vain and hypocritical pleas, whereas he represents this person afterwards, as with joy embracing the gospel, and so obtaining superior strength upon the full manifestation of pardoning grace there." ***The "Blank Bible" (WJE Online Vol. 24)***

Romans 7:20

Matthew 16:23. "Get thee behind me, Satan." We are not to understand it that Christ here calls Peter "Satan." No. Christ speaks to Satan, that he saw had a hand in this matter, and that influenced Peter thus to think and speak. He speaks to Peter's indwelling sin, which was as it were the devil in Peter. It was not an instance of Christ's severity towards Peter that he thus speaks, but his love and grace that he would not impute what Peter says to himself, but to Satan. He graciously makes a distinction between his disciple Peter and his indwelling corruption. As Paul says, *Romans 7:20*, "'Tis no more I, but sin that dwelleth in me." ***The "Blank Bible" (WJE Online Vol. 24)***

Romans 7:22

["I delight in the law of the Lord after the inward man."] This is so sure a trace of real piety as is represented in Scripture, as in this view so decisive, that if it be supposed a true representation of the character, we must surely allow it to have been that of a truly good man, whatever lamented imperfections might attend it. ***The "Blank Bible" (WJE Online Vol. 24)***

And 'tis most plain, that this putting off the old man, etc., is the very same thing with making the *heart and spirit new*. 'Tis apparent in itself: the spirit is called the "man" in the language of the Apostle; 'tis called the "inward man," and the "hidden man" (*Romans 7:22, 2 Corinthians 4:16, 1 Peter 3:4*). And therefore putting off the old man, is the same thing with the removal of the old heart, and the putting on the new man is the receiving a new heart and a new spirit. Yea, putting on the new man is expressly spoken of as the same thing with receiving a new spirit, or being renewed in spirit. *Ephesians 4:22–24*, "That ye put off the old man . . . and be renewed in the spirit of your mind, and that ye put on the new man." ***Original Sin (WJE Online Vol. 3)***

Romans 7:23

The best have a body of sin and death that they are in a degree of bondage to, and stand in need of a kind of work of conversion to deliver them. The apostle Paul, though so eminent a saint, was sensible that he greatly needed [it], and therefore is brought to cry out for it, "O wretched man that I am! who shall deliver [me from the body of this death?" (*Romans 7:23*)]. And he therefore earnestly sought conversion, or a spiritual resurrection, as though he had not yet attained it (*Philippians 3:11–12*). [And so] Job, though so eminent a saint. There are none of those in this world that are already converted but that God can still work a new change in them by his grace, so great that it shall make 'em new men and in a [sense] new creatures, not only from what they once were while they were natural men but also from what they are now. Thus the apostles, though some of them seemed to have been eminent saints before Christ's resurrection—particularly we have reason to think this of the apostle John—yet they passed under such a remarkable change after his resurrection, when the Spirit of God came to be so remarkably poured out upon them at the day of Pentecost, that they appeared, spoke and acted quite like new men, as if they had been made over again or had not been the same persons that they were before. ***Sermons and Discourses, 1739–1742 (WJE Online Vol. 22)***

Romans 7:24

First. Inquire whether your supposed grace has that influence as to render those things wherein you have failed to holy practice to be loathsome, grievous and humbling to you. Has it influence on your mind to render your past sinful practices hateful in your eyes, and has it made you a mourner for them? And does it render those things which have been in you since your supposed conviction, which are contrary to Christian practice, odious in your eyes? And is it the great burden of your life that you practice no better? Is it really grievous to you, and are you ready sometimes to loathe yourself for it after the example of Job? *Job 42:6*, "I abhor myself, and repent in dust and ashes." The apostle Paul cried out,

"O wretched man that I am! who shall deliver me from the body of this death?" [*Romans 7:24*]. ***Ethical Writings (WJE Online Vol. 8)***

"The state he [i.e., John Locke] had been describing was that of human weakness, wherein notwithstanding the law, even those who were under it, and sincerely endeavored to obey it, were frequently carried by their carnal appetites into the breach of it. The state of frailty he knew men in this world could not be delivered from."

So again in his [i.e., Locke's] note on this word δουλεύω, in the *Romans 7:25*, "'I serve, or make myself a vassal,' i.e. I intend and devote my whole obedience. The terms of life to those under grace St. Paul tells us at large, Romans 6, are δουλωθῆναι τῇ δικαιοσύνῃ, 'to become vassals to righteousness and to God.' Consonantly, he says here, αὐτὸς ἐγὼ, 'I myself, I the man,' being now a Christian, and so no longer under the law, but under grace, do what is required of me in that state. δουλεύω, I become a vassal to the law of God, i.e. dedicate myself to the service of it, in sincere endeavors of obedience; and so αὐτὸς ἐγὼ, I the man, shall be delivered from death. For he that under grace makes himself a vassal to God in a steady purpose of sincere obedience, shall from him receive the gift of eternal life, though his carnal appetite, which he cannot get rid of having its bent towards sin, makes him sometimes transgress, which would be certain death to him if he were still under the law." The Apostle says here in this *Romans 7:25* that though his flesh served "the law of sin," yet he himself served "the law of God," or as Mr. Locke interprets it, made himself a vassal to the law of God, or intended and devoted thereto his whole obedience. Thus does not a wicked man, or one that is after the flesh, by the Apostle's own testimony, in *Romans 8:5*. "For they that are after the flesh do mind the things of the flesh," φρονοῦσιν τὰ τῆς σαρκός, which, as Mr. Locke observes, signifies the employing the "bent of their minds," or subjecting the mind entirely to the fulfilling the lust of the flesh. This is inconsistent with their devoting themselves as vassals to the law of God, and their delighting in the law of God after the inner man, and their not allowing but hating those things that are contrary, which are the things the Apostle expresses in this context. See note[s] on *Romans 8:5*.

The beginning of the next chapter, which is a continuation of the same discourse, makes these things exceeding evident. "There is therefore now no condemnation to them that are in Christ Jesus, that walk not after the flesh, but after the Spirit." See note on *Romans 7:14–15 ff*. ***The "Blank Bible" (WJE Online Vol. 24)***

Are our souls now of such a nature that the remainders of sin are their continual burden; is sin that which we long to get rid of? Are we ready with the Apostle to cry out, "O wretched man that I am! Who shall deliver me from the body of this death" [*Romans 7:24*]? Cannot we rest and be quiet in the beholding of any sin in us, but that we must be continually laboring to cleanse ourselves from it more and more? Is that what we thirst after, to have sin more and more mortified? ***Sermons and Discourses, 1730–1733 (WJE Online Vol. 17)***

Romans 7:25

["With the mind *I myself* serve the law of God, but with the flesh the law of sin."] This Mr. Locke paraphrases thus. "To comfort myself therefore as that state requires for my deliverance from death, I myself with full purpose and sincere endeavors of mind, give up myself to obey the law of God, though my carnal inclinations are enslaved, and have a constant tendency to sin. This is all I can do, and this is all I, being under grace, that is required of me and through Christ, will be accepted." And in his notes he observes that "I myself" is in the original, "αὑτὸς ἐγὼ, i.e (says Mr. Locke), I, the man, with all my full resolution of mind. αὑτὸς, and ἐγὼ might have, both of 'em, been spared, if nothing more had been meant here than the nominative case to δουλεύω. See note, *Romans 7:20*." And in his note on *Romans 7:20* referred to on these words, "οὐ θέλω ἐθὼ, 'I would not.' *I* in the Greek is very, very emphatical, as is obvious, and denotes the man in that part which is chiefly to be counted himself, and therefore with the like emphasis, *Romans 7:25*, is called αὑτὸς ἐγὼ, 'I my own self.'" The Apostle would doubtless intimate that when he the saint was himself, and acted himself, he served the law of God, and when he served the law of sin, he was as it were not himself, but led captive by an enemy. This is agreeable to *Romans 7:17*, *Romans 7:20*, and *Romans 7:22*. These things plainly show that the Apostle speaks in the name of a saint, and not in the name of a wicked man. ***The "Blank Bible" (WJE Online Vol. 24)***

We find that true saints, or those persons who are sanctified by the Spirit of God, are in the New Testament called spiritual persons. And their being spiritual is spoken of as their peculiar character, and that wherein they are distinguished from those who are not sanctified. This is evident because those who are spiritual are set in opposition to natural men, and carnal men. Thus the spiritual man, and the natural man, are set in opposition one to another; *1 Corinthians 2:14–15*, "The natural man receiveth not the things of the Spirit of God, for they are foolishness unto him; neither can he know them; because they are spiritually discerned. But he that is spiritual judgeth all things." The Scripture explains itself to mean an ungodly man, or one that has no grace, by a natural man: thus the apostle Jude, speaking of certain ungodly men, that had crept in unawares among the saints, v. *4* of his Epistle, says, *v. 19*: "These are sensual, having not the Spirit." This the Apostle gives as a reason why they behaved themselves in such a wicked manner as he had described. Here the word translated "sensual," in the original is [*psuchikoi*]; which is the very same, which in those verses in 1 *Corinthians, ch. 2*, is translated "natural." In the like manner, in the continuation of the same discourse, in the next verse but one, spiritual men are opposed to carnal men: which the connection plainly shows mean the same, as spiritual men and natural men, in the foregoing verses; "and I, brethren, could not speak unto you, as unto spiritual, but as unto carnal"; i.e. as in a great measure unsanctified. That by carnal the Apostle means corrupt and unsanctified, is abundantly evident, by *Romans 7:25* and *Romans 8:1, 4–9, 12, 13*; *Galatians 5:16* to the end; *Colossians 2:18*. Now therefore, if by natural and carnal, in these texts, he intended "unsanctified"; then doubtless by spiritual, which is opposed thereto, is meant "sanctified" and gracious. ***Religious Affections (WJE Online Vol. 2)***

So again in his note on this word *δουλεύω*, in the *Romans 7:25*, "'I serve, or make myself a vassal,' i.e. I intend and devote my whole obedience. The terms of life to those under grace St. Paul tells us at large, *Romans 6*, are *δουλωθῆναι τῇ δικαιοσύνῃ*, 'to become vassals to righteousness and to God.' Consonantly, he says here, *αὐτὸς ἐγὼ*, 'I myself, I the man,' being now a Christian, and so no longer under the law, but under grace, do what is required of me in that state. *δουλεύω*, I become a vassal to the law of God, i.e. dedicate myself to the service of it, in sincere endeavors of obedience; and so *αὐτὸς ἐγὼ*, I the man, shall be delivered from death. For he that under grace makes himself a vassal to God in a steady purpose of sincere obedience, shall from him receive the gift of eternal life, though his carnal appetite, which he cannot get rid of having its bent towards sin, makes him sometimes transgress, which would be certain death to him if he were still under the law." The Apostle says here in this *Romans 7:25* that though his flesh served "the law of sin," yet he himself served "the law of God," or as Mr. Locke interprets it, made himself a vassal to the law of God, or intended and devoted thereto his whole obedience. Thus does not a wicked man, or one that is after the flesh, by the Apostle's own testimony, in the *Romans 8:5*. "For they that are after the flesh do mind the things of the flesh," *φρονοῦσιν τὰ τῆς σαρκός*, which, as Mr. Locke observes, signifies the employing the "bent of their minds," or subjecting the mind entirely to the fulfilling the lust of the flesh. This is inconsistent with their devoting themselves as vassals to the law of God, and their delighting in the law of God after the inner man, and their not allowing but hating those things that are contrary, which are the things the Apostle expresses in this context. See note on *Romans 8:5*. ***The "Blank Bible" (WJE Online Vol. 24)***

ROMANS CHAPTER 8

["There is therefore now no condemnation to them which are in Christ Jesus."] This is here mentioned because it was intimated, in the *Romans 7:24–25*, that it is Christ that delivers. "Who walk not after the flesh, but after the Spirit." The Apostle says that "walk not after the flesh, but after the Spirit," rather than that "have the Spirit," because walking "after the Spirit" is the proper evidence of having the Spirit.1 The Apostle hereby enforces a holy and spiritual walk.

The Apostle had this at heart, that those that "live in the Spirit" should also "walk in the Spirit" (*Galatians 5:25*), and guards against men of carnal and ungodly practice entertaining a hope of their having the Spirit, and being free from condemnation, that none might think that, because they professed Christianity and were baptized, that therefore they were free from condemnation. And the Apostle proceeds, in the next verse, to show why "there is no condemnation to them that in Christ Jesus walk not after the flesh, but after the Spirit," viz. because the law of the Spirit of life in Christ Jesus, or the Spirit that is become a principle of life in them, naturally bringing forth spiritual and eternal life (*John 4:14*), that they walk after, that is had in and by Christ Jesus, hath made them "free from the law of sin and death," i.e. hath freed them from the dominion and power of sin, or the "law of sin" (*Romans 7:23*) over them, as their enemy, that consists chiefly in its power to condemn and destroy them. And that it should be this kind of power and dominion of sin over us that the Apostle has respect to when he says we are made free from it, agrees well with the notion under which he here mentions sin, viz. as a law, calling it a "law of sin and death." So he called a law, in the latter part of the foregoing chapter. Now the power and dominion that a law has over us as an enemy consists in its power to condemn us. So that herein is the Apostle's reasoning. "There is no condemnation to them who are in Christ Jesus," because the Spirit that they have in Christ Jesus, dwelling in them as a principle of life, containing life and tending to life, delivers 'em from the condemning power of sin, by which it is that condemnation to death comes. The Spirit dwelling in believers as a principle of life and action, or as the Spirit that they walk after, delivers them from the power of sin over them, to bring them to condemnation, and to kill them, two ways. 1. As it unites them to Christ (For the Spirit is the bond of union. Hereby Christ is in them, as *Romans 8:9–10*), and so delivers them from the power that it has to hold them under the condemning sentence of the law. Sin maintains this dominion by the law; "the strength of sin is the law" (*1 Corinthians 15:56*). But this, this spiritual principle or law of the Spirit of life, frees from [the law], as 'tis the bond of union to Christ. The Spirit, as 'tis the bond of union with Christ, frees us from condemnation, not only as it frees from obligation to suffer the condemnation of the law in that Christ has satisfied the law, but also renders it impossible that we should suffer the condemnation of the law, for they are hereby united to Jesus Christ, who is the Son of God and fountain of life, and therefore must live. He is risen and lives forevermore; and if he lives, they must live also. His Spirit is the Spirit of life; they by partaking of his Spirit do necessarily partake of his life, and therefore necessarily are freed from death. They hereby partake of the nature of the Son, which is an immortal nature. "To be spiritually minded is life and peace" necessarily; and if we "through the Spirit do mortify the deeds of the flesh," we necessarily live (*Romans 8:6*, *Romans 8:13*).

And then if we partake of the spirit of the Son, we are children by nature; that is, we have the nature of children, as *Romans 8:14–16*. And therefore 'tis no way suitable that we should be condemned, for if we are sons, we are heirs of life, and partaking of the nature of the Son, are children with him, and joint-heirs with him of the same life, as *Romans 8:17*.

2. As it destroys the power of sin to bring them to condemnation effectively, or to work and produce death, which is the condemnation or thing condemned to. All this is "in Christ Jesus," as 'tis said in these *Romans 8:1–2*. 'Tis by their being in Christ that there is no condemnation to them, for 'tis by their being in Christ that they have the Spirit as a principle of life and action, or "walk not after the flesh, but after the Spirit." And 'tis by our having the Spirit in Christ Jesus that it becomes a Spirit of life, or 'tis by Christ that the Spirit has that virtue to deliver us from the power of sin to condemn and kill. If we had the Spirit, yet if it was not in Christ Jesus, uniting of us to him, and as his Spirit, it would not have this virtue. And therefore the Apostle proceeds, in the *Romans 8:3–4*, "For what the law could not do, in that it was weak through the flesh, God sending his

own Son in the likeness of sinful flesh, and for sin, condemned sin in the flesh, that the righteousness of the law might be fulfilled in us, who walk not after the flesh, but after the Spirit." By this the Apostle shows how there is no condemnation to us in Christ, and how by him way is made for our receiving the Spirit (*Galatians 3:13–14*), and how by that, in him we are freed from the condemning power of sin.

God has sent his Son, and has condemned sin, or the law of sin and death that had dominion over us. Therefore there is no condemnation to us that are in Christ. Sin has no longer power to condemn us, because God by Christ (whom we are in) has condemned that. And the Apostle tells us how God had condemned sin, viz. by condemning his Son that he made sin, that he sent in the likeness of sinful flesh and for sin, i.e. that he sent representing sinful flesh and standing for sin. And so God, by condemning him or laying the condemnation upon him, condemned sin or abolished it, abolished the forementioned power and dominion of it, "that the righteousness of the law might be fulfilled in us, that walk not after the flesh, but after the Spirit." Christ condemned sin in the flesh two ways, viz. by abolishing the guilt of sin by his expiation, and by actually fulfilling the righteousness of the law. And this he did "that the righteousness of the law might be fulfilled in us, who walk not after the flesh, but after the Spirit," by which it appears that it [is] by these two things conjunctly, or one by and with the other, that the righteousness of the law is fulfilled in us, viz. Christ's condemning sin in the flesh, or his satisfaction and righteousness, and our having and walking after the Spirit, which is these several ways. 1. Christ, by condemning sin in the flesh, has made way for our having the Spirit. He has procured the Spirit for us. 2. The Spirit in us is that by which we are united to Christ, for by the Spirit of Christ being in us, we have Christ in us (*Romans 8:10*), and so have his righteousness, which is the righteousness of the law made ours. And so the righteousness of the law is fulfilled in us. 3. By having the Spirit of Christ in us, we have union with him and communion in his nature. And so by the Spirit of the Son are become sons by nature, and so must necessarily as heirs have life, as *Romans 8:17*. 'Tis no way suitable that those who have the nature and state of sons should be condemned, but that they should have justification and life. And this may be meant by our having "the righteousness of the law fulfilled in us," viz. having fulfilled in us life, the reward of the righteousness of the law, for the Apostle here seems to mention the righteousness of the law as the opposite to condemnation and death that he had been speaking of. But 'tis the reward of the righteousness of the law that is the opposite of the condemnation for sin or the breach of the law. And this seems best to agree with the following verses. See notes upon them. 4. In having the Spirit, we have communion with Christ in his life, for to have the Spirit dwelling in us is life. The Spirit is the beauty and joy of the divine nature, and therefore must be the highest perfection and happiness of ours, and so must, by necessity of nature as well as condecency, have life and peace or happiness. 5. They that walk after the Spirit have the righteousness of the law fulfilled in them, as the Spirit of love fulfills that which is qualitatively the righteousness of the law in us. *Romans 13:10*, "Love is the fulfilling of the law." And *Galatians 5:14*, *Galatians 5:16*, "For all the law is fulfilled in one word, even in this: Thou shalt love thy neighbor as thyself. . . . This I say then, Walk in the Spirit, and ye shall not fulfill the lusts of the flesh." The Spirit effects in us the thing aimed at by the law, viz. holiness, which naturally tends to and produces life, the reward of the righteousness of the law. ***The "Blank Bible" (WJE Online Vol. 24)***

Romans 8:1

That by carnal the Apostle means corrupt and unsanctified, is abundantly evident, by *Romans 7:25* and *Romans 8:1, 4–9, 12, 13*; *Galatians 5:16* to the end; *Colossians 2:18*. Now therefore, if by natural and carnal, in these texts, he intended "unsanctified"; then doubtless by spiritual, which is opposed thereto, is meant "sanctified" and gracious. ***Religious Affections (WJE Online Vol. 2)***

A being under the law in this sense is the Apostles meaning, as is evident by the *Galatians 5:4* of this chapter, and by *Galatians 3 per totum*. See *Romans 8:1*. For what is said in that *Galatians 3*, introduces what follows in these two succeeding chapters. They can't be said to be under the law where the breaches of the law are not imputed to 'em. Sin is not imputed where there is no law, and vice versa (in a sense). There is no law, or persons are not under the law, where sin is not imputed. ***Notes on Scripture (WJE Online Vol. 15)***

But this damnation or condemnation is not to temporal death, because we are abundantly taught in the Scripture, that 'tis what believers shall not come into, as there, and *Romans 8:1*, *Romans 8:34*; *1 Corinthians 11:31–32*, *1 Corinthians 11:34*; *2 Corinthians 3:9*; *James 3:1*, and *James 5:12*; *John 3:17*; *Matthew 12:37*; *John 3:18*. That by the condemnation which sinners are exposed to, is meant the same with condemnation to suffer that death that God has threatened for sin, is particularly manifest by *John*

5:24. “Verily, verily, I say unto you, He that heareth my word, and believeth on him that sent me, hath everlasting life, and shall not come into condemnation; but is passed from death to life.” ***The “Miscellanies,” (Entry Nos. 501–832) (WJE Online Vol. 18)***

There is the same reason why it is necessary that the union with Christ should remain, as why it should be begun, why it should continue to be, as why it should once be: if it should be begun without remaining, the beginning would be in vain. In order to the soul’s being now in a justified state, and now free from condemnation, ‘tis necessary that it should now be in Christ, and not only that it should once have been in him. *Romans 8:1*, “There is no condemnation to them [which] are in Christ Jesus.” The soul is saved in Christ, as being now in him, when the salvation is bestowed, and not merely as remembering that it once was in him. ***Sermons and Discourses, 1734–1738 (WJE Online Vol. 19)***

“Therefore there is no condemnation to them that are in Christ Jesus, that walk not after the flesh, but after the Spirit” [*Romans 8:1*]. Here the Apostle evidently refers to the same two opposite principles warring one against another that he had been speaking of in the close of the preceding chapter, which he here calls flesh and spirit, as he does in his epistle to the Galatians. ***Writings on the Trinity, Grace, and Faith (WJE Online Vol. 21)***

[“There is therefore now no condemnation to them,” etc.] Wherefore? Why, for those reasons mentioned in the foregoing chapter. They ben’t condemned for their sins, because ‘tis not they that do it, but sin that dwells in them. What they do, they allow not; what they hate, that they do. ***The “Blank Bible” (WJE Online Vol. 24)***

Christ “condemned sin,” that there might be no condemnation to the believer. See *Romans 8:1*. ***The “Blank Bible” (WJE Online Vol. 24)***

In the *Romans 8:1*, the Apostle had intimated that if we walked after the flesh we should have condemnation. But in that and in the *Romans 8:2*, he had said that they that are after the Spirit shall have no condemnation, but shall be free from the condemning power of the flesh, or of “the law of sin.” ***The “Blank Bible” (WJE Online Vol. 24)***

Romans 8:2

This is yet more abundantly clear by the next words, which are, “For the law of the Spirit of life in Christ Jesus hath made me free from the law of sin and death” [*Romans 8:2*]. Here these two things that in the preceding verse are called flesh and spirit, are in this verse called “the law of the Spirit of life" and "the law of sin and death," evidently speaking still of the same law of our mind and the law of sin spoken of in the *Romans 7:25*. The Apostle goes on in the *Romans 8* to call corruption and grace by the names of flesh and spirit (*Romans 8:4–9*, and again *Romans 8:12–13*). These two principles are called by the same names in *Matthew 26:41*, "The spirit indeed is willing, but the flesh is weak." There can be no doubt but that the same thing is intended here by the flesh and spirit as (compare what is said of the flesh and spirit here and in these places) in the *Romans 7–8* and *Galatians 5*. Again, these two principles are called by the same words in *Galatians 6:8*. If this be compared with the *Galatians 5:18*, and with *Romans 8:6* and *Romans 8:13*, none can doubt but the same is meant in each place. ***Writings on the Trinity, Grace, and Faith (WJE Online Vol. 21)***

Because the Spirit of God dwells as a vital principle or a principle of new life in the soul, therefore 'tis called the Spirit of life (*Romans 8:2*); and the Spirit that "quickens" (*John 6:63*). ***Writings on the Trinity, Grace, and Faith (WJE Online Vol. 21)***

"For the law of the Spirit of life hath made me free from the law of sin and death." "It is to be observed, that the same person who spoke before is here represented as continuing his discourse, and speaks of himself as delivered from the bondage so bitterly complained [of]." Doddridge, *in loc.* 6 This shows that the beginning of this chapter is a continuation of the discourse in the latter part of the *Romans 7*, and together with the last part of the *Romans 7:25*, shows that the Apostle there don't speak in the person of a carnal or wicked man. ***The "Blank Bible" (WJE Online Vol. 24)***

Romans 8:3

But he [Dr. Taylor] supposes, no such law was ever given: and therefore there is need and room enough for the promises of grace; or as he argues (*Galatians 2:21*), it would have frustrated, or rendered useless the grace of God. For if justification came by the law, then truly Christ is dead in vain, then he died to accomplish what was, or *might have been effected* by law it self, without his death. Certainly the law was not brought in among the Jews to be a rule of justification, or to recover 'em out of a state of death, and to procure life by their sinless obedience to it: for in this, as well as in another respect, it was *weak*; not in itself, but through the *weakness* of our flesh (*Romans 8:3*). The law, I conceive, is not a dispensation suitable to the infirmity of the human nature in our present state; or it doth not seem congruous to the goodness of God to afford us no other way of salvation, but by law: which if we once transgress, we are ruined forever. ***Original Sin (WJE Online Vol. 3)***

One thing is particularly observable in that discourse of the Apostle in the seventh and eighth of Romans, in which he so often uses the term "flesh," as opposite to "spirit," which, as well as many other things in his discourse, makes it plain, that by flesh he means something in itself corrupt and sinful; and that is, that he expressly calls it "sinful flesh" (*Romans 8:3*). 'Tis manifest, that by "sinful flesh" he means the same thing with that flesh spoken of in the immediately foregoing and following words, and in all the context: and that when it is said, Christ was made in the likeness of sinful flesh, the expression is equipollent with those that speak of Christ as made sin, and made a curse for us. ***Original Sin (WJE Online Vol. 3)***

Christ "condemned sin," that there might be no condemnation to the believer. See *Romans 8:1*. ***The "Blank Bible" (WJE Online Vol. 24)***

In the *Romans 8:3*, that the law could not bring us to life by reason of the flesh, which would bring condemnation if we were under the law. ***The "Blank Bible" (WJE Online Vol. 24)***

Galatians 4:9. The law is here called "weak," because it could not give righteousness and life. See *Romans 8:3* and *Galatians 2:21*. ***The "Blank Bible" (WJE Online Vol. 24)***

8. Taylor, *Paraphrase*, p. 379, taking up immediately after passage quoted in n. 9: "Certainly the Law was not brought in among the *Jews* to be a Rule of Justification; or to recover them out of a State of Death, and to procure them Life by their sinless Obedience to it: For in this, as well as in another Respect it *was weak*, not in itself, but through the Weakness of our *Flesh*, *Romans 8:3*. The Law, I conceive, is not a Dispensation suitable to the Infirmity of the Human Nature, in our present State." ***"Original Sin" Notebook (WJE Online Vol. 34)***

Hebrews 1:9. "Thou hast loved righteousness," etc. "This refers to that unparalleled instance of the love of moral rectitude, which Christ hath given in becoming a sacrifice for sins, by his atonement doing more than ever hath been done by any rational agent towards displaying his love of righteousness, and hatred of iniquity." See *Romans 8:3*. ***The "Blank Bible" (WJE Online Vol. 24)***

His loveliness and his love have both their greatest and most affecting manifestation in those sufferings he endured for us at his death. Therein above all appeared his holiness, his hatred of sin, and his love to God in that when he desired to save sinners, rather than that a suitable testimony should not be borne against it, he would submit that strict justice should take place in its condemnation and punishment in his own soul's being poured out unto death (*Romans 8:3*). And such was his regard to God's honor that, rather than the desired happiness of himself should injure it, he would give up himself a sacrifice for sin. Thus, in the same act he appears in the greatest conceivable manifestation of his infinite hatred of sin and also infinite grace and love to sinners. His holiness appeared like a fire burning with infinite vehemence against sin, at the same time that his love to sinners appeared like a sweet flame burning with an infinite fervency of benevolence. ***Letters and Personal Writings (WJE Online Vol. 16)***

Romans 8:3–4

We are obliged to keep all positive precepts by the covenant of works. The Jews were obliged to observe the ceremonial law by the covenant of works; and therefore if they broke the ceremonial law, that breach exposed 'em to the penalty of the law, or covenant of works, viz. eternal death: and nothing exposes to death or damnation judicially but by the law which threatened, "Thou shalt surely die." The law is the eternal, unalterable rule of righteousness between God and man, and therefore is the rule of judgment by which all that a man does shall either be justified or condemned; and no sin exposes to damnation, but by the law. So now, he that refuses to obey the precepts that require an attendance on the sacraments of the New Testament, is exposed to damnation by virtue of the law, or covenant of works. It may be argued, that all sins whatsoever are breaches of the law, or covenant of works: because all sins, even breaches of positive precepts as well as others, have atonement by the death of Christ; but Christ died only to satisfy the law, or to bear the curse of the law for us (*Galatians 3:10–13; Romans 8:3–4*). ***The "Miscellanies": (Entry Nos. a–z, aa–zz, 1–500) (WJE Online Vol. 13)***

'Tis not by the gospel, but by the law, that unbelief is a sin that exposes to eternal damnation, as is evident, because we have the pardon of the sin of unbelief by the death of Christ, which shows that Christ died to satisfy for the sin of unbelief as well as oilier sins. But Christ was to answer the law, and satisfy that; he in his death endured the curse of the law (*Galatians 3:10–13*, and *Romans 8:3–4*). 'Tis absurd to say that Christ died to satisfy the gospel, or to bear the punishment of that. ***Notes on Scripture (WJE Online Vol. 15)***

What the law failed of, being weak through the flesh, Christ performed. *Romans 8:3–4*, "For what the law could not do, in that it was weak through the flesh, God sending his own Son in the likeness of sinful flesh, and for sin, condemned sin in the flesh: that the righteousness of the law might be fulfilled in us, that walk not after the flesh, but after the Spirit." So the old heavens and earth are destroyed because of their defects, and a new heavens and earth introduced, that are to remain forever. ***The "Miscellanies": (Entry Nos. a–z, aa–zz, 1–500) (WJE Online Vol. 13)***

Romans 8:4

They that comply with the terms of justification, in the way of the covenant of grace, they fulfill the righteousness of the law, in some sense. In that they "walk not after the flesh but after the Spirit" (*Romans 8:4*), "the righteousness of the law is fulfilled in us," in the sense of the same Apostle, in the same epistle, *Romans 13:8*, "He that loveth another hath fulfilled the law." ***The "Miscellanies," 833–1152 (WJE Online Vol. 20)***

In the *Romans 8:4*, it is implied that if we walk after the flesh, justification and the reward of righteousness can't "be fulfilled in us," but if we walked after the Spirit it would be. The substance and drift of each of these things is the same, viz. if we are after, or walk after, the flesh, we shall surely come to condemnation. But, on the contrary, if we are after, or walk after, the Spirit, it will surely bring us to life, the reward of righteousness . . . ***The "Blank Bible" (WJE Online Vol. 24)***

Romans 8:5

"For they that are after the flesh do mind the things of the flesh." The Apostle in these words has probably respect to what was said of a believer in the foregoing chapter, to whom there is no condemnation, viz. that though he did sometimes through infirmity obey the will or law of the flesh, yet they did not allow, but hate these things; and so it was not they, but sin that dwelt in them. But here the Apostle observes of them that *are* and *walk* "after the flesh," that they "mind the things of the flesh." They delight in them, and pursue them with the full bent of their minds. And therefore there is condemnation to them, and they shall have death, as in the next verse. ***The "Blank Bible" (WJE Online Vol. 24)***

St. Paul's words, *Romans 8:5*, confirm the true meaning of these words of our Savior. "For they that are after the flesh do mind the things of the flesh; but they that are after the Spirit, the things of the Spirit." Such phrases, "they that are after the flesh," and "they that are after the Spirit," with the Apostle signify much the same thing with "those that are born after the flesh," and "those that are born after the Spirit," as appears by *Galatians 4:29*, where the last expression, "they that are born after the Spirit," in the original is the same as in *Romans 8:5*, "they that are after the Spirit." ***The "Blank Bible" (WJE Online Vol. 24)***

The Apostle says here in this *Romans 7:25* that though his flesh served "the law of sin," yet he himself served "the law of God," or as Mr. Locke interprets it, made himself a vassal to the law of God, or intended and devoted thereto his whole obedience. Thus does not a wicked man, or one that is after the flesh, by the Apostle's own testimony, in the *Romans 8:5*. "For they that are after the flesh do mind the things of the flesh," φρονοῦσιν τὰ τῆς σαρκός, which, as Mr. Locke observes, signifies the employing the "bent of their minds," or subjecting the mind entirely to the fulfilling the lust of the flesh. This is inconsistent with their devoting themselves as vassals to the law of God, and their delighting in the law of God after the inner man, and their not allowing but hating those things that are contrary, which are the things the Apostle expresses in this context. ***The "Blank Bible" (WJE Online Vol. 24)***

The godly, having this experimental knowledge, it wonderfully enlightens to the understanding of the gospel and the spiritual and true meaning of the Scripture, because he finds the same things in his own heart that he reads of. He knows how it is, because he feels it himself. And this makes that [that] he reads, the Scripture and other spiritual books, [appear] with much more delight than otherwise he would do. This makes him delight much more in those discourses, books and sermons that are most spiritual, which others have the least relish of. *Romans 8:5*, "For they that are after the flesh do mind the things of the flesh; but they that are after the Spirit the things of the Spirit." ***Sermons and Discourses: 1723–1729 (WJE Online Vol. 14)***

Romans 8:5–8

But, on the contrary, if we are after, or walk after, the Spirit, it will surely bring us to life, the reward of righteousness, of which the Apostle now, in the *Romans 8:5–8*, proceeds to give the reason, viz. that if we are after the flesh, we shall mind the things of the flesh. The nature of our souls will be carnal, and that will necessarily bring us to death, because to be carnally minded is "enmity against God" *Romans 8:7*, and is not, nor can, be subject to the law of God, can't please God, and therefore must bring us to condemnation. But, on the contrary, "they that are after the Spirit" *Romans 8:5* do mind "the things of the Spirit, τὰ τοῦ πβεύματος φρονοῦσιν. The Spirit is become a principle of nature in them. The nature of their souls is spiritual, but this naturally and necessarily tends to life, τὸ φρόνημα τοῦ πνεύματος, "is life and peace" *Romans 8:6*. ***The "Blank Bible" (WJE Online Vol. 24)***

Romans 8:6

I Corinthians 2:13–14, "Which things also we speak, not in the words which man's wisdom teacheth, but which the Holy Ghost teacheth, comparing spiritual things with spiritual. But the natural man receiveth not the things of the Spirit of God." Here the Apostle himself expressly signifies, that by spiritual things, he means the things of the Spirit of God, and things which the Holy Ghost teacheth. The same is yet more abundantly apparent by viewing the whole context. Again, *Romans 8:6*, "To be carnally minded is death: but to be spiritually minded is life and peace." ***Religious Affections (WJE Online Vol. 2)***

And it must be here observed, that although it is with relation to the Spirit of God and his influences, that persons and things are called spiritual; yet not all those persons who are subject to any kind of influence of the Spirit of God, are ordinarily called spiritual in the New Testament. They who have only the common influences of God's Spirit, are not so called, in the places cited above, but only those, who have the special, gracious and saving influences of God's Spirit: as is evident, because it has been already proved, that by spiritual men is meant godly men, in opposition to natural, carnal and unsanctified men. And it is most plain, that the Apostle by spiritually minded, *Romans 8:6*, means graciously minded. ***Religious Affections (WJE Online Vol. 2)***

"But the Spirit is life because of righteousness. But if the Spirit of him that raised up," etc. The Apostle seems here to have respect to what he had said, *Romans 8:6*, that "to be spiritually minded is life and peace." ***The "Blank Bible" (WJE Online Vol. 24)***

"Is not subject to the law of God." This is to show the reason why "to be carnally minded is death" *Romans 8:6*, because the law condemns to death those that are not subject to it. ***The "Blank Bible" (WJE Online Vol. 24)***

"To be carnally minded is death: but to be spiritually minded is life and peace." The Apostle explains what he means by being carnally and spiritually minded, in what follows in the 9th verse, and shows that by being spiritually minded, he means a having the indwelling and holy influences of the Spirit of God in the heart. ***The "Blank Bible" (WJE Online Vol. 24)***

Romans 8:7

There is nothing in their nature, as they have it by the first birth, whence should arise any true subjection to God; as appears by *Romans 8:7*. If there were anything truly good in the flesh, or in man's nature, or natural disposition, under a moral view, then it should only be amended; but the Scripture represents as though we were to be enemies to it, and were to seek nothing short of its entire destruction, as has been observed. And elsewhere the Apostle directs not to the amending of the old man, but putting it off, and putting on the new man; and seeks not to have the body of death made better, but to be delivered from it. ***Original Sin (WJE Online Vol. 3)***

"Is not subject to the law of God." This is to show the reason why "to be carnally minded is death" *Romans 8:6*, because the law condemns to death those that are not subject to it. ***The "Blank Bible" (WJE Online Vol. 24)***

Romans 8:8

So long as men are in their natural state, they not only have no good thing, but it is impossible they should have, or do any good thing; as appears by *Romans 8:8*. ***Original Sin (WJE Online Vol. 3)***

Romans 8:9

'Tis agreeable to the order of persons in the Trinity and their manner of subsisting. The Father subsists of himself; he is neither begotten nor proceeds. 'Tis suitable therefore that he should be first in relation to what is done in the work of redemption, that he should be first orderer, provider, etc. The Son proceeds from the Father; 'tis suitable that he should be sent by him. The Holy Ghost proceeds both from the Father and the Son. He proceeds from the Son as well as Father, and so is sent by him as well as by the Father. 'Tis evident, because he is called "the Spirit of the Son."

Galatians 4:6, "God hath sent forth the Spirit of his Son into your hearts." *Romans 8:9*, he is called "the Spirit of Christ." ***Sermons and Discourses: 1723–1729 (WJE Online Vol. 14)***

Christ comes down from heaven in the saving influences of his Spirit on the hearts of men. The Holy Spirit that sanctifies and comforts the hearts of the elect is his Spirit. . . . Christ himself is said to be in the hearts of men by his Spirit›s being in them. ***Sermons and Discourses, 1739–1742 (WJE Online Vol. 22)***

We know whether we have the Spirit of Christ by the fruits of the Spirit, and therefore may argue well that they that han't such like fruits of the Spirit of Christ han't the Spirit of Christ. But the Scripture tells us expressly that they that han't the Spirit of Christ are none of his. *Romans 8:9*, "Now if any man have not the Spirit of Christ, he is none of his." If they are not Christ's, then certainly they are not in a state of salvation. ***Sermons and Discourses, 1743–1758 (WJE Online Vol. 25)***

Natural men, or those that are not savingly converted, have no degree of that principle from whence all gracious actings flow, viz. the Spirit of God, or of Christ; as is evident, because 'tis asserted both ways in Scripture that those that have not the Spirit of Christ are not his (*Romans 8:9*), and also that those that have the Spirit of Christ are his. ***The "Miscellanies," (Entry Nos. 501–832) (WJE Online Vol. 18)***

Romans 8:10

So that not only the persons are called spiritual, as having the Spirit of God dwelling in them; but those qualifications, affections and experiences that are wrought in them by the Spirit, are also spiritual, and therein differ vastly in their nature and kind from all that a natural man is or can be the subject of while he remains in a natural state; and also from all that men or devils can be the authors of; 'tis a spiritual work in this high sense; and therefore above all other works in peculiar to the Spirit of God. There is no work so high and excellent; for there is no work wherein God does so much communication himself, and wherein the mere creatures hath, in so high a sense, a participation of God; so that it is expressed in Scripture by the saints being made "partakers of divine nature" (*II Peter 1:4*), and having God dwelling in them, and they in God (*I John 4:12, 15–16* and ch. *3:21*), and having Christ in them (*John 17:21*, *Romans 8:10*), being the temple of the living God (*II Corinthians 6:16*), living by Christ's life (*Galatians 2:20*), being made partakers of God's holiness (*Hebrews 12:10*), having Christ's love dwelling in them (*John 17:26*), having his joy fulfilled in them (*John 17:13*), seeing light in God's light, and being made to drink of the river of God's pleasures (*Psalms 36:8–9*), having fellowship with God, or communication and partaking with him (as the word signifies, *I John 1:3*). ***Religious Affections (WJE Online Vol. 2)***

But by dying to ourselves, we mean the mortifying of that false, inordinate, irregular, mistaken self-love, whereby we seek to please only ourselves and none else, seek our own present pleasure without consideration of our future state. Now this strong inclination to please and pamper ourselves must die within us, and we must die to that: we must die to our lusts and to our natural corruptions, by mortification and the deepest humility, and a mean and lowly thought of ourselves. This dying to ourselves is very frequently spoken of in the Word of God:

He that findeth his life shall lose it, and he that loseth his life for my sake shall find it (*Matthew 10:39*). If any man come unto me and hate not his father and mother, and wife and children, and brethren and sisters, yea, and his own life also, he cannot be my disciple (*Luke 14:26*). And if Christ be in you, the body is dead because of sin; but the spirit is life because of righteousness (*Romans 8:10*). ***Sermons and Discourses 1720–1723 (WJE Online Vol. 10)***

Here the Apostle does fully explain himself what he means when he so often calls that holy principle that is in the hearts of the saints by the name "Spirit." This he means, the Spirit of God itself dwelling and acting in them. In the *Romans 8:9* he calls it the Spirit of God, and the Spirit of Christ in the *Romans 8:10*. ***Writings on the Trinity, Grace, and Faith (WJE Online Vol. 21)***

It is the same life; the same Spirit that quickened him, quickeneth us, *Romans 8:10*. If we be quickened truly, we live with the same life that Christ did." ***The "Miscellanies," (Entry Nos. 1153–1360) (WJE Online Vol. 23)***

Christ condemned sin in the flesh two ways, viz. by abolishing the guilt of sin by his expiation, and by actually fulfilling the righteousness of the law. And this he did "that the righteousness of the law might be fulfilled in us, who walk not after the flesh, but after the Spirit," by which it appears that it [is] by these two things conjunctly, or one by and with the other, that the righteousness of the law is fulfilled in us, viz. Christ's condemning sin in the flesh, or his satisfaction and righteousness, and our having and walking after the Spirit, which is these several ways. 1. Christ, by condemning sin in the flesh, has made way for our having the Spirit.

He has procured the Spirit for us. 2. The Spirit in us is that by which we are united to Christ, for by the Spirit of Christ being in us, we have Christ in us (*Romans 8:10*), and so have his righteousness, which is the righteousness of the law made ours. And so the righteousness of the law is fulfilled in us. 3. By having the Spirit of Christ in us, we have union with him and communion in his nature. ***The "Blank Bible" (WJE Online Vol. 24)***

"The body is dead." I.e. shall die. The body is mortal by reason of sin. But if Christ be in you, the spirit shall not die, but shall live forever. ***The "Blank Bible" (WJE Online Vol. 24)***

Romans 8:11

The same Spirit begat Christ in the grave, that begat him in his mother's womb. (The mother's womb is compared to the lower parts of the earth in [*Psalms 139:15*], and Christ's resurrection is called his being begotten [*Revelation 1:5*]). And without doubt, both these begettings were by the same Spirit. And therefore that Spirit that is spoken of, by which Christ was raised, was without doubt the Holy Ghost, and not the divine Logos as is generally supposed. 'Tis given as a reason in *Romans 8:11*, why believers should be raised from the dead, that the Spirit of him that raised up Christ from the dead dwells in them; they have an immortal, vivifying Spirit dwelling in them. 'Tis said, that God will quicken their mortal bodies by his Spirit that dwelleth in them; and without doubt God raised up Christ by the same Spirit. And this also was the reason why Christ was raised, and why it was impossible he should be detained in the grave: because that Spirit of God did in such a manner dwell in his human nature, viz. so as to cause a personal union between him and the Godhead. ***The "Miscellanies," (Entry Nos. 501–832) (WJE Online Vol. 18)***

Romans 8:12–13

And the Apostle, when he speaks of the testimony of the Spirit of God in *Romans 8:15–16*, in that very place he principally and most immediately has respect to such effective exercises of love as those whereby Christians deny themselves in times of trial; as appears by his manner of introducing what is there said, which is to be seen in *Romans 8:12–13*, "Therefore, brethren, we are debtors, not to the flesh, to live after the flesh. For if we live after the flesh, ye shall die: but if ye through the Spirit do mortify the deeds of the flesh, ye shall live"; and also by what immediately follows in

Romans 8:17–18, "And if children, then heirs; heirs of God, and joint heirs with Christ; if so be that we suffer with him, that we may also be glorified together. For I reckon that the sufferings of this present time are not worthy to be compared with the glory which shall be revealed in us." That exercise of love, or the filial spirit that the Apostle here speaks of as the highest ground of hope, is the same with that exercise of the love of God that Christians experience in bearing tribulation for his sake ***The "Miscellanies," (Entry Nos. 501–832) (WJE Online Vol. 18)***

Romans 8:13

Hence we may learn the reason why the apostle Paul so much insisted on this, intimating to those to whom he wrote that if any pretended to belong to the kingdom of God, and did not keep God's commandments, they were but vain words. *Ephesians 5:5–6*, "For this ye know, that no whoremonger, nor unclean person, nor covetous man, who is an idolater, hath any inheritance in the Kingdom of Christ and of God. Let no man deceive you with vain words." *Galatians 6:7*, "Be not deceived." *1 Corinthians 6:9–10*, "Know ye not that the unrighteous shall not inherit the Kingdom of God? Be not deceived: neither fornicators, nor idolaters, nor adulterers, nor effeminate, nor abusers of themselves with mankind, nor thieves, nor covetous, nor drunkards, nor revilers, nor extortioners, shall inherit the Kingdom of God." And he tells us that they who "are Christ's have crucified the flesh with the affections and lusts," *Galatians 5:24*. And he tells us that they who walk after the flesh shall die, *Romans 8:13*. And this teaches us the reason why this is so much insisted on by the apostle James in places which you have often read and heard, and which I need not now mention. And so by the apostle John in his epistles this is abundantly insisted on more than all other signs in places too numerous now to be mentioned. ***Ethical Writings (WJE Online Vol. 8)***

Mortifying our sensual and fleshly lusts. *Matthew 5:29*, "And if thy right eye offends thee, pluck it out, and cast it from thee: and it is better for thee that one of thy members should perish, than that thy whole body should be cast into hell." *Romans 8:13*, "If ye live after the flesh, ye shall die: but if ye through the Spirit do mortify the deeds of the body, ye shall live." ***Writings on the Trinity, Grace, and Faith (WJE Online Vol. 21)***

The old man is condemned and slain, but the new man lives to God, as the apostle Paul says, "If ye live *after*" or according "to the flesh, ye shall die; but if ye through the Spirit do mortify the deeds of the flesh, ye shall live" [*Romans 8:13*]. The word "according" is used in the same sense that it [is] in *Ephesians 4:22* and *Ephesians 4:24*. This verse is to be connected with the *1 Peter 4:1–4*, which speak of our dying unto the flesh, as we are according to the flesh, and living spiritually and unto God. And it also has respect to what was said in the *1 Peter 3*, especially *1 Peter 3:18–20*. Preaching the gospel of old to the old world before the flood is here spoken of as parallel to the preaching of the gospel to men now, because as then, the end of the old world was at hand by the deluge; so now "the end of all things is at hand," as in the next verse, viz. *1 Peter 4:7*, and also foregoing *1 Peter 4:5*. ***The "Blank Bible" (WJE Online Vol. 24)***

Romans 8:14

So from time to time the great promises of the Spirit in other places in the Prophets are to God's people Israel, or Israel's and Abraham's posterity. Hence a being endowed by the Spirit is by the Apostle spoken of as an evidence of being "the sons of God," as *Romans 8:14*, and in and "of Abraham," in this chapter. ***The "Blank Bible" (WJE Online Vol. 24)***

From what has been said, it is also evident, that it is not spiritual knowledge, for persons to be informed of their duty, by having it immediately suggested to their minds, that such and such outward actions or deeds are the will of God. If we suppose that it is truly God's manner thus to signify his will to his people, by immediate inward suggestions, such suggestions have nothing of the nature of spiritual light. Such kind of knowledge would only be one kind of doctrinal knowledge; a proposition concerning the will of God, is as properly a doctrine of religion, as a proposition concerning the nature of God, or a work of God: and an having either of these kinds of propositions, or any other proposition, declared to a man, either by speech, or inward suggestion, differs vastly from an having the holy beauty of divine things manifested to the soul, wherein spiritual knowledge does most essentially consist. Thus there was no spiritual light in Balaam; though he had the will of God immediately suggested to him by the Spirit of God from time to time, concerning the way that he should go, and what he should do and say. 'Tis manifest therefore, that a being led and directed in this manner, is not that holy and spiritual *leading of the Spirit of God*, which is peculiar to the saints, and a distinguishing mark of the sons of God, spoken of, *Romans 8:14*. "For as many as are led by the Spirit of God, are the sons of God." *Galatians 5:18*, "But if ye be led by the Spirit, ye are not under the law." ***Religious Affections (WJE Online Vol. 2)***

Those texts of Scripture that speak of the children of God as led by the Spirit, have been by some brought to defend a being guided by such impulses; as particularly those [in] *Romans 8:14*, "For as many as are led by the Spirit of God, they are the sons of God"; and *Galatians 5:18*, "But if ye are led by the Spirit, ye are not under the law." But these texts themselves confute them that bring them; for 'tis evident that the leading of the Spirit that the Apostle speaks of is a gracious leading, or what is peculiar to the children of God, and that natural men cannot have; for he speaks of it as a sure evidence of their being the sons of God, and not under the law: but a leading or directing a person by immediately revealing to him where he should go, or what shall hereafter come to pass, or what shall be the future consequence of his doing thus or thus, if there be any such thing in these days, is not of the nature of the gracious leading of the Spirit of God that is peculiar to God's children; 'tis no more than a common gift; there is nothing in it but what natural men are capable of, and many of them have had in the days of inspiration. A man may have ten thousand such revelations and directions from the Spirit of God, and yet not have a jot of grace in his heart: 'tis no more than the gift of prophecy, which immediately reveals what will be, or should be hereafter; but this is but a common gift, as the Apostle expressly shews, *1 Corinthians 13:2*, *1 Corinthians 13:8*. If a person has anything revealed to him from God, or is directed to anything by a voice from heaven, or a whisper, or words immediately suggested and put into his mind, there is nothing of the nature of grace merely in this; 'tis of the nature of a common influence of the Spirit, and is but dross and dung in comparison of the excellency of that gracious leading of the Spirit that the saints have. Such a way of being directed where one shall go, and what he shall do, is no more than what Balaam had from God, who from time to time revealed to him what he should do, and when he had done one thing, then directed him what he should do next; so that he was in this sense led by the Spirit for a considerable time [*Numbers 22*]. ***The Great Awakening (WJE Online Vol. 4)***

He calls it the "Spirit of him that raised up Jesus from the dead" dwelling in them; and in the *Romans 8:14* he calls it the Spirit of God. ***Writings on the Trinity, Grace, and Faith (WJE Online Vol. 21)***

So from time to time the great promises of the Spirit in other places in the Prophets are to God's people Israel, or Israel's and Abraham's posterity. Hence a being endowed by the Spirit is by the Apostle spoken of as an evidence of being "the sons of God," as *Romans 8:14*, and in and "of Abraham," in this chapter. ***The "Blank Bible" (WJE Online Vol. 24)***

Romans 8:15

And when the Apostle speaks of the witness of the spirit, in *Romans 8:15–17*; he has a more immediate respect to what the Christians experienced, in their exercises of love to God, in suffering persecution; as is plain by the context. He is, in the foregoing verses, encouraging the Christian Romans under their suffering, that though their bodies be dead, because of sin, yet they should be raised to life again. ***Religious Affections (WJE Online Vol. 2)***

Crying "Abba father," *Romans 8:15* is faith in the Lord as one's father, which must have, a being confident of one's good estate inseparable from it, or rather enwrapped in it. I suppose what I have mentioned is very consistent with what you say, "That faith, and persons believing that they have faith, are not the same"; for one's believing that he has faith, simply and by itself, has for its object the man's inward frame, or the actings and exercises of his spirit, and not a divine testimony; this is not divine faith, but as I have laid the matter, a being confident of one's good estate has for its foundation the word of God (*Hebrews 13:5*, etc.) ultimately—at least to be sure, this is *one* way in which faith is acted, or one thing in its exercise. ***Religious Affections (WJE Online Vol. 2)***

And whereas it is said, "Return, O backsliding children, saith the Lord; for I am married unto you, and I will take you one of a city," etc. (ver. *Jeremiah 3:14*). Indeed, "I am married," in the Hebrew, is in the preterperfect tense; but you know, Sir, that in the language of prophecy, the preter tense is very commonly put for the future; and whereas it is said, "How shall I put thee among the children? And I said, Thou shalt call me my father" (ver. *Jeremiah 3:19*). I acknowledge this expression here, "my Father," and that *Romans 8:15* is the language of faith. It is so two ways, 1st, it is such language of the soul as is the immediate effect of a lively faith. I acknowledge, that the lively exercises of faith do naturally produce satisfaction of a good estate *as their immediate effect*. ***Religious Affections (WJE Online Vol. 2)***

All gracious hope is hope arising from faith, and hope encourages and draws forth acts of faith. So love tends to hope. For a spirit of love is the spirit of a child. And the more one feels within himself this spirit of a child, the more natural it will be for him to look on God and go to God as his Father. This childlike spirit casts out the spirit of bondage or slavish fear. *Romans 8:15*, "Ye have not received the spirit of bondage again to fear, but ye have received the spirit of adoption, whereby we cry, Abba, Father." The apostle John tells us that perfect love casts out fear. *1 John 4:18*, "There is no fear in love; but perfect love casteth out fear." ***Ethical Writings (WJE Online Vol. 8)***

In ch. *Romans 7:4–6*, the Apostle speaks of them as those that once were in the flesh, and were under the law, but now delivered from the law, and dead to it. In ch. *Romans 8:15* and following verses, he tells them, they had received the "spirit of adoption," and speaks of them as having the witness of the Spirit that they were "the children of God, heirs of God, and joint heirs with Christ." ***Ecclesiastical Writings (WJE Online Vol. 12)***

Now how unaccountable would these things be, if the case was, that the members of the primitive Christian churches were not admitted into them under any such notion as their being really godly persons and heirs of eternal life, nor with any respect to such a character appearing on them; and that they themselves joined to these churches without any such pretense, as having no such opinion of themselves! But it is particularly evident that they had such an opinion of themselves, as well as the apostles of them, by many things the apostles say in their epistles. Thus, in *Romans 8:15–16* the Apostle speaks of them as having "received the spirit of adoption," the Spirit of God bearing witness with their spirits, that they were "the children of God." ***Ecclesiastical Writings (WJE Online Vol. 12)***

84. *Romans 8:15*. "For ye have not received the spirit of bondage again unto fear, but ye have received the Spirit of adoption, whereby we cry, Abba, Father." That is, ye have not the spirit of slaves and bondservants that works by slavish fear, but the spirit of children so that you ben't afraid, but dare cry, "Abba, Father," dare as children approach God with a holy boldness. The spirits are different: one is the spirit of God; the other is not. ***Notes on Scripture (WJE Online Vol. 15)***

The filial spirit, or Spirit of the Son, or Spirit of adoption, is a principle that, so far as it prevails, excludes and renders the saints incapable of fear, or a legal principle, or spirit of bondage. *1 John 4:18*, "Perfect love casteth out fear." It casts it out as Sarah and Isaac cast out the bondwoman and her son, that we read of in the chapter preceding the text that we are upon [*Galatians 4:30*]. It is in Christians a principle of love, of childlike confidence and hope, as in the *Galatians 4:6*, it cries, "Abba, Father." It evidences to 'em their being the children of God and begets that trust and assurance that renders 'em incapable of a legal principle. *Romans 8:15–16*, "For ye have not received the spirit of bondage again unto fear, but ye have received the Spirit of adoption, whereby we cry, Abba, Father. The Spirit itself beareth witness with our spirits, that we are the children of God." ***Notes on Scripture (WJE Online Vol. 15)***

This witness of the Spirit, or a Spirit of adoption, must be the experience of the exercise of such a spirit, or a spirit of love, which is a childlike spirit, in opposition to a spirit of fear, which is the spirit of bondage. But it has been already observed that the keeping Christ's commands that has been spoken of consists mainly in the exercise of grace in the heart; and that kind of exercise of love, or the spirit of adoption that there is in such practical exertions and effective exercises of love, are the highest and most essential and distinguishing kind of exercises of love: and therefore in them this testimony and seal and earnest of the Spirit of love is given in its clearest and fullest manner. And the Apostle, when he speaks of the testimony of the Spirit of God in *Romans 8:15–16*, in that very place he principally and most immediately has respect to such effective exercises of love as those whereby Christians deny themselves in times of trial . . . ***The "Miscellanies," (Entry Nos. 501–832) (WJE Online Vol. 18)***

Psalms 51:12. "Uphold me by thy free spirit." The same that in the New Testament is called the "Spirit of adoption," and set in opposition to a "spirit of bondage" [*Romans 8:15*], which David's sin had brought him under. ***The "Blank Bible" (WJE Online Vol. 24)***

"Ye have not received the spirit of bondage again." I.e. the dispensation you are now come under is not another dispensation like that of Moses, tending to fear, etc. ***The "Blank Bible" (WJE Online Vol. 24)***

We are within ourselves conscious to a childlike spirit towards God, a spirit of adoption, which naturally disposes us to come to God, and behave towards God as our Father. From the childlike spirit we feel, which our own spirits or consciousness testifies to, we naturally conclude that we are the children of God. The Spirit of adoption naturally cries, Abba, Father, calls God Father *Romans 8:15*. ***The "Blank Bible" (WJE Online Vol. 24)***

2 Corinthians 3:17–18 "Where the Spirit of the Lord is, there is liberty," because the Lord is the Son of God; and so those that have "the Spirit of the Lord" have a filial spirit, and therefore a free spirit, a "Spirit of adoption," which is opposite to a "spirit of bondage" [*Romans 8:15*]. If the Son gives us his own Spirit, we shall have a free spirit indeed; for whom the Son makes free, he shall be free indeed. See notes on *Galatians 5:18*, *Ans.* to *Inq.* 2, no. 196 ***The "Blank Bible" (WJE Online Vol. 24)***

3. Christ by his death abolished guilt, and held forth to the world a proper and complete atonement and full satisfaction for sin, which made that old legal dispensation no longer proper or meet to be kept up in the church; but a dispensation of greater liberty was suitable to succeed this. The legal way in which God treated his church had its ground very much

in the concealment of the proper atonement for sin, or its being but very obscurely revealed. Therefore they were kept under a yoke of bondage. The church, while a minor, differed nothing from a servant, but was under tutors and governors; and they received a spirit of bondage unto fear [*Romans 8:15*]. Their sacrifices and legal purifications were to renew and keep up a sense of guilt; and therefore all fell, of course, when once Christ crucified, the great sacrifice and perfect atonement of guilt, was revealed. The end of the ceremonial law was to cause that all might stand self-condemned, and be shut up to the grace that should afterwards be revealed. Thus Christ blotted out "the handwriting of ordinances that was against us, that was contrary to us, and took it out of the way, nailing it to his cross" (*Colossians 2:14*). ***The "Blank Bible" (WJE Online Vol. 24)***

Van Mastrict supposes there to be three things preparatory to actual faith and repentance, viz. 1. Contrition, which the Apostle calls "the spirit of bondage to fear" marginal, which he supposes is meant when the Psalmist speaks of a contrite heart, and Christ, when he speaks of those that labor and are heavy laden; which consists in the sinner's sense of the filthiness of his sins, and the anger of God and fear of punishment, and sense of his own folly and madness in sinning as he has done, and great grief and sorrow accompanying of it, and confession of sins before God and man and indignation against himself. 2. Humiliation, by which the contrite person, in the thoughts of his sins and misery that he is in danger of, is vile and abject in his own eyes, and condemns himself and acknowledges he deserves eternal damnation, is filled with shame and acknowledges himself to be wholly unworthy of any mercy. 3. Saving desperation, whereby a person is sensible that he has nothing to pay for his own deliverance, becomes poor in spirit, and that we can do nothing for our own deliverance. ***Documents on the Trinity, Grace and Faith (WJE Online Vol. 37)***

Romans 8:16

And the saints are the jewels of Jesus Christ, the great potentate, who has the possession of the empire of the universe: and these jewels have his image enstamped upon them, by his royal signet, which is the Holy Spirit. And this is undoubtedly what the Scripture means by the seal of the Spirit; especially when it is enstamped in so fair and clear a manner, as to be plain to the eye of conscience; which is what the Scripture calls *our spirit* [*Romans 8:16*]. ***Religious Affections (WJE Online Vol. 2)***

And indeed the Apostle, when in that, *Romans 8:16*, he speaks of the Spirit's bearing witness with our spirit, that we are the children of God, does sufficiently explain himself, if his words were but attended to. What is here expressed, is connected with the two preceding verses, as resulting from what the Apostle had said there, as every reader may see. The three verses together are thus: "For as many as are led by the Spirit of God, they are the sons of God: for ye have not received the spirit of bondage again to fear; but ye have received the spirit of adoption, whereby we cry, Abba, Father; the Spirit itself beareth witness with our spirits, that we are the children of God." Here, what the Apostle says, if we take it together, plainly shows, that what he has respect to, when he speaks of the Spirit's giving us witness or evidence that we are God's children; is his dwelling in us, and leading us, as a spirit of adoption, or spirit of a child, disposing us to behave towards God as to a Father. This is the witness or evidence the Apostle speaks of, that we are children, that we have the spirit of children, or spirit of adoption. And what is that, but the spirit of love? ***Religious Affections (WJE Online Vol. 2)***

And whereas the Apostle says, "the Spirit bears witness with our spirits" [*Romans 8:16*]; by "our spirit" here, is meant our conscience, which is called the spirit of man; *Proverbs 20:27*, "The spirit of man is the candle of the Lord, searching all the inward parts of the belly." We elsewhere read of the witness of this spirit of ours; *II Corinthians 1:12*, "For our rejoicing is this, the testimony of our conscience." And *I John 3:19–21*, "And hereby do we know that we are of the truth, and shall assure our hearts before him. For if our heart condemn us, God is greater than our heart, and knoweth all things. Beloved if our heart condemn us not, then have we confidence towards God." When the apostle Paul speaks of the Spirit of God bearing witness with our spirit, he is not to be understood of two spirits, that are two separate, collateral, independent witnesses; but 'tis by one, that we receive the witness of the other: the Spirit of God gives the evidence, by infusing and shedding abroad the love of God, the spirit of a child, in the heart; and our spirit, or our conscience, receives and declares this evidence for our rejoicing. ***Religious Affections (WJE Online Vol. 2)***

If God held sinners in a state of condemnation, and as the objects of his hatred and wrath, it would be utterly incongruous that they should have his Spirit. It is utterly unbeautiful and inharmonious that a person have anything of those holy, sweet, humble dispositions and motions of heart, which are a participation of the divine nature, given him while he is held as the object of God's utter displeasure and loathing. Therefore, when a person feels the Spirit of God in those divine dispositions and exercises, it assures him that God does not hold him as an enemy, but that he is in a state of favor with God. For when he feels those motions he knows what they be, and he sees that it would be utterly incongruous for him to have them, that God should give them to him, if he did not accept of him. This is that seal and that earnest of the Spirit that we read of; this is that white stone and new name, which no man knows but he that receives it [*Revelation 2:17*]. Thus the Spirit of God bears witness together with our spirits, that we are the children of God, *Romans 8:16*. ***The "Miscellanies": (Entry Nos. a–z, aa–zz, 1–500) (WJE Online Vol. 13)***

Sometimes the strong and lively exercises of love to God do give a kind of immediate and intuitive evidence of the soul's relation to God. Divine love is the bond by which the soul of the saint is united to God, and sometimes when this divine love is strong and lively, this bond of union can be seen as it were intuitively. The saint sees that he is united to God, and so is God's, for he sees and feels the union between God and his soul. He sees clearly and certainly that divine love that does evidently, beyond all contradiction or exception, unite his soul to God. He knows there is an union, for he sees it, or feels it, so strong that he can't question it, or doubt of it. *1 John 4:18*, "There is no fear in love; but perfect love casts out fear." How can the saint doubt but that he stands in a childlike relation to God, when he plainly sees a childlike union between God and his soul? He that has such a strong exercise of a divine and holy love to God, he knows at the same time that 'tis not from himself. This that he feels so strong in his own heart brings its own evidence with it that it is from God. It is a childlike union of his heart to God, that God himself gives; and therefore, in seeing and feeling this union, he sees and feels that God has taken his soul, and has united it as a child to him, so that he does as it were see that he is a child of God. This seems to be that in Scripture which is called the Spirit of God bearing witness within our spirits that we are the children of God (*Romans 8:16*); or "the Spirit of adoption, whereby we cry, Abba, Father," as in the preceding verse. The Spirit of God gives those motions and exercises of a childlike love to God that naturally inclines the heart to look on God as his Father, and behave towards him as such (see note on *Romans 8:16*). God, in giving this, does manifest himself to be our Father, for the soul does as it were feel itself to be God's child. It feels beyond doubting as it were a childlike union to God in the heart. ***The "Miscellanies," (Entry Nos. 501–832) (WJE Online Vol. 18)***

He that has such strong exercise of a divine and holy love to God, he knows at the same time that this is not from himself. This that he feels so strong in his own heart, brings its own evidence with it that it is from God. It is a childlike union of his heart to God that God himself gives. And therefore in seeing and feeling this union, he sees that God has taken his heart, and has united it as a child to him; so that he does as it were see that he is a child of God. This seems to be that "bearing witness with our spirit, that we are the children of God" (*Romans 8:16*); which in Scripture is called "the Spirit of God." The Spirit of God gives these holy motions, and exercises childlike love to God, that naturally inclines the heart to look on God as his Father. 'Tis called the "spirit of adoption, whereby we cry, Abba, Father," [in the] foregoing verse. God in giving this spirit does manifest himself to be our Father; for the soul does as it were feel itself to be God's child, as it feels the strong and clear exercises of childlike dispositions and affections, and so as it were feels a childlike union, and sees a childlike relation to God. ***Sermons and Discourses, 1734–1738 (WJE Online Vol. 19)***

Men don't know that they are godly by believing that they are godly. We know many things by faith. *Hebrews 11:3*, "By faith we understand that the worlds were framed by the word of God, so that things which are seen were not made of things which do appear." "Faith is the evidence of things not seen" (*Hebrews 11:1*). Thus men know the trinity of persons in the Godhead, that Jesus is the Son of God, that he that believes in him will have eternal life, the resurrection of the dead. And if God should tell a saint that he hath grace, he might know it by believing the word of God. But it is not in this way that godly men know that they have grace. It is not revealed in the Word, and the Spirit of God doth not testify it to particular persons. Some think that the Spirit doth testify it to some, and they ground it on *Romans 8:16*, "The Spirit itself beareth witness with our spirit, that we are the children of God." They think the Spirit reveals it by giving an inward testimony to it, and some godly men think they have had experience of it, but they may easily mistake. When the Spirit of God doth eminently stir up a spirit of faith and sheds abroad the love of God in the heart, it is easy to mistake it for a testimony. And that is not the meaning of Paul's words. The Spirit discovers the grace of God in Christ, and thereby draws forth special actings of faith and love; which are evidential, but it doth not work in way of testimony. If God do but help us to receive the revelations in the Word, we shall have comfort enough without new revelations. ***Sermons and Discourses, 1739–1742 (WJE Online Vol. 22)***

["The Spirit itself beareth witness with our spirit."] The Spirit of God and our spirit are not spoken of here as two witnesses separate and independent. But 'tis by one that we receive the witness of the other. 'Tis by 1 our own spirit that we receive the witness of the Spirit of God. We are within ourselves conscious to a childlike spirit towards God, a spirit of adoption, which naturally disposes us to come to God, and behave towards God as our Father. From the childlike spirit we feel, which our own spirits or consciousness testifies to, we naturally conclude that we are the children of God. The Spirit of adoption naturally cries, Abba, Father, calls God Father *Romans 8:15*. "The Spirit itself beareth witness with our spirit," etc. That in *Romans 9:1*, "My conscience bearing me witness in the Holy Ghost," or "in the Holy Spirit," may serve to ascertain the Apostle's meaning in this place. For in that place the Apostle speaks of witnessing to his grace or divine virtue in a particular instance, as here in the general. And the same two things are spoken of as concerned in testifying, viz. the Holy Spirit and his own spirit or conscience. ***The "Blank Bible" (WJE Online Vol. 24)***

Romans 8:17

The nation of Israel, whom God calls his son, his first-born, were heirs of the land of Canaan, that good land which was God's land, the land that God had set apart for himself. So the church of God, that consists of the children of God, that are "heirs of God and joint heirs with Christ" [*Romans 8:17*], are heirs of the world as Christ is heir of the world. And therefore, God promises that he that approves himself one of these, shall inherit all things; and he will be his God, and he shall be his son. ***Apocalyptic Writings (WJE Online Vol. 5)***

Consider what glorious rewards are promised to be hereafter bestowed on those who do willingly suffer for Christ. It is said that they shall receive a crown of life, *James 1:12*. And Christ promises that those who forsake houses or lands, or father or mother, or wife, or children for his name's sake, shall receive an hundredfold and shall inherit everlasting life, *Matthew 19:29*. And we are told that such shall be accounted worthy of the kingdom of God, *2 Thessalonians 1:5*. And to the like purport the same Apostle tells us in *2 Timothy 2:11–12*, "It is a faithful saying: For if we be dead with him, we shall also live with him. If we suffer, we shall also reign with him: if we deny him, he also will deny us." And so *Romans 8:17*, "If so be we suffer with him, that we also may be glorified together." ***Ethical Writings (WJE Online Vol. 8)***

Thus it is that souls espoused to Christ must reign over the world, because Christ reigns over the world. This is frequently promised. They must sit down in his throne because he is set down on his Father's throne, *Revelation 3:21*. Because Christ has power over all the nations, and rules [them] with a rod of iron, and breaks them in pieces as a potter's vessel, so Christ says, *Revelation 2:26–27*, that they also shall have power over me nations, and "shall rule them with a rod of iron," and break them in pieces as a potter's vessel, too. Because Christ is God's Son and heir of all God's estate, believers must be sons and heirs of all God's estate too, *Romans 8:17*. Because Jesus Christ is possessor of heaven earth and sea, sun moon and stars, so believers must be possessors of heaven earth and sea, sun moon and stars too (*Revelation 21:7*; *2 Corinthians 6:10*), and, as I could mention, in fifty other things. So, because Christ rose from the dead, which was a great part of his glorification, so shall saints rise from the dead too, which is a great part of their glorification. ***The "Miscellanies": (Entry Nos. a–z, aa–zz, 1–500) (WJE Online Vol. 13)***

"And if children, then heirs; heirs of God, and joint heirs with Christ; if so be that we suffer with him, that we may also be glorified together. For I reckon that the sufferings of this present time are not worthy to be compared with the glory which shall be revealed in us." That exercise of love, or the filial spirit that the Apostle here speaks of as the highest ground of hope, is the same with that exercise of the love of God that Christians experience in bearing tribulation for his sake . . . ***The "Miscellanies," (Entry Nos. 501–832) (WJE Online Vol. 18)***

"For two, saith he, shall be one flesh. But he that is joined [unto the Lord is one spirit]." They are received to the relation of children to God the Father, or of his family, "and of the household of God" (*Ephesians 2:19*); and have right to all the privileges of the children of God. They are "heirs of God, and joint-heirs with Christ" (*Romans 8:17*). The good that is promised them is of the highest kind. 'Tis a mansion, an inheritance in heaven, the highest and the most glorious part of the creation, [the most glorious] palace [in heaven] that God hath built. And then the happiness that is promised them is the full enjoyment of God, without restraint, in the boldness and nearness of excess, in the cold draughts they take. ***Sermons and Discourses, 1734–1738 (WJE Online Vol. 19)***

And then if we partake of the spirit of the Son, we are children by nature; that is, we have the nature of children, as *Romans 8:14–16*. And therefore 'tis no way suitable that we should be condemned, for if we are sons, we are heirs of life, and partaking of the nature of the Son, are children with him, and joint-heirs with him of the same life, as *Romans 8:17*. ***The "Blank Bible" (WJE Online Vol. 24)***

By having the Spirit of Christ in us, we have union with him and communion in his nature. And so by the Spirit of the Son are become sons by nature, and so must necessarily as heirs have life, as *Romans 8:17*. 'Tis no way suitable that those who have the nature and state of sons should be condemned, but that they should have justification and life. ***The "Blank Bible" (WJE Online Vol. 24)***

"And if children, then heirs," etc. "If children, then heirs" of life, and must live. This is to confirm what the Apostle had asserted in the *Romans 8:13*, and *Romans 8:11*, *Romans 8:10*, *Romans 8:6*, and *Romans 8:2*. ***The "Blank Bible" (WJE Online Vol. 24)***

By adoption, though far off, [you will be reborn] by a spiritual generation (*John 1:12–13*, *1 John 5:1*). [Your] nature as saints [will be] immediately from God, as his blessed children by a blessed affinity. This, above all other things, shows the height of the privilege [the redeemed enjoy: to be] treated as children [of God, with the] dear love and complacence of a Father. [You will have God's] tenderness and pity, [be] instructed, protected, counseled, provided [for, and] received [in]to his house [to] dwell with him. [You will] have fellowship [with Christ], be his heirs; *Romans 8:17*, "Heirs of God, and joint-heirs [with Christ]"; *Revelation 21:7*. ***Sermons and Discourses, 1743–1758 (WJE Online Vol. 25)***

And so when he ascended into heaven, and was exalted to great glory there, this also was as a public person: he took possession of heaven not only for himself, but his people, as their forerunner and head, that they might ascend also, "and sit together in heavenly places with him" (*Ephesians 2:5–6*). Christ "writes upon them his new name" (*Revelation 3:12*); i.e. he makes them partakers of his own glory and exaltation in heaven. His "new name" is that new honor and glory that the Father invested him with, when he set him on his own right hand: as a prince, when he advances anyone to new dignity in his kingdom, gives him a new title. Christ and his saints shall be glorified together (*Romans 8:17*). ***Sermons and Discourses, 1743–1758 (WJE Online Vol. 25)***

The saints while on earth pray and labor for the same thing that Christ labored for, viz. the advancement of the kingdom of God among men, the promoting the prosperity of Zion and flourishing of religion in this world, and most of them have suffered for that end, as Christ did; have been made partakers with their head in his sufferings, and "filled up" (as the Apostle expresses it) "that which is behind of the sufferings of Christ": and therefore they shall partake with him of the glory and joy of the end obtained; *Romans 8:17*, "We are joint-heirs with Christ; if so be that we suffer with him, that we may be also glorified together." *2 Timothy 2:12*, "If we suffer with him, we shall also reign with him." ***Sermons and Discourses, 1743–1758 (WJE Online Vol. 25)***

Again, *John 8:42*, "If God were your Father, ye would love me"; which certainly implies that all that are the children of God do love Christ. But none that are not the children of God are in a state of salvation, or have any title to eternal life. For the gospel way of coming to a title to eternal life is by inheritance, but none are heirs but children. "If children, then heirs," says the Apostle [*Romans 8:17*]; but if we are not children, then we are no heirs. And 'tis evident by [an] abundance of texts that the title is no other way than by inheritance. ***Sermons and Discourses, 1743–1758 (WJE Online Vol. 25)***

Romans 8:18

'Tis a bondage the creature is subject to, from which it was partly delivered when Christ came, and the gospel was promulgated in the world; and will be more fully delivered at the commencement of the glorious day we are speaking of; and perfectly at the day of judgment. This agrees with the context; for the Apostle was speaking of the present suffering state of the church [*Romans 8:18*]. The reason why the church in this world is in a suffering state, is that the world is subjected to the sin and corruption of mankind. ***Apocalyptic Writings (WJE Online Vol. 5)***

Romans 8:19

Doubtless, the world is to enjoy a sabbath, after all this labor, these wearisome changes and overturnings; the world shall enjoy a rest in the peaceable reign of the saints. This the strain of all prophecy seems to hold forth to us. The creature travails in pain, and groans for this manifestation of the sons of God, this rest that remaineth for the church [*Romans 8:19*, *Romans 8:22*]. ***Apocalyptic Writings (WJE Online Vol. 5)***

The "whole creation" is, as it were, earnestly waiting for that day, and constantly groaning and travailing in pain to bring forth the felicity and glory of it. For that day is above all other times, excepting the day of judgment, the day of "the manifestation of the sons of God," and of their "glorious liberty": and therefore that elegant representation the Apostle makes of the earnest expectation and travail of the creation, in *Romans 8:19–22*, is applicable to the glorious events of this day . . . ***Apocalyptic Writings (WJE Online Vol. 5)***

If at the same time that the creation (that "waiteth for the manifestation of the sons of God" [*Romans 8:19*]) appears especially in travail, the church of God appears remarkably as a woman with child, crying, and travailing in birth, and pained to be delivered, wrestling and agonizing with God in prayer, for the promised blessing, there is the more reason to hope that the time is nigh, when she shall bring forth that man-child that is to rule all nations. ***Letters and Personal Writings (WJE Online Vol. 16)***

'Tis represented in Scripture as though the whole creation were laboring and travailing to bring forth this perfect redemption of the elect. *Romans 8:19*, "For the earnest expectation of the creature waiteth for the manifestation of the sons of God" ***The "Miscellanies," (Entry Nos. 501–832) (WJE Online Vol. 18)***

The Apostle had been representing in the preceding verses that the whole creation was as it were in travail to bring forth that birth, viz. the birth of the children of God into a state of liberty, happiness, and glory. This in *Romans 8:19* he calls "the manifestation of the sons of God," alluding to children's being bought forth to the light when they are born. This was [to] have its highest fulfillment at the general resurrection, when they shall be born from the grave, and manifested in the most public manner in the proper glory of God's children, and shall receive the most public testimonies of God's fatherly love. ***The "Blank Bible" (WJE Online Vol. 24)***

That great outpouring of the Spirit (*Acts 2:4* [and] *Acts 2:13–17*). The Spirit of God, the chief subject matter of prayer, [is] the great purchase and promise of Christ. [We have] more encouragement to pray for this than any other [thing]. This very thing is what is the subject of half the Lord's Prayer. The church of God travailing (*Revelation 12:2*). The whole creation is represented as groaning (*Romans 8:19*, etc.). Singing (*Isaiah 49:13*, *Isaiah 44:23*). Prayer is represented as a principal means (*Revelation 8:2–3*). ***Sermons and Discourses, 1743–1758 (WJE Online Vol. 25)***

Romans 8:20

The reason why the church in this world is in a suffering state, is that the world is subjected to the sin and corruption of mankind. By "vanity"

[*Romans 8:20*], in Scripture, is very commonly meant sin and wickedness; and also by "corruption" [*Romans 8:21*], as might be shewn in very many places, would my intended brevity allow. ***Apocalyptic Writings (WJE Online Vol. 5)***

The sun is the greatest image of God [of] any inanimate creature in the whole universe (or at least it is so to us), in these two things, viz. as a fountain of light and life and refreshment, and also in being a consuming fire, an immense fountain as it were of infinitely fierce and burning heat. And since it is abused by wicked men in the former sort of influences, they shall suffer the latter. As it has been the creature that has been principally abused by sin, and as it were the fountain of all the rest that have been so abused, and so is that which chiefly groans under the bondage of corruption, so it will be the chief instrument of the punishment of sin. And if sinners will finally abuse the benefits they have by the sun, and thereby abuse the Creator of the sun, that is infinitely brighter and more excellent, and an infinitely more terrible and more consuming fire, he will make that sun, in conjunction with many millions more, the instruments of his wrath. 'Tis the visible creation that has been made subject to vanity and has been abused and groaned under the sin of men [*Romans 8:20*, *Romans 8:22*], and therefore, all together, in all the parts, with united force shall arise against them and execute God's vengeance upon them. ***The "Miscellanies," 833–1152 (WJE Online Vol. 20)***

The creature is "made subject to vanity" *Romans 8:20*, not only in the corruption and decay in their nature, that has been occasioned by the sin of man, whereby this world we live in is but the ruins of what it was once, but also as it is in a sort subjected to sin, and made a servant to that through the abusive use that man, who has the dominion over the creatures, puts them. Thus the sun is in a sort a servant to all manner of wickedness, as its light and other beneficial influences are abused by men, and made subservient to their lusts and sinful purposes. So of the rain, and fruits of the earth, and the brute animals, and all other parts of this visible creation. They all serve men's corruption, and obey their sinful will. And God doth in a sort subject them to it, for he continues influence and power to make them to be obedient, according to the same law of nature whereby they yield to men's command when used to good purposes. ***The "Blank Bible" (WJE Online Vol. 24)***

Romans 8:21

But they are greatly mistaken. The service of God is not a slavery as they imagine. They are [not] the worst and most miserable slaves that are the servants of him; but they enjoy the best and most desirable liberty that are holy; they have the "liberty of the children of God" [*Romans 8:21*]. They are free indeed; *John 8:36*, "If the Son therefore shall make you free, ye shall be free indeed." God's law is a perfect law of liberty; *James 1:25*, "But whoso looketh into the perfect law of liberty, and continueth therein, he being not a forgetful hearer, but a doer of the work, this man shall be blessed in his deed." ***Sermons and Discourses, 1730–1733 (WJE Online Vol. 17)***

Now in this world in many respects we enjoy not the "liberty of the children of God" (*Romans 8:21*), but are still in pain under bondage. The Old Testament church were treated as a servant in comparison of what the church is under the New Testament, but still the church is treated as a servant in comparison of what it will be after the resurrection. ***The "Blank Bible" (WJE Online Vol. 24)***

Romans 8:22

Though the creature is thus subject to vanity, yet it don't rest in this subjection, but is constantly acting and exerting itself, in order to that glorious liberty that God has appointed at the time we are speaking of, and as it were reaching forth towards it. All the changes that are brought to pass in the world, from age to age, are ordered in infinite wisdom in one respect or other to prepare the way for that glorious issue of things, that shall be when truth and righteousness shall finally prevail and he, whose right it is, shall take the kingdom. All the creatures, in all their operations and motions, continually tend to this. As in a clock, all the motions of the whole system of wheels and movements, tend to the striking of the hammer at the appointed time. All the revolutions and restless motions of the sun and other heavenly bodies, from day to day, from year to year, and from age to age, are continually tending hither; as all the many turnings of the wheels of a chariot, in a journey, tend to the appointed journey's end. The mighty struggles and conflicts of nations, and shakings of kingdoms, and those vast successive changes that are brought to pass, in the kingdoms and empires of the world, from one age to another, are as it were travail pangs of the creation, in order to bring forth this glorious event. And the

Scriptures represent the last struggles and changes that shall immediately precede this event, as being the greatest of all; as the last pangs of a woman in travail are the most violent [*Romans 8:22*]. ***Apocalyptic Writings (WJE Online Vol. 5)***

The sun is the greatest image of God [of] any inanimate creature in the whole universe (or at least it is so to us), in these two things, viz. as a fountain of light and life and refreshment, and also in being a consuming fire, an immense fountain as it were of infinitely fierce and burning heat. And since it is abused by wicked men in the former sort of influences, they shall suffer the latter. As it has been the creature that has been principally abused by sin, and as it were the fountain of all the rest that have been so abused, and so is that which chiefly groans under the bondage of corruption, so it will be the chief instrument of the punishment of sin. And if sinners will finally abuse the benefits they have by the sun, and thereby abuse the Creator of the sun, that is infinitely brighter and more excellent, and an infinitely more terrible and more consuming fire, he will make that sun, in conjunction with many millions more, the instruments of his wrath. 'Tis the visible creation that has been made subject to vanity and has been abused and groaned under the sin of men [*Romans 8:20*, *Romans 8:22*], and therefore, all together, in all the parts, with united force shall arise against them and execute God's vengeance upon them. ***The "Miscellanies," 833–1152 (WJE Online Vol. 20)***

This work is long a-doing and there are a very great number of mighty revolutions and events before 'tis completed. Already the bigger part of six thousand years [have passed, during which a] great many overturnings have been [achieved, but the end has] not yet [been] accomplished. And [there] yet remain many great changes. [It] has been foretold; God has promised. God's people have long been waiting, hoping, longing. All nature has been groaning, and as it were in travail to bring it to pass. *Romans 8:22*, "For we know that the whole creation groaneth and travaileth in pain together until now." [God's end has been] accomplished as yet but in small part: the Scriptures speak of vastly greater numbers. ***Sermons and Discourses, 1743–1758 (WJE Online Vol. 25)***

Romans 8:23

And this vital indwelling of the Spirit in the saints, in this less measure and small beginning, is the "earnest of the Spirit" [*II Corinthians 1:22*], the "earnest of the future inheritance" [*Ephesians 1:14*], and "the firstfruits of the Spirit," as the Apostle calls it, *Romans 8:23*, where, by the firstfruits of the Spirit, the Apostle undoubtedly means the same vital gracious principle, that he speaks of in all the preceding part of the chapter, which he calls Spirit, and sets in opposition to flesh or corruption. Therefore this earnest of the Spirit, and first fruits of the Spirit, which has been shown to be the same with the seal of the Spirit, is the vital, gracious, sanctifying communication and influence of the Spirit, and not any immediate suggestion or revelation of facts by the Spirit. ***Religious Affections (WJE Online Vol. 2)***

The time of the saints' glorious resurrection is often spoken of as the proper time of the saints' salvation, the day of their redemption, the time of their adoption, glory and recompense (as in *Ephesians 4:30*; *Romans 8:23*; *Luke 14:14* and *Luke 21:38*; *II Timothy 4:1, 9*; *Colossians 3:4*; *I Thessalonians 1:7*; *Hebrews 9:23*; *I Peter 1:13* and *I Peter 5:4*; *I John 3:2* and other places). ***Original Sin (WJE Online Vol. 3)***

That the Spirit of God is spiritual joy and delight, is confirmed by those places where we are told that the Holy Spirit is the "earnest" of our future inheritance [*Ephesians 1:14*] and the "first-fruits" (*Romans 8:23*). The earnest is a part of the inheritance; which shows that our future inheritance, that happiness spoken of that God will give his saints, is nothing but a fullness of his Spirit. This is that "river of water of life" which comes from the throne of God and the Lamb [*Revelation 22:1*]. ***The "Miscellanies": (Entry Nos. a–z, aa–zz, 1–500) (WJE Online Vol. 13)***

The redemption of the bodies of the saints is part of the work of redemption: the resurrection to life is called a redemption of their bodies (*Romans 8:23*). ***Sermons and Discourses 1720–1723 (WJE Online Vol. 10)***

As the work of redemption is the end of all God's other works, so it will in a sense be the last of God's works. It shall have its actual fulfillment and accomplishment at the consummation of all things. What shall then be fulfilled will be the redemption of the elect church in an eminent manner. *Luke 21:28*, "Lift up your heads, for your redemption draweth nigh"; *Ephesians 4:30*, "sealed to the day of redemption"; *Ephesians 1:14*, "till the redemption of the purchased possession"; *Romans 8:23*, "the adoption, to wit, the redemption of our body." That is the proper season of the church's actual redemption. ***The "Miscellanies," 833–1152 (WJE Online Vol. 20)***

Having the spirit of Christ. *Romans 8:9*, "But ye are not in the flesh, but in the Spirit, if so be that the Spirit of God dwell in you. Now if any man have not the Spirit of Christ, he is none of his"; and *Romans 8:14*, "For as many as are led by the Spirit of God, they are the sons of God." *1*

John 3:24, "Hereby we know that he abideth in us by the Spirit that he hath given us"; and *1 John 4:13*, "Hereby know we that we dwell in him, because he hath given us of his Spirit." Therefore, believers are said to be sealed by the Spirit and to have the earnest of the Spirit. *2 Corinthians 1:22*, "Who hath also sealed us, and given us the earnest of the Spirit in our hearts"; and *2 Corinthians 5:5*, "He who hath wrought for this selfsame thing is God, who hath also given us the earnest of the Spirit." *Ephesians 1:13–14*, "Ye were sealed with the holy Spirit of promise, which is the earnest of our future inheritance"; and *Ephesians 4:30*, "And grieve not the holy Spirit of God, whereby ye are sealed unto the day of redemption." The Spirit is called the firstfruits, *Romans 8:23*. ***Writings on the Trinity, Grace, and Faith (WJE Online Vol. 21)***

Our hope of the glory of God is not an hope that only occasions the grief of disappointment, but meets with success, and has already obtained the thing hoped for in some degree in the earnests of it, in the earnests of the Spirit that are given in our hearts (*Ephesians 1:13–14*, *2 Corinthians 5:5–6*, *2 Corinthians 1:20–22*, *Ephesians 4:30*, *Romans 8:23*), which we feel in that holy, sweet, and divine love that "is shed abroad" in us, which is the breathing, and the proper and natural act of the Holy Ghost. ***The "Blank Bible" (WJE Online Vol. 24)***

"Waiting for the adoption." Now God gives the Spirit of adoption, whereby we have the hope of being hereafter delivered to the liberty, and all the privileges, and blessings of children. But at the resurrection this shall be literally fulfilled. Now in this world in many respects we enjoy not the "liberty of the children of God" (*Romans 8:21*), but are still in pain under bondage. The Old Testament church were treated as a servant in comparison of what the church is under the New Testament, but still the church is treated as a servant in comparison of what it will be after the resurrection. Therefore is that perfecting of the saints' glory called their "adoption," because it is their admission to the complete enjoyment of the liberty, and privileges, and inheritance of children. 'Tis called the "adoption" in this place the rather, because the Apostle was speaking of the saints' being God's children, as [the] *Romans 8:17*, and from thence back. "The redemption of our body." The Apostle, in calling the resurrection of saints "the redemption of the body," probably has in his eye that passage in *Hosea 13:14*. "I will ransom them from the power of the grave. O death, I will be thy plagues; O grave, I will be thy destruction." ***The "Blank Bible" (WJE Online Vol. 24)***

Romans 8:24

Hope is so great a part of true religion, that the Apostle says we are saved by hope. ***Religious Affections (WJE Online Vol. 2)***

Faith is that by which we are built on that strong rock, so that we can't be overthrown; and the same is the anchor by which we are held fast, and can't be driven to and fro of wind and storms, and shipwrecked, and lost. That which is here called "hope" is the very same that is elsewhere called "faith"; and saving and justifying faith is often in the New Testament called by the name of hope, as in *Romans 8:24–25*. ***Notes on Scripture (WJE Online Vol. 15)***

Romans 8:26

But as to those that have been thought to be converted among us, in this time, they generally seem to be persons that have had an abiding change wrought on them: I have had particular acquaintance with many of them since, and they generally appear to be persons that have a new sense of things, new apprehensions and views of God, of the divine attributes, and Jesus Christ, and the great things of the Gospel: they have a new sense of the truth of them, and they affect them in a new manner; though it is very far from being always alike with them, neither can they revive a sense of things when they please. Their hearts are often touched, and sometimes filled, with new sweetnesses and delights; there seems to be an inward ardor and burning of heart that they express, the like to which they never experienced before; sometimes, perhaps, occasioned only by the mention of Christ's name, or some one of the divine perfections: there are new appetites, and a new kind of breathings and pantings of heart, and groanings that cannot be uttered [*Romans 8:26*]. There is a new kind of inward labor and struggle of soul towards heaven and holiness. ***The Great Awakening (WJE Online Vol. 4)***

'Tis the Spirit in the saints that seeks the blessing of God by faith and prayer; and, as the Apostle says, with groanings that cannot be uttered, *Romans 8:26*. Likewise, the Spirit also helpeth our infirmities. For we know not what we should pray for as we ought, but the Spirit itself maketh intercession for us with groanings that cannot be uttered. ***Sermons and Discourses 1720–1723 (WJE Online Vol. 10)***

64. Resolved, when I find those "groanings which cannot be uttered," of which the Apostle speaks [*Romans 8:26*], and those "breakings of soul

for the longing it hath," of which the Psalmist speaks, *Psalms 119:20*, that I will promote them to the utmost of my power, and that I will not be weary of earnestly endeavoring to vent my desires, nor of the repetitions of such earnestness. July 23 and Aug. 10, 1723. ***Letters and Personal Writings (WJE Online Vol. 16)***

And oftentimes for want of expressions they (the saints) are forced to content themselves with groans that cannot be uttered, *Romans 8:26*. But in heaven they shall have no such hindrance. They will have no dullness or unwieldiness, no corruption of heart to fight against divine love and hinder suitable expressions, no clog of a heavy lump of clay, or an unfit organ for an inward heavenly flame. They shall have no difficulty in expressing all their love. Their souls, which are like a flame of fire with love, shall not be like a fire pent up but shall be perfectly at liberty. The soul which is winged with love shall have no weight tied to the feet to hinder its flight. There shall be no want of strength or activity, nor any want of words to praise the object of their love. They shall find nothing to hinder them in praising or seeing God, just as their love inclines. Love naturally desires to express itself; and in heaven the love of the saints shall be at liberty to express itself as it desires, either towards God or one another. ***Ethical Writings (WJE Online Vol. 8)***

Romans 8:27

And being sensible of our own weakness, and the deceitfulness of our own hearts, and our proneness to forget our most solemn vows and lose our resolutions; we promise to be often strictly examining ourselves by these promises, especially before the sacrament of the Lord's Supper; and beg of God that he would, for Christ's sake keep us from wickedly dissembling in these our solemn vows; and that he who searches our hearts [*Romans 8:27*] and ponders the path of our feet [*Proverbs 4:26*] would from time to time help us in trying ourselves by this covenant, and help us to keep covenant with him, and not leave us to our own foolish wicked and treacherous hearts. ***The Great Awakening (WJE Online Vol. 4)***

And being sensible of our own weakness, and the deceitfulness of our own hearts, and our proneness to forget our most solemn vows and lose our resolutions; we promise to be often strictly examining ourselves by these promises, especially before the sacrament of the Lord's Supper; and beg of God that he would, for Christ's sake keep us from wickedly dissembling in these our solemn vows; and that he who searches our hearts

[*Romans 8:27*] and ponders the path of our feet [*Proverbs 4:26*] would from time to time help us in trying ourselves by this covenant, and help us to keep covenant with him and not leave us to our own foolish, wicked and treacherous hearts. ***Letters and Personal Writings (WJE Online Vol. 16)***

Romans 8:28

"And we know that all," etc. The Apostle had before observed that the whole creation groaned in earnest expectation of "the manifestation of the sons of God" *Romans 8:19*, and also that the Spirit of God made "intercession for us with groanings that cannot be uttered" *Romans 8:26*, and helped our infirmities in our groaning and waiting for the same thing, viz. the adoption or redemption of our body, and the perfecting of our salvation. And this leads the Apostle to observe that all things do befriend the saints in this matter, and work together for the bringing them to that perfected salvation. And the reason why they do so is given in the following verses, viz. because this is what God eternally decreed, and for this end called them, and is immutably resolved to bring them to it. And God being for it, he makes all others work together to bring it to pass, as [the] *Romans 8:31*. ***The "Blank Bible" (WJE Online Vol. 24)***

1st, that notwithstanding the truth of that saying of the Apostle, *Romans 8:28*, the saints have cause to lament their leanness and barrenness, and that they are guilty of so much sin, not only as it is to the dishonor of God, but also as that which is like to be to their own eternal loss and damage. ***Religious Affections (WJE Online Vol. 2)***

Love to God disposes men meekly to bear the injuries which they receive, because it sets persons very much above the injuries of men. It does so in two respects. It sets men above the reach of the injuries of men. None can hurt those who are true lovers of God. Their life is hid with Christ in God [*Colossians 3:3*]. God is their Father and Protector, and carries them on high on eagle's wings. *Romans 8:28*, "All things work together for good to them that love God." ***Ethical Writings (WJE Online Vol. 8)***

Another thing may be noted, which is, that if the saying of the Apostle, *Romans 8:28*, "All things shall work together for good to them that love God," holds true in this sense, that while a man continues in the love of God, that love of God will be an occasion of everything's turning to his good all trials and opposition, this excellent and divine principle is of so wholesome and salutary a nature that it sucks sweetness and happiness out of everything, even those things that in their direct tendency are most against the saints. ***Notes on Scripture (WJE Online Vol. 15)***

Nothing can be inferred from that promise in *Romans 8:28*, tending to set aside or abate the influence of motives to earnest endeavors to avoid all sin, and to increase in holiness, and abound in good works, from a view to an high and eminent degree of glory in the eternal world. ***Notes on Scripture (WJE Online Vol. 15)***

Because conversion is a work that is done at once, and not gradually. If saving grace differed only in degree from what went before, then the making a man a good man would be a gradual work; it would be the increasing the grace that he has, till it comes to such a degree as to be saving—at least it would be frequently so. But that the conversion of the heart is not a work that is thus gradually wrought, but that it is wrought at once, appears by Christ's converting the soul being represented by his calling of it. *Romans 8:28–30*. ***The "Miscellanies," (Entry Nos. 501–832) (WJE Online Vol. 18)***

All the creatures in all their motions, operations and changes are seeking this end, viz. the perfect redemption of the elect, and never will be at rest till that glorious and eternal reign of the saints is established. And therefore 'tis said there in that context, *Romans 8:28–30*. ***The "Miscellanies," (Entry Nos. 501–832) (WJE Online Vol. 18)***

Romans 8:29

Arg. II. If God don't foreknow the volitions of moral agents, then he did not foreknow the *fall* of man, nor of angels, and so could not foreknow the great things which are *consequent* on these events; such as his sending his Son into the world to die for sinners, and all things pertaining to the great work of redemption; all the things which were done for four thousand years before Christ came, to prepare the way for it; and the incarnation, life, death, resurrection and ascension of Christ; and the setting him at the head of the universe, as king of heaven and earth, angels and men; and the setting up his church and kingdom in this world, and appointing him the judge of the world; and all that Satan should do in the world in opposition to the kingdom of Christ: and the great transactions of the day of judgment, that men and devils shall be the subjects of, and angels concerned in; they are all what God was ignorant of before the fall. And if so, the following scriptures, and others like them, must be without any meaning, or contrary to truth: *Ephesians 1:4*, "According as he hath chosen us in him before the foundation of the world." *I Peter 1:20*: "Who verily was foreordained before the foundation of the world." *II Timothy 1:9*, "Who hath saved us, and called us with an holy calling; not according to our works, but according to his own purpose, and grace, which was given us in Christ Jesus before the world began." So, *Ephesians 3:11* (speaking of the wisdom of God in the work of redemption), "According to the eternal purpose which he purposed in Christ Jesus." *Titus 1:2*, "In hope of eternal life, which God, that cannot lie, promised before the world began." *Romans 8:29*, "Whom he did foreknow, them he also did predestinate," etc. *I Peter 1:2*, "Elect, according to the foreknowledge of God the Father." ***Freedom of the Will (WJE Online Vol. 1)***

The elect are all "predestinated to be conformed to the image of the Son of God, that he might be the first-born among many brethren" (*Romans 8:29*). "As we have borne the image of the first man, that is earthly, so we must also bear the image of the heavenly: for as is the earthy, such are they also that are earthy; and as is the heavenly, such are they also that are heavenly" (*I Corinthians 15:47–49*). Christ is full of grace; and Christians "all receive of his fullness, and grace for grace": i.e. there is grace in Christians answering to grace in Christ, such an answerableness as there is between the wax and the seal; there is character for character: such kind of graces, such a spirit and temper, the same things that belong to Christ's character, belong to theirs. That disposition wherein Christ's character does in a special manner consist, therein does his image in a special manner consist. Christians that shine by reflecting the light of the Sun of Righteousness, do shine with the same sort of brightness, the same mild, sweet and pleasant beams. These lamps of the spiritual temple, that are enkindled by fire from heaven, burn with the same sort of flame. The branch is of the same nature with the stock and root, has the same sap, and bears the same sort of fruit. The members have the same kind of life with the head. It would be strange if Christians should not be of the same temper and spirit that Christ is of . . . ***Religious Affections (WJE Online Vol. 2)***

This love that God has to his saints that is thus everlasting, is not only general, as God did from all eternity love saints, i.e. loved their character; the qualifications of saints were what he naturally delighted in. But his love to the particular persons is from eternity. He did as it were know them by name, and set his love in such particular saints. And therefore God is said to have foreknown his saints; i.e. he from all eternity saw them particularly, and knew them as his own. *Romans 8:29*, "For whom he did foreknow, he also did Predestinate." ***Sermons and Discourses, 1734–1738 (WJE Online Vol. 19)***

"For whom he did foreknow, he also did predestinate to be conformed to the image of his Son." This is the sum of what the elect are predestinated to, viz. "to be conformed to the image of his Son," to be made like his Son, and to have communion with him in his holiness and in his happiness. They are predestinated to be conformed to his Son in his death, in dying to sin and the world, and in his resurrection, by being quickened from being dead in trespasses and sins, and also in their bodies being raised, Christ the first fruits, and afterwards those that are Christ's at his coming. They are conformed to Christ in his justification. When Christ rose, he was justified; and believers in their justification do but partake with him in his justification, as *Romans 8:34*. They are conformed to Christ in his relation to the Father, or in his sonship, and are made also the children of God, so that they are his brethren, only he is the firstborn among them, as the Apostle here observes. They are conformed to Christ in the Father's love to him, and are partakers with him in it as members. They are conformed to Christ in his being heir of the world, and they are joint heirs. They are conformed to Christ in his exaltation and glorification, for he and they shall be glorified together. They are conformed to him in ascension into heaven; they shall also ascend. They are conformed to him in the glorification of his body, for their bodies shall be made like unto his glorious body. They are conformed to him in his enjoyment of the Father in heaven; they by being members of him partake with him in his enjoyment of the Father's infinite love, and in his joy in the Father. His joy is fufilled in them, and the glory which the Father has given him, he has given them. They are conformed to him in his reigning over the world. They sit with him in his throne, and they have power over the nations, and they shall rule them with a rod of iron, and as the vessels of a potter shall they be broken to shivers, even as he received of his Father. They shall be conformed unto him in his judging the world, for the saints shall judge the world; yea, they shall sit with Christ in judging angels. This glory, this excellency and happiness that consists in the saints' being conformed to Christ, is the sum of the good that they are predestinated to; and the whole of their conformity to Christ is what the Apostle has respect [to], and not only their being made like him in conversion and sanctification. "For whom he did foreknow." To judge of the force of this expression, see *Matthew 25:12*, *Deuteronomy 33:9*, and *John 9:21*, *Psalms 31:7*. In *Exodus 2:25*, "God had respect unto them"; in the original, "God knew them." Thus מוֹדַע in the

Hebrew is a kinsman or near friend, and מוֹדַעַת, kindred and affinity, from יָדַע, "to know." See *Job 9:21*, and *Proverbs 12:10*, "Regardeth the life of his beast"; in the original, "knoweth the life of his beast." ***The "Blank Bible" (WJE Online Vol. 24)***

Romans 8:30

And as God carries on the work of converting the souls of fallen men through all these ages, so he goes on to justify them, to blot out all their sins and to accept them as righteous in his sight through the righteousness of Christ, and to adopt them and receive them from being the children of Satan to be his own children. So he also goes on to sanctify, or to carry on the work of his grace which he has begun in them, and to comfort them with the consolation of his spirit and to glorify them, to bestow upon them when their bodies die that eternal glory which is the fruit of the purchase of Christ. That is the *Romans 8:30*: "Whom he did predestinate [them he also called: and whom he called, them he also justified: and whom he justified, them he also glorified]." ***A History of the Work of Redemption (WJE Online Vol. 9)***

Those that God is pleased to convert and call unto Jesus Christ, them he justified. *Romans 8:30*, "Whom he called, them he also justified." As soon as ever they accept of Jesus Christ and come to him, their sins are all blotted out. Whatsoever wickedness they have been guilty of, God remembers it no more, and they are released from punishment. And not only so, but they are taken into favor, and are adjudged to eternal life; they have a right given them to all those glorious blessings which Christ purchased. ***Sermons and Discourses: 1723–1729 (WJE Online Vol. 14)***

Nor did God choose men because he foresaw that they would believe and come to Christ. Faith is the fruit of election and not the cause of it; *Acts 13:48*, "As many as were ordained to eternal life believed." 'Tis because God hath chosen men that he calls them to Christ and causes them to come to him. To suppose that election is from the foresight of faith is to place calling before election, which is contrary to the order in which the Scriptures represents things; *Romans 8:30*, "Whom he did predestinate, them he also called." ***Sermons and Discourses, 1730–1733 (WJE Online Vol. 17)***

This verse proves perseverance two ways. First, it is said, "Whom he did predestinate, them he also called." We are to understand it, they and they only; so that all that are called are predestinated or elected. And those that are elected, they can't finally fall away (*Matthew 24:24*). Secondly, we are told that all that are called are justified and glorified; so that all that are called shall go to heaven. ***The "Blank Bible" (WJE Online Vol. 24)***

Romans 8:31

We go too far when we look upon the success that God gives to some persons, in making them the instruments of doing much good, as a testimony of God's approbation of those persons and all the courses they take. It is a main argument that has been made use of to defend the conduct of some of those ministers, that have been blamed as imprudent and irregular, that God has smiled upon them and blessed them, and given them great success, and that however men charge them as guilty of many wrong things, yet 'tis evident that God is with them, and then who can be against them [*Romans 8:31*]? And probably some of those ministers themselves, by this very means, have had their ears stopped against all that has been said to convince 'em of their misconduct. But there are innumerable ways that persons may be misled, in forming a judgment of the mind and will of God, from the events of providence. If a person's success be a reward of something that God sees in him, that he approves of, yet 'tis no argument that he approves of everything in him. ***The Great Awakening (WJE Online Vol. 4)***

Love to God disposes men meekly to bear the injuries which they receive, because it sets persons very much above the injuries of men. It does so in two respects. It sets men above the reach of the injuries of men. None can hurt those who are true lovers of God. Their life is hid with Christ in God [*Colossians 3:3*]. God is their Father and Protector, and carries them on high on eagle's wings. *Romans 8:28*, "All things work together for good to them that love God." Ver. *Romans 8:31*, "If God be for us, who can be against us?" ***Ethical Writings (WJE Online Vol. 8)***

This impulse to activism among children of Reformed Christianity derives chiefly from the high Calvinistic doctrine of divine sovereignty. One who is called to be the obedient servant of a God whose purposes in history cannot be thwarted is prepared to face every foe with indomitable courage: "If God is for us, who can be against us?" (*Romans 8:31*). The Calvinist's quest for assurance of his calling, moreover, took him quickly to the question, "How can I know I am of the elect?" Calvin warned that a univocal answer is impossible, since such matters are locked in the inscrutable counsels of God; but he suggested nevertheless some presumptive evidences of election, one of which was an upright life of strict obedience to the divine will. ***The Great Awakening (WJE Online Vol. 4)***

Romans 8:32

If we take good notice of the Apostle's discourse in the Romans 8, it will be apparent that his words by no means imply or intend so much. The context leads us to understand that God is for the saints, and works for them, each person of the Godhead: God the Father, who "spared not his own Son" (Romans 8:32), and justifies the saints (Romans 8:33) . . . ***Notes on Scripture (WJE Online Vol. 15)***

When I think how great this happiness is, sometimes it is ready to seem almost incredible. But the death and sufferings of Christ make everything credible that belongs to this blessedness; for if God would so contrive to show his love in the manner and means of procuring our happiness, nothing can be incredible in the degree of the happiness itself. If all that God doth about it be of a piece, he will also set infinite wisdom on work to make their happiness and glory great in the degree of it. If God "spared not his own Son, but delivered him up for us all, how shall he not with him also freely give us all things?" [*Romans 8:32*]. Nothing could have been such a confirmation of their blessedness as this. If nothing be too much to be given to man, and to be done for man in the means of procuring his happiness, nothing will be too much to be given to him as the end, no degree of happiness too great for him to enjoy. ***The "Miscellanies," (Entry Nos. 501–832) (WJE Online Vol. 18)***

Judges 15:18. "And called on the Lord, and said, Thou hast given this great deliverance into the hand of thy servant; and now shall I die for thirst, and fall into the hand of the uncircumcised?" As Sampson in most of his wonderful acts was certainly intended as a type of Christ, and his miraculous conflicts with and victories over his enemies shadows of Christ's great conflict with the powers of darkness and victory over them, so this that we have here an account of is probably a representation of Christ's intercession, by which he obtained the Holy Spirit after his sufferings, pleading those sufferings, that great battle and victory, and also the prayer of believers who are the members of Christ, or the church, which is as it were Christ, using that argument with God, that seeing God hath wrought that great redemption for us by that conflict and victory of Christ, may they not well think his mercy sufficient to give them the Holy Spirit, that living water, that they may not die for thirst and fall into the hands of the mortal enemies of their souls, which is the same argument which is mentioned, *Romans 5:6–10* and *Romans 8:32*. Christ pleads this argument in heaven, for if his elect people perish with thirst, 'tis all one in his view and God's view, as if he perished with thirst. And he pleads this argument by his spirit (the spirit of faith and prayer in his saints). ***The "Blank Bible" (WJE Online Vol. 24)***

The saints in heaven will praise God for bestowing glory upon them; but the actual bestowment of glory upon them, after it has been purchased by the blood of Christ, is in no measure so great a things as the purchasing of it by his blood. For Christ, the eternal Son of God, to become man, and to lay down his life, was a far greater thing than the glorifying of all the saints that ever have been, or ever will be glorified, from the beginning of the world to the end of it. The giving Christ to die, comprehends all other mercies: for all other mercies are through this. The giving of Christ is a greater thing than the giving of all things else for the sake of Christ. This evidently appears, from *Romans 8:32*. "He who spared not his own Son, but delivered him up for us all, how shall he not with him also freely give us all things?" ***Sermons and Discourses, 1734–1738 (WJE Online Vol. 19)***

Romans 8:32, If we would judge what God is willing to do, or what he can find it in his heart to do, for his people, let us consider what he actually hath done. He hath given his only begotten Son to die for them. The consideration of this great and wonderful act and gift of God, is argument enough. That single argument is in this case equivalent to a thorough demonstration; in *Romans 8:32*, "He that spared not his own Son, but delivered him up for us all, how shall he not with him also freely give us all things?" God gave his Son, a person that was God, to die and be made a curse for us. ***Sermons and Discourses, 1734–1738 (WJE Online Vol. 19)***

Romans 8:33

And which is much more, that which has been condemned in you by man, and for which you have suffered from them, is doubtless approved of by God; and I trust you will have a glorious reward from him: for the cause you suffer in is plainly the cause of God. And if God be for us, who can be against us? [*Romans 8:31*]. If he justifies, what need we care who condemns? [*Romans 8:33*]. ***Letters and Personal Writings (WJE Online Vol. 16)***

Romans 8:34

Christ's exaltation, viz. his rising from the dead and his ascending into heaven, is often insisted on in the gospel as being the great evidence that what Christ had done and suffered was sufficient for us. So it is, *Romans 8:34*, "Who is he that condemneth? It is Christ that died, yea rather, that is risen again, who is even at the right hand of God, who also maketh intercession for us." So it is said, "Christ was manifest in the flesh, justified in the Spirit" (*1 Timothy 3:16*), i.e. God justified him as mediator, declared by opening his prison doors that what he had done was sufficient. It was the highest demonstration that could be given: for Christ put himself in our stead, and took upon him our sins and became responsible for all. ***Sermons and Discourses: 1723–1729 (WJE Online Vol. 14)***

The context leads us to understand that God is for the saints, and works for them, each person of the Godhead: God the Father, who "spared not his own Son" (*Romans 8:32*), and justifies the saints (*Romans 8:33*), and is the Father of the saints (*Romans 8:14* ff.); and God the Son, who died for them, and rose again, and ascended to the right hand of God for them, and makes continual intercession for them (*Romans 8:34*); and God the Holy Ghost, who bears witness with their spirits, that they are the children of God, and helps their infirmities, and leads and conducts them, etc. (*Romans 8:14–16, Romans 8:23, Romans 8:26–27*). ***Notes on Scripture (WJE Online Vol. 15)***

And indeed the justification of a believer is no other than his being admitted to communion in, or participation of the justification of this head and surety of all believers; for as Christ suffered the punishment of sin, not as a private person but as our surety, so when after this suffering he was raised from the dead, he was therein justified, not as a private person, but as the surety and representative of all that should believe in him; so that he was raised again not only for his own, but also for our justification, according to the Apostle. *Romans 4:25*, "Who was delivered for our offenses, and raised again for our justification." And therefore it is that the Apostle says as he does in *Romans 8:34*, "Who is he that condemneth? it is Christ that died, yea rather that is risen again." ***Sermons and Discourses, 1734–1738 (WJE Online Vol. 19)***

And so long Jesus Christ ruleth in a way of conquest, destroying sin and death and all enemies and redeeming the body and bringing body and soul together, and lastly pronouncing a final sentence; and in this sense it is that the Scripture usually speaks of his sitting at God's right hand to intercede for us (as it is *Romans 8:34*, and by sitting there he meaneth reigning), to destroy enemies, to put us out of danger of death and condemnation. ***The "Miscellanies," (Entry Nos. 1153–1360) (WJE Online Vol. 23)***

They are predestinated to be conformed to his Son in his death, in dying to sin and the world, and in his resurrection, by being quickened from being dead in trespasses and sins, and also in their bodies being raised, Christ the first fruits, and afterwards those that are Christ's at his coming. They are conformed to Christ in his justification. When Christ rose, he was justified; and believers in their justification do but partake with him in his justification, as *Romans 8:34*. ***The "Blank Bible" (WJE Online Vol. 24)***

By these means true saints are brought into a state of freedom from condemnation and all the curses of the law of God. *Romans 8:34*, "Who is he that condemneth?" And by this means they are safe from that dreadful and eternal misery which naturally they are exposed to, and are set on high out of the reach of all their enemies, so the gates of hell and powers of darkness can never destroy them; nor can wicked men, though they may persecute them, ever hurt them. ***Sermons and Discourses, 1743–1758 (WJE Online Vol. 25)***

Romans 8:33–34. Dr. Doddridge renders these verses thus. "Who shall lodge any accusation against the elect of God? Is it God? He who justified!? Who is he that condemneth? Is it Christ? He who hath died? Yea rather, who is risen again, who is now at the right hand of God, and is also making intercession for us?" And the Doctor adds this note. "I here follow the pointing proposed by the learned and ingenious Dr. Samuel Harris in his *Observations*, which greatly illustrates the spirit of the passage, and shows, how justly that author adds, that it is remarkably in the grand manner of Demosthenes." ***The "Blank Bible" (WJE Online Vol. 24)***

Romans 8:35

And again, *Romans 8:35–37*, the Apostle speaks of the love of Christ, that tribulation, distress, persecution, famine, nakedness, peril nor sword could overcome [ver. *Romans 8:35*]. Now suffering in the cause of Christ being so great a fruit of charity, and that which the Apostle elsewhere often speaks of as a fruit of charity, it does not appear likely that he would omit it in this place where he professedly treats of the various fruits of charity. ***Ethical Writings (WJE Online Vol. 8)***

That the saying of the Apostle, "All things work together for good to them that love God," though it be fulfilled in some respect to all saints, and at all times, and in all circumstances, yet is fulfilled more especially and eminently to the saints continuing in the exercise of love to God, not falling from the exercises or failing of the fruits of divine love in times of trial. Then temptations, enemies, and sufferings will be best; such as be will be best for them, working that which is most for their good every way. And they shall be more than conquerors over tribulation, distress, persecution, famine, nakedness, peril, and sword (*Romans 8:35–37*). ***Notes on Scripture (WJE Online Vol. 15)***

But such changes won't change or alter the love of God to his saints. They are liable to feel changes: they may pass through great and sore affliction, may be brought very low, so as to be generally hated and despised by men. They may come down from earthly prosperity to embrace dunghills, and may become the object of the contempt of men, hated and persecuted even to death; as was the case of Job, "But now they that are younger than I have me in derision, whose fathers I would have disdained to have set with the dogs of my flock" (*Job 30:1*); and Heman, "Lover and friend hast thou put far from me, and mine acquaintance into darkness" (*Psalms 88:18*). But yet God's love to them won't fail. *Romans 8:35*, "Who shall separate us from the love of Christ? shall tribulation, or distress, or persecution, or famine, or nakedness, or peril, or sword?" ***Sermons and Discourses, 1734–1738 (WJE Online Vol. 19)***

Romans 8:35–39. In the *Romans 8:35*, the Apostle speaks of the love of the saints to Christ, as is evident by the two verses which follow; and here he asserts the perseverance of their love. In the *Romans 8:38–39*, the Apostle speaks of the constancy and immutability of Christ's love to them; and he gives the latter as the reason of the former. The saints' love will never fail to Christ, because Christ's love won't fail to them; and so he won't suffer their love to fail, as is evident by the manner in which the *Romans 8:37–38* are connected. ***The "Blank Bible" (WJE Online Vol. 24)***

Romans 8:37

We are told that true believers do overcome the world. *1 John 5:4*, "Whatsoever is born of God overcometh the world: and this is the victory that overcometh the world, even our faith." They overcome both the flatteries and the frowns of the world. The sufferings and difficulties of the world are its weapons; and if there be any of these which a believer has not a spirit to encounter for Christ's sake, then by these weapons or sufferings the world has them in subjection and has the victory. But Christ gives his soldiers the victory over the world; yea, they are more than conquerors through

Christ, who hath loved them [*Romans 8:37*]. The promises, we find, are from time to time made to them that overcome. But as to the fearful, or those who have not courage in the warfare, are cowardly soldiers of Christ, and so do not conquer, it is threatened concerning them as in *Revelation 21:8*, "But the fearful, and unbelieving, and the abominable, and murderers, and whoremongers, and sorcerers, and idolaters, and all liars, shall have their part in the lake which burneth with fire and brimstone: which is the second death." ***Ethical Writings (WJE Online Vol. 8)***

Romans 8:38

If we take good notice of the Apostle's discourse in the *Romans 8*, it will be apparent that his words by no means imply or intend so much. The context leads us to understand that God is for the saints, and works for them, each person of the Godhead: God the Father, who "spared not his own Son" (*Romans 8:32*), and justifies the saints (*Romans 8:33*), and is the Father of the saints (*Romans 8:14*ff.); and God the Son, who died for them, and rose again, and ascended to the right hand of God for them, and makes continual intercession for them (*Romans 8:34*); and God the Holy Ghost, who bears witness with their spirits, that they are the children of God, and helps their infirmities, and leads and conducts them, etc. (*Romans 8:14–16, Romans 8:23, Romans 8:26–27*). And all God's creatures, the whole creation groaning and travailing in pain, waiting "for the manifestation of the sons of God" (*Romans 8:19–22*), and even their persecuting enemies (*Romans 8:33–37*), and not only things in this world, but also in the world to come, not only all mankind, but angels and devils (*Romans 8:38*), and all dispensations of providence, not only in bestowing prosperity, but in bringing adversity and chastisements (*Romans 8:35–37*), not only in giving life, but bringing death (*Romans 8:38*)—all things shall befriend the saints and work for their good. But there is nothing in all the context that leads us to suppose that all dispensations of providence that are merely negative, and their negative consequences in withholding grace, or withholding means and advantages, so that no possible advantages could have been greater, or tending to higher degrees of holiness and happiness [also do good]. ***Notes on Scripture (WJE Online Vol. 15)***

ROMANS CHAPTER 9

Romans 9:1

"The Spirit itself beareth witness with our spirit," etc. That in *Romans 9:1*, "My conscience bearing me witness in the Holy Ghost," or "in the Holy Spirit," may serve to ascertain the Apostle's meaning in this place. For in that place the Apostle speaks of witnessing to his grace or divine virtue in a particular instance, as here in the general. And the same two things are spoken of as concerned in testifying, viz. the Holy Spirit and his own spirit or conscience. *The "Blank Bible" (WJE Online Vol. 24)*

Romans 9:1–3

The Apostle Paul, though a man as much resigned and devoted to God, and under the power of his love, perhaps as any mere man that ever lived, yet had a peculiar concern for his countrymen the Jews, the rather on that account that they were his brethren and kinsmen according to the flesh; he had a very high degree of compassionate grief for them, insomuch that he tells us he had great heaviness and continual sorrow of heart for them, and could wish himself accursed from Christ for them [*Romans 9:1–3*]. *The Great Awakening (WJE Online Vol. 4)*

Romans 9:3

["For I could wish that myself were accursed from Christ."] In the original, it is, "That myself were anathema from Christ." *Anathema* comes from *anatithemi*; *sepono*, [from] *seorsim pono*. The Apostle's meaning probably is that he was willing that Christ should so order it that he should in this world be cut off from the society and privileges of his visible people as an excommunicated person, and also be cut off from the earth by an accursed death, death at last, dying under the hidings of God's face, and dreadful fruits of his displeasure for a time, as Christ did, and thus to suffer from Christ for the Jews, as Christ, who was made a curse for us, suffered from God the Father, who was despised and rejected of men, cast out of the synagogue as an accursed person while he lived, and at last died an accursed death for us. As Christ loved us, so this apostle loved his brethren.

"For I could wish that myself were accursed from Christ," etc. Dr. Doddridge renders it, "'I could wish that I myself were made an anathema after the example of Christ,' i.e. like him exposed to all the execrations of an enraged people, and even to the infamous and accursed death of crucifixion itself. "And the Doctor adds this note." This sense is given by the learned Dr. Waterland, who urges the manner in which ἀπό is used, *2 Timothy 1:3*, ἀπὸ τῶν προγόνων, 'after the example of the forefathers.' Compare *1 John 3:16*, 'Hereby perceive we the love of God, that he laid down his life for us; and we ought to lay down our lives for the brethren.'" ***The "Blank Bible" (WJE Online Vol. 24)***

Why should it be thought strange that those that are full of the Spirit of Christ should be proportionably, in their love to souls, like to Christ, who had so strong a love to them and concern for them, as to be willing to drink the dregs of the cup of God's fury for them? And at the same time that he offered up his blood for souls, [he] offered up also, as their High Priest, "strong crying and tears" [*Hebrews 5:7*], with an extreme agony, wherein the soul of Christ was as it were in travail for the souls of the elect; and therefore in saving them he is said to "see of the travail of his soul" [*Isaiah 53:11*]. As such a spirit of love to, and concern for souls was the spirit of Christ, so it is the spirit of the church; and therefore the church, in desiring and seeking that Christ might be brought forth in the world, and in the souls of men, is represented, *Revelation 12:2*, as a woman crying, "travailing in birth, and pained to be delivered." The spirit of those that have been in distress for the souls of others, so far as I can discern, seems not to be different from that of the Apostle, who travailed for souls and was ready to wish himself "accursed from Christ" for others [*Romans 9:3*]. And that of the Psalmist, *Psalms 119:53*, "Horror hath taken hold upon me, because of the wicked that forsake thy law." And vs. *Psalms 119:136*, "Rivers of waters run down mine eyes because they keep not thy law." And that of the prophet Jeremiah, *Jeremiah 4:19*, "My bowels! My bowels! I am pained at my very heart! My heart maketh a noise in me! I cannot hold my peace! Because thou hast heard, O my soul, the sound of the trumpet, the alarm of war!" And so chap. *Jeremiah 9:1*, and *Jeremiah 13:17*, and *Jeremiah 14:17*; and *Isaiah 22:4*. We read of Mordecai, when he saw his people in danger of being destroyed with a temporal destruction, *Esther 4:1*, that he "rent his clothes, and put on sackcloth with ashes, and went out into the midst of the city, and cried with a loud and bitter cry." And why then should persons be thought to be distracted, when they can't forbear crying out at the consideration of the misery of those that are going to eternal destruction? ***The Great Awakening (WJE Online Vol. 4)***

Romans 9:3–5

Tis manifest, that something diverse from being visible saints, is often intended by that nation's being called God's people, and that that nation, the family of "Israel according to the flesh," and not with regard to any moral and religious qualifications, were in some sense adopted by God, to be his peculiar and covenant people; from *Romans 9:3–5*, "I could wish myself accursed from Christ for my brethren according to the flesh; who are Israelites; to whom pertaineth the adoption, and the glory, and the *covenants*, and the giving of the law, and the service of God, and the promises; whose are the fathers," etc. I observed, that these privileges here mentioned, are spoken of as belonging to the Jews, "not now as visible saints, not as professors of the true religion, not as members of the visible church of Christ (which they did not belong to) but only as a people of such a nation, such a blood, such an external carnal relation to the patriarchs, their ancestors; Israelites, 'according to the flesh': inasmuch as the Apostle is speaking here of the unbelieving Jews, professed unbelievers, that were out of the Christian church, and open visible enemies to it; and such as had no right at all to the external privileges of Christ's people." I observed further, that in like manner "this Apostle in *Romans 11:28–29* speaks of the same unbelieving Jews, that were enemies to the gospel, as in some respect an elect people, and interested in the calling, promises and covenants, God formerly gave their forefathers, and are still beloved for their sakes. 'As concerning the gospel, they are enemies for your sakes: But as touching the election, they are beloved for the fathers' sakes. For the gifts and calling of God are without repentance.'" ***Ecclesiastical Writings (WJE Online Vol. 12)***

Romans 9:4

["To whom pertaineth the adoption and the glory."] The same glory is doubtless here meant whose departure was lamented when the ark was taken, when it was cried by the true friends of Israel, "The glory is departed from Israel" [*1 Samuel 4:21*], meaning the ark and the cloud of glory in which God appeared above upon it, or rather, Jesus Christ, with respect to these tokens of his friendly presence. ***The "Blank Bible" (WJE Online Vol. 24)***

Romans 9:5

"Who is over all." Or "above all." This is mentioned with regard to their fathers, Abraham, Isaac, and Jacob, referred to in the foregoing words, who were excellent persons and high in dignity; but Christ is far above them. ***The "Blank Bible" (WJE Online Vol. 24)***

The great and main end of separating one particular nation from all others, as God did the nation of Israel, was to prepare the way for the coming of the Messiah, who was to proceed of that blood. God's covenant with Abraham and the other patriarchs implied that the Messiah should be of their blood, or their seed according to the flesh. And therefore it was requisite that their progeny according to the flesh should be fenced in by a wall of separation, and made God's people. If the Messiah had been born of some of the professors of Abraham's religion, but of some other nation, that religion being propagated from nation to nation, as 'tis now under the gospel, it would not have answered the covenant with Abraham, for the Messiah to have been born of Abraham's seed only in this sense. The Messiah being by covenant so related to Jacob's progeny according to the flesh, God was pleased, agreeable to the nature of such a covenant, to show great respect to that people on account of that external carnal relation. Therefore the Apostle mentions it as one great privilege, that of them according to the flesh Christ came, *Romans 9:5*. As the introducing the Messiah and his salvation and kingdom was the special design of all God's dealings and peculiar dispensations towards that people, the natural result of this was, that great account should be made of their being of that nation, in God's covenant dealings with them. ***Ecclesiastical Writings (WJE Online Vol. 12)***

Romans 9:6

"Not as though the word of God hath taken none effect." This is said with reference to the covenants and promises mentioned, *Romans 9:4*, "For they are not all Israel." *Psalms 125:5*. ***The "Blank Bible" (WJE Online Vol. 24)***

Those Jews of which the Christian church at first was made up, were the whole body of the people that were truly Israelites; they were the whole of God's Israel. The rest were rejected from being God's people, as much as the ten tribes were when they were removed out of God's sight. They forsook and went off from Israel; they were broken off from that stock by unbelief that the Gentiles might be grafted on. They forsook the God of Israel, the King of Israel, the priesthood, temple worship and ordinances of Israel; and God withdrew the tokens of his presence from among them, and removed 'em out of his sight by sending them into captivity, as he did the ten tribes. According to the Apostle's observation, "They are not all Israel, that are of Israel" [*Romans 9:6*]. So that those that the Christian proselytes joined themselves to were the remnant of Israel, or that part of the nation of Israel that yet remained and had not departed, and were not rejected from being any more of Israel, or God's people. God threatened (*Numbers 14:12*) that he would disinherit the whole congregation of Israel, and make of Moses a great nation. If he had so done, proselytes joining themselves to his posterity would have been Israelites nevertheless for his being but one of so many hundred thousands. ***The "Miscellanies," (Entry Nos. 501–832) (WJE Online Vol. 18)***

Romans 9:7

'Tis evident that the natural relation that any bare to Abraham or Israel, was not the main foundation of their being denominated children of Abraham or of Israel, in divine style, but some relation that is more spiritual; as appears by *Genesis 21:12*, "In Isaac shall thy seed be called." That is, he and his posterity shall be accounted thy seed, and not any other of thy posterity; and accordingly Ishmael, the son of his handmaid, and the children that he had by his lawful wife Keturah, were excluded. Thus the Apostle argues from hence, *Romans 9:7*, "Neither, because they are the seed of Abraham, are they children: but, In Isaac shall thy seed be called." And so in Esau and Jacob, that were both the sons of Isaac by the same woman and at the same birth, and though Esau was the first-born. ***The "Miscellanies," (Entry Nos. 501–832) (WJE Online Vol. 18)***

Romans 9:11–13

["For the children not being yet born, neither having done either good or evil. . . . Jacob have I loved, and Esau have I hated."] I.e. neither having been guilty of any actual sin, not but that they were respected as being both in their corruptness. Esau was hated as corrupt. For 'tis manifest, that drift and argument of the Apostle leads us to understand no more than that it was before either of them had actually done either good or evil, and therefore they either had or could distinguish themselves one from another by doing good or evil. And so they were looked upon as both in the same state, whence it appears that it was only the purpose of God, according to election, that distinguished them, and not they that distinguished themselves by doing either good or evil. ***The "Blank Bible" (WJE Online Vol. 24)***

Romans 9:11

That BY WORKS the Apostle means any *good works* whatsoever, and not only works of the ceremonial law, nor perfect obedience only, appears by *Romans 9:11*. "For the children not being yet born, NEITHER HAVING DONE ANY GOOD OR EVIL, that the purpose of God according to election might stand, not of works, but of him that calleth." ***Writings on the Trinity, Grace, and Faith (WJE Online Vol. 21)***

Romans 9:13

God in election set his love upon those that he elected; *Romans 9:13*, "Jacob have I loved, and Esau have I hated"; *Jeremiah 31:3*, "I have loved thee with an everlasting love: therefore with lovingkindness have I drawn thee"; and, in the forementioned place, *1 John 4:19*, "We love him, because he first loved us." God of infinite goodness and benevolence can love those that have no excellency to merit or attract it. The love of man is consequent upon some loveliness in the object, but the love of God is enticed out to it and the cause of it. ***Sermons and Discourses, 1730–1733 (WJE Online Vol. 17)***

Romans 9:15

'Tis an evidence that the Apostle, in the 9th of Romans, has not respect only to an election and dereliction of nations or public societies, because one instance that he produces to illustrate and confirm what he says, is the dereliction of a particular person, even Pharaoh, *Romans 9:17*. So 'tis an instance of God's mercy to a particular person, even Moses, when he says to Moses, "I will have mercy on whom I will have mercy, and will have compassion," etc. ***"Controversies" Notebook (WJE Online Vol. 27)***

Romans 9:15–16

ELECTION NOT FROM A FORESIGHT OF WORKS, or conditional, or depending on the condition of men's wills, as is evident by *2 Timothy 1:9*, "Who hath saved us, and called us with an holy calling, not according to our works, but according to his own purpose and grace, which was given us in Christ Jesus before the world began"; *Philippians 2:13*, "For 'tis God that worketh in you both to will and to do of his own good pleasure"; *Romans 9:15–16*, "I will have mercy on whom I will have mercy, . . . So then 'tis not of him that willeth, nor of him that runneth, but of God that showeth mercy." ***"Controversies" Notebook (WJE Online Vol. 27)***

Romans 9:16

God don't bestow this great mercy upon some and not upon others because some are more deserving of it than others, because they are of a better disposition naturally, or because they done more good, han't been so wicked in their lives as others. Those that are converted, before are as other men, under the same power of sin and living a sinful life. As the Apostle says in the third verse of the context, "We also were sometimes foolish, disobedient, deceived, serving divers lusts and pleasures, living in malice and envy, hateful, and hating one another." God takes them out of the midst of their sins and makes them partakers of the divine nature. *Romans 9:16*, "'Tis not of him that willeth, nor of him that runneth, but of God that showeth mercy." ***Sermons and Discourses: 1723–1729 (WJE Online Vol. 14)***

'Tis not from the foresight of any, neither moral nor natural qualifications, or any circumstances, that God chooses men: not because he sees that some men are of a more amiable make, a better natural temper, or genius, not because he foresees that some men will have better abilities and will have more wisdom than others and so will be able to do more service for God than others that he chooses, or because he foresees that they will be great and rich and so under greater advantages to do service for him; *1 Corinthians 1:27–28*, "God hath chosen the foolish things of this world to confound the wise; and God hath chosen the weak things of the world to confound the things which are mighty; and base things of the world, and things which are despised, hath God chosen, yea, and things which are not, to bring to naught things that are." Nor is it from any foresight of men's endeavors after conversion, because he sees that some will do much more than others to obtain heaven, that he chooses. But God chooses them and therefore awakens them and stirs them up to strive for conversion; *Romans 9:16*, "not of him that willeth, but of God that showeth mercy." ***Sermons and Discourses, 1730–1733 (WJE Online Vol. 17)***

"Tis not of him that willeth nor of him that runneth, but of God that showeth mercy." By such an expression in the Apostle's phraseology from time to time is meant the use of endeavors, whereby they seek the benefit they would obtain. So what he says is agreeable to what he says, *Romans 11:4–7*, where he particularly shows that 'tis God that preserves the remnant, and that it [is] of the election of his grace or free kind[ness], and not of their works, but in such a way of freedom as is utterly inconsistent with its being of their works; and in *Romans 11:7*, that it is not determined by their seeking but God's election. If the Apostle here, as Mr. Taylor says, has respect to bodies of men, to the posterity of Esau and Jacob, etc. yet this he applies to distinctions made in these days of the gospel, and that distinction made between those that were in the Christian church and those that were not—particularly some of the Jews that were in the Christian [church] and others of the same nation that were not—which [is] made by some believing and accepting Christ and others' rejection, [by] that faith which they professed to be with all their hearts, that faith which was a mercy and virtue, and the want of which was a fault, as by the objection the Apostle supposes, *Romans 9:19*, "Why doth he yet find fault"; the want of which argued hardness of heart (*Romans 9:18*), exposed 'em to wrath and destruction as a punishment of sin (*Romans 9:22*), and exposes persons to be like the inhabitants of Sodom and Gomorrah (*Romans 9:29*). ***Writings on the Trinity, Grace, and Faith (WJE Online Vol. 21)***

Romans 9:17

"Even for this same purpose have I raised thee up," etc. For this cause God raised up Pharaoh out of the corrupt mass of mankind, mentioned, *Romans 9:21*. See infra, note on *Romans 9:21*. This scripture will hardly justify our expressing ourselves so that God gives reprobates a being to that end, that he might glorify himself in their destruction. But the expression here used will allow of our supposing that God, in thus doing, viz. raising up Pharaoh to glorify himself in his destruction, had respect to Pharaoh as included in the common corrupt mass of mankind, and as fallen in Adam, being in his loins, where all future mankind by ordinary generation were when he fell, and so fell in him. And for this reason perhaps the word "raised up" is rather used than the word "made" or "created." ***The "Blank Bible" (WJE Online Vol. 24)***

Romans 9:18

The Apostle, in the former part of the verse, "he hath mercy on whom he will have mercy," [has respect] to what God said to Moses, mentioned in the Romans 9:18. In the latter part of the verse, he hath an eye to the case of Pharaoh (mentioned in the immediately foregoing verse), whose heart God so often hardened that he might destroy him. ***The "Blank Bible" (WJE Online Vol. 24)***

The Arminians ridicule our distinction of the secret and revealed will of God, or more properly expressed, our distinction between the decree and law [of God], because we say he may decree one thing and command another; and so they say we hold contrariety and contradiction in God, as if one will of his contradicted and was directly contrary to another. But however, if they will call this a contradiction of wills, we do certainly and absolutely know there is such a thing, so that it is the greatest absurdity to dispute about it. We and they [know it was] God's secret will that Abraham should not sacrifice his son, but yet his command was to do it. [We] do certainly know that God willed that Pharaoh's heart should be hardened, and yet that the hardness of his heart was his sin. We do know that God willed that [the] Egyptians should hate God's people. *Psalms 105:25*, "He turned their heart to hate his people and deal subtilely with his servants." We do know that it was God's will that Absalom should lie with David's wives. *2 Samuel 12:11–12*, "Thus saith the Lord, Behold, I will raise up evil against thee out of thine own house, and I will take thy wives before thine eyes and give them unto thy neighbor; and he shall lie with thy wives in the sight of this sun. For thou didst it secretly, but I will do this thing before all Israel and before the sun." We do certainly know that God willed that Jeroboam and the ten tribes should rebel. The same, we know, may be said of the plunder of the Babylonians; and other instances might be given. The Scripture plainly tells us that God wills to harden some men (*Romans 9:18*), that Christ should be killed by men, [etc.]. ***The "Blank Bible" (WJE Online Vol. 24)***

Romans 9:19

That is mentioned as an objection of some against something in divine revelation—whatever that was—and the objection was, that they could not see how it was agreeable to the moral perfections in God. But yet the Apostle sharply reproves it as a daring presumptuous objection. "Nay," says he, "but, O man, who art thou that repliest against God? Shall the thing formed say to him that formed it, Why hast thou made me thus?" ***Sermons, Series II, January–June 1740 (WJE Online Vol. 55)***

Romans 9:20

How have some of you risen up against God, and in the frame of your minds opposed him in his sovereign dispensations! And how justly upon that account, might God oppose you, and set himself against you! You never yet would submit to God; never could willingly comply with it that God should have dominion over the world, and that he should govern it for his own glory, according to his own wisdom. You a poor worm, a potsherd, a broken piece of an earthen vessel, have dared to find fault, and quarrel with God. *Isaiah 45:9*, "Woe to him that strives with his Maker. Let the potsherd strive with the potsherds of the earth: shall the clay say to him that fashioneth it, What makest thou?" But yet you have ventured to do it. *Romans 9:20*, "Who art thou, O man, that repliest against God?" But yet you have thought you was big enough; you have taken upon you to call God to an account, why he does thus and thus; you have said to Jehovah, "What dost thou?" ***Sermons and Discourses, 1734–1738 (WJE Online Vol. 19)***

Godly men never do actually attain to perfect holiness in this life, but are always very far from it. The most holy of men have found cause to complain of the abundance of corruption that they found remaining in their hearts. [The] apostle Paul [complains], *Romans 7:24*, "O wretched man that I am!" Job, though said to be one perfect and upright, yet says of himself, *Romans 9:20*, that if he should justify himself, his own mouth should condemn him; and if he should say he was perfect, it should also prove him perverse. And in the thirtieth [and thirty-first] verses, that if he should wash himself with snow water, and make his hands never so clean; yet God would plunge him in the ditch, and his own clothes shall abhor him. And we know how God reproved him, and how he was convinced, and humbled, and brought to cry out of himself that he abhorred himself. ***Sermons and Discourses, 1734–1738 [1734] (WJE Online Vol. 19)***

Romans 9:20–21

Isaiah 40:13–14, "Who hath directed the Spirit of the Lord, or being his counselor hath taught him? With whom took he counsel, and who instructed him; and who taught him in the path of judgment, and taught him knowledge, and shewed to him the way of understanding?" *John 3:8*, "The wind bloweth where it listeth; and thou hearest the sound thereof; but canst not tell whence it cometh, and whither it goeth." We hear the sound, we perceive the effect, and from thence we judge that the wind does indeed blow; without waiting, before we pass this judgment, first to be satisfied what should be the cause of the wind's blowing from such a part of the heavens, and how it should come to pass that it should blow in such a manner, at such a time. To judge a priori is a wrong way of judging of any of the works of God. We are not to resolve that we will first be satisfied how God brought this or the other effect to pass, and why he hath made it thus, or why it has pleased him to take such a course, and to use such and such means, before we will acknowledge his work, and give him the glory of it. This is too much for the clay to take upon it with respect to the potter [cf. *Jeremiah 18:6*; *Romans 9:20–21*]. "God gives not account of his matters: his judgments are a great deep: he hath his way in the sea, and his path in the great waters, and his footsteps are not known; and who shall teach God knowledge, or enjoin him his way, or say unto him, What doest thou? We know not what is the way of the Spirit, nor how the bones do grow in the womb of her that is with child; even so we know not the works of God who maketh all." No wonder therefore if those that go this forbidden way to work, in judging of the present wonderful operation, are perplexed and confounded. We ought to take heed that we don't expose ourselves to the calamity of those who pried into the ark of God, when God mercifully returned it to Israel, after it had departed from them [*1 Samuel 6:19*]. ***The "Blank Bible" (WJE Online Vol. 24)***

Romans 9:21

["Hath not the potter power over the clay, of the same lump to make one vessel unto honor, and another unto dishonor?"] 'Tis certainly most natural and most agreeable to the manner, by this lump or mass, to understand the corrupt mass of mankind. The mass intended is that wherein both vessels of honor and dishonor lay undistinguished, and out of which they were taken when they were first distinguished by the hands of the potter. But that mass, in which both the chosen and rejected lie undistinguished, and from whence their distinction first begins by the hands of God the potter, is the corrupt mass of fallen mankind. They are all found in this state; a state of sin and misery is common to 'em all, wherein they lie undistinguished till [God] calls some out of the world, and leaves others in it. And then these vessels, which are made out of this mass, are here called vessels of mercy and vessels of wrath. Now mercy and wrath both do presuppose sin in the very notion of them. ***The "Blank Bible" (WJE Online Vol. 24)***

Romans 9:21 (extended comments)

God has different uses for different men. Some are destined to a baser use as vessels unto dishonor; others are chosen for the most noble use, viz. the serving and glorifying of God, and that God may show the glory of divine grace upon them. Here are several things [that] may be observed concerning this election of God, whereby God chooses truly godly persons.

(1) This election supposes that the persons chosen are found amongst others. The word "election" denotes this; it signifies a choosing out. The elect are found by cleansing grace amongst the rest of mankind. They were of the company from amongst whom they are chosen. They were found amongst them not only as they dwell amongst them—elect and reprobate are found mixed together, as tares and wheat—and not only as they are of the same human nature: they are descended of the same first parents and are in the same outward condition.

But they are found amongst them in the same sinfulness and in the same misery. They are alike partakers of original corruption. They are amongst them in the guilt of the first transgression. They are amongst them in being destitute of anything in them that is good. They are amongst them in enmity against God in serving Satan and being in bondage to him. They are amongst them in condemnation to eternal destruction. They are amongst them in being without righteousness. And they are amongst them every way, so that there is no distinction between them prior to the distinction that election makes. There is no respect wherein the elect are not amongst the common multitude of mankind. 'Tis [that] they are chosen from amongst them, and election makes a distinction; *1 Corinthians 4:7*, "Who maketh thee to differ?"; *1 Corinthians 6:11*, "Such were some of you." And therefore,

(2) Nothing foreseen, foreseen excellency or endeavors of the elected, is the motive that influences God to choose them; but election is only from his good pleasure. God's election being the first thing that causes any distinction, it can be no distinction that is already the foresight of which is to [be] considered as prior, that it influences God to choose them.

It is not the seeing of any amiableness in these above the rest that causes God to choose them rather than the rest. God don't choose men because they are excellent, but he makes them excellent because he has chosen them. 'Tis not because God considers them as holy that he chooses them; he chooses them that they might be holy; *Ephesians 1:4–5*, "According as he hath chosen us in him before the foundation of the world, that we should be holy and without blame before him in love: having predestinated us unto the adoption of children by Jesus Christ to himself, according to the good pleasure of his will."

God don't choose them from any foresight of any respect they will have to him more than others. God don't choose men and set his love upon them because they love him, for he hath first loved us; *1 John 4:10*, "not that we loved him, but that he loved us"; and *1 John 4:19*, "because he first loved us."

'Tis not from any foresight of good works, either any good works that men do before or after conversion. But, on the contrary, men do good works because God hath chosen them; *John 15:16*, "Ye have not chosen me, but I have chosen you, and ordained you, that you should go and bring forth much fruit, and that your fruit should remain."

Nor did God choose men because he foresaw that they would believe and come to Christ. Faith is the fruit of election and not the cause of it; *Acts 13:48*, "As many as were ordained to eternal life believed." 'Tis because God hath chosen men that he calls them to Christ and causes them to come to him. To suppose that election is from the foresight of faith is to place calling before election, which is contrary to the order in which the Scriptures represents things; *Romans 8:30*, "Whom he did predestinate, them he also called."

'Tis not from the foresight of any, neither moral nor natural qualifications, or any circumstances, that God chooses men: not because he sees that some men are of a more amiable make, a better natural temper, or genius, not because he foresees that some men will have better abilities and will have more wisdom than others and so will be able to do more service for God than others that he chooses, or because he foresees that they will be great and rich and so under greater advantages to do service for him; *1 Corinthians 1:27–28*, "God hath chosen the foolish things of this world to confound the wise; and God hath chosen the weak things of the world to confound the things which are mighty; and base things of the world, and things which are despised, hath God chosen, yea, and things which are not, to bring to naught things that are." Nor is it from any foresight of men's endeavors after conversion, because he sees that some will do much more than others to obtain heaven, that he chooses. But God chooses them and therefore awakens them and stirs them up to strive for conversion; *Romans 9:16*, "not of him that willeth, but of God that showeth mercy."

Election in Scripture is everywhere referred to [as] God's mere good pleasure; *Matthew 11:26*, "Even so, Father: for so it seemed good in thy sight"; *2 Timothy 1:9*, "not according to our works, but according to his own purpose and grace, which was given us in Christ before the world began."

(3) True Christians are chosen of God from all eternity, not only before they were born but before the world was created. They were foreknown of God and chosen by him out of the world; *Ephesians 1:4*, "according as he hath chosen us in him before the foundation of the world"; and *2 Timothy 1:9*, "according to his own purpose and grace, which was given us in Christ before the world began."

(4) God in election set his love upon those that he elected; *Romans 9:13*, "Jacob have I loved, and Esau have I hated"; *Jeremiah 31:3*, "I have loved thee with an everlasting love: therefore with lovingkindness have I drawn thee"; and, in the forementioned place, *1 John 4:19*, "We love him, because he first loved us." God of infinite goodness and benevolence can love those that have no excellency to merit or attract it. The love of man is consequent upon some loveliness in the object, but the love of God is enticed out to it and the cause of it.

Believers were from all eternity beloved both by the Father and the Son. The eternal love of the Father appears in that, that he from all eternity contrived a way for their salvation and chose Jesus Christ to be their redeemer, and laid help upon him. 'Tis a fruit of this electing love that God sent his Son into the world to die. It was to redeem that certain number that were his chosen; he so loved the chosen; *1 John 4:10*, "Herein is love, not that we loved him, but that he loved us, and sent his Son to be a propitiation for our sins." It is a fruit of the eternal electing love of Jesus Christ that he was willing to come into the world and die for sinners, and that he actually came and died; *Galatians 2:20*, "who loved me, and gave himself for me."

And so conversion, and glorification, and all that is done for a believer from the first to the last is a fruit of electing love.

(5) This electing love of God is singly of every particular person. Some deny a particular election and say that there is no election; there [is] only a general determination that all that believe and obey shall be saved. Some own no more than an absolute election of nations. But God did from all eternally and singly and distinctly choose and set his love upon every particular person that ever believes, as is evident by that place in *Galatians 2:20*, "who loved me, and gave himself for me." God set his love from eternity upon this and that believer as particularly as if there were no others chosen but he. And therefore 'tis represented as though they were mentioned by name. Their names are written in the book of life; *Luke 10:20*, "Rejoice, that your names are written in heaven"; *Revelation 13:8*, "And all that dwell upon earth shall worship him, whose names are not written in the book of life of the Lamb slain from the foundation of the world."

(6) In election, believers were from all eternity given to Jesus Christ. As believers were chosen from all eternity, so Christ was from eternity chosen and appointed to be their redeemer, and he undertook the work of redeeming them. But there was a covenant about it between the Father and Son. Christ, as we have already observed, loved them. This is the account he gives of himself, how it was with him before the world, and one thing is that then he rejoiced in the habitable parts of God's earth and his delights were with the sons of men [*Proverbs 8:31*]. And when he undertook for them, he knew what success he should have. God promised him a certain number, and he had their names, as it were, written in a book; and therefore the book of life is called the Lamb's book; *Revelation 21:27*, "but they that are written in the Lamb's book of life." And he bears their names

upon his heart, as the high priest of old did the names of the tribes of the children of Israel on his breastplate [*Exodus 28:29*]. Christ often calls the elect those that God had given him; *John 17:2*, "As thou hast given him power over all flesh, that he should give eternal life to as many as thou hast given him"; and again, in *John 17:9*, "I pray not for the world, but for them which thou hast given me"; *John 17:11*, "Keep through thy name those whom thou hast given me." ***Sermons and Discourses, 1730–1733 (WJE Online Vol. 17)***

Romans 9:22

["And to make his power known."] The Apostle has reference to what was said of Pharaoh in the *Romans 9:17*, that God raised him up to show his power in him. See *Isaiah 33:13*. "Fitted to destruction." In this the Apostle has not respect to their creation, as if he had said, "created to be destroyed," but to their hardening, mentioned, *Romans 9:18*, which is done in the time of God's enduring them with "much long-suffering," as in the words immediately preceding. See notes on *Romans 9:11–13*, *Romans 9:17*, and *Romans 9:21*. See *Isaiah 32:13*, and *Isaiah 42:13*. ***The "Blank Bible" (WJE Online Vol. 24)***

In that forecited place in the *Romans 9*, we are told of two ends of God's damning wicked men: one is that he may show his wrath and make his power known in their destruction [*Romans 9:22*]; and the other is, as it follows in the *Romans 9:23*, "And that he might make known the riches of his glory on the vessels of mercy." That is, God shows the dreadfulness of his majesty and anger in the destruction of the wicked, in the sight of the godly, that the godly may thereby become the happier by knowing better the riches of his glory: for when they see how dreadful God's anger is, that will make them sensible of the worth of his favor and will make them prize it exceedingly. This argues also that the torments of the damned will be exceeding great. ***Sermons and Discourses: 1723–1729 (WJE Online Vol. 14)***

Hereby God will to a greater degree glorify the terribleness of his wrath. One design he has upon his heart is to [glorify his wrath]; God is willing to show his wrath and make the power of it known (*Romans 9:22*). The word of God, when it is not regarded by men, it is an occasion of filling up the measure of their sin, and so of filling up the measure of their punishments. When it does men no good, it ripens the grapes for the winepress, it fits them for fuel for hellfire. (2) It renders justice in their damnation the more conspicuous. And so God glorifies his justice the more in their destruction, for their guilt becomes greater and more notorious and they become more inexcusable; and their own consciences will condemn them the more and will justify the judge in the sentence he passes upon them. The iniquity of such men cries aloud for vengeance, and the justice of God in the destruction of such men as have refused his word will be especially clear and evident in the sight of men and angels. Thus God is not frustrated. His word don't return to him void. ***Sermons and Discourses, 1730–1733 (WJE Online Vol. 17)***

Romans 9:22–23

The saints and angels in heaven, before whom the wicked will be punished, will doubtless have a very great sight of the infinite greatness and awful majesty of God, against whom sin is committed, and so of the glorious excellency of that Savior and his dying love, that is rejected by sinners; and therefore, will have a sense of the horrible evil of sin that is committed against such a God, and such a Savior an evil in it that is answerable to what God says of it in *Jeremiah 2:12–13*. And therefore, if the punishment they see ben't agreeable to this sight and sense they have of God's glory, and the evil of sin, there will be a visible defect, an unharmoniousness, [an] unanswerableness in the things which they see, one to another. One thing that they behold will tend to depress that idea of God's majesty, that other things tend to raise. Whereas this punishment is designed to raise their idea of God's power and majesty, to impress it with exceeding strength and liveliness upon their minds, and so to raise their sense of the riches and excellency of his love to them. ***The "Miscellanies," 833–1152 (WJE Online Vol. 20)***

Romans 9:22–23

"To show his wrath, and make his power known. . . . And that he might make known the riches," etc.] He does not say, "to show his justice or righteousness," for that is as much showed in God's glorifying and making happy the saints, and much more in some respect. God's justice is more gloriously manifested in the sufferings of Christ for the elect than in the damnation of the wicked.

I am convinced that hell torments will be eternal from one great good the wisdom of God proposes by them, which is, by the sight of them to exalt the happiness, the love and joyful thanksgivings of the angels and men that are saved; which it tends exceedingly to do. I am ready to think that the beholding the sight of the great miseries of those of their species that are damned will double the ardor of their love, and the fullness of the joy of the elect angels and men. It will do it many ways. The sight of the wonderful power, the great and dreadful majesty and authority, and the awful justice and holiness of God manifested in their punishment, will make them prize his favor and love exceedingly the more; and will excite a most exquisite love and thankfulness to him, that he chose them out from the rest to make them thus happy, that God did not make them such vessels of wrath, according to *Romans 9:22–23*, "What if God, willing to show his wrath," etc. "and that he might make known the riches of his glory on the vessels of mercy." And then, only a lively sense of the opposite misery makes any happiness and pleasure double what it would be. Seeing therefore that this happiness of the blessed is to be eternal, the misery of the damned will be eternal also. ***The "Miscellanies": (Entry Nos. a–z, aa–zz, 1–500) (WJE Online Vol. 13)***

Romans 9:23

The word "glory," as applied to God or Christ, sometimes evidently signifies the communications of God's fullness, and means much the same thing with God's abundant and exceeding goodness and grace. So *Ephesians 3:16*, "That he would grant you, according to the riches of his glory, to be strengthened with might, by his Spirit in the inner man." The expression, "according to the riches of his *glory*" is apparently equivalent to that in the same Epistle, ch. *Ephesians 1:7*, "according to the riches of *his grace*." And [in] *Ephesians 2:7*, "The exceeding riches of his grace in his kindness towards us, through Christ Jesus." In like manner is the word "glory" used in *Philippians 4:19*, "But my God shall supply all your need, according to his riches in glory, by Christ Jesus." And *Romans 9:23*, "And that he might make known the riches of his glory, on the vessels of mercy." In this, and the foregoing verse, the Apostle speaks of God's making known two things, his great wrath and his rich grace. The former, on the vessels of wrath, ver. *Romans 9:22*. The latter, which he calls "the riches of his glory," on the vessels of mercy, ver. *Romans 9:23*. So when Moses says, "I beseech thee show me thy *glory*"; God granting his request, makes answer, "I will make all my *goodness* to pass before thee," *Exodus 33:18–19*. ***Ethical Writings (WJE Online Vol. 8)***

God is the giver of the pure heart, and he gives it for this very end, that it may be prepared for the blessedness of seeing. Thus we are taught in the Word of God. The people of God are sanctified and their hearts are made pure, that they may be prepared for glory, as vessels are prepared by the potter for the use he designs. They are elected from all eternity to eternal life, and have purity of heart given them, on purpose to fit them for that which they are chosen to; *Romans 9:23*, "And that he might make known the riches of his glory on the vessels of mercy, which he had afore prepared to glory." We read of the church being arrayed in fine linen, clean and white, by which is signified the church's purity; and it was to prepare her for the enjoyment of Christ (*Revelation 19:7–8*). And in *Revelation 21:2*, the church thus purified is said to be "as a bride adorned for her husband." ***Sermons and Discourses, 1730–1733 (WJE Online Vol. 17)***

But God's declared design in this grand affair is to magnify the infinite riches of his grace. *Romans 9:23*, "That he might make known the riches of his glory on the vessels of mercy." *Ephesians 1:5–7*, "Having predestinated us unto the adoption of children by Jesus Christ to himself, according to the good pleasure of his will, to the praise of the glory of his grace, wherein he hath made us accepted in the beloved. In whom we have redemption through his blood, the forgiveness of sins, according to the riches of his grace." And *Ephesians 2:4–7*, "But God, who is rich in mercy, for his great love wherewith he loved us, even when we were dead in sins, hath quickened us together with Christ, (by grace ye are saved); and hath raised us up together, and made us sit together in heavenly places in Christ Jesus: that in the ages to come he might show the exceeding riches of his grace in his kindness toward us through Christ Jesus." ***Sermons and Discourses, 1734–1738 (WJE Online Vol. 19)***

Romans 9:24

So with respect to calling men into Christ's fellowship and kingdom, this also is ascribed to God. *Romans 8:30*, "whom he did predestinate, them he also called." *Acts 2:39*, "as many as the Lord our God shall call." *1 Corinthians 1:9*, "God is faithful, by whom ye were called unto the fellowship of his Son Jesus Christ our Lord." *1 Thessalonians 2:12*, "That ye would walk worthy of God, who hath called you unto his kingdom and glory," *2 Thessalonians 2:13–14*, "God hath from the beginning chosen you to salvation . . . whereunto he called you by our gospel." *2 Timothy 1:8–9*, "according to the power of God; who hath saved us, and called us with an holy calling, not according to our works, but according to his own purpose and grace." *1 Peter 5:10*, "the God of all grace, who hath called us unto his eternal glory." See *Romans 9:24*, *1 Peter 1:15*. ***The "Miscellanies," (Entry Nos. 1153–1360) (WJE Online Vol. 23)***

Romans 9:27

Here is to [be] observed the success the gospel had among the Jews, for God first began with them. God, being about to reject the main body of that people, first calls in his elect from among them before he forsook them to turn to the Gentiles. It was so in former great and dreadful judgments of God on that nation; the bulk of them were destroyed, and only a remnant saved and reformed. So it was in the rejection of the ten tribes; long before this rejection the bulk of the ten tribes were rejected when they left the true worship of God in Jeroboam's time, and afterwards more fully in Ahab's time, but yet there was a number of them that God reserved. A number left their possessions in those tribes and went up [and settled in the tribes of Judah and Benjamin]. And afterwards, there were seven thousand in Ahab's time [who had not bowed the knee to Baal]. And so in the captivity into Babylon; but a remnant of them returned. So now again [the great part of the people were rejected; but some few were saved]. And therefore the Holy Ghost compares this reservation of a number that were converted by the preaching of the apostles to those former remnants, *Romans 9:27*, "Esaias also crieth concerning Israel, Though the number of the children of Israel [be as the sand of the sea, a remnant shall be saved]." ***A History of the Work of Redemption (WJE Online Vol. 9)***

Romans 9:27–29

We are not to look upon all this time of the rejection and dispersion of the Jews since they have been broken off and the Gentiles grafted in, to be so long a suspension of the fulfillment of the promises made to Abraham, Isaac and Jacob concerning their seed, or an intermission of the bestowment of promised mercies and blessings to them. Those promises are now in actual accomplishment in the mercy bestowed on the Christian church, as well as before in his mercy bestowed on the Jewish church, and in much more full and glorious accomplishment. God has not cast off the seed of Abraham and Israel now in the gospel times in no wise, but hath brought them nearer to himself, and hath, according to frequent prophecies of gospel times, abundantly increased their blessings and the manifestations of his favor to them. When the greater part of the nation of the Jews were broken off by unbelief, the seed of Israel were no more cast off then than in the time of the captivity of Israel and Judah into Assyria and Babylon. For then, by far the greater part of that nation were forever removed from being God's people, and it was but a remnant that was preserved and returned. So there was in the beginning of the gospel a remnant [of] that nation that God preserved to be his people that embraced the gospel and believed in Christ. There were many thousands in that one city, Jerusalem (*Acts 21:20*); and without doubt multitudes in other parts of Judea and in Galilee, and multitudes in other parts of the world where the Jews were dispersed, as we have an account. And this remnant might probably be as great in proportion to the whole nation, as the remnant that were continued and owned as God's people after the captivity into Assyria and Babylon. See *Romans 11*, at the beginning: "I say then, hath God cast away his people? God forbid. For I also am an Israelite, of the seed of Abraham, of the tribe of Benjamin. God hath not cast away his people which he foreknew. Wot ye not what the Scripture saith of Elias? how he maketh intercession to God against Israel saying, Lord they have killed thy prophets, and digged down thine altars; and I am left alone, and they seek my life. But what saith the answer of God unto him? I have reserved to myself seven thousand men, who have not bowed the knee to the image of Baal. Even so then at this present time also there is a remnant according to the election of grace." The prophets very often speak of those that shall be owned by God as his people as but a remnant, and that this remnant shall be but a small number in proportion to the whole. *Isaiah 6:13*, "But in it shall be a tenth, and it shall return, and shall be eaten: as a teil tree, and as an oak, whose substance is in them, when they cast their leaves: so the holy seed shall be the substance thereof." See *Isaiah 24:13*. *Isaiah 10:22*, "For though thy people Israel be as the sand of the sea, yet a remnant of them shall return." *Isaiah 1:9*, "Except the Lord of hosts had left unto us a very small remnant, we should have been as Sodom, and we should have been like unto Gomorrah." Which two last places the Apostle quotes to this purpose, *Romans 9:27–29*. The unbelieving Jews are not the children of Abraham any more than the Ishmaelites and Edomites, because they are disinherited. God threatened in the wilderness that he would disinherit the whole congregation of Israel, and make of Moses a great nation. If he had so done, the promises made to the fathers concerning their seed might have been fulfilled, though it had been only in Moses' posterity. The ten tribes, when they were carried away, they were the greater part of them disinherited and removed from being any more a people, or of Israel; so in gospel times the unbelieving Jews are disinherited. And 'tis only the remnant according to the election of grace that are the seed of Abraham and Israel, though that remnant be exceedingly multiplied by sons and daughters from among the Gentiles, agreeable to ancient prophecies. And this remnant of Israel hath been the mother of thousands of millions, agreeably to the blessing given to Rebekah (*Genesis 24:60*). The Gentiles are their children in the style of the prophets, and therefore the children of Abraham and Israel. As it was of old before Christ came, the people were not Israel because they all came from Israel by natural generation, but the people as a people were derived from him; and so it is now. ***The "Miscellanies," (Entry Nos. 501–832) (WJE Online Vol. 18)***

Romans 9:30–31

"Mr. Locke has offered another exposition of these words, and by the 'righteousness' here spoken of, understands the righteousness of God, in keeping his word with the nation of the Jews, notwithstanding their provocations; or, as he explains it more fully in his notes on *Romans 3:5* to which he refers, God's 'faithfulness' in keeping his promise of saving believers, Gentiles as well as Jews, by righteousness through faith in Jesus Christ. But this seems to be as ill supported as that of Grotius. For I cannot find one single passage in the whole New Testament, where *δικαιοσυνης θεο* is used in that sense. Most certainly it is used in a very different sense in this context, *Romans 3:21*, *Romans 3:23*, and throughout this epistle, where it always signifies, either the righteousness by which we are justified, or that perfection of God which makes such righteousness necessary to our justification. In the former sense it is used, *Romans 9:30–31*, and *Romans 10:4*. And both these senses seem to have place, *Romans 10:3*, where the word is used twice in one verse. And as to the sense which it bears in the *Romans 3:5*, which is the only passage Mr. Locke refers to in support of his opinion, 'tis evidently to be understood there of the justice of God, that perfection which is manifested and displayed in punishing the sin and unrighteousness of men; the sense it likewise bears in the text under consideration. Not to add, that the Apostle speaks here of the 'remission' of the sins of particular persons, even of all that died in faith under the dispensation of the Old Testament, and not of the remission of the sins of the Jews nationally considered, as Mr. Locke is obliged to understand it consistently with the sense of the text. Compare *Hebrews 9:15*." Rawlin on *Justification*, 94–95. *The "Miscellanies," (Entry Nos. 1153–1360) (WJE Online Vol. 23)*

Romans 9:31–32 (extended comments)

Trusting in our own righteousness for justification or acceptance with God, or the having the ground of our expectation of God's favor in a high and false apprehension of our own excellency, as related to God's favor, is a thing fatal to the soul, and what will prevent salvation. This is evident by *Romans 9:31–32*. "But Israel, which followed after the law of righteousness, hath not attained to the law of righteousness. Wherefore? because they sought it not by faith, but as it were by the works of the law." Here 'tis evident:

1. That this that Israel did that is here spoken of is fatal, because 'tis said they attained not to the law of righteousness for this reason; this is given as the main reason of their missing of it. And then it's evident by the context, for that is what the Apostle is speaking of, viz. how the greater part of that nation miss of salvation and shall be vessels of wrath; and indeed, this is what he is upon throughout the whole chapter.

2. That by seeking or following after the law of righteousness by the works of the law, is meant seeking justification by the works of the law. For what is here expressed by following after the law of righteousness, is in the preceding verse, where the Apostle is evidently speaking of the same thing, called following after righteousness, by which is doubtless intended a becoming righteous in the sight of God, or to his acceptance. When it is said, Israel sought or followed after the law of righteousness by the works of the law, 'tis as much as to say, Israel sought and expected to be found in God's appointed way of justification by performing the works of the law.

3. 'Tis evident that by the works of the law here is meant not only a conformity to Jewish ordinances of worship, but our own moral righteousness or excellency, consisting in our obedience to the laws of God in general, whether moral, ceremonial or whatever; because what is called here the works of the law, is called in the *Romans 10:3* their own righteousness, where the same thing is evidently intended by the reference the Apostle has there to what is said here. And doubtless by the works of the law is meant the same as the Apostle means by the righteousness of the law in the *Romans 10:5*, where that expression is evidently used as synonymous with our own righteousness (*Romans 10:3*), and so they

are used as synonymous (*Philippians 3:6*, *Philippians 3:9*). But doubtless by their own righteousness is meant the same as their own goodness or moral excellency, and not only that part of it that consisted in their obedience to the ceremonial law. And again, we often find the works of the law set by this Apostle in opposition to the free grace of God, and therefore thereby must be intended our own excellency. For wherein does grace appear, but in being bestowed on them that are no more excellent, that are so unworthy, so far from deserving anything? *Romans 3:20*, *Romans 3:24*, *Romans 3:27*, *Romans 3:28*; and *Titus 3:5*, where, instead of works of law, the Apostle says works of righteousness; *Romans 11:6* and *Romans 4:4*; *Galatians 5:4*; *Ephesians 2:8*, *Ephesians 2:9*.

And then where the Apostle speaks of the works of the law, when speaking of this matter of justification, he evidently means not only works of the ceremonial, but also moral law, as *Romans 3:20* with the context; and in other places where this matter is treated of, which it is needless to mention.

4. Seeking or following after justification by the works of the law or by our own righteousness, is fatal, as it is a self-exaltation, and upon the account of that high opinion there is of, and dependence upon, our own excellency in it. For doubtless 'tis fatal to our salvation upon the account of that in it, wherein it is especially opposite to God's design in the way of our salvation. This way of man's seeking his own salvation is fatal to man, doubtless because of that in it by which it is contrary to God's way, or to his aim in the way that he has contrived; which is that salvation should be wholly for Christ's sake, and that free grace alone should be exalted, and boasting be excluded, and all glory should belong to God and none to us (*Romans 3:27*, *Ephesians 2:19*, *Romans 4:2*, *1 Corinthians 1:29–31*). Doubtless, therefore, seeking justification by the works of the law is fatal upon the account of the boasting that is included in it. The end of the law is that men may be sensible they have nothing of their own to plead. *Romans 3:19*, "That every mouth may be stopped."

And then 'tis evident that this was the error of the Jews, that are those that are here spoken of, by the accounts we have of them, viz. that they had a high conceit of their own righteousness, and looked upon themselves as very acceptable, and highly valued in the sight of God upon that account. This kind of pride and self–dependence, is what the Pharisees are so often found fault with for, who were the leading sect among the Jews, and were heads and leaders in the Jews' opposition to the gospel (*Matthew 6:2*, *Matthew 6:5*, *Matthew 6:16*; *Matthew 7:3–5*; *Luke 16:15*; *Luke 18:9–12*). And this is mentioned as the fault of the Jews in general (*Romans 2:17–23*). And this is prophesied of as that for which the Jews should be rejected, when the gentiles should be called (*Isaiah 65:6*, with the context). ***The "Miscellanies," (Entry Nos. 501–832) (WJE Online Vol. 18)***

Romans 9:33

Trusting in Christ is implied in the nature of faith, as is evident by *Romans 9:33*, "As it is written, Behold I lay in Sion a stumbling stone and rock of offense: and whosoever believeth on him shall not be ashamed." The Apostle there in the context is speaking of justifying faith. And 'tis evident that trusting in Christ is implied in the import of the word "believeth": for being ashamed, as the word is used in Scripture, is the passion that arises upon the frustration of trust or confidence. ***Writings on the Trinity, Grace, and Faith (WJE Online Vol. 21)***

[*1 John 3:3*. "Every one that hath this hope *in him*."] I.e. "in God," or in Christ. The person spoken of in the foregoing and following words, *ἐπ' αὐτῷ*. The preposition *ἐπί* expresses not the relation of hope to the subject of it, but to its object, as in many places of the New Testament. It signifies the relation of faith, trust, and hope to their object, as *Matthew 27:43*, "He trusted in God"; *Luke 11:22*, "wherein he trusted"; *Luke 18:9*, "trusted in themselves"; *Luke 24:25*, "to believe on all the Prophets," etc.; *Acts 9:42*, "many believed in the Lord"; *Acts 11:17*, "who believed in the Lord"; *Acts 16:31*, "Believe on the Lord Jesus"; *Romans 4:24*, "believe on him"; *Romans 9:33*, "believeth on him"; *Romans 10:11*, "believeth on him"; *Romans 15:12*, "in him shall the Gentiles hope"; *2 Corinthians 1:9*, "should not trust in ourselves, but in God"; *2 Corinthians 2:3*, "confidence in you all"; *1 Timothy 1:16*, "believe on him"; *1 Timothy 4:10*, "hoped in the living God"; *1 Timothy 5:5*, "hoped in God"; *1 Timothy 6:17*, "hope not in uncertain riches"; *Hebrews 2:13*, "trusting in him"; *Hebrews 6:1*, "of faith in God"; *1 Peter 2:6*, "he that believeth on him"; *1 Peter 3:5*, "hoped in God." ***The "Blank Bible" (WJE Online Vol. 24)***

ROMANS CHAPTER 10

Romans 10:2

By having much knowledge, you will be under greater advantages to conduct yourselves with prudence and discretion in your Christian course, and so to live much more to the honor of God and religion. Many who mean well, and are full of a good spirit, yet, for want of prudence, conduct themselves so as to wound religion. Many have a zeal of God, which does more hurt than good, because it is "not according to knowledge" (*Romans 10:2*). The reason why many good men behave no better in many instances, is not so much that they want grace, as that they want knowledge. ***Sermons and Discourses, 1739–1742 (WJE Online Vol. 22)***

'Tis evident that there are counterfeits of all kinds of gracious affections; as of love to God, and love to the brethren, as has been just now observed: so of godly sorrow for sin, as in Pharaoh, Saul, and Ahab, and the children of Israel in the wilderness (*Exodus 9:27, I Samuel 24:16–17* and *I Samuel 26:21, I Kings 21:27, Numbers 14:39–40*); and of the fear of God, as in the Samaritans, who feared the Lord, and served their own gods at the same time (*II Kings 17:32–33*); and those enemies of God we read of, *Psalms 66:3*, who through the greatness of God's power, submit themselves to him, or, as it is in the Hebrew, lie unto him, i.e. yield a counterfeit reverence and submission: so of a gracious gratitude, as in the children of Israel, who sang God's praise at the Red Sea (*Psalms 106:12*), and Naaman the Syrian, after his miraculous cure of his leprosy (*II Kings 5:15*, etc.). So of spiritual joy, as in the stony-ground hearers (*Matthew 13:20*) and particularly many of John the Baptist's hearers (*John 5:35*). So of zeal, as in Jehu (*II Kings 10:16*), and in Paul before his conversion (*Galatians 1:14, Philippians 3:6*), and the unbelieving Jews (*Acts 22:3, Romans 10:2*). ***Religious Affections (WJE Online Vol. 2)***

Holy affections are not heat without light; but evermore arise from some information of the understanding, some spiritual instruction that the mind receives, some light or actual knowledge. The child of God is graciously affected, because he sees and understands something more of divine things than he did before, more of God or Christ and of the glorious things exhibited in the gospel; he has some clearer and better view than he had before, when he was not affected: either he receives some understanding of divine things that is new to him; or has his former knowledge renewed after the view was decayed; *I John 4:7*, "Everyone that loveth . . . knoweth God." *Philippians 1:9*, "I pray that your love may abound more and more, in knowledge and in all judgment." *Romans 10:2*, "They have a zeal of God, but not according to knowledge." ***Religious Affections (WJE Online Vol. 2)***

'Tis not all zealous persons that are truly Christians, nor is it all those that are zealous with a religious zeal. The Jews, that were the enemies of Christ and the apostles, as the apostle Paul bears record of them, had a "zeal of God," i.e. a religious zeal (*Romans 10:2*). And the Apostle himself, while he was a persecuter, had such a zeal, as he says of himself, *Acts 22:3*, "I am verily a man which am a Jew, born in Tarsus, a city of Cilicia, yet brought up in this city at the feet of Gamaliel, and taught according to the perfect manner of the law of the fathers, and was zealous towards God, as ye all are this day." ***Sermons and Discourses, 1739–1742 (WJE Online Vol. 22)***

Romans 10:3

The same is very manifest by *Romans 10:3–4*. "For they being ignorant of God's righteousness, and going about to establish their own righteousness, have not submitted themselves to the righteousness of God. For Christ is the end of the law for righteousness to everyone that believeth." The antithesis here makes it evident that by "God's righteousness" is meant a righteousness, in having which we are righteous. ***Notes on Scripture (WJE Online Vol. 15)***

A being saved by another's righteousness is a thing that men naturally can have no conception of the propriety of. [They are] ignorant of God's righteousness, can't see how they can be saved any other way. They have no faith, ben't taught by the spirit of God. They think right in thinking that it must be by righteousness, and they, being not enlightened, can't see any other righteousness [but their own]. And this makes them keep striving to get a righteousness of their own; *Romans 10:3*, "[they] being ignorant of God's righteousness, and going about to establish their own righteousness, have not submitted themselves unto the righteousness of God." ***Sermons and Discourses, 1730–1733 (WJE Online Vol. 17)***

'Tis evident that by the works of the law here is meant not only a conformity to Jewish ordinances of worship, but our own moral righteousness or excellency, consisting in our obedience to the laws of God in general, whether moral, ceremonial or whatever; because what is called here the works of the law, is called in the *Romans 10:3* their own righteousness, where the same thing is evidently intended by the reference the Apostle has there to what is said here (*Romans 9:31–32*). ***The "Miscellanies," (Entry Nos. 501–832) (WJE Online Vol. 18)***

Again, it is evident that trusting in our own righteousness is fatal to the soul by *Romans 10:3*, "For they, being ignorant of God's righteousness, and going about to establish their own righteousness, have not submitted themselves unto the righteousness of God." This is evidently spoken as a thing fatal to them, by the manner of the Apostle's introducing it, having said that it was his heart's desire and prayer for them that they might be saved, then shows how they fail of it. ***The "Miscellanies," (Entry Nos. 501–832) (WJE Online Vol. 18)***

The Apostle does in like manner argue against our being justified by our own righteousness, as he does against being justified by the works of the law; and evidently uses the expressions of our "own righteousness," and "works of the law," promiscuously, and as signifying the same thing. It is particularly evident by *Romans 10:3*, "For they being ignorant of God's righteousness, and going about to establish their own righteousness, have not submitted themselves to the righteousness of God." ***Sermons and Discourses, 1734–1738 (WJE Online Vol. 19)***

And therefore it follows that when the Apostle speaks of justification by the works of the law, as opposite to justification by faith, he don't mean only the ceremonial law, but also the works of the moral law, which are the things spoken of by Moses, when he says, "He that doth those things shall live in them"; and which are the things that the Apostle in this very place is arguing that we can't be justified by; as is evident by the context, the last verses of the preceding chapter, "But Israel which followed after the law of righteousness, hath not attained to the law of righteousness: Wherefore? Because they sought it not by faith, but as it were by the works of the law," etc. And in the *Romans 10:3* of this chapter, "For they being ignorant of God's righteousness, and going about to establish their own righteousness, have not submitted themselves to the righteousness of God." ***Sermons and Discourses, 1734–1738 (WJE Online Vol. 19)***

For though the Apostle speaks there particularly of circumcision, yet (I have shown already, that) it is not merely being circumcised, but trusting in circumcision as a righteousness, that the Apostle has respect to. He could not mean that merely being circumcised would render Christ of no profit or effect to a person; for we read that he himself for certain reasons, took Timothy and circumcised him (*Acts 16:3*). And the same is evident by the context, and by the rest of the epistle. And the Apostle speaks of trusting in their own righteousness, as fatal to the Jews. *Romans 9:31–32*, "But Israel, which followed after the law of righteousness, hath not attained to the law of righteousness: wherefore? Because they sought it not by faith, but as it were by the works of the law; for they stumbled at that stumbling-stone." Together with *Romans 10:3*, "For they being ignorant of God's righteousness, and going about to establish their own righteousness, have not submitted themselves unto the righteousness of God." And this is spoken of as fatal to the Pharisees, in the parable of the Pharisee and the publican, that Christ spake to them, to reprove them for trusting in themselves, that they were righteous. ***Sermons and Discourses, 1734–1738 (WJE Online Vol. 19)***

Before conversion, man seeks to cover himself with his own fig leaves (*Philippians 3:6–7*), and to lick himself whole with his own duties (*Micah 6:6–7*). He is apt to trust in himself (*Luke 16:15* and *Luke 18:9*), and set up his own righteousness, and reckon his counters for gold, and not submit to the righteousness of God (*Romans 10:3*). But conversion changes his mind; now he casts away his filthy rags, and counts his own righteousness, but a menstruous cloth: he casts it off, as a man would the verminous tatters of a nasty beggar (*Isaiah 64:7*). Now he is brought to poverty of spirit (*Matthew 5:3*), complains of and condemns himself (*Romans 7*), and all his inventory is poor, and miserable, and wretched, and blind, and naked (*Revelation 3:17*). He sees a world of iniquity in his holy things, and calls his once-idolized righteousness, but flesh, and loss, and dog's meat, and would not for a thousand worlds be found in himself. ***Documents on the Trinity, Grace and Faith (WJE Online Vol. 37)***

Romans 10:4

Not that I think that the law only should be preached: ministers may preach other things too little. The Gospel is to be preached as well as the law, and the law is to be preached only to make way for the Gospel, and in order to an effectual preaching of that; for the main work of ministers of the Gospel is to preach the Gospel: it is the end of the law; Christ is the end of the law for righteousness [*Romans 10:4*]. So that a minister would miss it very much if he should insist so much on the terrors of the law, as to forget his end, and neglect to preach the Gospel; but yet the law is very much to be insisted on, and the preaching of the Gospel is like to be in vain without it. ***The Great Awakening (WJE Online Vol. 4)***

It will be inquired concerning every one, both righteous and wicked, whether the Law stands against him or no, whether they have a fulfillment of the Law to show. As for the righteous, they will have this to show: they will have it to plead that the judge himself has fulfilled the Law for them; that he has both satisfied for their sins and fulfilled the righteousness of the Law for them. *Romans 10:4*, "Christ is the end of the law for righteousness to every one that believeth." And as for the wicked: when it shall be found by the book of God's remembrance that they have broken the Law and have no fulfillment of the Law to plead for themselves, they shall have the sentence of the Law pronounced upon them. ***Sermons and Discourses: 1723–1729 (WJE Online Vol. 14)***

The antithesis here makes it evident that by "God's righteousness" is meant a righteousness, in having which we are righteous. And the *Romans 10:4* shows that this righteousness was procured for every believer by Christ, as he was subject to the law. "Christ is the end of the law for righteousness," the natural meaning of which is that, as so what concerns the elect, or them that believe, the Lawgiver, in making the law and establishing of it as a rule for them, had respect to Christ only for its being answered. The law that requires righteousness looks to Christ only to produce that righteousness that it requires, who of God is made to be righteousness, and who is "the Lord our righteousness" [*Jeremiah 23:6*]. ***Notes on Scripture (WJE Online Vol. 15)***

Why the righteousness of Christ is called "the righteousness of God in him" (*Romans 10:4*), and "the righteousness of God" in other places. 'Tis because this principally shows the infinite value and excellency and merit of that righteousness, viz. that it was the righteousness of a divine person; and also because this shows our immediate and universal dependence on God for all our happiness, by the constitution of things in the covenant of grace. It shows how we are empty and are nothing, and God all in all. ***The "Miscellanies," 833–1152 (WJE Online Vol. 20)***

Romans 10:4, "Christ is the end of the law for righteousness to every one that believeth." *Acts 13:39*, "And by him all that believe are justified." In these and other places, a state of salvation is predicated of everyone that believeth or hath faith. 'Tis not said to every one that believeth and walks answerably, or to every one that believeth and takes up an answerable resolution to obey; which would be to limit the proposition and make an exception, and be as much as to say, not everyone that believes, but to such believers only as not only believe, but obey. But this don't consist with those universal expressions: "The gospel is the power of God to salvation to every one that believeth"; "The righteousness of God is unto all, and upon all them that believe"; "Christ is the end of the law for righteousness to every one that believeth." And by the supposition, they that have not saving faith are in a state of damnation; as it is also expressly said in Scripture, "He that believeth not shall [be] damned," and the like. ***Sermons and Discourses, 1743–1758 (WJE Online Vol. 25)***

Romans 10:5

So, *Deuteronomy 30:15*, "See, I have set before thee this day, life and good, and death and evil." V. 19, "I call heaven and earth to record this day against you, that I have set before you life and death, blessing and cursing." The life that is spoken of here, is doubtless the same that is spoken of in *Leviticus 18:5*, "Ye shall therefore keep my statutes and my judgments, which if a man do, he shall live in them." This the Apostle understands of eternal life; as is plain by *Romans 10:5* and *Galatians 3:12*—but that the death threatened for sin in the law of Moses meant eternal death, is what Dr. Taylor abundantly declares. So in his Note on *Romans 5:20*, "Such a constitution the law of Moses was, subjecting those who were under it to death for every transgression; meaning by death ETERNAL DEATH." These are his words. ***Original Sin (WJE Online Vol. 3)***

Concerning the objection from Ezekiel. God's saying in *Ezekiel 18:24*, "if the righteous shall fall from his righteousness, and commit iniquity, all his righteousness shall not be remembered; but in his iniquity that he hath done, shall he die," and the like, don't at all prove that 'tis supposed to be possible that a truly righteous man should fall from his righteousness; any more than God's saying, *Leviticus 18:4–5*, "Ye shall do my judgments, and keep mine ordinances, to walk therein: I am the Lord your God. Ye shall therefore keep my statutes, and my judgments: which if a man do, he shall live in them"; and in *Ezekiel 20:11*, "And I gave them my statutes, and showed them my judgments, which if a man do, he shall even live in them"; and the same, *Ezekiel 20:13* and *Ezekiel 20:21*; and to the same purpose, *Ezekiel 18:22*, the next verse but one before that whence the objection is taken, "In his righteousness that he hath done he shall live." These two assertions are again joined together in *Ezekiel 33:18–19*. I say, what is said in the forementioned place no more proves it to be possible for a truly righteous man to fall from righteousness, so as to die in his iniquity, than these places prove that 'tis possible for a man to do those things required in God's statutes and judgments, so as to live in them, or to perform righteousness, so that in the righteousness that he hath done, he shall live. But these last mentioned places do not prove that it is possible for a man to do righteousness, and the things required in God's statutes, so as to live in them, by the express sentence of the Apostle, when speaking of those very passages of the Old Testament, *Romans 10:5* and *Galatians 3:12*. The truth concerning both these assertions of the Old Testament seems to be that they are proposed to us as signifying and containing diverse verities, and for a diverse use in application to ourselves. ***The "Miscellanies," (Entry Nos. 501–832) (WJE Online Vol. 18)***

Romans 10:6

And now let us consider—Is it not strange that in a Christian, orthodox country, and such a land of light as this is, there should be many at a loss whose work this is, whether the work of God or the work of the Devil? Is it not a shame to New England that such a work should be much doubted of here? Need we look over the histories of all past times, to see if there ben't some circumstances and external appearances that attend this work, that have been formerly found amongst enthusiasts? Whether the Montanists had not great transports of joy, and whether the French Prophets had not agitations of body? Blessed be God! He don't put us to the toil of such inquiries. We need not say, "Who shall ascend into heaven" [*Romans 10:6*], to bring us down something whereby to judge of this work. Nor does God send us beyond the seas, nor into past ages, to obtain a rule that shall determine and satisfy us. But we have a rule near at hand, a sacred book that God himself has put into our hands, with clear and infallible marks, sufficient to resolve us in things of this nature; which book I think we must reject, not only in some particular passages, but in the substance of it, if we reject such a work as has now been described, as not being the work of God. The whole tenor of the Gospel proves it; all the notion of religion that the Scripture gives us confirms it. ***The Great Awakening (WJE Online Vol. 4)***

But here we have lain in groaning circumstances in our souls, in pinching want of spiritual supplies year after year, and but little appearance of a general concern about it. [We] ben't much engaged about to get supplies, though they have been ready at hand. And God has been ready to bestow if we had had an heart to seek it of him. *Romans 10:6–08*, "Say not in thine heart, Who shall ascend into heaven (that is, to bring Christ down from above)? Or, Who shall descend into the deep (that is, to bring up Christ again from the dead)? But what saith it? The word is nigh thee, even in thy mouth, and in thy heart: that is, the word of faith, which we preach." We have been bestirring ourselves about other things and making a great bustle and noise. We have bestirred ourselves about a market for our cattle, and we have bestirred ourselves about the inner commons, and have very notably bestirred ourselves in some other matters; but we have not stirred up ourselves to lay hold on God, or to turn from our sins and earnestly to seek the returns of God's Holy Spirit. ***Sermons and Discourses, 1739–1742 (WJE Online Vol. 22)***

Romans 10:8

And according[ly], the Apostle observes, this was not the ultimate revelation that Moses made to the people of a way for them to obtain righteousness; but he afterwards reveals another way that was not impossible, but easy, as the very manner of his expression intimates. "But the righteousness which is of faith speaketh on this wise, Say not in thine heart, Who shall ascend into heaven?" etc., as if the terms of life were impossible. "But what saith it? The word is nigh thee," etc. *Romans 10:8*. This is the way by Christ, or "this is the word of faith, which we preach." So that this is the ultimate revelation that Moses made; and the former revelation of an impossible way was only to make way for this. Thus "Christ is the end of the law for righteousness to everyone that believeth." ***The "Blank Bible" (WJE Online Vol. 24)***

The difference between the two covenants, here in this context represented by the Apostle, is that the one requires an actual full and perfect performance of the word of God in order to justification. The other requires no more than that the Word of God, revealing himself as our merciful God and Father, should be in our mouth or profession, and in our heart, whereby our profession is sincere, and become heartily disposed to yield to that Word of God. ***The "Blank Bible" (WJE Online Vol. 24)***

Romans 10:8, "Who shall go over the sea for us, to bring it to us, that we may hear it, and do it?" [*Deuteronomy 30:13*], and so have the benefit of it, that deliverance and salvation which is to be obtained by it, as is evident by the context. For this is the supposed interrogation of the people in captivity, seeking deliverance from that calamity. 'Tis deliverance or salvation they are inquiring after, as contained in the word, as in the gospel. Therefore the Apostle says, 'tis "the word of faith, that we preach" [*Romans 10:8*], implying a supposition, that if they could obtain the word, or the "commandment" (as it is called, [*Deuteronomy 30:11*]), and receive it, they therein received deliverance. They therein received God, whose law it was, as their Savior. In inquiring after the commandment, they inquire after a savior. And God tells 'em that the word is near 'em, so that if they would receive it in their heart, mouth and practice, they should therein have the benefit of salvation. The Lawgiver would become their Savior. In receiving it they would receive life, as is expressed in what follows: "I have set life and death before thee; the word and its salvation is nigh thee; God sends it to thine heart and thy mouth; if thou wilt but receive it, there thou shalt have it, and have life; thou shalt have it for accepting." So that obedience is here spoken of under the notion of an acceptance or reception of a savior, a receiving the Author of the word as the Author of the gospel of life. Being in the mouth and heart means a being received. "The word is very nigh thee, in thy mouth, and in thy heart, that thou mayest do it" [*Deuteronomy 30:14*], i.e. so nigh thee that there is need of nothing but the consent of your heart, or your cordial reception, and you have it in your heart and practice and have the benefit of it. ***The "Miscellanies," (Entry Nos. 1153–1360) (WJE Online Vol. 23)***

Romans 10:9

So *Romans 10:9–10*, "If thou shalt confess with thy mouth the Lord Jesus, and shalt believe in thine heart, that God hath raised him from the dead, thou shalt be saved: for with the heart man believeth unto righteousness, and with the mouth confession is made unto salvation." Where a public profession of religion with the mouth is evidently spoken of as a great duty of all Christ's people, as well as believing in him; and ordinarily requisite to salvation; not that it is necessary in the same manner that faith is, but in like manner as baptism is. Faith and verbal profession are jointly spoken of here as necessary to salvation, in the same manner as faith and baptism are, in *Mark 16:16*. ***Ecclesiastical Writings (WJE Online Vol. 12)***

When the Apostle speaks of a profession of our faith in Christ, as one duty which all Christians ought to perform as they seek salvation, 'tis the profession of a saving faith that he speaks of: his words plainly imply it. "If thou shalt confess with thy mouth the Lord Jesus, and shalt believe in thine heart that God hath raised him from the dead, thou shalt be saved" [*Romans 10:9*]. The faith which was to be professed with the mouth, was the same which the Apostle speaks of as in the heart, but that is saving faith. ***Ecclesiastical Writings (WJE Online Vol. 12)***

And by the way I must observe, that Mr. Williams would have done well, if he was able, to have reconciled these repugnant things, taken notice of in my book; "That with the heart man believeth to righteousness," and that if men believe with the heart that God raised Christ from the dead, they shall be saved; agreeable to *Romans 10:9–10*. And yet that men may believe this with their heart, yea, and with all their heart, and still not believe to righteousness, nor ever be saved. So likewise, that "whoever shall confess that Jesus is the Son of God, God dwelleth in him, and he in God"; as in *1 John 4:15*. And that "whosoever believeth that Jesus is the Christ, is born of God," *1 John 5:1*. And yet, that a man may believe this very thing with all his heart, and confess it with his mouth; and this in the language of the same apostles and primitive ministers; and still not be born of God, nor have a spark of grace in him. ***Ecclesiastical Writings (WJE Online Vol. 12)***

Romans 10:10

"For with the heart man believeth unto righteousness, and with the mouth confession is made unto salvation" [*Romans 10:10*]. Believing unto righteousness, is saving faith; but 'tis evidently the same faith which is spoken of, as professed with the mouth, in the next words in the same sentence. And that the gentiles, in professing the Christian religion or swearing to Christ, should profess saving faith, is implied, *Isaiah 45:23–24*, "Every tongue shall swear; surely shall one say, in the Lord have I righteousness and strength," i.e. should profess entirely to depend on Christ's righteousness and strength. ***Ecclesiastical Writings (WJE Online Vol. 12)***

Christ in his kingly office bestows salvation, and therefore accepting him in his kingly office, by a disposition to sell all and suffer all in duty to Christ, and giving proper respect and honor to him, is the proper condition of salvation. This is manifest by *Hebrews 5:9*, "And being made perfect, he became the author of eternal salvation to all them that obey him"; and by *Romans 10:10*, "For with the heart man believeth unto righteousness, and with the mouth confession is made unto salvation." The Apostle speaks of such a confessing of Christ, or outward and open testifying our respect to him, and adhering to our duty to him, as exposed to suffering, reproach and persecution. ***The "Miscellanies," 833–1152 (WJE Online Vol. 20)***

If Peter had not been converted after his fall, he would not have persevered in the faith and profession of Christ. He would have fallen under that threat, *Luke 12:9*, "He that denies me before men [shall be denied before the angels of God]." 'Tis necessary to our salvation that we should with our mouth make confession of Christ (*Romans 10:10*). They don't believe to the saving of the soul, but draw back. *Hebrews 10:38–39*, "Now the just shall live by faith: but if any man draw back, my soul shall have no pleasure in him. But we are not of them." ***Sermons and Discourses, 1739–1742 (WJE Online Vol. 22)***

The next thing that I would advise you to look to in order to your not resting in a common faith instead of a saving, is the seat of it. See to it that the seat of it ben't only in your understanding or speculation, but [in] your whole soul, and especially your heart; [that is, your] inclination and will. This is commonly intended by the heart in Scripture; *Romans 10:10*, "With the heart man believeth unto righteousness." See to it that you not only assent to the truth, but that you receive the love of the truth: that you are not only persuaded [of the truth], but do embrace [it]. [See to it] that you receive Christ with your heart, that you truly open the doors of your heart. Your heart is what he seeks. *Proverbs 23:26*, "My son, give me thine heart." Christ is a suitor: he seeks to win the heart; and not merely that you may believe as the devils do, with a mere assent of your understanding. See to it that you have an holy faith, that precious faith of God's elect, which is a good moral virtue. ***Sermons and Discourses, 1743–1758 (WJE Online Vol. 25)***

Romans 10:11

Romans 10:11, [132.] See no. [107]. [. . .] with *Isaiah 28:16* and *Romans 9:33* and *Romans 10:11*. These places show that waiting for God signifies the same as believing on him. And 'tis evident by what was observed, [No. 113], that waiting on God, or for God, signifies the same as trusting in him. ***Writings on the Trinity, Grace, and Faith (WJE Online Vol. 21)***

Romans 10:12

Romans 10:12, Compare:

1 Kings 8:39	*John 2:24* and *John 16:30*, and *Acts 1:24*
Jeremiah 17:10	*Revelation 2:3*
Isaiah 44:6	*Revelation 1:17*
Revelation 1:8	*Revelation 22:13*
1 Timothy 6:15	*Revelation 17:14, Revelation 19:16*
Isaiah 10:21	*Isaiah 9:6*
Romans 10:12	*Acts 10:36, Romans 9:5*
Psalms 90:2	*Proverbs 8:22 ff.*
Nehemiah 9:6	*John 1:3, Colossians 1:16–17*
Genesis 1:1	*Hebrews 1:10*
Exodus 20:3	*Luke 24:25, Hebrews 1:6*
Matthew 4:10	*John 5:23*

The "Miscellanies," (Entry Nos. 1153–1360)

Romans 10:13

Christ is the Lord mentioned in *Romans 10:13*, "For whosoever shall call upon the name of the Lord shall be saved." That it is Christ is spoken of is evident from the two foregoing verses, and also from the next verse, even the fourteenth. But the words are taken from *Joel 2:32*, where the word translated "Lord" is "Jehovah." See also *1 Corinthians 1:2*. ***The "Miscellanies," (Entry Nos. 1153–1360)***

Romans 10:14

But God has more especially made the word preached efficacious to the enlightening [of] the soul. Faith comes by hearing, and hearing by the word preached: *Romans 10:14*, "How then shall they call on him in whom they have not believed, and how shall they believe in him of whom they have not heard, and how shall they hear without a preacher?" ***Sermons and Discourses 1720–1723 (WJE Online Vol. 10)***

No speech can be any means of grace, but by conveying knowledge. Otherwise the speech is as much lost as if there had been no man there, and he that spoke, had spoken only into the air; as it follows in the passage just quoted, vv. *1 Corinthians 14:6–10*. He that doth not understand, can receive no faith, nor any other grace; for God deals with man as with a rational creature; and when faith is in exercise, it is not about something he knows not what. Therefore hearing is absolutely necessary to faith; because hearing is necessary to understanding, *Romans 10:14*. "How shall they believe in him of whom they have not heard?" ***Sermons and Discourses, 1739–1742 (WJE Online Vol. 22)***

But yet ministers of the gospel, as Christ's servants and officers under him, are appointed to promote the designs of that great work of Christ, the work of salvation. 'Tis the work that ministers are devoted to; and therefore they are represented as co-workers with Christ. *2 Corinthians 6:1*, "We then, as workers together with him, beseech you also that ye receive not the grace of God in vain." Christ is the Savior of the souls of men; ministers also, are spoken of in Scripture as saving men's souls. *1 Timothy 4:16*, "In doing this, thou shalt both save thyself and them that hear thee." *Romans 10:14*, "If by any means I may provoke to emulation them which are my flesh, and might save some of them." *1 Corinthians 9:22*, "That I might by all means save some." And whereas 'tis said, *Obadiah 21*, "Saviors shall come upon Mount Zion"; ministers of the gospel are supposed to be there intended. ***Sermons and Discourses, 1743–1758 (WJE Online Vol. 25)***

God deals with man as with a rational creature; and when faith is in exercise, it is not about something he knows not what. Therefore, hearing is absolutely necessary to faith; because hearing is necessary to understanding. *Romans 10:14*, "how shall they believe in him of whom they have not heard?" In like manner, there can be no love without knowledge. It is not according to the nature of the human soul, to love an object which is entirely unknown. The heart cannot be set upon an object of which there is no idea in the understanding. The reasons which induce the soul to love, must first be understood, before they can have a reasonable influence on the heart. ***Sermons, Series II, 1739 (WJE Online Vol. 54)***

Romans 10:15

I would not advise that any should take upon them the work of a minister or teacher, to go about and make a business of warning and exhorting others, and neglect the business of their proper calling. For any man to assume this to himself, unless [he] be orderly appointed thereto, is disorderly and presumptuous. *Romans 10:15*, "How can they preach, except they be sent?"; *Hebrews 5:4*, "No man taketh this honor to himself, except he that is called of God." ***Sermons and Discourses, 1734–1738 (WJE Online Vol. 19)***

Romans 10:16

Romans 10:16–18, So Christ rose from the grave to send forth his light and truth to the utmost ends of the earth, that had hitherto been confined to one nation, and to rule over all nations in the kingdom of his grace. Thus his line goes out through all the earth, and his words to the end of the world, so that "there is no speech or language, where his voice is not heard" *Psalms 19:3*, as is here said of the line and voice of the sun and heavenly bodies, in the two foregoing verses, which are by the Apostle interpreted of the gospel of Jesus Christ. *Romans 10:16–18*, "But they have not all obeyed the gospel. For Esaias saith, Lord, who hath believed our report? So then faith cometh by hearing, and hearing by the word of God. But I say, Have they not heard? Yes, verily, their sound went into all the earth, and their words unto the end of the world." ***Notes on Scripture (WJE Online Vol. 15)***

Romans 10:17

The testimony that is the proper ground of faith is in the Word of God, "Faith cometh by hearing, and hearing by the word of God" (*Romans 10:17*). There is such a testimony given us in the Word of God, that *he that believes shall be saved:* But there is no such testimony in the word of God, as that such an individual person, in such a town in Scotland or New England, believes. There is such a proposition in the Scripture, as that *Christ loves those that love him;* and therefore that everyone is bound to believe; and a firm believing it on divine testimony is properly of the nature of faith; and for any one to doubt of it, is properly the heinous sin of unbelief: But there is no such proposition in Scripture, or that is any part of the gospel of Christ, that such an individual person in Northampton loves Christ. If I know I have complacence in Christ, I know it the same way that I know I have complacence in my wife and children, viz. by the testimony of my own heart, or inward consciousness. Evangelical faith has the gospel of Christ for its foundation; but that *I love Christ* is a proposition not contained in the gospel of Christ. ***Religious Affections (WJE Online Vol. 2)***

Romans 10:19

As it was foretold in both Old Testament and New, that the Jews should reject the Messiah, so it was foretold that the Gentiles should receive him, and so be admitted to the privileges of God's people; in places too many to be now particularly mentioned. It was foretold in the Old Testament, that the Jews should envy the Gentiles on this account (*Deuteronomy 32:21* compared with *Romans 10:19*). Christ himself often foretold, that the Gentiles would embrace the true religion, and become his followers and people. ***Freedom of the Will (WJE Online Vol. 1)***

Romans 10:20

The prophet Isaiah is therefore deservedly called "the evangelical prophet." He seems to teach the glorious doctrines of the gospel almost as plainly as the apostles did who preached after Christ was actually come. The apostle Paul, therefore, takes notice that the prophet "Esaias is very bold," *Romans 10:20*, i.e. as the meaning of the word as used in the New Testament is very plain, he speaks out very plainly and fully, so being "very bold" is used; *2 Corinthians 3:12*, we use "great plainness of speech" or "boldness" as it is in the margin. How plainly and fully does the prophet Isaiah describe the manner and circumstances, nature and end, of the sufferings and sacrifice of Christ in the *Isaiah 53* of his prophecy. There is scarce a chapter in the New Testament itself is more full on it. And how much, and in what a glorious strain, does the same prophet speak from time [to] time of the glorious benefits of Christ, the unspeakable blessings which shall redound to his church through his redemption. Jesus Christ, the person that this prophet spoke so much of, once appeared to Isaiah in the form of an human nature, the nature that he should afterwards take upon him. We have an account of it in the *Isaiah 6* of his prophecy, at the beginning ["I saw also the Lord sitting upon a throne, high and lifted up, and his train filled the temple"]. This was Christ that Isaiah now saw, as we are expressly told in the New Testament, *John 12:39–41* ["Esaias said again . . . be converted . . . said Esaias, when he saw his glory, and spoke of him"]. ***A History of the Work of Redemption (WJE Online Vol. 9)***

Romans 10:16–21, Again, it is evident that trusting in our own righteousness is fatal to the soul by *Romans 10:3*, "For they, being ignorant of God's righteousness, and going about to establish their own righteousness, have not submitted themselves unto the righteousness of God." This is evidently spoken as a thing fatal to them, by the manner of the Apostle's introducing it, having said that it was his heart's desire and prayer for them that they might be saved, then shows how they fail of it. 'Tis evident also by the last verses of the preceding chapter, where the Apostle is speaking of the same thing in those forementioned words, which occasion these. 'Tis evident also by the *Romans 10:16–21. The "Miscellanies," (Entry Nos. 501–832) (WJE Online Vol. 18)*

ROMANS CHAPTER 11

Romans 11:1

["I say then," etc.] Dr. Doddridge renders it thus. "Do I say then that God hath rejected his people?" ***The "Blank Bible" (WJE Online Vol. 24)***

Romans 11:4

Here is to [be] observed the success the gospel had among the Jews, for God first began with them. God, being about to reject the main body of that people, first calls in his elect from among them before he forsook them to turn to the Gentiles. It was so in former great and dreadful judgments of God on that nation; the bulk of them were destroyed, and only a remnant saved and reformed. So it was in the rejection of the ten tribes; long before this rejection the bulk of the ten tribes were rejected when they left the true worship of God in Jeroboam's time, and afterwards more fully in Ahab's time, but yet there was a number of them that God reserved. A number left their possessions in those tribes and went up [and settled in the tribes of Judah and Benjamin]. And afterwards, there were seven thousand in Ahab's time [who had not bowed the knee to Baal]. And so in the captivity into Babylon; but a remnant of them returned. So now again [the great part of the people were rejected; but some few were saved]. And therefore the Holy Ghost compares this reservation of a number that were converted by the preaching of the apostles to those former remnants, *Romans 9:27*, "Esaias also crieth concerning Israel, Though the number of the children of Israel [be as the sand of the sea, a remnant shall be saved]." ***A History of the Work of Redemption (WJE Online Vol. 9)***

Romans 11:5

To observe particularly how invincible a proof of the Calvinist doctrine of election that place is, in *Romans 11:5*, "Even so, then at this present time also there is a remnant according to the election of grace." Dr. Doddridge observes upon it, that some explain this of having chosen grace, i.e. the gospel. But that term is very unnatural, and neither suits the phrase, nor the connection with the former clause or with the next verse, in which the Apostle comments on his own words. ***"Controversies" Notebook (WJE Online Vol. 27)***

To improve that argument, that election is said not to be of WORKS. *Romans 9:11*, "that the purpose of God according to election might stand, *not of works*, but of him that calleth"; v. 11, "neither of them *having done either good or evil*"; and *Romans 11:5–6*, "Even so at this present time also there is a remnant according to the *election of grace*. And if by grace, then it is no more *of works*: otherwise grace is no more grace. But if it be of works, then it is no more grace: otherwise work is no more work"; *2 Timothy 1:9*, "who hath saved us, and called us with an holy calling, *not according to our works*, but according to his own purpose and grace, which was given us in Christ Jesus before the world began." ***"Controversies" Notebook (WJE Online Vol. 27)***

"The election according to grace, mentioned, *Romans 11:5*, means the whole body of the Jewish converts, even all that did embrace the Christian faith, and were not hardened in or blinded by their prejudices and infidelity; as is apparent from the following words, v. 7, 'The election hath obtained, but the rest were blinded.'" ***Documents on the Trinity, Grace and Faith (WJE Online Vol. 37)***

Romans 11:6

The Apostle don't only say, that we are not justified by the works of the law, but that we are not justified by works, using a general term; as in our text it is said, "unto him that worketh not, but believeth on him that justifieth," etc. and in the *Romans 4:6*, "God imputeth righteousness without works." And *Romans 11:6*, "And if by grace, then is it no more of works, otherwise grace is no more grace: but if it be of works, then is it no more grace; otherwise work is no more work." So *Ephesians 2:8–9*, "For by grace are ye saved, through faith, not of works." By which, there is no reason in the world to understand the Apostle of any other than works in general, as correlates of a reward, or good works, or works of virtue and righteousness. When the Apostle says we are justified or saved not by works, without any such term annexed as "the law," or any other addition to limit the expression, what warrant have any to confine it to works of a particular law, or institution, excluding others? Are not observances of other divine laws works, as well as of that? It seems to be allowed by the divines in the Arminian scheme, in their interpretation of several of those texts where the Apostle only mentions works, without any addition, that he means our own good works in general; but then they say, he only means to exclude any proper merit in those works. But to say the Apostle means one thing when he says we ben't justified by works, another when he says we ben't justified by the works of the law, when we find the expressions mixed, and used in the same discourse, and when the Apostle is evidently upon the same argument, is very unreasonable, it is to dodge, and fly from Scripture, rather than to open and yield ourselves to its teachings. ***Sermons and Discourses, 1734–1738 (WJE Online Vol. 19)***

'Tis evident that by the works of the law here is meant not only a conformity to Jewish ordinances of worship, but our own moral righteousness or excellency, consisting in our obedience to the laws of God in general, whether moral, ceremonial or whatever; because what is called here the works of the law, is called in the *Romans 10:3* their own righteousness, where the same thing is evidently intended by the reference the Apostle has there to what is said here. And doubtless by the works of the law is meant the same as the Apostle means by the righteousness of the law in the *Romans 10:5*, where that expression is evidently used as synonymous with our own righteousness (*Romans 10:3*), and so they are used as synonymous (*Philippians 3:6*, *Philippians 3:9*). But doubtless by their own righteousness is meant the same as their own goodness or moral excellency, and not only that part of it that consisted in their obedience to the ceremonial law. And again, we often find the works of the law set by this Apostle in opposition to the free grace of God, and therefore thereby must be intended our own excellency. For wherein does grace appear, but in being bestowed on them that are no more excellent, that are so unworthy, so far from deserving anything? *Romans 3:20*, *Romans 3:24*, *Romans 3:27*, *Romans 3:28*; and *Titus 3:5*, where, instead of works of law, the Apostle says works of righteousness; *Romans 11:6* and *Romans 4:4*; *Galatians 5:4*; *Ephesians 2:8*, *Ephesians 2:9*. ***The "Miscellanies," (Entry Nos. 501–832) (WJE Online Vol. 18)***

But the great and most distinguishing difference between that covenant and the covenant of grace is, that by the covenant or grace we are not thus justified by our own works, but only by faith in Jesus Christ. 'Tis on this account chiefly that the new covenant deserves the name of a covenant of grace, as is evident by *Romans 4:16*, "Therefore it is of faith, that it might be by grace." And *Romans 3:20*, *Romans 3:24*, "Therefore by the deeds of the law there shall no flesh be justified in his sight; being justified freely by his grace, trough the redemption that is in Jesus Christ." And *Romans 11:6*, "And if by grace then is it no more of works: otherwise grace is no more grace: But if it be of works, then is it no more grace: otherwise work is no more work." *Galatians 5:4*, "Whosoever of you are justified by the law, ye are fallen from grace." And therefore the Apostle when he in the same epistle to the Galatians, speaks of the doctrine of justification by works as another gospel, he adds, "which is not another" (*Galatians 1:6–7*). 'Tis no gospel at all; 'tis law: 'tis no covenant of grace, but of works: 'tis not an evangelical, but a legal doctrine. Certainly that doctrine wherein consists the greatest and most essential difference between the covenant of grace and the first covenant, must be a doctrine of great importance. That doctrine of the gospel by which above all others it is worthy of the name of gospel, is doubtless a very important doctrine of the gospel. ***Sermons and Discourses, 1734–1738 (WJE Online Vol. 19)***

The following passages from Dr. Guise, in the *Berry Street Sermons*, Sermon 21, illustrate this point. "The Apostle states the notion of grace in justification, saying, 'If by grace, then it is no more of the works: otherwise grace is no more grace. But if it be of works, then it is no more grace: otherwise, work is no more work' (*Romans 11:6*). But lest we should take the term *grace* in some laxer sense, as it is concerned in our justification, it is further said to be 'freely by his grace' (*Romans 3:24*) to exclude all conceit, as though there were anything in us, for which this favor of God is extended to us. And in the following chapter, the Apostle excludes all our works from having any share in our title to this blessing, 'that the reward may be reckoned to be of grace, not of debt,' and speaks of God's 'justifying the ungodly,' to show what their character was, till he justified them (*Romans 4:4–5*). And what but grace could move him to justify persons of that character? Accordingly, in the next chapter, he seems to strain the powers of language to set out the freeness and riches of this grace, calling it 'the grace of God,' and 'the gift by grace, which had abounded unto many,' and 'the free gift' in delivering from 'many offenses unto justification' (*Romans 5:15–16*)." ***The "Miscellanies," 833–1152 (WJE Online Vol. 20)***

Taylor insists upon it, that our full and final justification is of works and not only of grace, and yet he allows that this final justification is spoken of in Scripture as being of grace, *2 Timothy 1:18* and *Jude 21*. But how does this consist with what the Apostle says, *Romans 4:4*, "Now to him that worketh the reward is not reckoned of grace, but of debt"; and *Romans 11:6*, "And if by grace, then it is no more of works: otherwise grace is no more grace. But if it be of works, then it is no more grace: otherwise work is no more work"? ***Writings on the Trinity, Grace, and Faith (WJE Online Vol. 21)***

Romans 11:7

There are multitudes of men that seek salvation that never obtain what they seek for. ***Sermons and Discourses, 1739–1742 (WJE Online Vol. 22)***

Though a people that live under means are wont in general to seek and hope for salvation, yet 'tis the election only that obtains, and the rest are blinded. ***Sermons and Discourses, 1739–1742 (WJE Online Vol. 22)***

If the Apostle here, as Mr. Taylor says, has respect to bodies of men, to the posterity of Esau and Jacob, etc. yet this he applies to distinctions made in these days of the gospel, and that distinction made between those that were in the Christian church and those that were not—particularly some of the Jews that were in the Christian [church] and others of the same nation that were not—which [is] made by some believing and accepting Christ and others' rejection, [by] that faith which they professed to be with all their hearts, that faith which was a mercy and virtue, and the want of which was a fault, as by the objection the Apostle supposes, *Romans 9:19*, "Why doth he yet find fault"; the want of which argued hardness of heart (*Romans 9:18*), exposed 'em to wrath and destruction as a punishment of sin (*Romans 9:22*), and exposes persons to be like the inhabitants of Sodom and Gomorrah (*Romans 9:29*). ***Writings on the Trinity, Grace, and Faith (WJE Online Vol. 21)***

"The election hath obtained, and the rest were blinded". That by "the election" is not meant the Gentiles, but the elect part of the Jews, is most apparent by the context. ***"Controversies" Notebook (WJE Online Vol. 27)***

Romans 11:8

So God is said to have given the wicked Jews a "spirit of slumber" (*Romans 11:8*), and to have given "a lying spirit in the mouth" of the false prophets (*1 Kings 22:23*), and to have given to the enemies of the church "to take peace from the earth" (*Revelation 6:4*, *Revelation 6:8*), and to have given to the Beast to speak blasphemies (*Revelation 13:5*). And to these and all sayings of the like nature, he gives this as a general explanation, viz. that God gives those faculties by which we are enabled to obtain those things, and means and motives sufficient to excite those faculties to the performance of their proper actions. So God givest riches, he gives our daily bread, he gives all things to all men; but yet they must employ these faculties which God has given to procure 'em. Thus the Jews say God hath given repentance to the Gentiles, when Peter, preaching to them and proposing motives, they repented and believed (*Acts 10:36*, *Acts 10:43*). So faith is said to be the gift of God, because the objects of our faith are only by divine revelation, and are confirmed to us and made credible by the evidence which God has given. ***Writings on the Trinity, Grace, and Faith (WJE Online Vol. 21)***

Romans 11:9–10

That Christ indeed suffered the full punishment of the sin that was imputed to him, or offered that to God that was fully and completely equivalent to what we owed to divine justice for our sins, is evident by *Psalms 69:5*, "O God, thou knowest my foolishness, and my sins" (*my guiltiness*, it is in the Hebrew) "are not hid from thee." That the person that is the subject of this Psalm, and that is here speaking, is the Messiah, is evident from many places in the New Testament, in which it is applied to Christ, as *John 15:25* and *John 2:17* and *Romans 15:3*, *2 Corinthians 6:2*, *John 19:28–30*, with *Matthew 27:34*, *Matthew 27:48* and *Mark 15:23* and *Romans 11:9–10*, *Acts 1:20*; and by the Psalm itself, especially when compared with other psalms and prophecies of the Old Testament. It is plain that David in this Psalm did not speak in his own name, but in the name of the Messiah. ***The "Miscellanies," 833–1152 (WJE Online Vol. 20)***

Romans 11:12

Concerning the CALLING of the JEWS, see my "Treatise on the Apocalypse," no. 22. As to the time of it, see note on Luke 21:24. As the redemption and salvation of Christ respects chiefly the soul, and yet that the restoration of men by him may be every way complete, the body also shall at last rise and be restored. So Christ's redemption and the glorious prophecies of the blessed fruits of it to Israel respects mainly the spiritual Israel; yet through God's abundant grace, and that all things may be restored by Christ in due time, the external and literal Israel shall be restored by him. So likewise, as something equivalent to the restoration of the body, not only shall the spiritual state of the Jews be hereafter restored, but their external state as a nation in their own land. ***The "Blank Bible" (WJE Online Vol. 24)***

The prophecies of the New Testament do no less evidently shew, that a time will come when the gospel shall universally prevail, and the kingdom of Christ be extended over the whole habitable earth, in the most proper sense. Christ says (*John 12:32*), "I, if I be lifted up from the earth, will draw all men unto me." 'Tis fit, that when the Son of God becomes man, he should have dominion over all mankind: 'tis fit, that since he became an inhabitant of the earth, and shed his blood on the earth, he should possess the whole earth: 'tis fit, seeing here he became a servant, and was subject to men, and was arraigned before them, and judged, condemned and executed by them, and suffered ignominy and death in a most public manner, before Jews and Gentiles, being lifted up to view on the cross upon an hill, near that populous city Jerusalem, at a most public time, when there were many hundred thousand spectators, from all parts, that he should be rewarded with an universal dominion over mankind; and it is here declared he shall be. The Apostle, in the *Romans 11*, teaches us to look on that great outpouring of the Spirit and ingathering of souls into Christ's kingdom, that was in those days, first of the Jews, and then of the Gentiles, to be but as the "first fruits" of the intended harvest, both with regard to Jews and Gentiles, and to look on the ingathering of those first fruits as a sign that all the remainder both of Jews and Gentiles should in due time be gathered in (*Romans 11:16*). "For if the first fruit be holy, the lump is also holy; and if the root be holy, so are the branches." And in that context, the Apostle speaks of the fullness of both Jews and Gentiles, as what shall hereafter be brought in, as distinct from that ingathering from among both, that was in those primitive ages of Christianity: in *Romans 11:12* we read of the "fullness of the Jews," and in the *Romans 11:25* of the "fullness of the Gentiles": and there in *Romans 11:30–32*, the Apostle teaches us to look upon that infidelity and darkness, that first prevailed over all Gentile nations, before Christ came, and then over the Jews after Christ came, as what was wisely permitted of God, as a preparation for the manifestation of the glory of God's mercy, in due time, on the whole world, constituted of Jews and Gentiles. "God hath concluded them all in unbelief, that he might have mercy upon all" [*Romans 11:32*]. These things plainly shew, that the time is coming when the whole world of mankind shall be brought into the church of Christ; and not only a part of the Jews, and a part of the Gentile world, as the first fruits, as it was in the first ages of the Christian church; but the fullness of both, the whole lump, all the nation of the Jews, and all the world of Gentiles. ***Apocalyptic Writings (WJE Online Vol. 5)***

Though we don't know the time in which this conversion of the nation of Israel will come to pass, yet this much we may determine by Scripture, that it will [be] before [the] glory of the Gentile part of the church shall be fully accomplished, because it is said that their coming in shall be life from the dead to the Gentiles, *Romans 11:12*, *Romans 11:15* ["Now if the fall of them be the riches of the world . . . how much more their fullness? . . . For if the casting away of them be the reconciling of the world, what shall the receiving of them be, but life from the dead?"]. ***A History of the Work of Redemption (WJE Online Vol. 9)***

The word "fullness," in the former part of this verse, is doubtless to be understood in like manner as the word "filleth," in the latter part. By Christ's filling "all in all" seems evidently to be intended that he supplies all the creatures in heaven and in earth, angels, and blessed spirits, and men, with all good, as in *Ephesians 4:10*. "He that descended is the same also that ascended far above all heavens, that he might fill all things," viz. that he might supply all intelligent creatures in heaven and earth with good. So when it is said, *Ephesians 3:19*, "that ye might be filled with all the fullness of God," the meaning seems to be, that ye might have your souls satisfied with a participation of God's own good, his beauty and joy. "For our communion is with the Father, and with his Son Jesus Christ" (*1 John 1:3*). So when the Apostle says, Christ emptied himself, as *Philippians 2:7*, he means he appeared in the world without his former glory and joy. See *John 17:5*. So that here the Apostle teaches that Christ, who fills all things, all elect creatures in heaven and earth, himself is filled by the church. He, who supplies angels and men with all that good in which they are perfect and happy, receives the church as that in which he himself is happy. He, from whom and in whom all angels and saints are adorned and made perfect in beauty, himself receives the church as his glorious and beautiful ornament, as the virtuous wife is a crown to her husband. The church is the garment of Christ, and was typified by that coat of his that was without seam [*John 19:23*], [which] signified the union of the various members of the church, and was typified by those garments of the high priest that were made "for glory and for beauty" (*Exodus 28:2*), as seems evident by the *Psalms 133:2*, and by the precious stones of his breastplate in a particular manner, on which were engraven the names of the children of Israel. *Isaiah 62:3*, "Thou shalt also be a crown of glory in the hand of the Lord, and a royal diadem in the hand of thy God," i.e. in the possession of God. So *Zechariah 9:16–17*, "And the Lord their God shall save them in that day as the flock of his people, for they shall be as the stones of a crown, lifted up as an ensign upon his land." As 'tis from and in Christ that all are supplied with joy and happiness, so Christ receives the church as that in which he has exceeding and satisfying delight and joy. *Isaiah 62:5*, "As the bridegroom rejoiceth over the bride, so shall thy God rejoice over thee." This seems to be the good that Christ sought in the creation of the world, who is the beginning of the creation of God, when all things were created by him and for him, viz. that he might obtain a spouse that he might give himself to and give himself for, on whom he might pour forth his love, and in whom his soul might eternally be delighted. Till he had attained this, he was pleased not to look on himself as complete, but as wanting something, as Adam was not complete till he had obtained his Eve (*Genesis 2:20*). ***Notes on Scripture (WJE Online Vol. 15)***

There is yet remaining a future glorious advancement of the church and kingdom of God in this world. *Isaiah 44:3*, etc., "Pour water"; *Isaiah 32:15*, "until the spirit [be poured upon us]"; *Isaiah 45:8*, "drop down, [ye heavens, from above]." *Ezekiel 39:29*, "Neither will I hide my face any more from them: for I have poured out my spirit upon the house of Israel, saith the Lord God." After the destruction of Antichrist, *Daniel 2:43*, "they shall mingle themselves with the seed of men: but they shall not cleave one to another." *Daniel 7:18*, "But the saints of the most High shall take the kingdom, and possess the kingdom forever, even forever and ever." After the calling of the Jews, *Romans 11:12*, [we read of the "fullness" of the Jews]; *Romans 11:15*, "life from the dead." [Also, in] *Romans 11:24–26*, "until the fullness of the Gentiles be come in: and so all Israel shall be saved." [The] utter abolishing of heathenism, *Jeremiah 10:11*, "[The gods that have not made the heavens and the earth, even they] shall perish from the earth." ***Sermons and Discourses, 1743–1758 (WJE Online Vol. 25)***

Romans 11:14

'Tis the will of Christ to convey this golden oil, this most excellent and precious benefit that ever he bestows, by ministers; whereby as Christ himself is the author of eternal salvation, so ministers become a kind of subordinate saviors. Thus the Apostle speaks of his saving his hearers, *Romans 11:14, 1 Corinthians 9:22*, and tells in Timothy that in following his counsel he will save "both himself and them that hear him" (*1 Timothy 4:16*); and in the prophecy, *Obadiah 21*, ministers are called saviors. In this way we shall not only have that anointing that will qualify us for a most honorable office in this world, but we shall be anointed to an eternal priesthood; and not only so, but an eternal royalty in heaven, and [we] shall be there kings and priests to God, even the Father. In this way we shall stand by the God of the earth in this world, and we shall enjoy much holy and sweet communion with him, and in this way we shall come to be near his throne in heaven: faithful and holy ministers will be, probably, some that will be next to Christ in heaven; [as] in John's vision of the glory of God in heaven (*Revelation 5*), the twenty-four elders were represented as having their seats next the throne. ***Sermons and Discourses, 1743–1758 (WJE Online Vol. 25)***

Romans 11:15

I say, by this it seems that the world of the Gentiles shall be, as it were, revived from the dead after this. By which it appears, that very great events for the advancement of religion and the kingdom of Christ shall be accomplished after the calling of the Jews, which shall be extensive, that it may be called a reviving of the world from the dead. And this last event must doubtless be before the millennium begins. Probably it will be thus. First, Turkey in Europe shall be overthrown, and the true religion established in those parts of Europe possessed by the Turks, which will be accomplished in pouring out the 6th vial. Concerning which, see no. 78. Nextly, Antichrist shall be overthrown, and the true religion embraced by the nations that formerly were the subjects of Antichrist. And perhaps religion shall begin to be gloriously propagated among heathen. Thirdly, the Jews shall be called. And fourth, this will be succeeded by an universal propagation of religion through the vast regions of the earth, that had been many ages covered with ignorance and darkness, and had as it were lain dead in paganish and Mahometan barbarism and brutality (which are to revive from the dead, after this calling of the Jews), and [by] the last great battle, wherein the remains of Antichrist, Mahometanism and heathenism shall be united and shall be conquered. Which victory shall be the revival of the world from the dead, and is the first resurrection spoken of in *Revelation*

20. And then the millennium shall begin. ***Apocalyptic Writings (WJE Online Vol. 5)***

Though we don't know the time in which this conversion of the nation of Israel will come to pass, yet this much we may determine by Scripture, that it will [be] before [the] glory of the Gentile part of the church shall be fully accomplished, because it is said that their coming in shall be life from the dead to the Gentiles, *Romans 11:12*, *Romans 11:15* ["Now if the fall of them be the riches of the world . . . how much more their fulness? . . . For if the casting away of them be the reconciling of the world, what shall the receiving of them be, but life from the dead?"]. ***A History of the Work of Redemption (WJE Online Vol. 9)***

Romans 11:16

The Apostle, in the *Romans 11*, teaches us to look on that great outpouring of the Spirit and ingathering of souls into Christ's kingdom, that was in those days, first of the Jews, and then of the Gentiles, to be but as the "first fruits" of the intended harvest, both with regard to Jews and Gentiles, and to look on the ingathering of those first fruits as a sign that all the remainder both of Jews and Gentiles should in due time be gathered in (*Romans 11:16*). "For if the first fruit be holy, the lump is also holy; and if the root be holy, so are the branches." And in that context, the Apostle speaks of the fullness of both Jews and Gentiles, as what shall hereafter be brought in, as distinct from that ingathering from among both, that was in those primitive ages of Christianity: in *Romans 11:12* we read of the "fullness of the Jews," and in the *Romans 11:25* of the "fullness of the Gentiles": and there in *Romans 11:30–32*, the Apostle teaches us to look upon that infidelity and darkness, that first prevailed over all Gentile nations, before Christ came, and then over the Jews after Christ came, as what was wisely permitted of God, as a preparation for the manifestation of the glory of God's mercy, in due time, on the whole world, constituted of Jews and Gentiles. "God hath concluded them all in unbelief, that he might have mercy upon all" [*Romans 11:32*]. These things plainly shew, that the time is coming when the whole world of mankind shall be brought into the church of Christ; and not only a part of the Jews, and a part of the Gentile world, as the first fruits, as it was in the first ages of the Christian church; but the fullness of both, the whole lump, all the nation of the Jews, and all the world of Gentiles. ***Apocalyptic Writings (WJE Online Vol. 5)***

[*1 Corinthians 15:20*. "But now is Christ risen from the dead, and become the first fruits of them that slept."] "Where he refers to the law concerning the first fruits. When the harvest was ripe, they were to bring a sheaf of the first fruits for a wave offering, with a burnt offering at the same time (*Leviticus 23:9–11*). Nor might they eat bread, parched corn, or green ears, till they had made their offering of first fruits. But having done this as the law required, the whole mass and substance of the harvest was hallowed, this offering of the first fruits being instead of all the rest, to which he alludes, *Romans 11:16*. 'If the first fruits be holy, the lump is holy.' Now with reference hereto, the Apostle calls the resurrection of Christ the 'first fruits'; it having as it were hallowed the dead bodies of the saints, and consecrated them to a new life. He rose not only as first in order, but his resurrection was a representation and figure of ours; showed not only that it might be, but that it should be; he rose as our head; when the natural body was raised, the mystical was raised also. 'By his resurrection he dissolved the tyranny of death,' saith one of the Fathers, 'and raised the whole world or church.' Which is no more than what the Apostle intimates in these words, 'He hath raised us up together with Christ' (*Ephesians 2:6*). He rose for us, went into heaven for us, as our 'forerunner' (*Hebrews 6:20*)." Bennet's *Christian Oratory*, 165.2 See *Isaiah 26:19*. ***The "Blank Bible" (WJE Online Vol. 24)***

Romans 11:17

The words are remarkable and very significant if we look into all the foregoing discourse, from the beginning of *Romans 9*, of which this is the conclusion. By not giving to God, but having all this wholly *from, through* and *in* God, is intended that these things, these great benefits forementioned, are thus from God without being from or through us. That some of the Jews were distinguished from others in enjoying the privileges of Christians, was not of themselves: "Not of him that willeth, nor him that runneth, but of God that showeth mercy." 'Tis of him who has "mercy on whom he will have mercy." 'Tis of God, whom makes of the same lump a vessel of honor and a vessel unto dishonor. 'Tis not of us nor our works, but of the calling of God, or "of him that calleth" (*Romans 9:11*, *Romans 9:16*, *Romans 9:21*). Not first of our own choice, but of God's election (*Romans 9:11*, *Romans 9:27* and *Romans 11:5*). All of the grace of God in such a manner as not to be of our works at all, yea, and so as to be utterly inconsistent with its being of our works (*Romans 11:5–7*). In such a manner as not firstly to be of their seeking; their seeking don't determine, but God's election (*Romans 11:7*). 'Tis of God, and not of man, that some were grafted in that were wild olive branches in themselves, and were unlikely as to any [thing] in themselves to be branches than others (*Romans 11:17*). Their being grafted in is owing to God's distinguishing goodness, while he was pleased to use severity towards others (*Romans 11:22*). Yea, God has so ordered it on purpose that all should be shut up in unbelief, be left to be so sinful, that he might have mercy on all, so as more visibly to show the salvation of all to be merely dependent on mercy. Then the Apostle fitly concludes all this discourse with, "Who hath first given to him, [and it shall be recompense unto him again? For] of him, through him, and to him, are all things: to whom be glory for ever. Amen." ***Writings on the Trinity, Grace, and Faith (WJE Online Vol. 21)***

If it should here be further objected, that 'tis an evidence that gentile Christians are visible saints, according to the New Testament notion of visible saintship, in the very same manner as the whole Jewish nation were till they were broken off by their obstinant rejection or the Messiah; and the gentile Christians represented as being grafted into the same olive [tree], from whence the Jews were broken off by unbelief, *Romans 11:17*, etc. ***Ecclesiastical Writings (WJE Online Vol. 12)***

If it be as Mr. Williams expressly says, that persons are not visible saints without a credible profession, visibility and moral evidence, not only of moral sincerity, but true holiness (p. 139), then all is wholly insignificant and vain, that is said to prove, that the children of Israel were visible saints without any evidence of such holiness, by reason of the idolatry and gross and open wickedness of vast multitudes of 'em, who are yet called God's people: and so likewise, all that is said to prove, that the members of the primitive Christian church had no other visibility of saintship than they, because they are grafted into the same olive [tree (*Romans 11:17*)]: and also all that Mr. Williams has said to prove, that many of the members of the primitive churches were as grossly wicked as they. ***Ecclesiastical Writings (WJE Online Vol. 12)***

Romans 11:18

["But if thou boast, thou bearest not the root, but the root thee."] I.e. consider that "thou bearest," etc. 'Tis unreasonable that you should boast of your relation to the root, or of your being branches from that root, against the branches that are broken off, for your present relation to the root is not from you, but from the root. The union or relation of the branches to the root don't begin from the branches, but from the root. It is owing to the root, and not to the branches; the root bears the branch, and not the branch the root. ***The "Blank Bible" (WJE Online Vol. 24)***

Romans 11:20

That perseverance is thus necessary to salvation not only as a *sine qua non*, but by reason of such an influence and dependence, seems manifest from Scripture, as particularly, *Hebrews 10:38–39*, "Now the just shall live by faith: but if any man draw, back my soul shall have no pleasure in him. But we are not of them who draw back unto perdition; but of them that believe to the saving of the soul." *Romans 11:20*, "Well; because of unbelief they were broken off, but thou standest by faith. Be not high-minded, but fear." *John 15:7*, "If ye abide in me, and my words abide in you, ye shall ask what ye will, and it shall be done unto you." *Hebrews 3:14*, "For we are made partakers of Christ, if we hold the beginning of our confidence firm unto the end." *Hebrews 6:12*, "Be ye followers of them who through faith and patience inherit the promises." ***The "Miscellanies," (Entry Nos. 501–832) (WJE Online Vol. 18)***

Hence gracious affections don't tend to make men bold, forward, noisy and boisterous; but rather to speak trembling (*Hosea 13:1*, "When Ephraim spake trembling, he exalted himself in Israel; but when he offended in Baal, he died"); and to clothe with a kind of holy fear in all their behavior towards God and man; agreeable to *Psalms 2:11, 1 Peter 3:15, 2 Corinthians 7:15, Ephesians 6:5, 1 Peter 3:2, Romans 11:20*. ***Religious Affections (WJE Online Vol. 2)***

And, that perseverance in faith is thus necessary to salvation, not merely as a sine qua non, or as an universal concomitant of it, but by reason of such an influence and dependence, seems manifest by many Scriptures; I would mention two or three. *Hebrews 3:6*, "Whose house are we, if we hold fast the confidence, and the rejoicing of the hope, firm unto the end." *Hebrews 3:14*, "For we are made partakers of Christ, if we hold the beginning of our confidence, steadfast unto the end." *Hebrews 6:12*, "Be ye followers of them, who through faith and patience inherit the promises." *Romans 11:20*, "Well, because of unbelief they were broken off, but thou standest by faith: Be not high-minded, but fear." ***Sermons and Discourses, 1734–1738 (WJE Online Vol. 19)***

You were many of you, as I well remember, much alarmed with the apprehension of the danger of the prevailing of these corrupt principles, near sixteen years ago. But the danger then was small in comparison of what appears now: these doctrines at this day are much more prevalent than they were then: the progress they have made in the land, within this seven years, seems to have been vastly greater than at any time in the like space before: and they are still prevailing and creeping into almost all parts of the land, threatening the utter ruin of the credit of those doctrines, which are the peculiar glory of the gospel, and the interests of vital piety. And I have of late perceived some things among yourselves, that show that you are far from being out of danger, but on the contrary remarkably exposed. The elder people may perhaps think themselves sufficiently fortified against infection: but 'tis fit that all should beware of self-confidence and carnal security, and should remember those needful warnings of Sacred Writ, "Be not high-minded, but fear" [*Romans 11:20*], and "let him that stands take heed lest he fall" [*1 Corinthians 10:12*]. But let the case of the elder people be as it will, the rising generation are doubtless greatly exposed. These principles are exceedingly taking with corrupt nature, and are what young people, at least such as have not their hearts established with grace, are easily led away with. ***Sermons and Discourses, 1743–1758 (WJE Online Vol. 25)***

Romans 11:22

So believers being overthrown in their faith, or their [not] knowing Christ's voice and following him, is called a being plucked out of Christ's hand; and it is implied that the consequence would be their perishing. And it also seems to be implied [that] their possession to eternal life by Christ's gift depends on their perseverance. *John 10:27–28*, "My sheep hear my voice, and I know them, and they follow me: and I give unto them eternal life; and they shall never perish, neither shall any pluck them out of my hand." And in the *John 15*, believers persevering in faith in Christ, or their abiding in him, is spoken of as necessary to the continuance of the saving union and relation that is between Christ and believers, and Christ's abiding in them; as *John 15:4–5*, "Abide in me and I in you. As the branch cannot bear fruit of itself, except it abide in the vine; no more can ye, except ye abide in me. I am the vine, ye are the branches. He that abideth in me, and I in him, the same bringeth forth much fruit." And in the *John 15:6* it is spoken of as the necessary consequence of their not abiding in Christ, if that were possible, that the union should be utterly broken between Christ and them, and that damnation should be the consequence. "If a man abide not in me, he is cast forth as a branch, and is withered; and men gather them, and cast them into the fire, and they are burned." And in the *John 15:7* this perseverance of faith is spoken of as the necessary means of the success of faith, as expressed in prayer, which is faith's voice, necessary to obtain those good things that faith and prayer seek. "If ye abide in me, and my words abide in you, ye shall ask what ye will, and it shall be done unto you." And in the *John 15:9–10* it is implied that Christ's acceptance of us, and favor to us as his, depends on our perseverance. "As the Father hath loved me, so have I loved you: continue ye in my love. If ye keep my commandments, ye shall abide in my love; even as I have kept my Father's commandments, and abide in his love." So the same perseverance is spoken of as necessary to our continuing in the favor and grace of God. "Now when the congregation was broken up, many of the Jews and religious proselytes followed Paul and Barnabas: who, speaking to them, persuaded them to continue in the grace of God" [*Acts 13:43*]. And so it is spoken [of] as necessary to continuing in the goodness of God, and a being cut off is spoken of as the certain consequence of the contrary. *Romans 11:22*, "Behold therefore the goodness and severity of God: on them which fell, severity; but towards thee, goodness, if thou continue in his goodness: otherwise thou also shalt be but off." That expression of standing fast IN THE LORD (*1 Thessalonians 3:8* and *Philippians 4:1*) implies that perseverance is necessary to a continuing in Christ, or in a saving relation to him; and more plainly still in *1 John 2:24*, "Let that therefore abide in you, which ye have heard from the beginning. If that which ye have heard from the beginning shall remain in you, ye also shall continue in the Son, and in the Father." See *1 Corinthians 15:2*, and *2 Timothy 4:7–8*, and *Hebrews 12:28*. See *Jeremiah 3:19*. ***The "Miscellanies," (Entry Nos. 501–832) (WJE Online Vol. 18)***

As the benefit and advantage of the good improvement of such a season is extraordinary great; so the danger of neglecting and misimproving it, is proportionably great. 'Tis abundantly evident by the Scripture, that as a time of great outpouring of the Spirit is a time of great favor to those that are partakers of the blessing; so it is always a time of remarkable vengeance to others. So in *Isaiah 61:2*, the same that is called "the acceptable year of the Lord," is called also "the day of vengeance of our God." So it was amongst the Jews in the apostles' days: the Apostle in *2 Corinthians 6:2* says of that time that it was "the accepted time," and "day of salvation";

and Christ says of the same time, *Luke 21:22*, "These are the days of vengeance." At the same time that the blessings of the kingdom of heaven were given to some, there was an ax laid at the root of the trees, that those that did not bear fruit might be "hewn down, and cast into the fire," *Matthew 3:9–11*. Then was glorified both the goodness and severity of God, in a remarkable manner, *Romans 11:22*. The harvest and the vintage go together: at the same time that the earth is reaped, and God's elect are gathered into the garner of God, the angel that has power over fire thrusts in his sickle, and gathers the cluster of the vine of the earth, and casts it into the great winepress of the wrath of God, *Revelation 14*, at the latter end. So it is foretold that at the beginning of the glorious times of the Christian church, at the same time that the hand of the Lord is known towards his servants, so shall his indignation towards his enemies, *Isaiah 66:14*. So when that glorious morning shall appear, wherein "the Sun of righteousness shall arise," to the elect, "with healing in his wings," the day "shall burn as an oven" to the wicked, *Malachi 4:1–3*. There is no time like such a time for the increase of guilt, and treasuring up wrath, and desperate hardening of the heart, if men stand it out; which is the most awful judgment, and fruit of divine wrath, that can be inflicted on any mortal. So that a time of great grace and pouring out of the Spirit and the fruits of divine mercy, is evermore also a time of great outpouring of something else, viz. divine vengeance on those that neglect and misimprove such a season. ***The Great Awakening (WJE Online Vol. 4)***

Though Christ receives 'em now and treats them as children, yet if they appear to be false, guileful and deceitful when the light of that day comes to shine through all their veils, [then will Christ cast them off]. If they appear as they pretend when the fire of that day comes to burn up all coverings and disguises, then will Christ own them and never will cast them off. (See No. 722.) But perseverance in good works is the main condition of this covenant, in case there be opportunity for this trial (*1 John 2:24–26, Romans 11:22*). If there be, they will be judged by this in the day of judgment, for everyone shall be judged according to his works. ***The "Miscellanies," (Entry Nos. 501–832) (WJE Online Vol. 18)***

Here the enjoyment of the saving goodness of God, is mentioned as the consequent continuing in his goodness; and a being cut off, is mentioned as the certain consequence of falling away; and so in other places that might be mentioned. Here I would briefly show how it is necessary to salvation. ***Sermons and Discourses, 1734–1738 (WJE Online Vol. 19)***

John 8:31, "Ye continue in my word, then are ye my disciples indeed." *Romans 2:7*, "To them who by patient continuance in well doing seek for glory and honor and immortality, eternal life." *Romans 11:22*, "Behold therefore the goodness and severity of God: on them which fell, severity; but towards thee, goodness, if thou continue in his goodness: otherwise thou also shalt be cut off." *Colossians 1:21–23*, "You [. . .] hath he reconciled [. . .], to present you holy and unblameable and unreproveable in his sight: if ye continue in the faith grounded and settled, and be not moved away from the hope of the gospel." *Galatians 6:9*, "We shall reap, if we faint not." ***Writings on the Trinity, Grace, and Faith (WJE Online Vol. 21)***

That, in the Apostle's account, 'tis a proper consideration to prevent our boasting, that our distinction from others is not of ourselves, not only in being distinguished in having better gifts and better ministers; but in our being made partakers of the great privileges of Christians, such as being ingrafted into Christ and partaking of the fitness of that olive tree. *Romans 11:17–18*, "And if some of the branches be broken off, and thou, being a wild olive tree, wert grafted in amongst them, and with them partakest of the root and fatness of the olive tree; boast not against the branches." Here 'tis manifest, 'tis the distinction that was made between some and others that is the thing insisted on by the Apostle. Others were broken off; they were grafted in. And the Apostle, *Romans 11:22*, calls upon them to consider this great distinction, and to ascribe it only to the distinguishing goodness of God: "Behold therefore the goodness and severity of God: on them which fell, severity; but towards thee, goodness." And its being owing not to them but to God and his distinguishing goodness, is the thing the Apostle urges as a reason why they should not boast but magnify God's grace or distinguishing goodness. And if it was a good reason, and the scheme [of] our salvation be anyway so contrived (as the Apostle elsewhere signifies) that all occasion of boasting should be precluded and all reasons given to ascribe all to God's grace, then doubtless 'tis so ordered that the greatest privileges, excellency, honor and happiness of Christians should be that wherein they don't distinguish themselves, but the distinction is owing to God's distinguishing goodness. ***Writings on the Trinity, Grace, and Faith (WJE Online Vol. 21)***

Romans 11:24

Another emblem here to be taken notice of is the stock or root of which those are the branches. Though this is not here expressly mentioned, yet [the meaning is clear enough]. 'Tis plain this is Jesus Christ, the head of the church, the root and offspring of David, that branch spoken of in the context. Those are the branches of that eminent Branch of the Lord, as Christ said to his disciples. *John 15:15*, "I am the vine, ye are the branches." The Prophet, when he first inquired what these were, called them trees; but then the angel made him no answer, perhaps signifying by his silence that he gave them not a right denomination. Christ himself is the olive tree into which all true members of the church are ingrafted. This is that good olive tree spoken of, *Romans 11:24*, "For if thou wert cut out of the olive tree which is wild by nature, and wert graffed contrary to nature into a good olive tree: how much more shall these, which be the natural branches, be graffed into their own olive tree?" The matter is explained in the last verse of the text: "These are the two anointed ones, that stand by the Lord of the whole earth." Christ [is] most properly called the Lord of the earth. [He is] God with us, Lord of the whole earth, having respect to what was said in the *Zechariah 4:10*, "They are the eyes of the Lord." The union of these offices, that are the instruments of the spiritual good of the church, to Christ, or their standing by him as depending on him, is represented by the union of the branch to the stock of the good olive tree. ***Sermons and Discourses, 1743–1758 (WJE Online Vol. 25)***

Romans 11:25

The prophecies of the New Testament do no less evidently shew, that a time will come when the gospel shall universally prevail, and the kingdom of Christ be extended over the whole habitable earth, in the most proper sense. Christ says (*John 12:32*), "I, if I be lifted up from the earth, will draw all men unto me." 'Tis fit, that when the Son of God becomes man, he should have dominion over all mankind: 'tis fit, that since he became an inhabitant of the earth, and shed his blood on the earth, he should possess the whole earth: 'tis fit, seeing here he became a servant, and was subject to men, and was arraigned before them, and judged, condemned and executed by them, and suffered ignominy and death in a most public manner, before Jews and Gentiles, being lifted up to view on the cross upon an hill, near that populous city Jerusalem, at a most public time, when there were many hundred thousand spectators, from all parts, that he should be rewarded with an universal dominion over mankind; and it is here declared he shall be. The Apostle, in the *Romans 11*, teaches us to look on that great outpouring of the Spirit and ingathering of souls into Christ's kingdom, that was in those days, first of the Jews, and then of the Gentiles, to be but as the "first fruits" of the intended harvest, both with regard to Jews and Gentiles, and to look on the ingathering of those first fruits as a sign that all the remainder both of Jews and Gentiles should in due time be gathered in (*Romans 11:16*). "For if the first fruit be holy, the lump is also holy; and if the root be holy, so are the branches." And in that context, the Apostle speaks of the fullness of both Jews and Gentiles, as what shall hereafter be brought in, as distinct from that ingathering from among both, that was in those primitive ages of Christianity: in *Romans 11:12* we read of the "fullness of the Jews," and in the *Romans 11:25* of the "fullness of the Gentiles": and there in *Romans 11:30–32*, the Apostle teaches us to look upon that infidelity and darkness, that first prevailed over all Gentile nations, before Christ came, and then over the Jews after Christ came, as what was wisely permitted of God, as a preparation for the manifestation of the glory of God's mercy, in due time, on the whole world, constituted of Jews and Gentiles. "God hath concluded them all in unbelief, that he might have mercy upon all" [*Romans 11:32*]. These things plainly shew, that the time is coming when the whole world of mankind shall be brought into the church of Christ; and not only a part of the Jews, and a part of the Gentile world, as the first fruits, as it was in the first ages of the Christian church; but the fullness of both, the whole lump, all the nation of the Jews, and all the world of Gentiles. ***Apocalyptic Writings (WJE Online Vol. 5)***

Luke 14:22–23. Here in this parable is represented to us, first, the rejection of the Jews and the calling of the Gentiles (*Luke 14:22*); but in the twenty-third [verse], there is manifestly another general calling of the Gentiles spoken of. The first is that which is called "the calling of the Gentiles," the next that which is called in Scripture the bringing in "the fullness of the Gentiles" [*Romans 11:25*]. 'Tis manifest therefore by this text that there remains yet another calling of the Gentiles than hath yet been. ***Notes on Scripture (WJE Online Vol. 15)***

[*Proverbs 3:7*. "Be not wise in thine own eyes."] This forbids a man's being disposed to have an high thought of his own piety and holiness, as well as his own reason and judgment, for we know that wisdom is understood most commonly in this book for holiness or true virtue. This is confirmed by the sense in which the Apostle uses the same phrase (*Romans 11:25*). ***The "Blank Bible" (WJE Online Vol. 24)***

["Until the fullness of the Gentiles be come in."] "The fullness of the Jews (*Romans 11:12*) is the whole body of the Jewish nation professing Christianity. And therefore here 'the fullness of the Gentiles' must be the whole body of the Gentiles professing Christianity." Mr. Locke's note. That the whole world shall one day be brought into the Christian church is further evident by *Romans 11:32*. ***The "Blank Bible" (WJE Online Vol. 24)***

Romans 11:25–26

There is a time coming that there will be very great change in the world: those nations which now are covered with the darkness of heathenism and idolatry, or other false religions, shall be enlightened with the truth, and there shall be a more extraordinary appearance of the power of godliness amongst those that profess it, when God's spirit shall be poured out on old and young, and the knowledge of God shall cover the earth "as the waters cover the seas" (*Isaiah 11:9*); "When they shall teach no more every man his neighbor, and every man his brother, saying, Know the Lord; for they shall all know him, from the least to the greatest" [*Jeremiah 31:34*]; "When the fullness of the Gentiles shall come in and all Israel shall be saved" (*Romans 11:25–26*). These, and suchlike expressions, signify that all nations shall be Christianized and be visibly holy, and that multitudes—great multitudes all over the face of the earth—shall be brought to the saving knowledge of God. All those that are truly sensible of the worth of souls will think these very glorious times and will long for them. They are generally thought to be very near, which is a consideration that ought to stir up all Christians earnestly to pray for them, for though God has appointed the time of these things in his own counsels, yet he will be enquired of for them by his people before he accomplishes them: *Ezekiel 36:37–38*, "Thus saith the Lord God, I will yet for this be enquired of by the house of Israel, to do it for them; I will increase them with men like a flock. As the holy flock, as the flock of Jerusalem in her solemn feasts; so shall the waste cities be filled with flocks of men: and they shall know that I am the Lord." ***Sermons and Discourses 1720–1723 (WJE Online Vol. 10)***

Romans 11:26

Therefore the time of tribulation here spoken [of] is, as the prophet Jeremy expresses it, the time of Jacob's tribulation. *Jeremiah 30:7*, "Alas, for that day is great, so that none is like it: it is even the time of Jacob's trouble, but he shall be saved out of it." It is the time of the trouble, both of the literal and spiritual Jacob. The literal Jacob shall be saved out of it, when the time come that the Apostle speaks of in the *Romans 11*, when "all Israel shall be saved" *Romans 11:26*]. And the spiritual Jacob shall be saved out of it, as appears by the words of *Daniel 12:1*, where there seems to be reference to those words of Jeremiah. "And at that time shall Michael stand up, the great prince which standeth for the children of thy people. And there shall be a time of trouble, such as never was since there was a nation, even to that same time. And at that time thy people shall be delivered, everyone that are found written in the book." And that the spiritual Jacob, or the elect, shall be delivered out of it, appears by the words of Christ in this place, where Christ seems to have reference to what had been before said by both these other prophets. ***Notes on Scripture (WJE Online Vol. 15)***

Jewish infidelity shall then be overthrown. However obstinate they have now been for above seventeen hundred years in their rejecting Christ, and instances of conversion of any of that nation have been so very rare ever since the destruction of Jerusalem, but they have against the plain teachings of their own prophets continued to approve of the cruelty of their forefathers in crucifying [Christ]; yet when this day comes the thick veil that blinds their eyes shall be removed, *2 Corinthians 3:16*, and divine grace shall melt and renew their hard hearts, "And they shall look on him whom they [have pierced, and they shall mourn for him, as one mourneth for his only son, and shall be in bitterness for him, as one that is in bitterness for his firstborn]," *Zechariah 12:10* etc. And then shall all Israel be saved. The Jews in all their dispersions shall cast away their old infidelity, and shall wonderfully have their hearts changed, and abhor themselves for their past unbelief and obstinacy; and shall flow together to the blessed Jesus, penitently, humbly, and joyfully owning him as their glorious king and only savior, and shall with all their hearts as with one heart and voice declare his praises unto other nations. ***A History of the Work of Redemption (WJE Online Vol. 9)***

Romans 11:28.

How is the gospel "the power of God to salvation to those that believe, to the Jew first?" And so it is said in the *Romans 2:10*, that God will render "glory, honor, and peace to every man that worketh good, to the Jew first." *Arts.* God was ready to justify all that believed in Christ, and to reward all that work good, but especially the Jews, for the peculiar favor he bore to that nation for their forefathers' sakes, as *Romans 11:28*, and because they were born in covenant, or were his covenant people by descent. See *Romans 2:25*, "For circumcision verily profiteth," etc. ***The "Blank Bible" (WJE Online Vol. 24)***

Romans 11:28–29

And with regard to the people of Israel, 'tis very manifest, that something diverse is oftentimes intended by that nation's being God's people, from their being visible saints, or visibly holy, or having those qualifications which are requisite in order to a due admission to the ecclesiastical privileges of such. That nation, that family of Israel according to the flesh, and with regard to that external and carnal qualification, were in some sense adopted by God to be his peculiar people, and his covenant people. This is not only evident by what has been already observed, but also indisputably manifest from *Romans 9:2–5*, "I have great heaviness and continual sorrow of heart; for I could wish that myself were accursed from Christ for my brethren, my kinsmen according to the flesh, who are Israelites, to whom pertaineth the adoption, and the glory, and the covenants, and the giving of the law, and the service of God, and the promises; whose are the fathers; and of whom, concerning the flesh, Christ came." 'Tis to be noted, that the privileges here mentioned are spoken of as belonging to the Jews, not now as visible saints, not as professors of the true religion, not as members of the visible church of Christ; but only as people of such a nation, such a blood, such an external and carnal relation to the patriarchs their ancestors, Israelites, "according to the flesh." For the Apostle is speaking here of the unbelieving Jews, professed unbelievers, that were out of the Christian church, and open visible enemies to it, and such as had no right to the external privileges of Christ's people. So in *Romans 11:28–29* this Apostle speaks of the same unbelieving Jews, as in some respect an elect people, and interested in the calling, promises and covenants God formerly gave to their forefathers, and as still beloved for their sakes. "As concerning the gospel, they are enemies for your sake; but as touching the election they are beloved for the fathers' sakes: for the gifts and calling of God are without repentance." These things are in these places spoken of, not as privileges belonging to the Jews now as a people of the right religion, or in the true church of visible worshippers of God; but as a people of such a pedigree or blood; and that even after the ceasing of the Mosaic administration. But these were privileges more especially belonging to them under the Old Testament: they were a family that God had chosen in distinction from all others, to show special favor to above all other nations. 'Twas manifestly agreeable to God's design to constitute things so under the Old Testament, that the means of grace and spiritual privileges and blessing should be, though not wholly, yet in a great measure confined to a particular family, much more than those privileges and blessings are confined to any posterity or blood now under the gospel. God did purposely so order things that that nation should by these favours be distinguished, not only from those who were not professors of the worship of the true God but also in a great measure from other nations by a wall of separation that he made. This was not merely a wall of separation between professors and non-professors (such a wall of separation as this remains still in the days of the gospel) but between nation and nations. God, if he pleases, may by his sovereignty annex his blessing, and in some measure fix it, for his own reasons, to a particular blood, as well as to a particular place or spot of ground, to a certain building, to a particular heap of stones, or altar of brass, to particular garments, and other external things. And 'tis evident, that he actually did affix his blessing to that particular external family of Jacob, very much as he did to the city of Jerusalem, that he chose to place his name there, and to Mount Zion where he commanded the blessing. God did not so affix his blessing to Jerusalem or Mount Zion, as to limit himself, either by confining the blessing wholly to that place, never to bestow it elsewhere; nor by obliging himself always to bestow it on those that sought him there; nor yet obliging himself never to withdraw his blessing from thence, by forsaking his dwelling place there, and leaving it to be a common or profane place: but he was pleased so to annex his blessing to that place, as to make it the seat of his blessing in a peculiar manner, in great distinction from other places. In like manner did he fix his blessing to that blood or progeny of Jacob. It was a family which he delighted in, and which he blessed in a peculiar manner, and to which he in a great measure confined the blessing; but not so as to limit himself, or so as to oblige himself to bestow it on all of that blood, or not to bestow it on others that were not of that blood. He affixed his blessing to both these, both to the place and nation, by sovereign election (*Psalms 132:13–15*). He annexed and fixed his blessing to both by covenant. To that nation he fixed his blessing by his covenant with the patriarchs. Indeed the main thing, the substance and marrow of that covenant which God made with Abraham and the other patriarchs, was the covenant of grace, which is continued in these days of the gospel, and extends to all his spiritual seed, of the gentiles as well as Jews: but yet that covenant with the patriarchs contained other things that were as it were appendages to that great everlasting covenant of grace, promises of lesser matters, subservient to the grand promise of the future seed, and typical of things appertaining to him. Such were those promises, that annexed the blessing to a particular country, viz. the land of Canaan, and a particular blood, viz. the progeny of Isaac and Jacob. Just so it was also as to the covenant God made with David that we have an account of, *2 Samuel 7* and *Psalms 132*. If we consider that covenant with regard to what the soul and marrow of it was, it was the covenant of grace: but there were other promises which were as it were appendages of things subservient to the grand covenant, and typical of its benefits; such were promises of the blessing to the nation of the literal Israel, and of continuing the temporal crown of Israel to David's posterity, and of fixing the blessing to Jerusalem or Mount Zion, as the place that he chose to set his name there. And in this sense it was that the very family of Jacob were God's people by covenant, or his covenant people, and his chosen people; yea and this even when they were no visible saints, when they were educated and lived in idolatry, and made no profession of the true religion. ***Ecclesiastical Writings (WJE Online Vol. 12)***

Romans 11:28–29

'Tis manifest, that something diverse from being visible saints, is often intended by that nation's being called God's people, and that that nation, the family of "Israel according to the flesh," and not with regard to any moral and religious qualifications, were in some sense adopted by God, to be his peculiar and covenant people; from *Romans 9:3–5*, "I could wish myself accursed from Christ for my brethren according to the flesh; who are Israelites; to whom pertaineth the adoption, and the glory, and the *covenants*, and the giving of the law, and the service of God, and the promises; whose are the fathers," etc. I observed, that these privileges here mentioned, are spoken of as belonging to the Jews, "not now as visible saints, not as professors of the true religion, not as members of the visible church of Christ (which they did not belong to) but only as a people of such a nation, such a blood, such an external carnal relation to the patriarchs, their ancestors; Israelites, 'according to the flesh': inasmuch as the Apostle is speaking here of the unbelieving Jews, professed unbelievers, that were out of the Christian church, and open visible enemies to it; and such as had no right at all to the external privileges of Christ's people." I observed further, that in like manner "this Apostle in *Romans 11:28–29* speaks of the same unbelieving Jews, that were enemies to the gospel, as in some respect an elect people, and interested in the calling, promises and covenants, God formerly gave their forefathers, and are still beloved for their sakes. 'As concerning the gospel, they are enemies for your sakes: But as touching the election, they are beloved for the fathers' sakes. For the gifts and calling of God are without repentance.'" ***Ecclesiastical Writings (WJE Online Vol. 12)***

Romans 11:30–32

In *Romans 11:12* we read of the "fullness of the Jews," and in the *Romans 11:25* of the "fullness of the Gentiles": and there in *Romans 11:30–32*, the Apostle teaches us to look upon that infidelity and darkness, that first prevailed over all Gentile nations, before Christ came, and then over the Jews after Christ came, as what was wisely permitted of God, as a preparation for the manifestation of the glory of God's mercy, in due time, on the whole world, constituted of Jews and Gentiles. "God hath concluded them all in unbelief, that he might have mercy upon all" [*Romans 11:32*]. These things plainly shew, that the time is coming when the whole world of mankind shall be brought into the church of Christ; and not only a part of the Jews, and a part of the Gentile world, as the first fruits, as it was in the first ages of the Christian church; but the fullness of both, the whole lump, all the nation of the Jews, and all the world of Gentiles. ***Apocalyptic Writings (WJE Online Vol. 5)***

Romans 11:32

The representations of the redemption by Christ, everywhere in Scripture, lead us to suppose, that *all* whom he came to redeem, are *sinners*; that his salvation, as to the term from which (or the evil to be redeemed from) in all is sin, and the deserved punishment of sin. 'Tis natural to suppose, that when he had his name Jesus, or Savior, given him by God's special and immediate appointment, the salvation meant by that name should be his salvation in general; and not only a part of his salvation, and with regard only to some of them that he came to save. But this name was given him to signify his saving his people from their sins (*Matthew 1:21*). And the great doctrine of Christ's salvation is, that "he came into the world to save sinners" (*1 Timothy 1:15*), and that "Christ hath once suffered, the just for the unjust" (*1 Peter 3:18*). "In this was manifested the love of God towards us" (towards such in general as have the benefit of God's love in giving Christ) "that God sent his only begotten Son into the world, that we might live through him. Herein is love . . . that he sent his Son to be the propitiation for our sins" (*1 John 4:9–10*). Many other texts might be mentioned, which seem evidently to suppose, that all who are redeemed by Christ, are saved from sin. We are led by what Christ himself said, to suppose, that if any are not sinners, they have no need of him as a Redeemer, any more than a well man of a physician (*Mark 2:17*). And that men, in order to being the proper subjects of the mercy of God through Christ, must first be in a state of sin, is implied in *Galatians 3:22*. "But the scripture hath concluded all under sin, that the promise by faith of Jesus Christ might be given to them that believe." To the same effect is *Romans 11:32*. ***Original Sin (WJE Online Vol. 3)***

The prophecies of the New Testament do no less evidently shew, that a time will come when the gospel shall universally prevail, and the kingdom of Christ be extended over the whole habitable earth, in the most proper sense. Christ says (*John 12:32*), "I, if I be lifted up from the earth, will draw all men unto me." 'Tis fit, that when the Son of God becomes man, he should have dominion over all mankind: 'tis fit, that since he became an inhabitant of the earth, and shed his blood on the earth, he should possess the whole earth: 'tis fit, seeing here he became a servant, and was subject to men, and was arraigned before them, and judged, condemned and executed by them, and suffered ignominy and death in a most public manner, before Jews and Gentiles, being lifted up to view on the cross upon an hill, near that populous city Jerusalem, at a most public time, when there were many hundred thousand spectators, from all parts, that he should be rewarded with an universal dominion over mankind; and it is here declared he shall be. The Apostle, in the *Romans 11*, teaches us to look on that great outpouring of the Spirit and ingathering of souls into Christ's kingdom, that was in those days, first of the Jews, and then of the Gentiles, to be but as the "first fruits" of the intended harvest, both with regard to Jews and Gentiles, and to look on the ingathering of those first fruits as a sign that all the remainder both of Jews and Gentiles should in due time be gathered in (*Romans 11:16*). "For if the first fruit be holy, the lump is also holy; and if the root be holy, so are the branches." And in that context, the Apostle speaks of the fullness of both Jews and Gentiles, as what shall hereafter be brought in, as distinct from that ingathering from among both, that was in those primitive ages of Christianity: in *Romans 11:12* we read of the "fullness of the Jews," and in the *Romans 11:25* of the "fullness of the Gentiles": and there in *Romans 11:30–32*, the Apostle teaches us to look upon that infidelity and darkness, that first prevailed over all Gentile nations, before Christ came, and then over the Jews after Christ came, as what was wisely permitted of God, as a preparation for the manifestation of the glory of God's mercy, in due time, on the whole world, constituted of Jews and Gentiles. "God hath concluded them all in unbelief, that he might have mercy upon all" [*Romans 11:32*]. These things plainly shew, that the time is coming when the whole world of mankind shall be brought into the church of Christ; and not only a part of the Jews, and a part of the Gentile world, as the first fruits, as it was in the first ages of the Christian church; but the fullness of both, the whole lump, all the nation of the Jews, and all the world of Gentiles. ***Apocalyptic Writings (WJE Online Vol. 5)***

Romans 11:33

Dr. Doddridge renders it, "O the depth of the riches, and wisdom, and knowledge of God." And by "riches" he understands treasures of divine mercy. ***The "Blank Bible" (WJE Online Vol. 24)***

How great and how adorable does God appear, in having planned out the whole scheme of future events in his eternal counsels! Thus is his work all before him; it has always lain under his eye, and under his hand nothing can ever arise to surprize him or cast any difficulty or perplexity on his way, he having already from eternity settled the proper measures of conduct in every case that shall emerge. How incomprehensible and wonderful in counsel, as well as excellent in working, is God! and what reason have we to cry out, "O the depth of the riches both of the wisdom and knowledge of God! how unsearchable are his judgments, and his ways past finding out!," *Romans 11:33*. ***"Controversies" Notebook (WJE Online Vol. 27)***

Romans 11:33–36

But God's wisdom and omnisciency shines clearest of all in his perfect knowledge of himself, who is the infinite object of his own knowledge. That eternity of his, whereby he was from everlasting to everlasting, which so confounds us miserable worms, is clearly understood by him with the greatest ease, at one simple view; he also comprehends his own infinite greatness and excellency, which can be done by none but an infinite understanding. Well might the Apostle cry out: O the depths of the riches both of the wisdom and knowledge of God! how unsearchable are his judgments, and his ways past finding out! For who hath known the mind of the Lord, or who hath been his counsellor; or who hath first given to him, and it shall be recompensed to him again? For of him and through him, and to him, are all things: to whom be glory forever. Amen [*Romans 11:33–36*]. ***Sermons and Discourses 1720–1723 (WJE Online Vol. 10)***

Romans 11:34

These things can be said of none but Christ, who "is in the bosom of the Father" [*John 1:18*], and hath seen the Father, and hath known his mind, is the man that is his fellow, is worthy and able to open the book of his decrees, though sealed with seven seals, was as it were God's counselor, to whom God said, "Let us make" [*Genesis 1:26*]. And he is God's first-born, that was before the hills, that hath "heard the secret of God" (*Job 15:7–8*); he was as it were brought up with him. ***The "Blank Bible" (WJE Online Vol. 24)***

Romans 11:35

["Or who hath first given unto him, and it shall be recompensed to him again?"] I.e. who of mankind, either Jews or Gentiles, seeing both were shut up in unbelief? All were first concluded under sin, or a state of visible total impiety, as in the *Romans 11:35*. This confirms the greatness of "the depth of the riches of God," mentioned in the preceding verse, i.e. the grace of God. See note on that verse above. ***The "Blank Bible" (WJE Online Vol. 24)***

Romans 11:36

And when God is so often spoken of as the last as well as the first, and the end as well as the beginning, what is meant (or at least implied) is, that as he is the first efficient cause and fountain from whence all things originate, so he is the last final cause for which they are made; the final term to which they all tend in their ultimate issue. This seems to be the most natural import of these expressions; and is confirmed by other parallel passages, as *Romans 11:36*, "For of him and through him and to him are all things." *Colossians 1:16*, "For by him were all things created, that are in heaven, and that are in earth, visible and invisible, whether they be thrones or dominions, principalities or powers, all things were created by him, and for him." *Hebrews 2:10*, "For it became him, by whom are all things, and for whom are all things." In *Proverbs 16:4* 'tis said expressly, "The Lord hath made all things for himself." ***Ethical Writings (WJE Online Vol. 8)***

The doctrine that makes God's creatures and not himself to be his last end is a doctrine the farthest from having a favorable aspect on God's absolute self-sufficience and independence. It far less agrees therewith than the doctrine against which this is objected. For we must conceive of the efficient as depending on his ultimate end. He depends on this end in his desires, aims, actions and pursuits; so that he fails in all his desires, actions and pursuits, if he fails of his end. Now if God himself be his last end, then in his dependence on his end he depends on nothing but himself. If all things be of him, and to him, and he the first and the last, this shows him to be all in all: he is all to himself. He goes not out of himself in what he seeks; but his desires and pursuits as they originate from, so they terminate in himself; and he is dependent on none but himself in the beginning or end of any of his exercises or operations. But if not himself, but the creature, be his last end, then as he depends on his last end, he is in some sort dependent on the creature. ***Ethical Writings (WJE Online Vol. 8)***

And when God is so often spoken of as the last as well as the first, and the end as well as the beginning, what is meant (or at least implied) is, that as he is the first efficient cause and fountain from whence all things originate, so he is the last final cause for which they are made; the final term to which they all tend in their ultimate issue. This seems to be the most natural import of these expressions; and is confirmed by other parallel passages, as *Romans 11:36*, "For of him and through him and to him are all things." *Colossians 1:16*, "For by him were all things created, that are in heaven, and that are in earth, visible and invisible, whether they be thrones or dominions, principalities or powers, all things were created by him, and for him." *Hebrews 2:10*, "For it became him, by whom are all things, and for whom are all things." In *Proverbs 16:4* 'tis said expressly, "The Lord hath made all things for himself." ***Ethical Writings (WJE Online Vol. 8)***

The emanation or communication of the divine fullness, consisting in the knowledge of God, love to God, and joy in God, has relation indeed both to God and the creature: but it has relation to God as its fountain, as it is an emanation from God; and as the communication itself, or thing communicated, is something divine, something of God, something of his internal fullness; as the water in the stream is something of the fountain; and as the beams are of the sun. And again, they have relation to God as they have respect to him as their object: for the knowledge communicated is the knowledge of God; and so God is the object of the knowledge: and the love communicated, is the love of God; so God is the object of that love: and the happiness communicated, is joy in God; and so he is the object of the joy communicated. In the creature's knowing, esteeming, loving, rejoicing in, and praising God, the glory of God is both exhibited and acknowledged; his fullness is received and returned. Here is both an *emanation* and *remanation*. The refulgence shines upon and into the creature, and is reflected back to the luminary. The beams of glory come from God, and are something of God, and are refunded back again to their original. So that the whole is *of God*, and *in* God, and *to* God; and God is the beginning, middle and end in this affair. ***Ethical Writings (WJE Online Vol. 8)***

Thus 'tis God that has given us the Redeemer, and 'tis of him that our good is purchased; so 'tis God that is the Redeemer, and the price: and 'tis God also that is the good purchased. So that all that we have is *of* God, and *through* him, and *in* him; *Romans 11:36*, "For of him, and through him, and to him," or "in him," "are all things." The same in the Greek, that is here rendered "to him," is rendered "in him" (*1 Corinthians 8:6*). ***Sermons and Discourses, 1730–1733 (WJE Online Vol. 17)***

The Holy Ghost being a comprehension of all good things promised in the gospel, we may easily see the force of the Apostle's arguing, *Galatians 3:2*, "This only would I know, Received ye the Spirit by the works of the law, or by the hearing of faith?" So that in the offer of redemption, 'tis of God of whom our good is purchased, and 'tis God that purchases it, and 'tis God also that is the thing purchased. Thus all our good things are of God, and through God, and in God, as *Romans 11:36*, "For of him, and through him, and to him, and in him" (as εις is rendered in *1 Corinthians 8:6*), "are all things: to whom be glory forever." All our good is of God the

Father, and through God the Son, and all is in the Holy Ghost, as he is himself all our good. And so God is himself the portion and purchased inheritance of his people. Thus God is the Alpha and Omega in this affair of redemption. ***Writings on the Trinity, Grace, and Faith (WJE Online Vol. 21)***

ROMANS CHAPTER 12

Romans 12:1

As it is with spiritual discoveries and affections given at first conversion, so it is in all illuminations and affections of that kind, that persons are the subjects of afterwards; they are all *transforming*. There is a like divine power and energy in them, as in the first discoveries: and they still reach the bottom of the heart, and affect and alter the very nature of the soul, in proportion to the degree in which they are given. And a transformation of nature is continued and carried on by them, to the end of life; till it is brought to perfection in glory. Hence the progress of the work of grace in the hearts of the saints, is represented in Scripture, as a continued conversion and renovation of nature. So the Apostle exhorts those that were at Rome, beloved of God, called to be saints, and that were the subjects of God's redeeming mercies, to be transformed by the renewing of their mind; *Romans 12:1–2*, "I beseech you therefore by the mercies of God, that ye present your bodies, a living sacrifice; . . . And be not conformed to this world; but be ye transformed, by the renewing of your mind." ***Religious Affections (WJE Online Vol. 2)***

Christians, by offering obedience to God in their lives and conversation, they do what the Apostle calls, in *Romans 12:1*, offering their bodies to God "a living sacrifice, holy, and acceptable to God," as their "rational service." They offer their bodies; that is, they dedicate their bodies to holy uses and purposes. They yield their members as instruments of righteousness unto holiness. The soul, while here, acts by the body as to the external conversation, but in this Christians do serve God. They yield their eyes, their ears, their tongues, their hands and feet as servants to God, to be obedient to the dictates of his Word and of his Holy Spirit in the soul. ***Sermons and Discourses, 1730–1733 (WJE Online Vol. 17)***

So the Apostle exhorts those that were at Rome, "beloved of God, called to be saints" (*Romans 1:7*), and those that were the subjects of God's redeeming mercies, to be transformed by the renewing of their mind; *Romans 12:1–2*, "I beseech ye therefore by the mercies of God to present your bodies a living sacrifice, holy, acceptable unto God, which is your reasonable service. And be not conformed to this world, but be ye transformed by the renewing of your mind." ***The "Miscellanies," 833–1152 (WJE Online Vol. 20)***

By not continuing in sin, but walking in newness of life, and not serving sin; yielding obedience to God and being servants of righteousness; and bringing forth the fruits of righteousness. The Apostle in Romans 6 has a special respect to external works that are performed, because he particularly explains it by sin's not reigning in our mortal bodies; and yielding our members as "instruments of righteousness unto God"; and yielding our members as "servants of righteousness unto holiness" (see *Romans 6:1*, *Romans 6:3*, *Romans 6:6*, *Romans 6:12*, *Romans 6:13*, *Romans 6:16*, *Romans 6:18*, *Romans 6:19*). So the Apostle in *Romans 12:1* insists upon it. By good works and keeping God's commandments and bringing forth fruit, when spoken of as signs of sincerity, are chiefly intended properly voluntary behavior; because the same is expressed by walking before God and being perfect, walking before him in truth and with a perfect heart, running a race, fighting a good fight. ***Writings on the Trinity, Grace, and Faith (WJE Online Vol. 21)***

So the Apostle, in the beginning of his epistle to the Romans, says that he writes to those at Rome that were "beloved of God, called to be saints" [*Romans 1:7*], and yet he exhorts 'em to be transformed by the renewing of their mind. *Romans 12:1–2*, "I beseech you therefore, by the mercies of God, that ye present your bodies a living sacrifice, holy, acceptable unto God, which is your reasonable service. And be not conformed unto this world: but be ye transformed by the renewing of your mind." ***Sermons and Discourses, 1739–1742 (WJE Online Vol. 22)***

"I beseech you therefore, brethren, by the mercies of God." I.e. it being so that you Christians are so distinguished by the sovereign electing grace of God, as has been set forth in the three foregoing chapters. ***The "Blank Bible" (WJE Online Vol. 24)***

He was made capable of reasoning, that he might be capable by his reason to see God in his works, and capable of rational actions, that he might be capable of serving God; God seeks of us a "rational service" [*Romans 12:1*]. A creature is not capable of serving God without understanding and reason. A creature may be capable of serving that has no reason, as the brute creatures are capable of serving men; but God can be served only by rational creatures. ***Sermons and Discourses, 1730–1733 (WJE Online Vol. 17)***

Romans 12:2

There is a more excellent way that the Spirit of God leads the sons of God, that natural men cannot have, and that is by inclining them to do the will of God, and go in the shining path of truth and Christian holiness, from an holy heavenly disposition, which the Spirit of God gives them, and enlivens in them which inclines 'em and leads 'em to those things that are excellent and agreeable to God's mind, whereby they are "transformed by the renewing of their minds, and prove what is that good, and acceptable, and perfect will of God," as in *Romans 12:2*. And so the Spirit of God does in a gracious manner teach the saints their duty; and teaches 'em in an higher manner than ever Balaam, or Saul, or Judas, were taught, or any natural man is capable of while such. The Spirit of God enlightens 'em with respect to their duty by making their eye single and pure, whereby the "whole body is full of light" [*Matthew 6:22*]. The sanctifying influence of the Spirit of God rectifies the taste of the soul, whereby it savors those things that are of God, and naturally relishes and delights in those things that are holy and agreeable to God's mind, and like one of a distinguishing taste, chooses those things that are good and wholesome, and rejects those things that are evil; for the sanctified ear tries words, and the sanctified heart tries actions, as the mouth tastes meat. And thus the Spirit of God leads and guides the meek in his way, agreeable to his promises; he enables them to understand the commands and counsels of his Word, and rightly to apply them. Christ blames the Pharisees that they had not this holy distinguishing taste, to discern and distinguish what was right and wrong. *Luke 12:57*, "Yea, and why, even of your own selves, judge ye not what is right?" ***The Great Awakening (WJE Online Vol. 4)***

A Christian spirit seeks to please and glorify God. The things which are well pleasing to God and Christ, and tend to the glory of Christ, are called the things of Jesus Christ in opposition to our own things. *Philippians 2:21*, "For all seek their own, not the things which are Jesus Christ's." Christianity requires that we should make God and Christ our main end. Christians, so far as they live like Christians, live so that for them to live is Christ [*Philippians 1:21*]. Christians are required to live so as to please

God. *Romans 12:2*, "That ye may prove what is that good, and acceptable, and perfect will of God." ***Ethical Writings (WJE Online Vol. 8)***

In the *Romans 12:2* they are directed to make experiment of that which is eminently and far above the Jewish services, the "good, and acceptable, and perfect will of God." ***The "Blank Bible" (WJE Online Vol. 24)***

When a holy and amiable action is suggested to the thoughts of a holy soul; that soul, if in the lively exercise of its spiritual taste, at once sees a beauty in it, and so inclines to it, and closes with it. On the contrary, if an unworthy unholy action be suggested to it, its sanctified eye sees no beauty in it, and is not pleased with it; its sanctified taste relishes no sweetness in it, but on the contrary, it is nauseous to it. Yea its holy taste and appetite leads it to think of that which is truly lovely, and naturally suggests it; as a healthy taste and appetite naturally suggests the idea of its proper object. Thus a holy person is led by the Spirit, as he is instructed and led by his holy taste, and disposition of heart; whereby, in the lively exercise of grace, he easily distinguishes good and evil, and knows at once, what is a suitable amiable behavior towards God, and towards man, in this case and the other; and judges what is right, as it were spontaneously, and of himself, without a particular deduction, by any other arguments than the beauty that is seen, and goodness that is tasted. Thus Christ blames the Pharisees, that they did not, even of their own selves (*Luke 12:57*) judge what was right, without needing miracles to prove it. The Apostle seems plainly to have respect to this way of judging of spiritual beauty, in *Romans 12:2*. "Be ye transformed by the renewing of your mind, that ye may prove what is that good, and perfect, and acceptable will of God." ***Religious Affections (WJE Online Vol. 2)***

Romans 12:3

But humility is an excellency proper to all created intelligent beings, for they are all infinitely mean and little before God, and most of them mean in comparison with some of their fellow creatures. Humility implies a compliance with that rule of the Apostle, *Romans 12:3*, "For I say, through the grace given unto me, to every man that is among you, not to think of himself more highly than he ought to think; but to think soberly, according as God hath dealt to every man the measure of faith." Humility, as it is a virtue in man, contains a sense of his own comparative meanness, both as compared with God and with his fellow creatures. ***Ethical Writings (WJE Online Vol. 8)***

Here are perfect rules, which, if followed, will make us excel in the duties more immediately relating to ourselves. *Romans 12:3*, "For I say, through the grace given to me, to every man that is among you, not to think of himself more highly than he ought to think; but to think soberly, according as God hath dealt to every man the measure of faith." ***Sermons and Discourses: 1723–1729 (WJE Online Vol. 14)***

"For by virtue of that commission, to be the apostle of the Gentiles, which by the favor of God is bestowed on me, I bid everyone of you," etc. Mr. Locke's *Paraphrase*. ***The "Blank Bible" (WJE Online Vol. 24)***

That it is St. Paul's design here to prevent or regulate such disorder, and to keep everyone in the exercising his particular gift within its due bounds, is evident in that exhorting them, *Romans 12:3*, to a sober use of their gifts. He makes the measure of that sobriety to be that measure of faith or spiritual gift, which everyone in particular enjoyed by the favor of God. ***The "Blank Bible" (WJE Online Vol. 24)***

Romans 12:4

And the Scriptures represent as though every Christian should in all things he does be employed for the good of God's church, as each particular member of the body is in all things employed for the good of the body: *Romans 12:4* ff. ***Ethical Writings (WJE Online Vol. 8)***

Romans 12:5

1. Christians' union with Christ. They are spoken of as the body of Christ; for when the Apostle says, "We, being many, are one body," he means one body of Christ, as is manifest by what he says more expressly elsewhere, as particularly *Romans 12:5*, "For we, being many, are one body of Christ." And 1 Corinthians 12:20, "Now we are many members, yet one body." And *1 Corinthians 12:27*, "Now ye are the body of Christ, and members in particular," and the like in many other places. Christians' union with Christ is further represented by their being the food or the bread of Christ—sometimes his house—sometimes his apparel—sometimes his food: his wheat, good fruits, first fruits, his pleasant fruits, etc. 2. These representations express the union of Christians one with another, not only the body—one body. This is agreeable to what the Apostle says, *Romans 12:5*, "For we, being many, are one body of Christ, and every one members one of another." ***Sermons and Discourses, 1743–1758 (WJE Online Vol. 25)***

Romans 12:6

"Let us prophesy according to the proportion of faith." "The context in this and the three preceding verses leads us, without any difficulty, into the meaning of the Apostle in this expression. *1 Corinthians 12* and *1 Corinthians 14* show us how apt the new converts were to be puffed up with the several gifts that were bestowed on them; and everyone, as in like cases, is usual, forward to magnify his own, and to carry it further than in reality it extended. That it is St. Paul's design here to prevent or regulate such disorder, and to keep everyone in the exercising his particular gift within its due bounds, is evident in that exhorting them, *Romans 12:3*, to a sober use of their gifts. He makes the measure of that sobriety to be that measure of faith or spiritual gift, which everyone in particular enjoyed by the favor of God. But besides this, which is very obvious, there is another passage in that verse, which, rightly considered, strongly inclines this way. 'I say, through the grace that is given unto me,' says St. Paul. He was going to restrain them in the exercise of their distinct spiritual gifts, and he could not introduce what he was going to say in the case with a more persuasive argument than his own example. The same rule concerning the same matter St. Paul gives, *Ephesians 4:7*. *1 Corinthians 14:29–32* may also give light to this place." Mr. Locke's notes. ***The "Blank Bible" (WJE Online Vol. 24)***

Romans 12:8

God gives a strict charge that our hearts should not be grieved when we give to our poor brother. ***Ethical Writings (WJE Online Vol. 8)***

A spirit of government, or an extraordinary and miraculous qualification for the exercise of that part of the pastor's office which consists in judging, reproving, rebuking, admonishing, etc., he that had this gift was authorized to do this part of a pastor's work; and the church submitted to him herein that they discerned had this gift, for they had a discerning of spirits (among other gifts of the Spirit) among them. But this no more argues that government was a distinct standing office than that exhorting was, for some that had a gift of exhorting were in the exercise of that gift to do the part of a pastor, and no otherwise (*Romans 12:8*). ***The "Blank Bible" (WJE Online Vol. 24)***

Romans 12:10

What has been felt in late great transports is known to be nothing new in kind, but to be of the same nature with what was felt formerly, when a little child of about five or six years of age; but only in a vastly higher degree. These transporting views and rapturous affections are not attended with any enthusiastic disposition to follow impulses, or any supposed prophetical revelations; nor have they been observed to be attended with any appearance of spiritual pride, but very much of a contrary disposition, an increase of a spirit of humility and meekness, and a disposition in honor to prefer others [cf. *Romans 12:10*]. ***The Great Awakening (WJE Online Vol. 4)***

This love the apostles are often directing Christians to exercise towards fellow members of the visible church; as in *Romans 12:10*. "Be kindly affectioned one to another with brotherly love." The words are much more emphatical in the original, and do more livelily represent that peculiar endearment that there is between gracious persons, or those that look on one another as such; ***τη φιλαδελφία είς αλληλουω φιλόσο⊠γοι.*** The expression properly signifies, cleaving one to another with brotherly natural strong endearment. ***Ecclesiastical Writings (WJE Online Vol. 12)***

Romans 12:11

That religion which God requires, and will accept, does not consist in weak, dull and lifeless wouldings, raising us but a little above a state of indifference: God, in his Word, greatly insists upon it, that we be in good earnest, fervent in spirit, and our hearts vigorously engaged in religion: *Romans 12:11*, "Be ye fervent in spirit, serving the Lord." ***Religious Affections (WJE Online Vol. 2)***

In lively true devotion, in dispositions and duties more immediately respecting God, which are here most livelily represented and powerfully urged. *Romans 12:1–2*, "I beseech you therefore, brethren, by the mercies of God, that ye present your bodies a living sacrifice, holy, acceptable unto God, which is your reasonable service. And be not conformed to this world: but be ye transformed by the renewing of your mind, that ye may prove what is that good, and acceptable, and perfect, will of God." And *Romans 12:11*, "Not slothful in business; fervent in spirit; serving the Lord." ***Sermons and Discourses: 1723–1729 (WJE Online Vol. 14)***

Romans 12:12

Here are perfect rules, which, if followed, will make us excel in the duties more immediately relating to ourselves. *Romans 12:3*, "For I say, through the grace given to me, to every man that is among you, not to think of himself more highly than he ought to think; but to think soberly, according as God hath dealt to every man the measure of faith." And *Romans 12:12*, "Rejoicing in hope; patient in tribulation." ***Sermons and Discourses: 1723–1729 (WJE Online Vol. 14)***

Romans 12:13

Acts 2:42. "And fellowship." The original shows plainly that "the apostles' doctrine, and the fellowship," or communication (as it should have been rendered), "and the breaking of bread, and the prayers," are mentioned as four distinct parts of the public service of the church. And by "the communication" is doubtless meant communicating to the poor, which was a part of the stated service of every Sabbath. See the use of the word *κοινωνία* (*Romans 15:26*; *2 Corinthians 8:4*, and *2 Corinthians 9:13*; *Hebrews 13:16*; *1 Timothy 6:18*, *κοινωνικός*). See the meaning of the word *κοινωνέω* (*Romans 12:13*, *Galatians 6:6*, *Philippians 4:15*). ***The "Blank Bible" (WJE Online Vol. 24)***

Romans 12:14

And here I would also observe by the way, that some have a way of joining a sort of imprecations with their petitions for others, though but conditional ones, that appear to me wholly needless and improper: they pray that others may either be converted or removed. I never heard nor read of any such thing practiced in the church of God till now, unless it be with respect to some of the most visibly and notoriously abandoned enemies of the church of God. This is a sort of cursing men in our prayers, adding a curse with our blessing; whereas the rule is, "Bless and curse not" [*Romans 12:14*]. To pray that God would kill another is to curse him with the like curse wherewith Elisha cursed the children that came out of Bethel [*2 Kings 2:23–24*]. And the case must be very great and extraordinary indeed to warrant it, unless we were prophets, and did not speak our own words but words indited by the immediate inspiration of the Spirit of God. ***The Great Awakening (WJE Online Vol. 4)***

For we are not allowed to entertain ill will towards others in any case, but good will to all. We are required heartily to wish well and to pray for the prosperity of all men, our enemies and those that despitefully use us [*Matthew 5:44*]. The rule is to bless, and curse not. *Romans 12:14*, "Bless them which persecute you: bless, and curse not." That is, we should only wish good and pray for good to others, and in no case wish evil. All revenge, excepting revenge of public authority wherein men act not for themselves but for God, is forbidden. ***Ethical Writings (WJE Online Vol. 8)***

Romans 12:15

A Christian spirit disposes persons to rejoice in others' prosperity. It not only mortifies a disposition to grieve at it, but on the contrary gives a disposition to rejoice in it. A Christian spirit disposes to a compliance with that rule, *Romans 12:15*, "Rejoice with them that do rejoice, and weep with them that weep." ***Ethical Writings (WJE Online Vol. 8)***

The tenderness of the heart of a true Christian, is elegantly signified by our Savior, in his comparing such a one to a little child. The flesh of a little child is very tender: so is the heart of one that is new born. This is represented in what we are told of Naaman's cure of his leprosy, by his washing in Jordan, by the direction of the prophet; which was undoubtedly a type of the renewing of the soul, by washing in the laver of regeneration. We are told, *II Kings 5:14*, that "he went down, and dipped himself seven times in Jordan, according to the saying of the man of God; and his flesh came again, like unto the flesh of a little child." Not only is the flesh of a little child tender, but his mind is tender. A little child has his heart easily moved, wrought upon and bowed: so is a Christian in spiritual things. A little child is apt to be affected with sympathy, to weep with them that weep, and can't well bear to see others in distress: so it is with a Christian (*John 11:35*, *Romans 12:15*, *I Corinthians 12:26*). A little child is easily won by kindness: so is a Christian. A little child is easily affected with grief at temporal evils, and has his heart melted, and falls a weeping: thus tender is the heart of a Christian, with regard to the evil of sin. ***Religious Affections (WJE Online Vol. 2)***

The Christian spirit will make us apt to sympathize with our neighbor when we see him under any difficulty; *Romans 12:15*, "Rejoice with them that do rejoice, and weep with them that weep." When our neighbor is under difficulty, he is afflicted; and we ought to have such a spirit of love to him that we should be afflicted with him in his affliction. And if we ought to be afflicted, then it will follow that we ought to be ready to relieve, because if we are afflicted with him, we relieve ourselves in relieving him; his relief is so far our relief as his affliction is our affliction. Christianity teaches [us] to be afflicted in our neighbor's affliction; and nature teaches us to relieve ourselves when afflicted. ***Sermons and Discourses, 1730–1733 (WJE Online Vol. 17)***

Romans 12:16

Humility tends to prevent a scornful behavior. Treating others with scorn and contempt is the worst manifestation of pride towards men. But they that are under the influence of an humble spirit are far from such a behavior. They are not apt to despise those that are below them and, as it were, to look down upon them with a haughty, supercilious air, as though they were scarce worthy to come near them or to have any regard from them. They are sensible that there is no such vast difference between them and their fellow worms as warrants such a behavior. They are not apt to treat with scorn and contempt what others say, or to speak of what they do with ridicule and jeering reflections; to sit and relate over what such an one said and did at such and such a time, and make themselves sport with it. On the contrary, humility disposes persons to a condescending behavior to the meekest and meanest, to treat inferiors with courtesy and affability, as being sensible of their own meanness and despicableness before God, and that it is God alone, who makes them in any respect to differ in any advantage they have above them, agreeable to that precept, *Romans 12:16*, "Condescend to men of low estate." If they are great men, men in places of public trust and power, humility will dispose them to treat their inferiors in such a manner as this, and not in an haughty and scornful manner as vaunting themselves in their greatness. ***Ethical Writings (WJE Online Vol. 8)***

For a man to be highly conceited of his spiritual and divine knowledge, is for him to be wise in his own eyes, if anything is. And therefore it comes under those prohibitions, *Proverbs 3:7*, "Be not wise in thine own eyes"; *Romans 12:16*, "Be not wise in your own conceits." And brings men under that woe, *Isaiah 5:21*, "Woe unto them that are wise in their own eyes, and prudent in their own sight." Those that are thus wise in their own eyes, are some of the least likely to get good of any in the world. Experience shows the truth of that, *Proverbs 26:12*, "Seest thou a man wise in his own conceit? There is more hope of a fool than of him." ***Religious Affections (WJE Online Vol. 2)***

False and delusive experiences evermore tend to this; though oftentimes under the disguise of great and extraordinary humility. Spiritual pride, is the prevailing temper, and general character of hypocrites, deluded with false discoveries and affections. They are in general, of a disposition directly contrary to those two things belonging to the Christian temper, directed to by the Apostle; the one in *Romans 12:16*, "Be not wise in your own conceit"; and the other in *Philippians 2:3*, "Let each esteem others better than themselves." ***Sermons and Discourses, 1743–1758 (WJE Online Vol. 25)***

Romans 12:17

We should do good to those that do ill to us. This should be the Christian's way of retaliating, not returning evil for evil but good for evil. ***Ethical Writings (WJE Online Vol. 8)***

Romans 12:18

So he directs the Christian Romans not to please themselves, but everyone [to] please his neighbor for his good, to edification, *Romans 15:1–2*, and to follow after the things that make for peace, chap. *Romans 14:19*. And he presses it in terms exceeding strong, *Romans 12:18*, "If it be possible, as much as lieth in you, live peaceably with all men." ***The Great Awakening (WJE Online Vol. 4)***

James and John were for calling for fire from heaven on the Samaritans, because they would not receive them into their villages. But Christ rebuked 'em, and told 'em they knew not what manner of spirit they were of. *Romans 12:18*, "If it be possible, as much as lieth in you, live peaceably with all men." *Philippians 4:5*, "Let your moderation be known unto all men." ***The "Miscellanies," 833–1152 (WJE Online Vol. 20)***

Romans 12:19

God will undertake to plead your cause, and he is more able to put a stop to the injuries offered you than you. He hath said, Vengeance is mine, I will repay [*Romans 12:19*]. So God undertook for David. If you undertake,

God will leave it with you. *Proverbs 24:17–18*, "Rejoice not when thine enemy falleth, and let not thine heart be glad when he stumbleth: lest the Lord see it, and it displease him, and he turn away his wrath from him." ***Ethical Writings (WJE Online Vol. 8)***

All revenge, excepting revenge of public authority wherein men act not for themselves but for God, is forbidden. *Leviticus 19:18*, "Thou shalt not avenge, nor bear any grudge against the children of thy people, but thou shalt love thy neighbor as thyself: I am the Lord." And *Romans 12:19*, "Dearly beloved, avenge not yourselves, but rather give place unto wrath: for it is written, Vengeance is mine; I will repay, saith the Lord." Therefore all that anger which contains ill will or a desire of revenge is what Christianity is contrary to. Sometimes "anger" as it is spoken of in Scripture means only an ill sense, or only that sort of anger which consists in a desire of revenge, and so all anger is forbidden. ***Ethical Writings (WJE Online Vol. 8)***

Romans 12:20

"Thou shalt heap coals of fire on his head." I.e. this is the way to have God plead your cause, and execute vengeance for you, the way to have his vengeance brought upon his head if his evil is not overcome with your good, as in the words following. See that God's vengeance is meant by "burning coals," is confirmed by *Psalms 140:10*. ***The "Blank Bible" (WJE Online Vol. 24)***

Romans 12:21

We should do good both to friends and enemies. We are obliged to do good to our friends. Besides the obligations which we are under to do good to men as our fellow creatures, and those that are made in the image of God, we are under the obligations of friendship and gratitude. *Proverbs 18:24*, "A man that hath friends, must show himself friendly." But we are not only obliged to do good to them, but also to our enemies. *Matthew 5:43–44*, "Ye have heard that it hath been said, Thou shalt love thy neighbor, and hate thine enemy. But I say unto you, Love your enemies, bless them that curse you, do good to them that hate you, and pray for them which despitefully use you and persecute you." We should do good to those that do ill to us. This should be the Christian's way of retaliating, not returning evil for evil but good for evil. *Romans 12:17*, "Recompense to no man evil for evil." Ver.

Romans 12:21, "Be not overcome of evil, but overcome evil with good." *1 Thessalonians 5:15*, "See that none render evil for evil unto any man; but ever follow that which is good among yourselves, and to all men." *1 Peter 3:9*, "Not rendering evil for evil, or railing for railing: but contrariwise blessing; knowing that ye are thereunto called, that ye should inherit a blessing." ***Ethical Writings (WJE Online Vol. 8)***

ROMANS CHAPTER 13

Romans 13:1

["Let every soul be subject to the higher powers, for there is no power but of God. The powers that be are ordained of God."] "'Everyone,' however endowed with miraculous gifts of the Holy Ghost, or advanced to any dignity in the church of Christ. For that these things were apt to make men overvalue themselves is obvious from what St. Paul says to the Corinthians, *1 Corinthians 12*, and here to the Romans, *Romans 12:3–5*. But above all others, the Jews were apt to have an inward reluctancy and indignation against the power of any heathen over them, taking it to be an unjust and tyrannical usurpation upon them, who were the people of God, and their betters." ***The "Blank Bible" (WJE Online Vol. 24)***

Romans 13:1–2

Much is said about the way how civil government first came to be set up in the world. It seems to me, much most probable and most agreeable to Scripture, to suppose that in the beginning of things God appointed civil government. He taught men to form themselves into civil societies, and to appoint judges and rulers, and that all nations derived the custom from thence. And the ambition of particular men, and the necessity of the people, conspiring together, easily maintained the custom universally and in all ages.

'Tis to be observed that almost everything that was good and any way commendable in the heathen world was originally from revelation, not only what they had of truth among them in moral and divine things, but marriage and civil government. See *"Miscellanies," no. 350*.

God took care of the heathen world to restrain the wickedness of it, and to prevent those things that would have issued in the utter desolation of it. One instance of this merciful care of them was his ordering so in his providence that civil government should be maintained among them for the terror of evildoers and the praise of them that do well, so that some of the heathen nations were under a very good civil constitution, and were governed by very wholesome laws. So that the civil powers of the heathen were "ordained of God" two ways, viz. 1. As civil government was at first a thing of divine institution; 2. As the civil government that was then in being in the heathen world was a fruit of the merciful disposal of God's providence to the world for their good. ***The "Blank Bible" (WJE Online Vol. 24)***

Romans 13:3

This, the Apostle tells us, is one end of civil government, not only to be a terror to evildoers but to reward with honor them that do that which is good; *Romans 13:3*, "For rulers are not a terror to good works, but to the evil. Wilt thou then not be afraid of the power? Do that which is good, and thou shalt have praise of the same." So the apostle Peter to the same purpose; *1 Peter 2:14*, "or unto governors, as unto them that are sent by him for the punishment of evildoers, and for the praise of them that do well." ***Sermons and Discourses, 1730–1733 (WJE Online Vol. 17)***

Romans 13:4

[The] power of the sword [is], *Romans 13:4*, "to execute wrath upon him that doeth evil." Those that violate the rights [of mankind in society] are punished by the civil sword only as acting the part of enemies. If there should, instead of a single offender, arise a great number—as in a public riot or mob or rebellion—'tis lawful [to punish them]; and this is the same thing with here, if a particular town or city or province [should offend]. This is war. If war be lawful to defend a society from domestic enemies, then doubtless if a particular man should come from a foreign country and should set himself to do mischief, [he should be similarly punished]. Thus the light of nature [justifies war]. But besides, God has abundantly shown his approbation: directing, encouraging, commanding, [and] ordering the affairs of war, [and] rewarding [the defenders of the people]. And that God approves [of some war] appears not only from the Old Testament, but the New. The New Testament approves of the civil magistracy, and of the magistrates' using the sword to restrain open violence with force. ***Sermons and Discourses, 1743–1758 (WJE Online Vol. 25)***

Romans 13:6

The reason here given why subjects should pay tribute for the support of magistrates is that the work that God has called them to, mentioned, *Romans 13:4*, is enough to take up all their time. 'Tis what they should be devoted [to] for the good of their subjects, and so having no time any other way to provide for their own support. 'Tis reasonable that they should be supported by their subjects in a manner agreeable to the dignity of their station, being God's ministers, and the beneficialness of their office to the subject, being God's ministers for their good. ***The "Blank Bible" (WJE Online Vol. 24)***

Romans 13:7

Another effect of spiritual pride is a certain unsuitable and self–confident boldness before God and men. Thus some in their great rejoicings before God, han't paid a sufficient regard to that rule in *Psalms 2:11*. They han't rejoiced with a reverential trembling, in a proper sense of the awful majesty of God, and the awful distance between God and them. And there has also been an improper boldness before men, that has been encouraged and defended by a misapplication of that Scripture, *Proverbs 29:25*, "The fear of man bringeth a snare." As though it became all persons, high and low, men, women and children, in all religious conversation, wholly to divest themselves of all manner of shamefacedness, modesty or reverence towards man; which is a great error, and quite contrary to Scripture. There is a fear of reverence that is due to some men: *Romans 13:7*, "Fear to whom fear, honor to whom honor." And there is a fear of modesty and shamefacedness, in inferiors towards superiors, that is amiable and required by Christian rules: *1 Peter 3:2*, "While they behold your chaste conversation, coupled with fear." And *1 Timothy 2:9*, "In like manner also, that women adorn themselves in modest apparel, with shamefacedness and sobriety." ***The Great Awakening (WJE Online Vol. 4)***

Humility will tend to prevent a leveling behavior. They who are under the influence of a humble spirit will not be opposite to giving to others the honor which is due to them. They will be willing that their superiors should be known and acknowledged in their place, and it will not seem hard to them. They will not desire that all should be upon a level; for they know it is best that some should be above others and should be honored and submitted to as such, and therefore they are willing to comply with it agreeable to those precepts: *Romans 13:7*, "Render therefore to all their dues: tribute to whom tribute is due; custom to whom custom; fear to whom fear; honor to whom honor." *Titus 3:1*, "Put them in mind to be subject to principalities and powers, to obey magistrates." ***Ethical Writings (WJE Online Vol. 8)***

Romans 13:8

Sometimes by the law is meant the Ten Commandments, as containing the sum of the duty of mankind and all that is required, as of universal and perpetual obligation. But whether we take the law as signifying the Ten Commandments, or the whole written Word of God, the Scripture teaches us that the sum of what is required is love. So when by the law is meant the Ten Commandments, *Romans 13:8*, "He that loveth another hath fulfilled the law," and therefore several of the Commandments are rehearsed. And thus again in the tenth verse the Apostle says, "Love is the fulfilling of the law." Now unless love was the sum of what the law requires, the law could not be wholly fulfilled in love. A law is not fulfilled but by obedience to the sum, or whole of what it contains. So the same Apostle again in *1 Timothy 1:5*, "Now the end of the commandment is charity." Or if we take the law in a yet more extensive sense for the whole written Word of God, the Scripture still teaches us that love is the sum of what is required in it, as in *Matthew 22:40*. There Christ teaches that on those two precepts of loving God with all the heart, and our neighbor as ourselves, hang all the law and the prophets. That is, all the written Word of God. For that which was then called the law and the prophets was the whole written Word of God which was then extant. ***Ethical Writings (WJE Online Vol. 8)***

There is one place where the same word in the original is used as here, and also speaking of the end of the law or commandment, that exceedingly confirms this interpretation, viz. *1 Timothy 1:5*. "Now the end of the commandment is charity," i.e. the accomplishment or fulfillment of the law, as the same Apostle says, "Charity is the fulfilling of the law," in this epistle of *Romans 13:8, Romans 13:10*. So that 'tis manifest from this place that that righteousness, which this Apostle calls the "righteousness of God," consists in Christ's fulfilling or answering the law; and therefore that 'tis the same thing with what we call the "righteousness of Christ." ***Notes on Scripture (WJE Online Vol. 15)***

What is a full proof of this is that the Ten Commandments, that were given at Mt. Sinai, were delivered both [as] a revelation of the covenant of works and the covenant of grace to that people. Here particularly to prove this, see *Exodus 20:6* and *Deuteronomy 7:9*, *Deuteronomy 7:12*. There, the fulfillment of God's covenant with their fathers is promised to them that do God's commandments, but that, the Apostle teaches us in the epistle to the Galatians, was the covenant of grace. And there also, *Deuteronomy 7:9*, as in *Exodus 20:6*, mercy is promised on these terms; but mercy is not promised by the covenant of works, but the covenant of grace. See *Exodus 19:5–6*, *Exodus 24:4–8*, *Exodus 34:28*, *Deuteronomy 4:13*, with *Deuteronomy 4:23*, *Deuteronomy 9:9–11*, *Deuteronomy 29:1*, *Jeremiah 11:3–6*. See also "Scripture" no. 441. Those Ten Commands are often spoken of as containing the covenant of grace, and as revealing the terms of that covenant by which God espoused that church of Israel to himself; and as such, the two tables of stone were laid up in the ark and kept in the sanctuary. This could not be unless the same duties therein prescribed, that were the terms of the covenant of works, were in another respect the terms of the covenant of grace. 'Tis the same law that in one respect is the law of works that in the other is the law of faith; the same law is a law of subjection to those that are under the covenant of works that is the law of liberty to those that are under the covenant of grace. Christ in this respect, as well as others, did not come to destroy the law but to fulfill, as he says in *Matthew 5:17*. 'Tis evident, by the following part of the same sermon of Christ, that it was his fulfilling the law in this respect that he had especially in view, viz. teaching and leading and influencing his disciples to a true, sincere and real fulfillment of the duties of the law of God, as understood in its spiritual and true meaning; and this is especially evident by *Matthew 5:19–20*, immediately following. They that comply with the terms of justification, in the way of the covenant of grace, they fulfill the righteousness of the law, in some sense. In that they "walk not after the flesh but after the Spirit" (*Romans 8:4*), "the righteousness of the law is fulfilled in us," in the sense of the same Apostle, in the same epistle, *Romans 13:8*, "He that loveth another hath fulfilled the law." ***The "Miscellanies," 833–1152 (WJE Online Vol. 20)***

The Scripture teaches us that all our duty is summed up in love, or, which is the same thing, that 'tis the sum of all that is required in the law; and that, whether we take the law as signifying the Ten Commandments, or the whole written Word of God. So when by the Law is meant the Ten Commandments, *Romans 13:8*, "Owe no man anything, but to love one another: for he that loveth another hath fulfilled the law"; and, therefore, several of these commandments are there rehearsed. And again, in *Romans 13:10*, "Love is the fulfilling of the law." And unless love was the sum of what the law required, the law could not be fulfilled in love. A law is not fulfilled but by obedience to the sum of what it contains. So the same Apostle again, *1 Timothy 1:5*, "Now the end of the commandment is charity." ***Writings on the Trinity, Grace, and Faith (WJE Online Vol. 21)***

Romans 13:9

So in *Matthew 22:36–38*, that commandment, "Thou shalt love the Lord thy God with all thy heart, and with all thy soul, and with all thy mind," is given by Christ himself as the sum of the first table of the Law, in answer to the question of the lawyer, who asked him, "Which is the great commandment of the law?" And in the next verse, loving our neighbors as ourselves is mentioned as the sum of the second table, as it is also in *Romans 13:9*, where most of the precepts of the second table are rehearsed over in particular: "For this, Thou shalt not commit adultery, Thou shalt not kill, Thou shalt not steal, Thou shalt not bear false witness, Thou shalt not covet; and if there be any other commandment, it is briefly comprehended in this saying, namely, Thou shalt love thy neighbor as thyself." ***Writings on the Trinity, Grace, and Faith (WJE Online Vol. 21)***

The Scripture teaches this of each table of the law in particular. That command, "Thou shalt love the Lord thy God, with all thy heart, and with all thy soul, and with all thy mind," is given as the sum of the first table of the law, in the twenty-second chapter of Matthew, in answer to the question of the lawyer, who asked him, "Which is the great Commandment in the law?" Ver. *Matthew 22:36–38*, "Master, which is the great commandment in the law? Jesus said unto him, thou shalt love the Lord thy God with all thy heart, and with all thy soul, and with all thy mind. This is the first and great commandment." And in the next verse, the loving of our neighbor is mentioned as the sum of the second table, as it is in *Romans 13:9*, where the precepts of the second table are rehearsed over in particular. "For this, thou shalt not commit adultery, thou shalt not kill, thou shalt not steal, thou shalt not bear false witness, thou shalt not covet; and if there be any other commandment, it is briefly comprehended in this saying, viz. thou shalt love thy neighbor as thyself." And so again *Galatians 5:14*, "For all the law is fulfilled in one word, even in this; thou shalt love thy neighbor as thyself." The apostle [James] seems to teach the same thing in *James 2:8*, "If ye fulfill the royal law according to the Scripture, Thou shalt love thy neighbor as thyself, ye do well." Hence love appears to be the sum of all that virtue and duty which God requires of us; and therefore must undoubtedly be the most essential thing, or the sum of all that virtue which is essential and distinguishing in real Christianity. That which is the sum of all duty is the sum of all real virtue. ***Ethical Writings (WJE Online Vol. 8)***

Romans 13:10

So a due consideration of the nature of love will show that it will dispose men to all duties towards their neighbors. If men have a hearty love to their neighbors, it will dispose them to all acts of justice towards them. Men are not disposed to wrong those whom they truly love. Real love and friendship will dispose persons to give others their due. *Romans 13:10*, "Love worketh no ill to his neighbor." Love will dispose to truth towards neighbors, and will tend to prevent all lying, fraud and deceit. For men are not disposed to treat those with fraud and treachery whom they sincerely love. To treat men so is to treat them like enemies. But love destroys enmity. ***Ethical Writings (WJE Online Vol. 8)***

The Scripture teaches us that all our duty is summed up in love, or, which is the same thing, that 'tis the sum of all that is required in the law; and that, whether we take the law as signifying the Ten Commandments, or the whole written Word of God. So when by the Law is meant the Ten Commandments, *Romans 13:8*, "Owe no man any thing, but to love one another: for he that loveth another hath fulfilled the law"; and, therefore, several of these commandments are there rehearsed. And again, in *Romans 13:10*, "Love is the fulfilling of the law." And unless love was the sum of what the law required, the law could not be fulfilled in love. A law is not fulfilled but by obedience to the sum of what it contains. So the same Apostle again, *1 Timothy 1:5*, "Now the end of the commandment is charity." ***Writings on the Trinity, Grace, and Faith (WJE Online Vol. 21)***

Reason shows that all good dispositions and duties are wholly comprehended in, and will flow from, divine love. Love to God and men implies all proper respect or regard to God and men; and all proper acts and expressions of regard to both will flow from it, and therefore all duty to both. To regard God and men in our heart as we ought, and to have that nature of heart towards them that we ought, is the same thing. And therefore, a proper regard or love comprehends all virtue of heart; and he that shows all proper regard to God and men in his practice, performs all that in practice towards them which is his duty. The Apostle says, *Romans 13:10*, "Love works no ill to his neighbor." 'Tis evident by his reasoning in that place, that he means more than is expressed: that love works no ill, but all good, all our duty, to our neighbor; which reason plainly shows. And as the Apostle teaches that love to our neighbor works no ill but all good towards our neighbor, so, by a parity of reason, love to God works no ill, but all our duty, towards God. ***Writings on the Trinity, Grace, and Faith (WJE Online Vol. 21)***

This obedience of love was the very end of the covenant, the obedience God aimed at in giving his commandments. *1 Timothy 1:5*, "The end of the commandment is charity out of a pure heart." Yea, love is spoken [of] as the sum total of what is required in the commandments. *Romans 13:10*, "Love is the fulfilling of the law." And this is the fulfilling of the law that Christ teaches to be what is required in order to inherit eternal life. *Luke 10:25–28*, "And, behold, a certain lawyer stood up, and tempted him, saying, Master, what shall I do to inherit eternal life? He said unto him, What is written in the law? how readest thou? And he answering said, Thou shalt love the Lord thy God with all thy heart, and with all thy soul, and with all thy strength, and with all thy mind; and thy neighbor as thyself. And he said unto him, Thou hast answered right: this do, and thou shalt live." What he asks is what he should do to inherit eternal [life], or which is the same thing, to be an heir or to have a title to eternal [life]; and then [Christ] tells him that if he fulfills that great command of love, he should live: "This do, and thou shalt live"; which is as much as to say, "This do, and thou shalt be in a state of salvation. Thou [shalt] be an heir of eternal life, which is the thing thou inquirest after." The devil himself was sensible that, however strict a man was externally, yet if his obedience was only from self-love and not from love to God, there was no sincerity [and] nothing good in it. And therefore, when God gloried of Job to Satan as a perfect and upright man, one that feared God and eschewed evil, Satan answered the Lord, "Doth Job serve God for nought?" (*Job 1:9–10*). And God, in his reply, don't deny that Satan's consequences would be good if his assertion were true; and therefore, God puts that assertion to the proof. He allows that it shall be proved whether Job served God only out of self-love, without any love to him, and puts the determination of Job's uprightness on that issue. ***Sermons and Discourses, 1743–1758 (WJE Online Vol. 25)***

Romans 13:11

So, we should so desire heaven so much more than the comforts and enjoyments of this life that we should long to change these things for heaven. We should wait with earnest desire for the time when we shall arrive to our journey's end. The Apostle mentions it as an encouraging, comfortable consideration to Christians, when they draw nigh their happiness; *Romans 13:11*, "now is our salvation nearer than when we believed." ***Sermons and Discourses, 1730–1733 (WJE Online Vol. 17)***

Romans 13:11–12

We can't understand this, as though the Apostle concluded the day of judgment would come while they lived, because he had before explained himself otherwise; but only that the day of Christ's kingdom, which is the day of the salvation of the church of Christ, was at hand—that which the Holy Ghost had before intended by the kingdom of heaven—which indeed, in some things that the Holy Ghost meant by it, was near at hand; and, therefore, the Holy Ghost directed the Apostle to use such words. ***The "Miscellanies," 833–1152 (WJE Online Vol. 20)***

Romans 13:13

If we consider how much a spirit and practice which are contrary to a spirit of envy is insisted on in the precepts which Christ hath given. How full is the New Testament of precepts of good will to others, principles of meekness, humility and beneficence, which are all opposite to a spirit of envy! And how often are we particularly warned there against envy. *Romans 13:13*, "Let us walk honestly, as in the day; not in strife and envying." The same Apostle [blames] the Corinthians as being carnal, because there was envying among them. *1 Corinthians 3:3*, "Ye are yet carnal: for whereas there is among you envying, and strife, and divisions, are ye not carnal?" So the same Apostle mentions his fears concerning the Corinthians, lest he should find envy among them. *2 Corinthians 12:20*, "I fear lest when I come I shall not find you such as I would, and that I shall be found unto you such as ye would not: lest there be debates, envyings, etc." And envy is banded among other works of the flesh, *Galatians 5:19–21*, "Now the works of the flesh are manifest"; and then follows a catalogue of them, and among them are mentioned hatred, variance, wrath, strife, seditions, envyings. And the same Apostle warns them against it, ver. *Galatians 5:26*, "Let us not be desirous of vainglory, provoking one another, envying one another." Again envy is condemned, *1 Timothy 6:4–6*, "Doting about questions and strifes of words, whereof cometh envy, strife, railings, evil surmisings, etc." And envy is mentioned by the Apostle as one of those things that the Christians lived in before their conversion but were now redeemed from, and therefore counsels them to forsake it. *Titus 3:3*, "For we ourselves also were sometimes foolish, disobedient, deceived, serving divers lusts and pleasures, living in malice and envy, hateful, and hating one another." So the apostle James speaks of envy as exceedingly contrary to Christianity and all that is good. *James 3:14–16*, "But if ye have bitter envying and strife in your hearts, glory not, and lie not against the truth. This wisdom descendeth not from above, but is earthly, sensual, devilish. For where envying and strife is, there is confusion and every evil work." And he warns against this, ch. *James 5:9*, "Grudge not one against another, brethren, lest ye be condemned; behold, the judge standeth before the door." So the apostle Peter warns against the same, *1 Peter 2:1–2*, "Wherefore laying aside all malice, and all guile, and hypocrisies, and envies, and all evil speakings. As newborn babes, desire the sincere milk of the word, that ye may grow thereby." Thus the New Testament of Jesus Christ is full of precepts which are opposite to a spirit of envy. ***Ethical Writings (WJE Online Vol. 8)***

With many young people, he is the best man, that shows most of that kind of wit and boldness that appears in lascivious jesting. Their diversion consists very much in such kind of mirth. This [is] exceeding unbecoming Christians. Such persons, how much soever they may value themselves on their impudence and unclean wit, appear more like brutes than Christians. True Christianity is abhorrent to any such thing, as light is to darkness, and a due exercise of Christian holiness will make men more to abhor to take such talk into their mouths, than they would abhor to take a piece of a dead rotten carcass full of crawling worms into their mouths. The Apostle advises that such unclean communication be not so much as once named among Christians. *Ephesians 5:3–4*, "But fornication, and all uncleanness, and covetousness, let it not be once named amongst you, as becometh saints. Neither filthiness, nor foolish talking, nor jesting, which are not convenient." It requires Christians, whose bodies are the temples of God and who are persons devoted to the holy Jesus, to be pure in heart and mouth. They should follow after "whatsoever things are pure" (*Philippians 4:8*). Christians are the children of the light and of the day, and therefore should walk as children of the light. *Romans 13:13*, "Let us walk honestly, as in the day; not in chambering and wantonness." Christians are advised by the Apostle in *Colossians 3:5*, *Colossians 3:8*, to put away all filthy communication out of their mouths; and again in *Colossians 4:6*, that their speech should be "always with grace, seasoned with salt." Salt is used to preserve meats from putrefying and becoming rotten carrion, as otherwise they would do; so our words should be kept from uncleanness, which makes 'em like filthy noisome corruption. ***Sermons and Discourses, 1739–1742 (WJE Online Vol. 22)***

Romans 13:14

Jeremiah 2:32. "Can a maid forget her ornaments, or a bride her attire? Yet my people have forgotten me days without number." For our holiness is all the righteousness of God; all the beauty of the soul is wholly and only divine light reflected. All grace is nothing but the Holy Spirit dwelling in us; and all those graces and spiritual beauties, which are to the mind as attire, and ornament are to the body, are Christ in the soul, and nothing else. Wherefore we are commanded to put on Christ [*Romans 13:14*]. ***Notes on Scripture (WJE Online Vol. 15)***

ROMANS CHAPTER 14

Romans 14:1

Romans 14:1, I am sorry to hear of the threatening aspect of the present controversy upon your church and town. I heartily wish you may be led into healing methods, or to the proper means of preventing the evils feared. And though it be very desirable that both minister and people should be of the same mind and judgment, yet it may deserve the serious consideration of yourselves and of your reverend pastor whether, retaining your several sentiments in the present case, you may not, consistently therewith, accord and unite in affection and practice and in all the holy administrations of the house of God, as has been usual? Especially considering what an eminent branch of gospel holiness that charity is which is directed to express itself in a condescension to the infirmities of the weak and in a mutual forbearance in love, under different apprehensions among Christians, against the mischievous consequences whereof there is no remedy but this charity; and how earnestly it is recommended in the evangelical writings as a means to prevent the violation of unity in Christian churches, *Romans 14:1–5* ***Ecclesiastical Writings (WJE Online Vol. 12)***

Romans 14:2

"For one believeth he may eat all things; another, who is weak, eateth herbs." There was no meat that was killed and sold among the heathen but what was some way or other offered to an idol. So that the first Christians, in such populous cities as Rome, where they must buy all their provision at the heathen markets, could scarce come at any meat but what was offered to idols, or some way polluted, not being drained of the blood, etc. ***The "Blank Bible" (WJE Online Vol. 24)***

Romans 14:3

Judge and "set at nought" has reference to the same spoken of in the *Romans 14:3*, where we read of judging and despising. One party judged the other as licentious and wicked; the other party despised and set at nought him that differed from him as silly, superstitious, foolishly scrupulous, etc. ***The "Blank Bible" (WJE Online Vol. 24)***

Romans 14:4

That sort of judging which is God's proper business is forbidden, as *Romans 14:4*, "Who art thou that judgest another man's servant? To his own master he standeth or falleth." ***The Great Awakening (WJE Online Vol. 4)***

Judging our brethren and passing a condemnatory sentence upon them seems to carry in it an act of authority, especially in so great a case, to sentence them with respect to that state of their hearts, on which depends their liableness to eternal damnation; as is evident by such interrogations as those (to hear which from God's mouth is enough to make us shrink into nothing with shame and confusion, and sense of our own blindness and worthlessness). *Romans 14:4*, "Who art thou that judgest another man's servant? To his own master he standeth or falleth." And *James 4:12*, "There is one law-giver that is able to save and destroy; who art thou that judgest another?" Our wise and merciful Shepherd has graciously taken care not to lay in our way such a temptation to pride; he has cut up all such poison out of our pasture; and therefore we should not desire to have it restored. Blessed be his name, that he has not laid such a temptation in the way of my pride! I know that in order to be fit for this business, I must not only be vastly more knowing, but more humble than I am. ***The Great Awakening (WJE Online Vol. 4)***

And an aptness to judge and condemn shows an arrogant, proud disposition. It has a show of persons' setting up themselves above others, as though they were fit to be the lords and judges of their fellow servants, as if it were fit that they should stand or fall at their sentence. This seems implied in *James 4:11*, "He that speaketh evil of his brother, and judgeth his brother, speaketh evil of the law, and judgeth the law: but if thou judge the law, thou art not a doer of the law, but a judge." That is, you do not act as a fellow servant with him, or one that is under the law as well as he, but the giver and judge of the law. Therefore it follows in the next verse, "There is one Lawgiver, who is able to save and to destroy: who art thou that judgest another?" So *Romans 14:4*, "Who art thou that judgest another man's servant? To his own master he standeth or falleth." ***Ethical Writings (WJE Online Vol. 8)***

Not to [be] forward to judge others, to judge others' thoughts, to judge their hearts upon particular occasions, to determine as to the principles, motives and ends of their actions.

This is to assume God's province, to set up ourselves as lords and judges. *Romans 14:4*, "Who art thou that judgest another man's servant?" And *James 4:12*, "Speak not evil one of another, brethren. He that speaketh evil of his brother, and judgeth his brother, speaketh evil of the law, and judgeth the law; but if thou judge the law, thou are not a doer of the law but a judge."

This is the way to be judged and condemned ourselves. *Matthew 7:1–2*, "Judge not, that ye be not judged. For with what judgment ye judge; ye shall be judged." ***Sermons and Discourses: 1723–1729 (WJE Online Vol. 14)***

When we are so often forbidden to judge that we be not judged [*Luke 6:37*], without doubt [is meant] a judging of men's state, or of their sincerity and hypocrisy, good and evil principles, of their hearts in general as well as of particular actions; for what is meant by that prohibition is doubtless that we should not take God's work out of his hands, and anticipate the proper business of the day of judgment. In the place just now mentioned, we are forbidden to judge; in I Corinthians we are forbidden to judge others upon that account, because it is before the time. And in the *Romans 14:4*, we are forbidden to judge others upon the other account, because we therein go out of our place, and take God's work into our hands. *Romans 14:4*, "Who art thou that judgest another man's servant? To his own master he standeth or falleth." And *James 4:12*, "There is one Lawgiver, that is able to save and to destroy. Who art thou that judgest another?" ***Notes on Scripture (WJE Online Vol. 15)***

The Apostle, in this chapter, is upon the duty of bridling the tongue, and he has a special respect to that part of the government of the tongue which consists in refraining from talking against others and expressing with the tongue an ill-spirit towards our neighbors. He begins, "my brethren, be not many masters" [*James 3:1*], i.e. don't set up for judges of others; let not every man take upon him to be his neighbor's judge; it is not fit you should be all masters, all judges. The apostle Paul informs us that if we talk against our neighbors and judge them, we take upon us to treat men as if they were our servants; *Romans 14:4*, "Who art thou that judgest another man's servant? to his own master he standeth or falleth." And this Apostle, in the next chapter, [writes] that if we judge our neighbors we don't act like God's servants, or doers of the law, but as if we were the lawgivers and judges (*James 4:11–12*). ***Sermons and Discourses, 1730–1733 (WJE Online Vol. 17)***

But he that is [peaceable and faithful in Israel], he wisely holds his peace. He don't take upon him to judge others: he bows to their own master: he attends these rules of Christianity. *Matthew 7:1*, "Judge not"; *1 Corinthians 4:5*, "Therefore judge nothing before the time, until the Lord come, who will both bring to light the hidden things of darkness, and make manifest [the counsels of the hearts]"; *Romans 14:4*, "Who art thou that judgeth another man's servant to his own masters?" He avoids the condemnation of that scripture, *1 Timothy 6:4–5*, "Whereof cometh envy, strife, railings, evil surmisings, perverse disputings of men of corrupt minds." ***Sermons and Discourses, 1734–1738 (WJE Online Vol. 19)***

Romans 14:5

And then probably the Apostle feared that the Galatians made a righteousness of these observances, because he knew the character of those false teachers that endeavored to lead them into it, that they were a proud, pharisaical, self-righteous sort of persons. There were some that observed days and times that the Apostle had charity for. *Romans 14:5–6* ***The "Miscellanies," (Entry Nos. 501–832) (WJE Online Vol. 18)***

Romans 14:6

Tis exceeding manifest, that error or mistake may be the occasion of a gracious exercise, and consequently a gracious influence of the Spirit of God, by *Romans 14:6*. "He that eateth to the Lord, he eateth, and giveth God thanks; and he that eateth not to the Lord, he eateth not, and giveth God thanks." The Apostle is speaking of those, who through erroneous and needless scruples, avoided eating legally unclean meats. By this it is very evident, that there may be true exercises of grace, a true respect *to the Lord*, and particularly, a true thankfulness, which may be occasioned, both by an erroneous judgment and practice. And consequently, an error may be the occasion of those truly holy exercises that are from the infallible Spirit of God. And if so, 'tis certainly too much for us to determine, to how great a degree the Spirit of God may give this holy exercise, on such an occasion. ***Religious Affections (WJE Online Vol. 2)***

Lukewarmness in religion is abominable, and zeal an excellent grace; yet above all other Christian virtues, it needs to be strictly watched and searched; for 'tis that with which corruption, and particularly pride and human passion, is exceeding apt to mix unobserved. And 'tis observable that there never was a time of great reformation, to cause a revival of much of a spirit of zeal in the church of God, but that it has been attended in some notable instances, with irregularity, running out some way or other into an undue severity. Thus in the apostles' days, a great deal of zeal was spent about unclean meats, with heat of spirit in Christians one against another, both parties condemning and censuring one another, as not true Christians; when the Apostle had charity for both, as influenced by a spirit of real piety: "he that eats," says he, "to the Lord he eats, and giveth God thanks; and he that eateth not, to the Lord he eateth not, and giveth God thanks" [*Romans 14:6*]. ***The Great Awakening (WJE Online Vol. 4)***

So the primitive Christians, from their zeal for and against unclean meats, censured and condemned one another: this was a bad effect, and yet the Apostle bears them witness, or at least expresses his charity towards them, that both sides acted from a good principle, and true respect to the Lord, *Romans 14:6*. The zeal of the Corinthians with respect to the incestuous man, though the Apostle highly commends it, yet at the same time saw that they needed a caution lest they should carry it too far, to an undue severity, and so as to fail of Christian meekness and forgiveness, *2 Corinthians 2:6–11* and chap. *2 Corinthians 7:11* to the end. Luther, the great Reformer, had a great deal of bitterness with his zeal. ***The Great Awakening (WJE Online Vol. 4)***

Romans 14:7

The apostle Paul speaks expressly, and from time to time, of the members of the churches he wrote to, as all of them in esteem and visibility truly gracious persons. *Philippians 1:6–7*, "Being confident of this very thing, that he which has begun a good work in you will perform it until the day of the Lord Jesus Christ: even as it is meet for me to think this of you all" (that is, all singly taken, not collectively, according to the distinction before observed). So *Galatians 4:26*, "Jerusalem which is above, which is the mother of us all." *Romans 6:13*, "As many of us as have been baptized into Christ, have been baptized into his death." Here he speaks of *all* that have been baptized; and in the continuation of the discourse [*Romans 6:11–18*], explaining what is here said he speaks of their being dead to sin; no longer "under the law, but under grace"; having obeyed the "form of doctrine" from the heart being "made free from sin" and become "the servants of righteousness," etc. *Romans 14:7–8*, "None of us liveth to himself, and no man dieth to himself" (taken together with the context). *2 Corinthians 3:18*, "We all with open face beholding as in a glass," etc. And *Galatians 3:26*, "Ye are all the children of God by faith." ***Ecclesiastical Writings (WJE Online Vol. 12)***

Romans 14:8

For Christ, who is made head over all things to the church, will have all things so disposed as shall be most to His own glory and the welfare of His members; so that whether he die or live, or whatever becomes of him, he attains his end: "For whether we live, we live unto the Lord; and whether we die, we die unto the Lord: whether we live therefore, or die, we are the Lord's" (*Romans 14:8*). ***Sermons and Discourses 1720–1723 (WJE Online Vol. 10)***

Romans 14:9

For God the Father would have nothing to do with fallen man in a way of mercy but by a mediator. But in order to Christ's carrying on the Work of Redemption and accomplishing the success of his own purchase as God-man, it was necessary that he should be alive, and so that he should rise from the dead. Therefore Christ, after he had finished this purchase by death and by continuing for a time under the power of death, rises from the dead to fulfill the end of his purchase and himself to bring about that which he died for. For this matter God the Father had committed unto him, that he might as Lord of all manage all to his own purposes, *Romans 14:9*, "For to this end Christ both died, and rose, and revived, that he might be Lord both of the dead and of the living." ***A History of the Work of Redemption (WJE Online Vol. 9)***

And these things are spoken of Christ God-man. For in this last-mentioned place, 'tis mentioned as the reward of his being found in fashion as a man and humbling himself; and in that other place, and in that place in Romans, his being universal Judge, and every knee's bowing to him, and every tongue's confessing to him, is spoken of him as God-man:

for it is said that he died, rose, and revived that he might have this honor and authority [*Romans 14:9*]. So in *John 5:27*, 'tis said that the Father "hath given him authority to execute judgment also, because he is the Son of man." So that if he has acted the part of a judge towards the elect angels, it must be since his incarnation; and we know that he is to judge angels at the last day as God-man. ***The "Miscellanies," (Entry Nos. 501–832) (WJE Online Vol. 18)***

By "things in heaven" in that place in Philippians, and so doubtless here is meant the angels; and by "things in earth" is meant elect men living on earth. By "things under the earth," or in the lower parts of the earth, is meant the souls of departed saints whose bodies are gone under the earth, and especially the saints that were dead and buried before Christ came, or before Christ descended into the lower parts of the earth. Christ died and was buried that he might fill those that were dead and buried. *Romans 14:9*, "For to this end Christ both died, and rose, and revived, that he might be Lord both of the dead and of the living." By things or creatures under the earth is meant souls of buried saints, and not devils and damned souls in hell, is manifest from *Revelation 5:13*, "And every creature which is in heaven, and on the earth, and under the earth, and such as are in the sea, and all that are in them, heard I saying, Blessing, and honor, and glory, and power, be unto him that sitteth upon the throne, and unto the Lamb forever and ever." This would not be said of devils and wicked damned souls, who are far from thus praising and extolling God and Christ with such exultation; instead of that, they are continually blaspheming them. ***The "Miscellanies," (Entry Nos. 501–832) (WJE Online Vol. 18)***

And then Christ descended into the lower parts of the earth in a state of death, that he might bless those that were in a state of death; agreeable to *Romans 14:9*, "For to this end Christ both died, and rose, and revived, that he might be Lord both of the dead and of the living." So we read that when he died the graves of many saints were opened, and that many bodies of saints that slept arose and came out of their graves after his resurrection, and went into the holy city and appeared unto many. And then Christ ascended into heaven and filled them, bestowing eternal life and blessedness upon them, that the angels in heaven might all receive the reward of confirmed and eternal glory from him and in him. ***The "Miscellanies," (Entry Nos. 501–832) (WJE Online Vol. 18)***

Romans 14:10

Judge and "set at nought" has reference to the same spoken of in the *Romans 14:3*, where we read of judging and despising. One party judged the other as licentious and wicked; the other party despised and set at nought him that differed from him as silly, superstitious, foolishly scrupulous, etc. ***The "Blank Bible" (WJE Online Vol. 24)***

And Christ tells us that all power is given him in heaven and in earth (*Matthew 28:18*); and we are often particularly told as to the good angels, that he is made their Lord and Sovereign, and that they are put under him. The Apostle, in *Romans 14:10–12*, speaking of Christ's being universal Judge, before whose judgment seat all must stand and to whom all must give an account, speaks of it as meant by those words in the Old Testament: "As I live, saith the Lord, every knee shall bow to me, and every tongue shall confess to God"; which place of the Old Testament the Apostle refers to in *Philippians 2:9–11*, "Wherefore God also hath highly exalted him, and given him a name above every name: that at the name of Jesus every knee should bow, of things in heaven, and things in earth, and things under the earth; and that every tongue should confess that Jesus is Lord, to the glory of God the Father." ***The "Miscellanies," (Entry Nos. 501–832) (WJE Online Vol. 18)***

Romans 14:11

That glorious day we are speaking of is the proper and appointed time, above all others, for the bringing to pass the things requested in each of these petitions: as the prophecies everywhere represent that as the time, which God has especially appointed for the hallowing or glorifying his own great name in this world, causing "his glory to be revealed, that all flesh may see it together" [*Isaiah 40:5*], causing it "openly to be manifested in the sight of the heathen" [*Psalms 98:2*], filling the whole world with the light of his glory to such a degree that "the moon shall be confounded and sun ashamed" [*Isaiah 24:23*] before that brighter glory: the appointed time for the glorifying and magnifying the name of Jesus Christ, causing "every knee to bow, and every tongue to confess to him" [*Romans 14:11*]. ***Apocalyptic Writings (WJE Online Vol. 5)***

Another remarkable place wherein it is plainly foretold that the like method of professing religion should be continued in the days of the gospel, which was instituted in Israel, by swearing or public covenanting, is that, *Isaiah 45:22–25*, "Look unto me, and be ye saved, all ye ends of the earth; for I am God, and there is none else: I have sworn by myself, the word is gone out of my mouth in righteousness, and shall not return, that unto me every knee shall bow, every tongue shall swear: truly shall one say, in the Lord have I righteousness and strength: even to him shall men come: . . . In the Lord shall all the seed of Israel be justified and shall glory." This prophecy will have its last fulfillment at the day of judgment; but 'tis plain, that the thing most directly intended is the conversion of the gentile world to the Christian religion. What is here called "swearing," the Apostle in citing this place once and again calls "confessing" (*Romans 14:11*), "Every tongue shall confess to God." *Philippians 2:10–11*, "That every tongue should confess that Jesus Christ is Lord." ***Ecclesiastical Writings (WJE Online Vol. 12)***

We also may learn what is meant by swearing to the Lord, by *Isaiah 45:23–24*, "Unto me every knee shall bow, and every tongue shall swear. Surely, shall one say, in the Lord have I righteousness and strength"; together with the Apostle's citation and explication of this place, which instead of the word "swear" uses "confess," in *Romans 14:11*, and *Philippians 2:10*, which, in the Apostle's language, signifies the same as making open and solemn profession of Christianity. ***Notes on Scripture (WJE Online Vol. 15)***

Swearing to God and swearing by his name, by which seems to signify a solemnly giving up themselves to God in covenant, and vowing to receive him as their God, to obey and serve him, and entirely to give up themselves as his people, is spoken of as a duty to be performed by all God's visible Israel, *Deuteronomy 6:13* and *Deuteronomy 10:20*, *Psalms 63:11*. *Isaiah 45:23–24*, "I have sworn by myself: the word is gone out of my mouth in righteousness, and shall not return, that unto me every knee shall bow, every tongue shall swear. Surely, shall one say, in the Lord have I righteousness and strength: even to him shall men come"; compared with *Romans 14:11*, "and every tongue shall *confess* to God," and *Philippians 2:10–11*, "[That at the name of Jesus,] every knee should bow, . . . and every tongue should confess that Jesus is Lord." ***The "Miscellanies," 833–1152 (WJE Online Vol. 20)***

And the word "confess," ὁμολογέω, as used in the Scripture, don't only own a thing to be true, but implies the sincere, respectful, and joyful respect, acknowledgment, honor, and praise of heart, mouth, and practice, and a being devoted to. See *Hebrews 13:15*. In *Matthew 14:7*, it signifies vowing or promising to God. It has a like signification in the Septuagint,

Jeremiah 44:25. ὁμολογία is put for voluntary offering (*Deuteronomy 12:6, Deuteronomy 12:17*; *Ezekiel 46:12*; *Amos 4:5*), for avow (*Leviticus 22:18, Jeremiah 44:25*). ὁμόλόγως signifies "with freedom of heart" (*Hosea 14:4*). ἐξομολογέω is used for praise, and extol, and the like (*Romans 15:9*), and to adore and glorify (*Romans 14:11*, *Philippians 2:11*), and abundantly in the Septuagint. ***The "Blank Bible" (WJE Online Vol. 24)***

Romans 14:12

"EVERY ONE *of us shall give Account of* HIMSELF, and of no other, *to God, Romans 14:12*. Everyone shall be judged according to the particular Powers and Talents God has given *him*, and not according to the Powers and Talents which God originally gave to Adam. ***"Original Sin" Notebook (WJE Online Vol. 34)***

And they shall be called to an account concerning them, to see what answer they can make for themselves. *Matthew 12:36*, "But I say unto you, that every idle word that men shall speak, they shall give account thereof in the day of judgment." *Romans 14:12*, "So then every one of us shall give account of himself to God." ***Sermons and Discourses 1720–1723 (WJE Online Vol. 10)***

Romans 14:13

In matters that concern your temporal interest, we would have God in his providence deal so by us. We are often commanded to avoid those things that tend to lead others into sin . . . ***Sermons and Discourses, 1739–1742 (WJE Online Vol. 22)***

Romans 14:15

"Destroy not him with thy meat, for whom Christ died." That is as much as to say, Will you not put yourself so much out of the way as to restrain your appetite, though you thereby expose your brother to be destroyed, for whom Christ put himself so much out of the way as to die to save him from being destroyed? ***The "Blank Bible" (WJE Online Vol. 24)***

In matters that concern your temporal interest, we would have God in his providence deal so by us. We are often commanded to avoid those things that tend to lead others into sin. *1 Corinthians 8:8–13*, "But meat commendeth us not to God: for neither, if we eat, are we the better; neither, if we eat not, are we the worse. But take heed lest by any means this liberty of yours become a stumblingblock to them that are weak. For if any man see thee which hast knowledge sit at meat in the idol's temple, shall not the conscience of him which is weak be emboldened to eat those things which are offered to idols; and through thy knowledge shall the weak brother perish, for whom Christ died? But when ye sin so against the brethren, and wound their weak conscience, ye sin against Christ. Wherefore, if meat make my brother to offend, I will eat no flesh while the world standeth, lest I make my brother to offend." *Romans 14:13*, "Let us not therefore judge one another any more: but judge this rather, that no man put a stumblingblock or an occasion to fall in his brother's way." *Romans 14:15*, "But if thy brother be grieved with thy meat, now walkest thou not charitably. Destroy not him with thy meat, for whom Christ died." [Verses] *Romans 14:20–21*, "For meat destroy not the work of God. All things indeed are pure; but it is evil for that man who eateth with offense. It is good neither to eat flesh, nor to drink wine, nor any thing whereby thy brother stumbleth, or is offended, or is made weak." ***Sermons and Discourses, 1739–1742 (WJE Online Vol. 22)***

The Apostle so far uses their language, or speaks as they "spake," that he calls conformity to these things, "knowing the depths." But herein he differs, that whereas they called it "knowing the depths of such a god," he calls it "the depths of Satan." In that expression, "I will put upon you none other burden," he seems to have respect to the expression used at the Council of Jerusalem, when they exhorted to abstain from these two things, eating things sacrificed to idols, and fornication, and two more, things strangled and blood (*Acts 15:28–29*), it being thought necessary that these should be added, by reason of the then present circumstances of the church in its infant state, great part of the church being lately converted from Judaism, from which the Holy Ghost saw meet gradually to wean them, as a child has some bauble given to quiet it when weaned from the mother's breast, to eat stronger meat, not to put new wine into old bottles, agreeably to the maxims of the Apostle, in *Romans 14:15*. "But if thy brother be grieved with thy meat, now walkest thou not charitably. Destroy not him with thy meat, for whom Christ died." ***The "Blank Bible" (WJE Online Vol. 24)***

Romans 14:16

To the like purpose, the same Apostle directs Christians to walk in wisdom towards them that are without, *Colossians 4:5*, and to avoid giving offense to others if we can, that our good mayn't be evil spoken of, *Romans 14:16*. So that 'tis evident that the great and most zealous and most successful propagator of vital religion that ever was, looked upon it to be of great consequence to endeavor, as much as possible, by all the methods of lawful meekness and gentleness, to avoid raising the prejudice and opposition of the world against religion. When we have done our utmost there will be opposition enough against vital religion, against which the carnal mind of man has such an enmity (we should not therefore needlessly increase and raise that enmity); as in the Apostle's days, though he took so much pains to please men, yet because he was faithful and thorough in his work, persecution almost everywhere was raised against him. ***The Great Awakening (WJE Online Vol. 4)***

Romans 14:17

If we take the Scriptures for our rule, then the greater and higher are the exercises of love to God, delight and complacence in God, desires and longings after God, delight in the children of God, love to mankind, brokenness of heart, abhorrence of sin, and self-abhorrence for sin; and the "peace of God which passeth all understanding" [*Philippians 4:7*], and "joy in the Holy Ghost" [*Romans 14:17*], "joy unspeakable and full of glory" [*1 Peter 1:8*]; admiring thoughts of God, exulting and glorying in God; so much the higher is Christ's religion, or that virtue which he and his apostles taught, raised in the soul. ***The Great Awakening (WJE Online Vol. 4)***

"The kingdom of God is righteousness, peace, and joy in the Holy Ghost." *Acts 9:31*, "Walking in the fear of the Lord, and comfort of the Holy Ghost." But how well doth this agree with the Holy Ghost being God's joy and delight. *Acts 13:52*, "And the disciples were filled with joy, and with the Holy Ghost," meaning, as I suppose, that they were filled with spiritual joy. ***Writings on the Trinity, Grace, and Faith (WJE Online Vol. 21)***

From what has been said, it follows that the Holy Spirit is the sum of all good. 'Tis the fullness of God. The holiness and happiness of the Godhead consists in it; and in the communion or partaking of it consists all the true loveliness and happiness of the creature. All the grace and comfort that persons have here, and all their holiness and happiness hereafter, consists in the love of the Spirit, spoken of, *Romans 15:30*; and joy and comfort in the Holy Ghost, spoken of, *Romans 14:17*; *Acts 9:31*, *Acts 13:52*. And therefore, that in *Matthew 7:11*, "If ye then, being evil, know how to give good gifts unto your children, how much more shall your Father which is in heaven give good things to them that ask him?" is in *Luke 11:13* expressed thus: "If ye then, being evil, know how to give good gifts unto your children: how much more shall your heavenly Father give the Holy Spirit [to them] that ask him?" Doubtless there is an agreement in what is expressed by each Evangelist, and giving the Holy Spirit to them that ask is the same as giving good things to them that ask: for the Holy Spirit is the sum of all good. ***Writings on the Trinity, Grace, and Faith (WJE Online Vol. 21)***

Men are much more convinced of the truth of a profession by seeing [acts of righteousness and mercy accompany it] than by seeing men abound in a show of religion in words and gestures. All men have that within them that approves [righteous behavior]. *Romans 14:17–18*, "For the kingdom of God is not meat and drink; but righteousness, and peace, and joy in the Holy Ghost. For he that in these things serveth Christ is acceptable to God, and approved of men." The two former of these things here mentioned are moral duties towards men. ***Sermons and Discourses, 1739–1742 (WJE Online Vol. 22)***

And in this work it is that the heart is put in tune, and it is put into a capacity and disposition truly and sincerely to praise God and to make that heavenly melody, which is made in singing this new song, by exercising these divine principles of divine love and divine joy. "The love of God is shed abroad" in the heart by the Holy Ghost (*Romans 5:5*). And spiritual rejoicing is called "joy in the Holy Ghost" [*Romans 14:17*]. This saving work of God in the heart is redemption by power, as the other is redemption by purchase. And seeing it is thus—that this knowledge of the things to be sung, and the ability to make the melody of the song, is imparted no other way than by the saving work of the Spirit, whereby the soul is redeemed by power—hence we may see another reason why no man can learn that song but they that are redeemed. Other men are dumb and dead as to any such heavenly exercise as this. They can exalt their idols, but they can't exalt God. They can rejoice in the objects of their lusts, in their worldliness and in their carnal pleasures, but they can't rejoice in Christ Jesus. They can howl, but they can't sing the new song. ***Sermons and Discourses, 1739–1742 (WJE Online Vol. 22)***

Romans 14:19

1 Corinthians 10:32–33, "Give none offense, neither to the Jews, nor to the Gentiles, nor to the church of God: even as I please all men in all things, not seeking mine own profit, but the profit of many, that they may be saved." Yea, he declares that he laid himself out so much for this, that he made himself a kind of a servant to all sorts of men, conforming to their customs and various humors, in everything wherein he might, even in things that were very burdensome to him, that he might not fright men away from Christianity and cause them to stand as it were braced and armed against it, but on the contrary, if possible, might with condescension and friendship win and draw them to it; as you may see, *1 Corinthians 9:19–23*. And agreeable hereto, are the directions he gives to others, both ministers and people. So he directs the Christian Romans not to please themselves, but everyone [to] please his neighbor for his good, to edification, *Romans 15:1–2*, and to follow after the things that make for peace, chap. *Romans 14:19*. ***The Great Awakening (WJE Online Vol. 4)***

How amiable a thing is it to see a society living together in peace and unity. *Psalms 133*, "Behold, how good and how pleasant it is for brethren to dwell together in unity! 'Tis like the precious ointment upon the head, that ran down upon the beard, even Aaron's beard: that went down to the skirts of his garments; and as the dew of Hermon, and as the dew that descended on the mountains of Zion." Let us all therefore of this town, as we regard its temporal and spiritual prosperity, its reputation and beauty, do all that in us lies for the sake of unity. O that peace may continue with us and reign in the midst of us! O that there may be nothing but perfect amity and agreement! Let us therefore by all means abstain from anything that either directly or indirectly tends to contention. Let us not only follow peace immediately, but everything that makes for peace. *Romans 14:19*, "Let us therefore follow after things that make for peace, and things wherewith one may edify another." ***Sermons and Discourses 1720–1723 (WJE Online Vol. 10)***

Romans 14:20

"Destroy not the work of God." Christians are God's "workmanship, created in Christ Jesus unto good works" [*Ephesians 2:10*]. We are God's husbandry. We are God's building. We should not destroy this building, but edify it or build it up, as in the preceding verse. ***The "Blank Bible" (WJE Online Vol. 24)***

In matters that concern your temporal interest, we would have God in his providence deal so by us. We are often commanded to avoid those things that tend to lead others into sin. *1 Corinthians 8:8–13*, "But meat commendeth us not to God: for neither, if we eat, are we the better; neither, if we eat not, are we the worse. But take heed lest by any means this liberty of yours become a stumblingblock to them that are weak. For if any man see thee which hast knowledge sit at meat in the idol's temple, shall not the conscience of him which is weak be emboldened to eat those things which are offered to idols; and through thy knowledge shall the weak brother perish, for whom Christ died? But when ye sin so against the brethren, and wound their weak conscience, ye sin against Christ. Wherefore, if meat make my brother to offend, I will eat no flesh while the world standeth, lest I make my brother to offend." *Romans 14:13*, "Let us not therefore judge one another any more: but judge this rather, that no man put a stumblingblock or an occasion to fall in his brother's way." [Verse] *Romans 14:15*, "But if thy brother be grieved with thy meat, now walkest thou not charitably. Destroy not him with thy meat, for whom Christ died." *Romans 14:20–21*, "For meat destroy not the work of God. All things indeed are pure; but it is evil for that man who eateth with offense. It is good neither to eat flesh, nor to drink wine, nor any thing whereby thy brother stumbleth, or is offended, or is made weak." ***Sermons and Discourses, 1739–1742 (WJE Online Vol. 22)***

Romans 14:21

"Stumbleth, or is offended, or is made weak." They were made weak thus. The Jewish converts had been bred up in an extraordinary reverence for the ceremonial law. And when they saw that other Christians did not observe those laws, but allowed themselves to eat things that had been by those laws forbidden, and that they had been bred up in an abhorrence of as unclean, and argued that it was agreeable to the Christian institution for 'em so to do, and that it was a liberty allowed them by the gospel, they were in danger of being put out of concert of the gospel by that means, and to be weakened in their esteem and faith of it, that it indulged those liberties that they had such an inrooted and habitual abhorrence of, that they were stumbled and made weak in Christianity, or they were offended by being led in the same practice while they doubted of the lawfulness of it, for "he that doubteth is damned," as *Romans 14:23*. ***The "Blank Bible" (WJE Online Vol. 24)***

Romans 14:22

The apostles were in the same manner careful and tender of those they preached and wrote to. 'Twas very gradually that they ventured to teach them the cessation of the ceremonial laws of circumcision and abstinence from unclean meats. How tender is the apostle Paul with such as scrupled in *Romans 14*. He directs those that had knowledge to keep it to themselves for the sake of their weak brethren (*Romans14:22*). ***Sermons and Discourses, 1730–1733 (WJE Online Vol. 17)***

"Hast thou faith?" That is, to believe this doctrine of the gospel that these things are lawful, such a faith as the Apostle professes in the *Romans 14:14*. ***The "Blank Bible" (WJE Online Vol. 24)***

Romans 14:23

We ought to consider the nature of our actions which respect God: whether they are done in his service and to his glory; whether all that we do is part of the work that God has appointed for us and commanded, for everything that we do that is not part of God's service is part of the devil's service. "Whatever is not of faith is sin" (*Romans 14:23*). ***Sermons and Discourses 1720–1723 (WJE Online Vol. 10)***

"Stumbleth, or is offended, or is made weak." They were made weak thus. The Jewish converts had been bred up in an extraordinary reverence for the ceremonial law. And when they saw that other Christians did not observe those laws, but allowed themselves to eat things that had been by those laws forbidden, and that they had been bred up in an abhorrence of as unclean, and argued that it was agreeable to the Christian institution for 'em so to do, and that it was a liberty allowed them by the gospel, they were in danger of being put out of concert of the gospel by that means, and to be weakened in their esteem and faith of it, that it indulged those liberties that they had such an inrooted and habitual abhorrence of, that they were stumbled and made weak in Christianity, or they were offended by being led in the same practice while they doubted of the lawfulness of it, for "he that doubteth is damned," as *Romans 14:23*. ***The "Blank Bible" (WJE Online Vol. 24)***

ROMANS CHAPTER 15

Romans 15:1

Taylor says it should have been translated, "But we that are strong ought to bear the infirmities of the weak," this verse standing "in immediate connection with the Romans 14:23." See Taylor's notes. *The "Blank Bible" (WJE Online Vol. 24)*

Romans 15:1–2

So he directs the Christian Romans not to please themselves, but everyone [to] please his neighbor for his good, to edification, *Romans 15:1–2*, and to follow after the things that make for peace, chap. *Romans 14:19*. And he presses it in terms exceeding strong, *Romans 12:18*, "If it be possible, as much as lieth in you, live peaceably with all men." And he directs ministers to endeavor if possible, to gain opposers by a meek condescending treatment, avoiding all appearance of strife or fierceness, *2 Timothy 2:24–26*. To the like purpose, the same Apostle directs Christians to walk in wisdom towards them that are without, *Colossians 4:5*, and to avoid giving offense to others if we can, that our good mayn't be evil spoken of, *Romans 14:16*. So that 'tis evident that the great and most zealous and most successful propagator of vital religion that ever was, looked upon it to be of great consequence to endeavor, as much as possible, by all the methods of lawful meekness and gentleness, to avoid raising the prejudice and opposition of the world against religion. When we have done our utmost there will be opposition enough against vital religion, against which the carnal mind of man has such an enmity (we should not therefore needlessly increase and raise that enmity); as in the Apostle's days, though he took so much pains to please men, yet because he was faithful and thorough in his work, persecution almost everywhere was raised against him. ***The Great Awakening (WJE Online Vol. 4)***

Romans 15:2

They who have a Christian spirit have a spirit to seek the good of their fellow creatures. Thus the Apostle commands, *Philippians 2:4*, "Look not every man on his own things, but every man also on the things of others." We ought to seek others' spiritual good. A Christian spirit will dispose us to seek others' spiritual happiness; it will dispose us to seek their salvation from hell, and that they may obtain eternal glory, as it did the great Apostle. And it will incline persons to seek to edify others in holiness and comfort. "Edify one another" [*1 Thessalonians 5:11*]. A Christian spirit will dispose persons to seek others' wealth and outward estate. *1 Corinthians 10:24*, "Let no man seek his own, but every man another's wealth." So we should seek others' pleasure, wherein we can at the same time seek their profit. *1 Corinthians 10:33*, "Even as I please all men in all things, not seeking mine own profit, but the profit of many, that they may be saved." *Romans 15:2*, "Let every one of us please his neighbor for his good to edification." ***Ethical Writings (WJE Online Vol. 8)***

Romans 15:3

Christ, as it were, spent himself for us. Though we were enemies, yet he so loved us that from love to us he had a heart not only to look at our things, but to spend his own things for us, to forego his own ease and comfort, and outward honor, and to become poor for us. *Romans 15:3*, "For even Christ pleased not himself; but as it is written, The reproaches of them that reproached thee fell on me." And not only so, but to spend himself for us, to spend his blood, to offer up himself a sacrifice to the justice of God for our sakes. ***Ethical Writings (WJE Online Vol. 8)***

Romans 15:5

["Like-minded according to Christ Jesus."] That is, of a mind like unto Christ's mind, in the respect mentioned in the *Romans 15:3*. ***The "Blank Bible" (WJE Online Vol. 24)***

When God comes to dwell amongst a people, he makes of those that were a company of poor, naked, destitute, polluted, helpless creatures an eternal excellency, a holy and blessed people. He clothes them "with change of raiment" [*Zechariah 3:4*], and adorns them with the most "excellent ornaments" [*Ezekiel 16:7*]. He in infinite grace says to them, as *Isaiah 52:1*, "Awake, awake; put on thy strength, O Zion; put on thy beautiful garments, O Jerusalem, the holy city"; and as in the *Isaiah 54:11–12*, "Oh thou afflicted, tossed with tempest, and not comforted, behold, I will lay thy stones with fair colors, and lay thy foundations with sapphires. And I will make thy windows of agates, and thy gates of carbuncles, and all thy borders of pleasant stones." A people that have such an one dwelling in the midst of them have the best comforter. He is the "God that comforts those that are cast down" [*2 Corinthians 7:6*]; yea, he is the God of all consolation [*Romans 15:5*]. He is a fountain of peace and comfort to such a people. ***Sermons and Discourses, 1734–1738 (WJE Online Vol. 19)***

Romans 15:5–6

It is a thing well agreeing with the wisdom of Christ, and that peculiar favor he had manifested to his saints, and with his dealings with them in many other respects, to suppose, he has made provision in his institutions, that they might have the comfort of uniting, with such as their hearts are united within that holy intimate affection which has been spoken of, in some special religious exercises and duties of worship, and visible intercourse with their Redeemer, joining with those concerning whom they can have some satisfaction of mind that they are cordially united to them in ordering and expressing their love to their common Lord and Savior, that they may with one mind, with one heart, and one soul, as well as with one mouth glorify him; as in the forementioned *Romans 15:5–6*, compared with *Acts 4:32*. This seems to be what this heavenly affection naturally inclines to. And how eminently fit and proper for this purpose is the sacrament of the Lord's Supper, the Christian church's great feast of love; wherein Christ's people sit together as brethren in the family of God, at their father's table, to feast on the love of their Redeemer, commemorating his sufferings for them, and his dying love to them, and sealing their love to him and one another? It is hardly credible, that Christ has so ordered things as that there are no instituted social acts of worship, wherein his saints are to manifest their respect to him, but such as wherein they ordinarily are obliged (if the rule for admissions be carefully attended) to join with a society of fellow worshippers, concerning whom they have no reason to think but that the bigger part of them are unconverted (and are more provoking enemies to that Lord they love and adore, than most of the very heathen) which Mr. Stoddard supposes to be the case with the members of the visible church. ***Ecclesiastical Writings (WJE Online Vol. 12)***

Romans 15:6–12.

The Apostle, in the preceding part of the chapter, had been exhorting the Jewish and Gentile Christians to receive one another, notwithstanding differences of opinion about lesser matters. He exhorts those Jewish Christians that were scrupulous about unclean meats to receive the Gentile Christians that were not so, and also exhorts those Gentile Christians not to despise the Jewish Christians for their scrupulousness. And here in the *Romans 15:6*, he makes use of this as an argument, "That ye may with one mind and one mouth glorify God, even the Father of our Lord Jesus Christ," intimating that a respect to the glory and praise of God, that has been so gracious to both of them in giving Christ to them, and who is the Father of Jesus Christ that is the common Lord and Savior of both of them, should induce them thus to receive one another. And therefore [he] adds, *Romans 15:7*, "Wherefore receive ye one another, as Christ also received us to the glory of God." I.e. receive ye one another "to the glory of God," as Christ has received both of you, both Jews and Gentiles, "to the glory of God," or that the glory of God might be shown forth upon and declared by both. And then he goes on, in the *Romans 15:8–9*, to show how Christ glorified God in receiving each of them, and how he by receiving them gave each occasion to glorify him. In the *Romans 15:8* he shows how he glorified God by receiving the Jews, and gave them occasion to glorify him. He glorified the truth and faithfulness of God in fulfilling the promises made to their fathers, and so the Christian Jews have great reason to glorify him. "Now I say that Jesus Christ was a minister of the circumcision for the truth of God, to confirm the promises made unto the fathers." And in the *Romans 15:9* he shows the great cause he had given the Gentile Christians to glorify him by the great and wonderful mercy he had showed them in bringing of them out of so miserable a state of heathenish darkness, wherein they were aliens and strangers, etc., to be the people of God. So that both had great cause to glorify God, the same Father, for being received by Christ, the same Lord, unto the same privilege of a blessed union and communion with him, and therefore ought with one head and mouth to glorify God, as the Apostle had said before, *Romans 15:6*.

The texts he here cites from the Old Testament are very pertinent to these two things he had insisted, viz. how Jews and Gentiles should cordially join one with another, as with one heart and mouth, in glorifying God, and also how God had glorified himself in what he had done for each in sending Christ, etc. *Romans 15:9*, "I will confess thee among the Gentiles, and sing unto thy name." That shows how the Jews should unite with the Gentiles in glorifying God. The words next cited, *Romans 15:10*, show how the Gentiles should join with the Jews in glorifying God. "Rejoice, ye Gentiles, with his people." And the next words, *Romans 15:11*, show how both should unite in praising God: "all the Gentiles," and "all the people," i.e. the Jews. And the former part of the next verse, viz. *Romans 15:12*, "There shall be a root of Jesse," confirms what the Apostle had said, *Romans 15:8*, that God had glorified his truth to the Jews in sending Christ of their nation. "There shall be a root of Jesse." And the latter part of the verse confirms *Romans 15:9*, viz. God's mercy to the Gentiles, etc. ***The "Blank Bible" (WJE Online Vol. 24)***

Romans 15:9

And 'tis to be observed that the word "confess," as it is often used in the New Testament, signifies more than merely allowing; it implies an establishing and confirming a thing by testimony, and declaring it with manifestation of esteem and affection: so *Matthew 10:32*, "Whosoever therefore shall confess me before men, him will I confess also before my Father which is in heaven." *Romans 15:9*, "I will confess to thee among the Gentiles, and sing unto thy name." And *Philippians 2:11*, "That every tongue shall confess that Jesus Christ is Lord, to the glory of God the Father." And that this is the force of the expression, at the Apostle John uses it in this place, is confirmed by that other place in the same epistle, in the next chapter, at the first verse: "Whosoever believeth that Jesus is the Christ, is born of God; and everyone that loveth him that begat, loveth him also that is begotten of him." And by that parallel place of the Apostle Paul, where we have the same rule given to distinguish the true Spirit from all counterfeits, *1 Corinthians 12:3*, "Wherefore I give you to understand, that no man speaking by the Spirit of God, calleth Jesus accursed (or will shew an ill or mean esteem of him), and that no man can say that Jesus is the Lord, but by the Holy Ghost." ***The Great Awakening (WJE Online Vol. 4)***

Romans 15:12

There may be a strong belief of divine things in the understanding, and yet no saving faith; as is manifest, *1 Corinthians 13:2*, "Though I have faith, so that I could remove mountains, and have no charity, I am nothing." Not only trusting in Christ as one that has undertaken to save us, and as believing that he is our Savior, is faith, but applying to him or seeking to him that he would become our Savior, with a sense of his reality and goodness as a Savior, is faith; as is evident by *Romans 15:12*, "In him shall the Gentiles trust," compared with the place whence it is cited, *Isaiah 11:10*, "To it shall the Gentiles seek," together with *Psalms 9:10*, "And they that know thy name will put their trust in thee: for thou, Lord, hast not forsaken them that seek thee": which agrees well with faith's being called a looking to Christ, or coming to him for life, or flying for refuge to him, or flying to him for safety. And this is the first act of saving faith. And prayer's being the expression of faith confirms this. This is further confirmed by *Isaiah 31:1*, "Woe to them that go down into Egypt for help; and *stay* on horses, and *trust* in chariots, because they are many; and in horsemen, because they are very strong; but they *look* not unto the Holy One of Israel, neither *seek* the Lord!" When it is said, *Psalms 69:6*, "Let not them that wait on thee, O Lord, be ashamed for my sake: let not those that seek thee be confounded for my sake," it is equivalent to that in the scripture, "He that believeth shall never be confounded" [*1 Peter 2:6*]; and when it is said, *Psalms 69:32*, "And your heart shall live that seek the Lord," 'tis equivalent to that in the scripture, "The just shall live by faith" [*Romans 1:17*, *Galatians 3:11*]. So *Psalms 22:26* and *Psalms 70:4*. And so *Amos 5:4*, "For thus saith the Lord unto the house of Israel, Seek ye me, and ye shall live"; and *Amos 5:6*, "Seek the Lord, and ye shall live"; and *Amos 5:8*, "Seek him that made the seven stars and Orion, and turneth the shadow of death into the morning." *Canticles 4:8*, "Look from the top of Amana." *Isaiah 17:7–8*, "At that day shall a man look to his Maker, and his eyes shall have respect to the Holy One of Israel. And he shall not look to the altars, the work of his hands, neither shall respect that which his fingers have made, either the groves, or the images." *Isaiah 45:22*, "Look unto me, and be ye saved, all ye ends of the earth." *Jonah 2:4*, "I will look again towards thine holy temple." *Micah 7:7*, "Therefore I will look unto the Lord; I will wait for the God of my salvation: my God will hear me." *Psalms 34:5*, "They looked unto him, and were lightened: their faces were not ashamed." ***Writings on the Trinity, Grace, and Faith (WJE Online Vol. 21)***

Romans 15:12–13

These two verses confirm that by "hope" is meant faith in Christ, for when it is said, "in him shall the Gentiles trust," in the original it is, "in him shall the Gentiles hope"; and then it follows, "the God of hope fill you with all joy and peace in believing," referring to the joy of the Gentiles in trusting in Christ, spoken of, *Romans 15:10–11*. (See note on *Hebrews 6:19*, no. 284.) So where the word in our translation is "trust," it is "hope" in the original, in the following places: *1 Timothy 4:10*, *1 Timothy 6:17*, *John 5:45*, *Ephesians 1:12*, *1 Timothy 5:5*, *1 Peter 3:5*.

This confirms that the Old Testament "trust" is the same with the New Testament "faith," for 'tis evident trusting in God and hoping in God are often used in the Old Testament, as faith and hope are in the New. ***The "Blank Bible" (WJE Online Vol. 24)***

Romans 15:13

["And peace."] In this the Apostle refers to the unanimity between Jews and Gentiles he had been so much insisting on. ***The "Blank Bible" (WJE Online Vol. 24)***

He affords the best relief to poor, sad, and burdened souls. In him they may find rest [*Matthew 11:29*]. Those that have wandered, and have been tossed to and fro, and have found no rest, in him they have rest. They that have been afraid and terrified, in him they may have quietness and assurance forever. He is to a people that he dwells with, "as an hiding place from the wind, and a covert from the tempest" [*Isaiah 32:2*]. The comforts he bestows are not sensual and fleshly, but spiritual and holy: "all joy and peace in believing" [*Romans 15:13*]. He gives peace, "not as the world giveth" [*John 14:27*]. That comfort and quietness that he bestows on his people, is vastly more valuable than all that they can have from their worldly enjoyments. He puts joy and gladness into the heart better than when corn and wine and oil are increased. God is a tender father to his people, ready to pity them under all their affliction, and takes care of them. "In all their affliction he is afflicted, and the angel of his presence saves them: in his love and in his pity he redeems them; he bears them, and carries them" continually [*Isaiah 63:9*]. He has a most constant love to them and care for them than has a tender mother to her sucking child. *Isaiah 49:15–16*, "Can a woman forget her sucking child, that she should not have compassion on the son of her womb? yea, she may forget, yet will not I forget thee. Behold, I have graven thee upon the palms of my hands; thy walls are continually before me." God's comforting his people is compared to a mother's tenderly comforting a child that is hurt. *Isaiah 66:13*, "As one whom his mother comforteth, so will I comfort you." Christ comes to such a people on that errand "to preach good tidings unto the meek, and to bind up the brokenhearted, to proclaim liberty to the captives, and the opening of the prison to them that are bound; to comfort all that mourn" [*Isaiah 61:1–2*]; [and] to appoint to them that mourn amongst them, "beauty for ashes, the oil of joy for mourning, the garment of praise for the spirit of heaviness," that so everlasting joy may be to them; so that they may greatly rejoice in the Lord, and their soul be joyful in their God, who clothes them with "the garments of salvation," and covers them with "the robe of righteousness" [*Isaiah 61:3*, *Isaiah 61:10*]. Whatever afflictions and sorrows such a people might labor under before, yet if God be amongst them, they shall no more be termed forsaken. God will be amongst them as their shepherd, who will "gather his lambs with his arm, and gently lead those that are with young" [*Isaiah 40:11*]. ***Sermons and Discourses, 1734–1738 (WJE Online Vol. 19)***

Romans 15:14

The godly often need to be admonished and warned by others. Let the godly amongst us maintain a watchful eye not only over themselves, but over one another. And if they observe any of their brethren that seem to grow dull, and to lose the sense of things of religion, or to grow worldly, or in any respect to carry themselves unsuitably; let them friendly be stirring one another up. The godly have dullness and hardness, and often great corruption of heart, and many enemies to grapple with, and need one another's help. The wise virgins are apt to slumber and sleep, and need to be wakened by one another. This [is] a duty required in Scripture (*Romans 15:14*; *Colossians 3:16*). And there is generally much too little of this done amongst Christians. If it was done as it ought to be, it would have a great tendency to uphold religion among us. [It would be] proper for older Christians to be exhorting younger. And here I would particularly desire that you would not suffer those that sit by you, to sit sleeping at meeting; but wake one another, when anything of that appears. And let none of the godly give way so much to their corruption as to take it ill, when others admonish them, when others jog them to wake them, either out of their natural sleep in time of public worship, or their spiritual sleep, by friendly admonition. ***Sermons and Discourses, 1734–1738 (WJE Online Vol. 19)***

Romans 15:17

["I have therefore whereof I may glory through Jesus Christ in things pertaining to God."] The Apostle by this phrase, "things pertaining to God," means sacred things pertaining to the temple or the priesthood, or those affairs of God's people wherein their intercourse with God is maintained, and God is most immediate[ly] ministered to. Thus this phrase is used by this Apostle in *Hebrews 2:17*, and *Hebrews 5:1*. This phrase the Apostle uses here, because that thing he has respect to as his great honor, and which he speaks of in the preceding verse, is what he did as God's priest in "offering up the Gentiles," etc. Dr. Doddridge has this note on this place. "Raphelius very justly observes, that this phrase has a peculiar propriety when applied to sacerdotal affairs, and especially victims presented to God, of which the Apostle is here speaking. Other texts are illustrated by this remark, particularly *Hebrews 2:17*. ***The "Blank Bible" (WJE Online Vol. 24)***

Romans 15:18

'Tis something more than merely the assent of the understanding, because 'tis called an "obeying the gospel" (*Romans 10:16*; see no. [104]; *1 Peter 4:17*; *Romans 15:18*; *1 Peter 2:7–8*; *1 Peter 3:1*. 'Tis obeying the form of doctrine from the heart (*Romans 6:17*). This expression of obeying the gospel seems to denote the heart's yielding to the gospel in what it proposes to us in its calls. ***Writings on the Trinity, Grace, and Faith (WJE Online Vol. 21)***

It is further manifest from this place [*Galatians 5:6*] of the Apostle, wherein he speaks of faith as working by love, that all Christian exercises of heart, and works of life, are from love. For we are abundantly taught in the New Testament that all Christian holiness is begun with faith in Jesus Christ. All Christian obedience is in Scripture called the obedience of faith. *Romans 16:26*, "Is made known to all nations for the obedience of faith." The obedience here spoken of is doubtless the same with that mentioned in the preceding chapter, ver. *Romans 15:18*, "For I will not dare to speak of those things, which Christ hath not wrought by me, to make the Gentiles obedient by word and deed." And the Apostle tells us that the life he now lived in the flesh, he lived by the faith of the Son of God, *Galatians 2:20*. And we are often told that Christians *live* by faith, which carries in it as much as that all graces and holy exercises and works of their spiritual life are by faith. But how does faith work these things? Why, in this place in Galatians it works whatsoever it does work, and that is by love. Hence the truth of the doctrine follows, and that it is indeed so that all which is saving and distinguishing in Christianity does radically consist and is summarily comprehended in love. ***Ethical Writings (WJE Online Vol. 8)***

Romans 15:25

By ministering, as the word used in the New Testament is most commonly meant, [is] meant giving or communicating of our goods to others. So the apostle Paul, when he was going to Jerusalem to carry the contributions of other churches to the poor saints there, he says, *Romans 15:25*, "But now I go to Jerusalem to minister to the saints." So in *2 Corinthians 8:4*, speaking of the same contribution, he says, "Praying us with much entreaty that we would receive the gift, and take upon us the fellowship of ministering to the saints." So when he exhorts the Corinthians to the same contribution, he says, *ch. 9:1*, "For as touching the ministering to the saints, it is needless that I write unto you." So when the Apostle commends the Christian Hebrews for their charity to the saints, he says, *Hebrews 6:10*, "For God is not unrighteous to forget your work and labor of love, which ye have showed towards his name, in that ye have ministered to the saints, and do minister." And so in innumerable other places that might be mentioned. ***Sermons, Series II, 1739 (WJE Online Vol. 54)***

Romans 15:26

We find in the New Testament mention often made of a certain collection that was made by the churches abroad in the world for the relief of the saints in Judea; the occasion of which was a great dearth that there was in the world, which seems to have fallen heavy especially on the Christians in Judea, either because the scarcity was greater in that country, or because they suffered more through persecution, and by that means felt more of the calamity through the unkindness of their neighbors; who instead of relieving of them, and bestowing anything on them in this time of distress, rather opposed them, and took from them. The first mention we have of it is in the *Acts 11*, on [the] occasion of relating a prophecy that there was of it beforehand, [the] *Acts 11:28–29*: "And there stood up one of them named Agabus, and signified by the spirit that there should be great dearth throughout all the world: which came to pass in the days of Claudius Caesar. Then the disciples, every man according to his ability, determined to send relief unto the brethren which dwelt in Judea." And the Apostle mentioned it in his defense before Felix. *Acts 24:17*, "Now after many years I came to bring alms to mine own nation, and offerings." We read particularly of this collection being made in the churches that were in Galatia, and Macedonia, and Achaia. The two latter are mentioned by the Apostle in his epistle to the Romans. *Romans 15:26*, "For it hath pleased them of Macedonia and Achaia to make a certain contribution for the poor saints which were at Jerusalem." And there is mention of the church of Galatia in *1 Corinthians 16:1*"Now concerning the collection for the saints, as I have given order to churches of Galatia, even so do ye." And there seems to be a reference to it in the Epistle to the Galatians, chapter two, [verse] ten, "Only they would that we should remember the poor; the same which I also was forward to do." The church of Corinth was one of the churches of Achaia, and we find this collection much insisted on in both the epistles to this church. 'Tis particularly insisted, urged, and directed to in the last chapter of the First Epistle, and also throughout two chapters of this Second Epistle, viz. that wherein is our text and the foregoing. Corinth seems to have been a great and wealthy city, and their church one of the principal Christian churches that had been planted by the apostles. The Apostle is therefore much in stirring them up to bountifulness in their contributions. And among many other things he says to excite 'em to it, there is this in the text: "He which soweth sparingly shall reap also sparingly; but he which soweth bountifully shall reap also bountifully." ***Sermons and Discourses, 1734–1738 (WJE Online Vol. 19)***

Romans 15:30

The Scripture seems in many places to speak of love in Christians as if it were the same with the Spirit of God in them, or at least as the prime and most natural breathing and acting of the Spirit in the soul. *Philippians 2:1*, "If there be therefore any consolation in Christ, any comfort of love, any fellowship of the Spirit, any bowels and mercies, fulfill ye my joy, that ye be like-minded, having the same love, being of one accord, of one mind." *2 Corinthians 6:6*, "By kindness, by the Holy Ghost, by love unfeigned." *Romans 15:30*, "Now I beseech you, brethren, for the Lord Jesus Christ's sake, and for the love of the Spirit." *Colossians 1:8*, "Who declared unto us your love in the Spirit." *Romans 5:5*, having "the love of God shed abroad in our hearts by the Holy Ghost which is given to us" (see notes on this text). *Galatians 5:13–16*, "Use not liberty for an occasion to the flesh, but by love serve one another. For all the law is fulfilled in one word, even in this: Thou shalt love thy neighbor as thyself. But if ye bite and devour one another, take heed that ye be not consumed one of another. This I say then, Walk in the Spirit, and ye shall not fulfill the lust of the flesh." The Apostle argues that Christian liberty don't make way for fulfilling the lusts of the flesh, in biting and devouring one another and the like, because a principle of love, which was the fulfilling of the law, would prevent it; and in the *Galatians 5:16* he asserts the same thing in other words: "This I say then, Walk in the Spirit, and ye shall not fulfill the lust of the flesh." ***Writings on the Trinity, Grace, and Faith (WJE Online Vol. 21)***

It is from the breathings of the same Spirit that the Christian's love arises, both towards God and men. The Spirit of God is a spirit of love. And therefore when the Spirit of God enters into the soul, love enters. God is love, and he who has God dwelling in him by his Spirit will have love dwelling in him. The nature of the Holy Spirit is love; and it is by communicating himself, or his own nature, that the hearts of the saints are filled with love or charity. Hence the saints are said to be "partakers of the divine nature" [*2 Peter 1:4*]. And Christians' love is called the love of the Spirit. *Romans 15:30*, "Now I beseech you, brethren, for the Lord Jesus Christ's sake, and for the love of the Spirit." And having bowels of love and mercy seems to signify the same thing with having the fellowship of the Spirit in *Philippians 2:1*, "If there be therefore any consolation in Christ, if any comfort of love, if any fellowship of the Spirit, if any bowels and mercies." It is the Spirit which infuses love to God. *Romans 5:5*, "The love of God is shed abroad in our hearts by the Holy Ghost." And it is by the indwelling of this Spirit that the soul dwells in love to men. *1 John 4:12–13*, "If we love one another, God dwelleth in us, and his love is perfected in us. Hereby know we that we dwell in him, and he in us, because he hath given us of his Spirit." And ch. *1 John 3:23–24*, "And this is his commandment, that we should believe on the name of his Son Jesus Christ, and love one another, as he gave us commandment. And he that keepeth his commandments dwelleth in him, and he in him. And hereby we know that he abideth in us, by the Spirit which he hath given us." ***Ethical Writings (WJE Online Vol. 8)***

From what has been said, it follows that the Holy Spirit is the sum of all good. 'Tis the fullness of God. The holiness and happiness of the Godhead consists in it; and in the communion or partaking of it consists all the true loveliness and happiness of the creature. All the grace and comfort that persons have here, and all their holiness and happiness hereafter, consists in the love of the Spirit, spoken of, *Romans 15:30*; and joy and comfort in the Holy Ghost, spoken of, *Romans 14:17*; *Acts 9:31*, *Acts 13:52*. And therefore, that in *Matthew 7:11*, "If ye then, being evil, know how to give good gifts unto your children, how much more shall your Father which is in heaven give good things to them that ask him?" is in *Luke 11:13* expressed thus: "If ye then, being evil, know how to give good gifts unto your children: how much more shall your heavenly Father give the Holy Spirit [to them] that ask him?" Doubtless there is an agreement in what is expressed by each Evangelist, and giving the Holy Spirit to them that ask is the same as giving good things to them that ask: for the Holy Spirit is the sum of all good. ***Writings on the Trinity, Grace, and Faith (WJE Online Vol. 21)***

Romans 15:32

When such a minister and such a people are thus united, it is attended with *great joy:* the minister joyfully devoting himself to the service of his Lord in the work of the ministry, as a work that he delights in; and also joyfully uniting himself to the society of the saints that he is set over, as having complacence in them, for his dear Lord's sake, whose people they are; and willingly and joyfully, on Christ's call, undertaking the labors and difficulties of the service of their souls. And they, on the other hand, joyfully receiving him as a precious gift of their ascended Redeemer. Thus a faithful minister and a Christian people are each other's joy; *Romans 15:32*, "That I may come unto you with joy by the will of God, and may with you be refreshed." *2 Corinthians 1:14*, "As you have acknowledged us in part, that we are your rejoicing, even as ye are ours." ***Sermons and Discourses, 1743–1758 (WJE Online Vol. 25)***

Romans 15:33

And of all the external things that we can do to have the Spirit of God continued amongst [us], I believe the most likely thing to be successful to that end, of any one thing whatsoever, is abounding in deeds of love and charity. The abounding in deeds of love is the likeliest way to have the God of love and peace always dwelling with us (*Romans 15:33*). If we would now manifest our thankfulness for what God does for us by obeying that precept of Christ, *Matthew 10:8*, "Freely ye have received, freely give," and should be much in deeds of love and charity, in helping one another under our difficulties and straits, and promoting any design that tends to encourage that duty, I believe no one external thing whatsoever is so likely to be successful to this end. We see how God has smiled upon the charitable disposition that was manifested when the Reverend Mr. Whitefield was here. ***Sermons and Discourses, 1739–1742 (WJE Online Vol. 22)***

ROMANS CHAPTER 16

Romans 16:1

"Sister" is to be understood in the same sense here, as in *1 Corinthians 7:15*, *Romans 16:1*, *James 2:15*. ***The "Blank Bible" (WJE Online Vol. 24)***

Romans 16:7

1 Corinthians 15:11. "Therefore whether it were I or they," etc. There was no such thing as any difference among the Apostles in the doctrines that they preached, or as one's finding fault with what another taught; but all acknowledged each other's doctrine. It appears by this and several other places, as *2 Peter 3:15–16*; *Jude 3* and *Jude 17*; *Galatians 1:17–19*, *Galatians 1:22–24*; *Galatians 2:7–9*; *Galatians 2:9* of this context; *Romans 16:7* ***The "Blank Bible" (WJE Online Vol. 24)***

When they are excommunicated, they are avoided and rejected with abhorrence as visibly wicked. We are to cast them out as an unclean thing that defiles the church of God. In this sense the Psalmist professes hatred of those that were visible enemies of God. *Psalms 139:21–22*, "Do I not hate them, O Lord, that hate thee? and am I not grieved with those that rise up against thee? I hate them with perfect hatred." Not that he hated them with a hatred of malice or ill will, but with displicency and abhorrence of their wickedness. In this respect, we are to be the children of our Father which is in heaven, who, though he loves many wicked men with a love of benevolence, yet he don't love them with a love of complacence. Thus excommunicate persons are cut off from the charity of the church. They are cut off from the society that Christians have together as brethren. I speak now of that common society that Christian brethren have together. Thus we are commanded to withdraw from such, to avoid 'em, to have no company with 'em (*Romans 16:17*), to treat 'em as heathens and publicans. God's people are not only to avoid society with visibly wicked men in sacred things, but, as much as may be, avoid them and withdraw from them as to that common society which is proper towards Christians. Not that they should avoid speaking to 'em on any occasion—all manner and all degrees of society are not forbidden—but all unnecessary society, all such society as holds forth complacence in them, or such as is wont to be among those that delight in the company one of another. ***Sermons and Discourses, 1739–1742 (WJE Online Vol. 22)***

Romans 16:17–18

The Devil transformed himself into an angel of light, as there was in them a shew, and great boasts of extraordinary knowledge in divine things; *Colossians 2:8*; *1 Timothy 1:6–7* ***and chap. 6:3–5;*** *2 Timothy 2:14*, *2 Timothy 2:16–18*; *Titus 1:10*, *Titus 1:16*. Hence their followers called themselves Gnostics, from their great pretended knowledge: and the Devil in them mimicked the miraculous gifts of the Holy Spirit, in visions, revelations, prophecies, miracles, and the immediate conduct of the Spirit in what they did. Hence they are called false apostles and false prophets: see *Matthew 24:24*. Again, there was a false shew of, and lying pretenses to great holiness and devotion in words: *Romans 16:17–18* ***The Great Awakening (WJE Online Vol. 4)***

Romans 16:20

Then shall he also stand at the bar of the saints that he has so hated and afflicted and molested, for the saints shall judge him with Christ, *1 Corinthians 6:3*, "Know ye not that we shall judge angels?" Now shall he be, as it were, subdued under the church's feet, agreeable to *Romans 16:20*. Satan when he first tempted our first parents to fall, deceitfully and lyingly told them that they should be as gods; but little did he think that the consequence should be that they should indeed and be so much as gods as to be assessors with God, to judge. ***A History of the Work of Redemption (WJE Online Vol. 9)***

The day of the marriage of the Lamb is the day of Christ's rejoicing. *Isaiah 62:5*, *Zephaniah 3:17*. So it is the day of the gladness and rejoicing of the hearts of saints in heaven. See *Revelation 19:1–9*. When he rides forth in this world, girding his sword on his thigh, in his glory and majesty to battle against Antichrist and other enemies, they are represented as riding forth in glory with him, *Revelation 19:14*, and in his triumph they triumph. They appear on Mt. Zion with him with palms in their hands [*Revelation 7:9*], and as Satan is bruised under his feet [*Romans 16:20*], he is bruised under their feet. The saints therefore have no more done with the state of the church and kingdom on earth, because they have left this world and have ascended into heaven, than Christ himself had, when he left the earth and ascended into heaven; who was so far from having done with the prosperity of his church and kingdom here, as to any immediate concern in these things by reason of his ascension, that he ascended to that very end, that he might be more concerned, that he might receive the glory and reward of the enlargement and prosperity of his church and conquest of his enemies here, that he might reign in this kingdom, and be under the best advantages for it, and might have the fullest enjoyment of the glory of it, as much as a king ascends a throne in order to reign over his people, and receive the honor and glory of his dominion over them. ***The "Miscellanies," 833–1152 (WJE Online Vol. 20)***

"Bruise Satan under your feet shortly." Agreeably to what God promised of the seed of the woman [*Genesis 3:15*]. The Apostle probably has respect to the Christian church prevailing to the overthrow of heathenism in the empire in Constantine's time. It was suitable to intimate this to those Christians who were Romans, and dwelt in the capital city of that heathen empire. ***The "Blank Bible" (WJE Online Vol. 24)***

Romans 16:22

"I Tertius." Which Dr. Doddridge supposes to be the same with Silas, being a name signifying the same with the Latin word *Tertius*. ***The "Blank Bible" (WJE Online Vol. 24)***

Romans 16:23

3 John 1. "Gaius." Dr. Doddridge thinks it probable that this was the same person with "Gaius of Corinth, who hospitably received the apostle Paul when he went forth to preach the gospel gratis," whom he calls his "host" (*Romans 16:23*). ***The "Blank Bible" (WJE Online Vol. 24)***

Romans 16:25

The sum of the wisdom of God in all his works appears in bringing to pass this great event; and thus the manifold wisdom of God appeared by it to the angels, who desire to look into these things, in that by this his wise and great design now was made manifest in all his manifold works that they had seen, and till now never understood the meaning of. ***The "Miscellanies," (Entry Nos. 501–832) (WJE Online Vol. 18)***

"According to the revelation of the mystery, which was kept secret since the world began," And *Colossians 1:26–27*, "Even the mystery which hath been hid from ages and generations, but is now made manifest to his saints; to whom God would make known what is the riches of the glory of this mystery among the Gentiles, which is Christ in you, the hope of glory." The Apostle, in this text we are upon, speaks of it as being now made known for the present and all future ages, brought to light for the last ages of the world, which were now begun. ***Notes on Scripture (WJE Online Vol. 15)***

"None have heard, seen or perceived, *O God, besides thee*." The meaning is not only that no works had been already done that ever any had seen or heard of, parallel to this work. For if the meaning was that no works that were past had been seen or heard of like this work, those words *O God, besides thee*, would not be added. For if that were the sense, these words would signify that, though others had not seen any past works parallel with this, yet God had; which would not have been [true], for himself had not seen any past works parallel with this. The same may also be argued from *Ephesians 3:9–11*, compared with *Romans 16:25–26*, *Colossians 1:26*. Not only are the words of *Ephesians 3:10* very manifest to my present purpose, but those words in the verse preceding are here worthy of remark: "The mystery which, from the beginning of the world, hath been hid in God." Which seems plainly to imply that it was a secret that [God] kept within himself, was hid and sealed up in the divine understanding, and never had as yet been divulged to any other; was hid in God's secret counsels, which as yet no other being had never been made acquainted with. And so the words imply as much as those in the forementioned place in Isaiah, that "none had perceived besides God." ***The "Miscellanies," 833–1152 (WJE Online Vol. 20)***

Romans 16:26

It is further manifest from this place [*Galatians 5:6*] of the Apostle, wherein he speaks of faith as working by love, that all Christian exercises of heart, and works of life, are from love. For we are abundantly taught in the New Testament that all Christian holiness is begun with faith in Jesus Christ. All Christian obedience is in Scripture called the obedience of faith. *Romans 16:26*, "Is made known to all nations for the obedience of faith." The obedience here spoken of is doubtless the same with that mentioned in the preceding chapter, ver. *Romans 15:18*, "For I will not dare to speak of those things, which Christ hath not wrought by me, to make the Gentiles obedient by word and deed." And the Apostle tells us that the life he now lived in the flesh, he lived by the faith of the Son of God, *Galatians 2:20*. And we are often told that Christians *live* by faith, which carries in it as much as that all graces and holy exercises and works of their spiritual life are by faith. But how does faith work these things? Why, in this place in Galatians it works whatsoever it does work, and that is by love. Hence the truth of the doctrine follows, and that it is indeed so that all which is saving and distinguishing in Christianity does radically consist and is summarily comprehended in love. ***Ethical Writings (WJE Online Vol. 8)***

1 Peter 1:14. "As obedient children." In the Greek, τέκνα ὑπακοῆς, "children of obedience." The word ὑπακοῇ is often in the New Testament put for that compliance and yielding to the gospel that appertains to true faith. So it is in two other verses in this chapter, as *1 Peter 1:2* and *1 Peter 1:22*, and in other parts of the New Testament, as *Romans 1:5*, and *Romans 15:18*, and *Romans 16:26*, *II Cor. 10:5*, *1 Peter*, and other places, τέκνα ὑπακοῆς, "children of obedience," are in the language of the apostles opposite to υἱοὺς τῆς ἀπειθείας "children of disobedience" (*Ephesians 5:6*). These two sorts of persons are spoken of together, and set in opposition one to another, in the *1 Peter 4:17*. "And if it first begin at us, what shall the end be of them that obey not the gospel of God?" And again, *1 Peter 2:7–8*, "Unto you therefore which *believe* he is precious, but unto them which be *disobedient*," etc. ***The "Blank Bible" (WJE Online Vol. 24)***

Romans 16:27

For that, my brethren, the Scripture often expresseth it in the plural also. You read of the phrase, "forever and ever"; you have it in Revelation again and again. We shall reign with Christ "forever and ever"; it is for ages and ages. You have the same in *Romans 16:27*; and in the *Ephesians 3:21*, you shall find it is in the plural as well as here. "Unto him be glory in the church by Christ Jesus throughout all ages, world without end." He means not only this world, but the world that is to come too. And why? Because that to come is "the age of ages"; it is the *secula seculorum*. ***Notes on Scripture (WJE Online Vol. 15)***

The glory of God appears, by the account given in the Word of God, to be that end or event in the earnest desires of which, and in their delight in which, the best part of the moral world, and when in their best frames, do most naturally express the direct tendency of the spirit of true goodness, and give vent to the virtuous and pious affections of their heart, and do most properly and directly testify their supreme respect to their Creator. This is the way in which the holy Apostles, from time to time, gave vent to the ardent exercises of their piety, and expressed and breathed forth their regard to the Supreme Being. *Romans 11:36*, "To whom be glory forever and ever, Amen." Ch. *Romans 16:27*, "To God only wise, be glory, through Jesus Christ, forever, Amen." *Galatians 1:4–5*, "Who gave himself for our sins, that he might deliver us from this present evil world, according to the will of God and our Father, to whom be glory forever and ever, Amen." 2 *Timothy 4:18*, "And the Lord shall deliver me from every evil work, and will preserve me to his heavenly kingdom: to whom be glory forever and ever, Amen." *Ephesians 3:21*, "Unto him be glory in the church, by Christ Jesus throughout all ages, world without end." ***Ethical Writings (WJE Online Vol. 8)***

JONATHAN EDWARDS' ROMANS SERMON EXPLICATIONS

Sermon Explication on Romans 12:1 (Preached 1720–23)

Dedication to God

"I beseech you therefore, brethren, by the mercies of God, that ye present your bodies a living sacrifice, holy, acceptable to God, which is your reasonable service." *Romans 12:1.*

The Apostle, in the foregoing part of this epistle having insisted upon the great doctrines of Christianity, against Jews and heathens, and clearly proved and brightly illustrated those gospel truths which are so bright and glorious, the Apostle breaks out in a sort of a rapture at the conclusion of the doctrinal part of the epistle in the last words of the foregoing chapter:

"O the depth of the riches both of the wisdom and knowledge of God! How unsearchable are his judgments, and his ways past finding out! For who hath known the mind of the Lord, or who hath been his counsellor? Or who hath first given to him, and it shall be recompensed to him again? For of him, and through him, and to him are all things: to whom be glory forever. Amen" [*Romans 11:33–36*]

And now he begins in this twelfth chapter the practical part of the epistle, as an improvement of the foregoing glorious truths, and this he begins with the words of our text, with urging this greatest of all the duties of a Christian: of offering up ourselves to God. The Apostle begins with this because it comprehends all other duties. At this present time, we shall only consider these two things in the words:

1. The duty enjoined and urged, and that is the presenting our bodies, which is to be understood metonymically of our whole persons—body and soul—a living sacrifice to God. The sacrifices that were enjoined under the law were of bulls, goats, and calves, etc., which were but types of

the great sacrifice of the gospel: Jesus Christ, who was once offered up. And therefore, all the standing sacrifices that remain are of our own bodies which we are to offer up alive to God.

2. The argument by which it is urged, and that is that it is our most reasonable service; most reasonable by reason of those things of which the Apostle had been speaking in the foregoing part of the epistle.

Sermon Explication on Romans 1:24. (Preached 1723–26)

Romans 1:24, "Wherefore God also gave them up to uncleanness through the lust of their own heart to dishonor their own bodies, between themselves."

One thing wherein the Christian faith appears to be more excellent and better suited to the end of religion than any other in the world is not only that the reward of holiness it promises is greater and infinitely more excellent. But that the punishment of sin also that it threatens is more dreadful, and thereby more gloriously declares the Justice of God. And honors his holiness and his law but it tends more effectually to bring men off from a wicked life which has such a horrible Punishment affixed to it.

And it wonderfully unfolds those things which were so difficult and perplexing to men before. even God's dispensations in his providence towards wicked men in suffering them to live and prosper in the world, it show us the justice of God in so dealing with sinners and that instead of its 'being from God's injustice or unmindfullness of their wickedness that it is Part of their Punishment. And that the most dreadful part too in its consequences to obstinate sinners. *Rom 9:22*, "What if God, willing to show his wrath and to make his power known, endured with much long suffering the vessels of wrath fitted to destruction." And by our text also we may be instructed in the reasons of God's letting men alone in their sin.

The Apostle here is speaking of the inexcusableness of the heathen, yea although they had no light but the light of nature to go by. And how God was provoked by them and his anger stirred up against them. In that even they who are in so great darkness sinned against their light. Inasmuch as they might know much of God by the book of the creatures though not by the book of the Scriptures.

In the 23rd verse the sins that they committed and were what in them was chiefly provoking to God are mentioned, "And changed the Glory of the incorruptible God into and image make like to corruptible men and to birds and four footed beasts and creeping things . . ." which are the proper sins of heathenism. In our text we have an account of the punishment that God inflicted upon them for their sins particularly for their Idolatry. Wherefore God also gave them up to uncleanness through the lusts of their own hearts to dishonor their own bodies between themselves. We may herein observe:

1. What manner of punishment that is, which God inflicts upon the heathen. He gave them up to uncleanness &c. God gave them up to sin. Sin is the punishment. God leaves them to sin, gives them up to it. Suffers them to commit more sin and that is their punishment.

2. We are led by the first word of the verse to observe what this was a punishment of. Hereby we are led to the former verses. And there we find that it was because that thing became vain in their imaginations, & professing themselves wise they became fools and worshipped and served creatures and earthly corruptible things instead of God. The same thing is spoken of in the 25th verse: They changed the truth of God into a lie & worshipped and served the Creature more than the creator who is blessed forever.

3. Who they are that are thus punish'd by God. They were heathen who had nothing but the dim light of nature to walk by. Whose sins therefore were nothing aggravated as gospel sinners are.

Sermon Explication on Romans 12:18 (Preached 1723–26)

Living Peaceably One With Another. *Romans 12:18*. "If it be possible, as much as lieth in you, live peaceably with all men."

This chapter is a sort of a summary of those virtues and graces, amiable actions and heavenly dispositions, which more especially adorn the Christian, and make 'em shine brighter than other men. If the rules of this chapter were but followed universally in the world, it would most surprisingly transform and alter it, and make it another in comparison, but little differing from Jerusalem (*Romans 12:1*, above). The chapter is well worth our most diligent and frequent reading, and that we should bind the words and rules thereof, that we should bind them upon our hearts; yea, that they should be written in indelible characters there, that it should be the object of continual meditation, lying down and rising up, and that we should frequently examine our lives by it, as by an excellent catalog of those duties and practices, which, if performed, will make us appear Christians indeed, and will mold our hearts and regulate our lives according to Jesus Christ and his image. If this chapter were but eyed, and so put in practice by us, we should excel,

1. In lively true devotion, in dispositions and duties more immediately respecting God, which are here most livelily represented and powerfully urged. *Romans 12:1–2*, "I beseech you therefore, brethren, by the mercies of God, that ye present your bodies a living sacrifice, holy, acceptable unto God, which is your reasonable service. And be not conformed to this world: but be ye transformed by the renewing of your mind, that ye may prove what is that good, and acceptable, and perfect, will of God." And *Romans 12:11*, "Not slothful in business; fervent in spirit; serving the Lord."

2. Here are perfect rules, which, if followed, will make us excel in the duties more immediately relating to ourselves. *Romans 12:3*, "For I say, through the grace given to me, to every man that is among you, not to think of himself more highly than he ought to think; but to think soberly, according as God hath dealt to every man the measure of faith." And *Romans 12:12*, "Rejoicing in hope; patient in tribulation." But more especially,

3. Here are directions for behavior with relation unto men, which exceedingly tend to make mankind happy, and to make each particular person both excellent and blessed in human and Christian society, and every particular society to flourish. Here are rules how to behave ourselves in our particular stations, and duties from thence arising incumbent on us, from the fourth verse to the eighth; and then the duties which are undistinguishedly incumbent upon all towards each other, as verses nine and ten, "Let love be without dissimulation. Abhor that which is evil; cleave to that which is good. Be kindly affectioned one to another with brotherly love; in honor preferring one another"; and from the thirteenth verse to the end. Here we are exhorted to distribute to the necessity of saints, and to be given to hospitality; to bless them by whom we are wronged and abused; to bless always and never to curse; to sympathize with others, either in their prosperity or adversity, from love to them; and to rejoice with those that do rejoice, and weep with those that weep, as if their prosperity were our own. This is not only our friends, but, if we would be as Christians, we must rejoice at the happiness of those that persecute us, and weep and be grieved for their misfortunes. Here we are exhorted to unanimity, and to be of the same mind one towards another; not to mind high things, but to condescend to men of low degree, those that are below

ourselves, and not to be wise in our own conceit; to recompense to no man evil for evil, and to provide things honest in the sight of all. If these things were but followed, what [is] exhorted to in the next verse, the verse of our text, would of course follow. If men did use themselves to be kind unto those that abused them, to bless those that persecuted them, and did not mind high things, but were humble and lowly, and would condescend one to another, and were not wise in their own conceits—that is, if they were not tenacious of their own opinions, as thinking themselves wiser than any other—if men were slower in resenting injuries, and would never recompense evil for evil, and would be fair and open and sincere in all their dealings, and honest in the sight of the world, there would need no more in order to obtaining peace with all men.

That which follows this verse seems to be directions by what means we shall thus obtain peace with all men: "Dearly beloved, avenge not yourselves, but rather give place unto wrath." If we would maintain peace, we must not avenge ourselves and go about violently to resist what is done in opposition to ourselves; no, but we must give place to wrath, for God has challenged vengeance as his own prerogative. Therefore if our enemies hunger, we are to feed him; if he thirst, we must give him drink. This is all the revenge that we must make use of. We must not be overcome of evil, but overcome evil with good.

But to return to the words under consideration, in them we observe,

1. The thing that is exhorted to, that is, peace, a living peaceably with our fellow men.

2. The universality of this peace with others that we are to seek: "live peaceably with all men."

3. The extent of our obligation to this duty of living peaceably with all men: if it be possible, not only if it can be done without private inconveniences, not only when we are not injured by others, but if it be any way in the world possible, by any lawful means.

4. How we are to seek this living peaceably with all men: with all our might and power, as much in us lies. If there be any power, or any advantage, or any knowledge, how to live peaceably with all men, we are [to seek them]

Sermon explication on Romans 2:16. (Preached 1727–28)

Romans 2:16. "In the day when God shall judge the secrets of men by Jesus Christ according to my gospel."

The Apostle is speaking in the foregoing verses, beginning with the sixth verse, how God will judge all sorts of men universally according to their deeds; that he will render indignation and wrath, tribulation and anguish upon everyone that doth evil, whether he be Jew or Gentile; and on the contrary will render glory, honor and peace to every soul that works good, whether he be Jew or Gentile, for there is no respect of persons with God [*Romans 2:9–11*]. God won't favor the Jews because they are the seed of Abraham, nor shall the Gentiles be excused because of their ignorance. For says the Apostle, "as many as have sinned without law shall perish without law" [*Romans 2:12*]. That is, they shall perish for their breach of the law of nature, written in their hearts; as the Apostle afterwards explains himself, "and as many as have sinned under the law shall be judged by the law," as in the twelfth verse. What follows in three next verses comes in by way of parenthesis, and the words of our text are to be connected with the twelfth verse. There, he told by what rule they should be judged; in our text he tells the time when: "in the day when God shall judge the secrets of men according to my gospel."

This day is deciphered:

1. By the business of the day, which is judgment. It will be day appointed for this very end and business; it is a day to be noted for the great work of it. And therefore it is called the great and notable day, Acts 2:20.

2. The judge, who is Jesus Christ, that crucified man that the Apostle preached to the Romans.

3. The things judged, namely, the secrets of men; things that are out of the way of other judgments that human judges can have nothing to do with, because they are secret and hid from the world.

4. The revelation which God has made of it, which the Apostle calls his gospel, that is, the gospel which he had preached. As if he had said, "It will be on that day that I have told you of and preached to you, and which has been so clearly revealed in that gospel that I have preach[ed] to you and to other Gentiles."

Sermon explication on Romans 6:14 (Preached on 1728–29)

Romans 6:14. "For ye are not under the law but under grace"

The Apostle is answering an objection against what he had said in the foregoing chapter in the two Last verses of that chapter he had said that where sin abounded Grace did much more abound.

The objection which the apostle proposes is: why mayn't we continue in sin that grace may abound? Or why will it open a door for more unrestrained wickedness if grace reigns to eternal life as sin reigns unto death? The apostle spends this whole chapter in answering this objection, and in our text and the following verses he argues that the dominion abounding & reigning of grace will have a directly contrary tendency in those that receive it. That the gospel, which is such a dispensation of grace, instead of encouraging sin tends to deliver from its [dominion] and deliver from its [power] all that heartily entertain it.

Maybe there is a twofold dominion of sin that it has over wicked men. 1. It has dominion in them whereby it governs their hearts & behavior & 2. It has power over him with respect to his state as by the guilt of it he is held bound to Punishment.

Now those that are under the law they are under the dominion of sin in both these Respects: 1. Because in law no provision is made for man's deliverance from sin either from the guilt or strength of it. . the law indeed strictly forbids sin and not only so but very severely threatens the commission of it, but yet administers no other principle to preserve from it but only a servile fear of the spirit of bondage, which principle can never deliver the heart from the love, and so the power, of sin or make them sincere and hearty in their obedience, and therefore is called a dead letter. And then 2. It is the strength of sin both with respect to its obligation to punish. For 'tis only by virtue of the law that sin does infer an obligation and also with respect to the prevailing influence of sin as it is the occasion of corruption the more violently raging in the heart, as the apostle himself argues in the next 8 verses &c.

It was needful to observe this in order to see the force of the apostle's reasoning why they should be the less under the dominion for not being under the law, but under grace.

By grace is meant the dispensation of God's grace in Christ as the covenant of grace or the gospel as appears by the scope of the apostle and by its being set in opposition to the law or covenant of works . The word is so used in other places in the new testament, *2 Cor 6:1*. "we beseech you also that ye receive not the grace of God. in vain. That is the gospel of grace. And so *Gal 5:4* "whosoever of you are Justified by the law ye are fallen from grace," i.e. if you seek to be justified by the covenant of works then ye have departed from the gospel or covenant of grace. This dispensation of grace has quite another tendency from the law; it gives another principle of obedience besides servile fear. It gives the spirit of adoption or a principle of love, esteem and gratitude, which alone can render obedience, and by it is given the spirit of God to change the heart and deliver from the dominion of sin. Now persons may be under this covenant of grace in a twofold sense either only as they are under the preaching of it, and are under it by profession, or as their hearts are brought into subjection to it and entire compliance with it. 'Tis only that in the verse that we have respect to at this time the gospels being called grace and from thence we raise this doctrine.

Sermon explication on Romans 4:16 (Preached 1729–30)

Romans 4:16. "Therefore it is of faith that it might be by Grace."

The apostle in this chapter is arguing for the truth of the doc of justification by faith only from the instance of Abraham. He mentions this instance as that which would be most likely to be of weight with the Jews, the principal opposers of this doctrine, because that was the thing that they so highly valued themselves upon that they were the children of Abraham, and supposed that they had a right to the blessings of the covenant of Abraham by virtue of their being circumcised and [their] observance of other legal rites that were peculiar to the children of Abraham according to the flesh. The apostle therefore to convince them shows that Abraham himself to whom God first gave the ordinance of circumcision was not justified by works but by faith only, and this he evinces several ways: 1st in that the scripture says expressly though Abraham believed God and it was counted to him for righteousness, and secondly that he was justified before circumcision, the work which the Jews above all others built upon for justification. 10 v. "how was it Reckon then when he was in Circumcision or in Uncircumcision not in Circumcision but in uncircumcision." And in 11 v. he proceeds and argues that circumcision was so far from being that by which he was justified that it was a seal of the justification which he had already received it was a seal of the righteousness of faith which he had yet being uncircumcised, and then 3rd he argues that Abraham was justified not by the works of the law but by faith because that the promise that he should be the heir of the world was not to Abraham or to his seed through the law but through the righteousness of faith. 'Tis in this promise that God's covenant with Abraham chiefly consisted and this promise was not through the law or which is the same thing Abraham did received a title to the Blessing Promised by the works of the law, that is evident because if the promise were made through the law the promise would be of no effect because the law worketh wrath. There are none of the seed of Abraham that ever perfectly kept the law and so if the [promise] was made through the law the promise never would have been fulfilled to our [our/em?] soul as in the 13, 14, and 15 v. But the [soul/such?] promise being not through the law but of faith, and so a promise of sovereign grace that surmounts our transgressions and unworthiness it is sure to all the seed whereas otherwise none of the seed of Abraham would have obtained it as this v. of our text: Therefore it is of faith that it might be by Grace to the End that the promise [might be sure to all the seed]

Sermon Explication on Romans 7:14 (Preached 1729–30)

"But I am Carnal sold under sin." *Romans 7:14*. That the apostle in the foregoing part of the chapter had occasion to mention one thing that is a very remarkable evidence of the corruption of man's nature and that was that the law of God proved to man that his lust was the stronger for the Commandment. God's Prohibition excited the more lively exercises of the sinful appetite 8 v. The Apostle is here showing that its being thus was not from any fault in the law. The Law's proving an occasion of sin was no sign that the law was not good but that the blame is ours and that it denotes the exceeding sinfulness of our natures v. 11 and 12. Wherefore the Law is holy and the commandment holy just and good. And v. 14, For we know that the Law is spiritual but I am carnal sold under sin. The reason that what is good in itself becomes an occasion of our sin 'tis because we are sold under sin. Our natures are so universally and entirely depraved that everything, even that which is in itself the most good and holy, is turned by it into poison. There is nothing that will better it.

But on the contrary, that which is most opposite to the corruption enrages it which argues the absolute dominion of sin in the heart as a master over his slave that is sold to him

---

The Apostle here speaks of himself for as he is bought with a price Christ has redeemed him from this slavery that he might not serve sin and that sin no longer might have dominion over him, for which he praises God in the last verse in the chapter when he was crying out, Wretched man that I am! who shall deliver me from the body of this death? He makes answer to himself, I thank God through Jesus Christ our Lord. So then with the mind I myself serve the law of God. But the apostle explains himself in the eighteenth verse, For I know that in me that is in my flesh dwelleth no good thing. In my flesh, that is, in myself as I am by nature, which the apostle often calls "the flesh" and the "old man," or the "body of sin & death."

Sermon Explication on Romans 9:31–32 (Preached 1730–31)

Rom. 9:31–32. "But Israel, which followed after the law of righteousness, hath not attained to the law of righteousness. Wherefore? Because they sought it not by faith, but as it were by the works of the law."

In this chapter the apostle has been speaking of that sovereign dispensation of God of casting off the nation of the Jews excepting a remnant and his calling the Gentiles and he shows that this is agreeable to several prophecies of the O.T. as of Hosea and Esaias.

In these verses and the foregoing 30 the apostle takes notice of that wherein the favor of God in this dispensation does especially appear. That is that the Gentiles did not seek the Law of righteousness and yet they attained to it, and Israel that did seek it attained it not. Agreeable to what the apostle said in the sixteenth verse, 'tis not of him that willeth nor of him that runneth but of God that showeth mercy.

In the text we have first a thing laid down or asserted viz. that Israel which followed after the Law of righteousness did not attain to the Law of righteousness. They aimed at recommending themselves to God's favour. They sought and hoped to be justified by him and hoped that they were in the right way to obtain it by the Law of righteousness.

2 . the Reason why they did not attain to it is because they did not seek it in a right way. They sought it not by Faith but as it were by the word of the Law. They sought justification by their own righteousness.

Sermon Explication on Romans 5:7–8

Rom. 5:7–8. "For scarcely for a righteous man will one die: yet peradventure for a good man some would even dare to die. But God commendeth his love toward us, in that, while we were yet sinners, Christ died for us."

The comparison that is here made between the love of men one to another and the dying love of God is a short digression from the argument that the apostle is upon in the context. In the beginning of the chapter the apostle describes the hope of a Christian by the greatness of the good that is and the joyfulness of it and the effectualness of it to enable the

Christian to glory in tribulation, Therefore being Justified. . . . In the first three verses it shows how the tribulation of a true Christian is a means of increasing and establishing hope viz that a patient bearing of affliction that greatly confirms hope so that hope don't maketh ashamed. Men are made ashamed by their hope in scripture when their experience is not according to their hope.

But Christians when they are in tribulation and bear it with patience they ben't disappointed and that for the reason that the apostle gives because that in that way of enduring the tribulation the love of God was shed abroad in their hearts by the Holy Ghost which was given to them. God gives fresh supplies of Grace to them that patiently bear tribulation.

He pours forth the holy Ghost upon them, which is the earnest of their future inheritance and is often mention'd as such. And then the apostle proceeds to show what reason Christians have to be assured that their hope of future Glory shall not be disappointed from this argument that Christ died for them even while ungodly, which was the greatest thing Christ having done. Even while under the guilt of sin the apostle argues that no doubt but that when that guilt was removed by his death the salvation would be bestowed because it is not now so great a thing for God to bestow salvation after guilt is removed as it is for Christ to die to remove that guilt.

This of Christ dying for us while ungodly is mentioned to take notice of the wonderfulness of the love of God that Christ should die for us while sinners. To show how unparalleled the love of Christ is the apostle in the first place declares the utmost extent of the love of men: For scarcely for a righteous man will one die: yet peradventure for a good man some would even dare to die. By a good man here may be understood either a man with a qualification beyond righteousness. And then by a righteous man must be understood a man of moral justice one that is willing not to wrong any man but to give every his due; by a good man a bountiful man a of a kind spirit; by goodness sometimes is meant holiness godliness and sometimes bounty and kindness. When we speak of the goodness of God and if we understand it in this sense the meaning of the apostle is this: that men will scarcely die for another, though that other is a righteous man has always done fairly by him and never injured or did him any hurt. Yet possibly some would even die for one that not only never did them no hurt but have been good to those that they have received a great deal of kindness from and lie under special obligation. And this is the utmost that men's love extends to agreeable to what Christ says in John 15:13, Greater love hath no man than this that a man lay down his life for his friends. Or else we may understand a righteous man and good as synonymous terms and signifying the same thing and both in opposition to ungodly and sinners that it is here said that Christ died for. And so the word is changed from righteous to good only for sake of elegance of speech. None have scarcely ever gone so far as to lay down their lives for good and righteous men. But it may be sometimes the love of men have gone so far. But Christ died for those that there were the reverse of righteous and good he died for ungodly and sinners the apostle herein takes notice of one instance wherein the love of Christ transcends all the love of men one to another.

Explication on Romans 2:5 (Preached 1731)

Rom 2:5. "But after thy hardness and impenitent heart treasurest up unto thyself wrath against the day of wrath and revelation of the righteous judgment of God."

The principal aim of the apostle in the three first chap. of this epistle is to show that all mankind are naturally guilty or as the apostle expresses are all under sin

The apostle under this head distinctly of Jews and Gentiles in the first chapter the apostle had been setting forth the abominations that were prevailing among the Gentiles in this chapter the apostle begins upon the Jews to show that they in themselves are not a whit better though they were very apt to judge and condemn the Gentiles as looking upon themselves as much better than they.

The Apostle begins therefore "thou art inexcusable O man. . . . They were exceeding self righteous and exceeding censorious. They accounted themselves purer by nature than the Gentiles because they were the children of Abraham. They were very forward to take notice of the abominable wickedness of the Gentiles and sentenced all that were uncircumcised and did not join with their nation as utterly cast off by God. But they were very insensible of their own wickedness they never considered that they had the very same inclinations in their own hearts and did things that were of a like nature. They thought that the Gentiles were liable to the judgment of God but expected to escape the judgment of God themselves. [is Looked upon themselves] as wicked as they were. That they should be accepted of God because they were the children of Abraham and were circumcised this makes the apostle say "and thinkest thou this, O man, that judgest them which do such things, and doest the same, that thou shalt escape the judgment of God?"

This is the commonly if not universally the case with censorious persons those that are ready to spy out others' wickedness and the aggravations of it and to doom others to hell that they are a sort of men that are very insensible of their own wickedness and their own being judged and condemned of God themselves.

And the Case was with them as with other secure sinners. They flattered themselves from the mercy of God. Because God had not executed judgment on them already they flattered themselves that he never would. They at present saw no tokens of God's anger and so were emboldened to go on in sin as in the verse preceding the text.

They as yet falling nor feeling any thing of God's anger went on boldly in sin whenas they did but the time of God's patience in treasuring up wrath against the wrath. In the words we may observe: 1. the manner of those ungodly men that the apostle is speaking of they treasure up wrath to themselves. They treasure up something.

And what is that? It is not gold and silver or pearls or any other wealth. 'Tis not any precious or desirable thing. 'Tis wrath and vengence. That they heap up as if it were their wealth and 'tis wrath upon themselves. They treasure up their own misery. If any man should be industrious in augmenting another's calamity it would be monstrous. But when men heap up misery for themselves 'tis more strange.

2. Against what time they do this? "Against the day of wrath and revelation of the righteous judgment of God." The apostle was speaking how they encouraged themselves in sin because now God bore with them. Let 'em alone. But God lets men alone for the present only because the day is not come. This is not the day of wrath. That is the reason that they [neither] feel nor see anything of it at present. The wrath of God has its appointed day and then God will render to every man according to his deeds. [*Romans 2:6*]

Wicked men don't see any manifestations of God's anger now and they don't believe there is any nor can others see there is at present no[t] knowing either love or hate by all. But there is a day when God will reveal it. That is the day of the revelation of the righteous judgment [of God].

1. From what principle wicked men act in so doing from hardness and impenitency of heart according to thy hardness, it shows a most sottish . . .

Sermon Explication on Romans 3:13–18 (Preached 1731–32)

Rom 3.13–18. "Their throat is an open sepulcre. With their tongues they have used deceit the Poison of asps is under their Lips."

It is to be observed that the main drift of these three first Chapters to the Romans is to prove that all the world both Jews & Gentiles are under sin that hereby he may prove that none can be saved but by Jesus Christ nor justified but by faith.

In the first chapter he shows how the Gentiles or heathens are under sin. He there sets forth the dreadful corruption and wickedness that prevailed in the heathen world.

When he is done with the heathen then in the second chapter he comes to the Jews who used to judge the Gentiles and justify themselves. They accounted all the Gentiles sinners but esteemed themselves by nature holy. So the apostle shows that they also are under sin and that wherein they judged others they condemned themselves, in that they did the same things that the Gentiles did. Though they were called Jews and rested in the law and made their boast of God they were all by nature sinners as well as the Gentiles. He still is upon the same argument in this chapter showing that the Jews are by nature no better than the Gentiles as in verse nine, "what then are we no better than they" . . .

The apostle confirms what he says by citing several passages of the Old Testament that do teach the same thing viz the universal corruption of mankind. The words from the tenth to the eighteenth verse are texts quoted out of the Old Testament.

If it could be proved that the Jews were under sin from the Old Testament that was most likely to convince 'em for they universally acknowledged the Old Testament had been brought up since their infancy in a belief the of the divine authority & Certain truth of them.

There are two things that the apostle aims at the proof of by these vitations out of the Old Testament.

1. That all mankind are corrupt and

2. That they are all altogether corrupt. The first he proves in verses 10, 11 and 12 by a citation out of the fourteenth Psalm. This is to prove that they are all corrupt as it is written: 'there is none righteous.

Then by the citations that follow in the words that we propose now to insist on he proves that all are altogether corrupt. All Jews and Gentiles are corrupt and that not only in a measure but altogether. This is proved by various passages out of the Old Testament. These words: "their throat is an open sepulcre" are taken from the fifth verse of *Psalm 9*. "These the Poison of asps is under" 140 *Ps. 3* etc.

Sermon Explication on Romans 12:17 (Preached 1733)

Rom. 12.17. "Provide things honest in the sight of all men."

This chapter is one of the most excellent summaries of Christian duties that we have any where in the scriptures.

It may be observed to be commonly the manner of the apostle in the beginning of his epistle to insist chiefly on doctrine, but towards the latter upon practice and the duties of the Christian religion.

So the apostle in this epistle to the Romans in the eleven preceding chapters had insisted on an explication of the important doctrine of religion, but in the five last chapters which succeed he insists upon the various branches of Christian practice.

This chapter, which is the first of them, is an excellent summary of all rules for the directing our practice both towards God and our neighbor.

The text is one of those given for our direction in our behavior towards our neighbor in which we may observe:

1. The matter of the duty to provide things honest, i.e., that we should [be] strictly just and upright in all our dealings with our neighbor about the things of the present life, distinctly for the sake of gain, 'tis to make provision for ourselves or our families or others that we are interested in. The apostle exhorts that we should see to it that all those good things that we thus provide for ourselves be such as we come honestly by. That we may endeavor to add to our outward substance or to prevent its being diminished to better our outward circumstances in any respect or avoid our being damnified in them dishonestly. All such things as either gained dishonestly or kept dishonestly are dishonest things and provided dishonestly in the sense of the text.

2. The circumstance of the duty that the apostle directs to viz that it be done in the sight of all men, not that the apostle would have them to be ostentatious of their honesty. Ostentation of goodness is very opposite to the nature and spirit of Christianity. But the apostle's meaning rather is that they should be strictly and universally honest in their behavior towards all men that it may be evident unto all.

When persons walk very strictly and regularly at all times and towards all sorts of persons it can't fail to be taken notice, though they are never so far from being ostentatious of it. This is like that command of

Christ in *Matthew 5:16*, Let your light so shine before men, that they may see your good works, and glorify your Father which is in heaven.

The Apostle would have the Christian Romans to treat heathen with justice and honesty and by no means to wrong any in anything though they were their enemies. To behave so that those that are most their enemies and watch for occasions to accuse them may find no just occasion. To this purpose the apostle Peter 1 epistle 2.12, having your conversation honest among the Gentiles: that, whereas they speak against you as evildoers, they may by your good works, which they shall behold, glorify God in the day of visitation. To this Purpose the apostle directs 'em elsewhere to avoid the appearance of evil. The apostle would have them to be so far from being dishonest that they should avoid those things that look suspiciously; that they choose those ways of living behave in such a manner as would give the least room for suspicion of any dishonesty.

Sermon Explication on Romans 4:5. (Preached 1734)

JUSTIFICATION BY FAITH ALONE

"But to him that worketh not, but believeth on him that justifieth the ungodly, his faith is counted for righteousness." *Romans 4:5*

The following things may be noted in this verse:

1. That justification respects a man as ungodly: this is evident by those words—"that justifieth the ungodly." Which words can't imply less than that God in the act of justification, has no regard to anything in the person justified, as godliness, or any goodness in him; but that nextly, or immediately before this act, God beholds him only as an ungodly or wicked creature; so that godliness in the person to be justified is not so antecedent to his justification as to be the ground of it. When it is said that God justifies the ungodly, 'tis as absurd to suppose that our godliness, taken as some goodness in us, is the ground of our justification, as when it is said that Christ gave sight to the blind, to suppose that sight was prior to, and the ground of that act of mercy in Christ, or as if it should be said that such an one by his bounty has made a poor man rich, to suppose that it was the wealth of this poor man that was the ground of this bounty towards him, and was the price by which it was procured.

2. It appears that by "him that worketh not" in this verse, is not meant only one that don't conform to the ceremonial law, because "he that worketh not," and "the ungodly" are evidently synonymous expressions, or what signify the same; it appears by the manner of their connection; if it

ben't so, to what purpose is the latter expression "the ungodly" brought in? The context gives no other occasion for it, but only to show that the grace of the gospel appears in that God in justification has no regard to any godliness of ours: the foregoing verse is, "Now to him that worketh is the reward not reckoned of grace, but of debt": in that verse 'tis evident, that gospel grace consists in the rewards being given without works; and in this verse which nextly follows it and in sense is connected with it, 'tis evident that gospel grace consists in a man's being justified that is "ungodly"; by which it is most plain that by "him that worketh not," and him that is "ungodly," are meant the same thing; and that therefore not only works of the ceremonial law are excluded in this business of justification, but works of morality and godliness.

3.'Tis evident in the words, that by the faith that is here spoken of, by which we are justified, is not meant the same thing as a course of obedience, or righteousness, by the expression, by which this faith is here denoted, viz. "believing on him that justifies the ungodly." They that oppose the Solifidians, as they call them, do greatly insist on it, that we should take the words of Scripture concerning this doctrine, in their most natural and obvious meaning; and how do they cry out of our clouding this doctrine with obscure metaphors, and unintelligible figures of speech! But is this to interpret Scripture according to its most obvious meaning, when the Scripture speaks of our "believing on him that justifies the ungodly," or the breakers of his law, to say that the meaning of it is performing a course of obedience to his law, and avoiding the breaches of it? Believing on God as a justifier, certainly is a different thing from submitting to God as a lawgiver; especially a believing on him as a justifier of the ungodly, or rebels against the Lawgiver.

4.'Tis evident that the subject of justification is looked upon as destitute of any righteousness in himself, by that expression, "it is counted," or imputed to him "for righteousness"; the phrase, as the Apostle uses it here, and in the context, manifestly imports, that God of his sovereign grace is pleased in his dealings with the sinner, to take and regard, that which indeed is not righteousness, and in one that has no righteousness, so that the consequence shall be the same as if he had righteousness; (which may be from the respect it bears to something that is indeed righteousness). 'Tis plain that this is the force of the expression in the preceding verses: in the last verse but one, 'tis manifest the Apostle lays the stress of his argument for the free grace of God, from that text he cites out of text of the Old Testament about Abraham, on the word counted or imputed, and that this is the thing that he supposed God to show his grace in, viz. in his counting something for righteousness, in his consequential dealings with Abraham, that was no righteousness in itself. And in the next verse which immediately precedes the text, "Now to him that worketh is the reward not reckoned of grace, but of debt"; the word there translated reckoned, is the same that in the other verses is rendered imputed, andcounted: and 'tis as much as if the Apostle had said, "As to him that works, there is no need of any gracious reckoning, or counting it for righteousness, and causing the reward to follow as if it were a righteousness; for if he has works he has that which is a righteousness in itself, to which the reward properly belongs." This is further evident by the words that follow, *Romans 4:6*, "Even as David also described the blessedness of the man unto whom God imputeth righteousness without works"; what can here be meant by imputing righteousness without works, but imputing righteousness to him that has none of his own? *Romans 4:7–8*, "Saying blessed are they whose iniquities are forgiven, and whose sins are covered: Blessed is the man to whom the Lord will not impute sin." How are these words of David to the Apostle's purpose? Or how do they prove any such thing, as that righteousness is imputed without works, unless it be because the word imputed is used and the subject of the imputation is mentioned, as a sinner, and consequently destitute of a moral righteousness? For David says no such thing, as that he is forgiven without the works of the ceremonial law; there is no hint of the ceremonial law, or reference to it, in the words. I will therefore venture to infer this doctrine from the words, for the subject of my present discourse, viz.

Sermon Explication on Romans 3:19 (Preached 1735)

THE JUSTICE OF GOD IN THE DAMNATION OF SINNERS

"That every mouth may be stopped." *Romans 3:19*

The main subject of the doctrinal part of this epistle, is the free grace of God, in the salvation of men by Jesus Christ; especially as it appears in the doctrine of justification by faith alone. And the more clearly to evince this doctrine, and show the reason of it, the Apostle, in the first place, establishes that point, that no flesh living can be justified by the deeds of the law. And to prove it, he is very large and particular in showing, that all mankind, not only the Gentiles, but Jews, are under sin, and so under the condemnation to the law; which is what he insists upon from the beginning of the epistle to this place. He first begins with the Gentiles;

and in the *Romans 1*, shows that they are under sin, by setting forth the exceeding corruptions and horrid wickedness, that overspread the Gentile world: and then through the *Romans 2–3*, to the text and following verse, he shows the same of the Jews, that they also are in the same circumstances with the Gentiles, in this regard. They had an high thought of themselves, because they were God's covenant people, and circumcised, and the children of Abraham. They despised the Gentiles, as polluted, condemned, and accursed; but looked on themselves, on account of their external privileges, and ceremonial and moral righteousness, as a pure and holy people, and the children of God; as the Apostle observes in the *Romans 2*. It was therefore strange doctrine to them, that they also were unclean and guilty in God's sight, and under the condemnation and curse of the law. The Apostle does therefore, on account of their strong prejudices against such doctrine, the more particularly insist upon it, and shows that they are no better than the Gentiles; as in the *Romans 3:9*, "What then? Are we better than they? No, in no wise: for we have before proved both Jews and Gentiles, that they are all under sin." And to convince them of it, he then produces certain passages out of their own law, or the Old Testament (whose authority they pretended a great regard to), from the *Romans 3:9*. And it may be observed, that the Apostle first, cites certain passages to prove that mankind are all corrupt, in the *Romans 3:10–12*; "As it is written, There is none righteous, no not one: there is none that understandeth: there is none that seeketh after God: they are all gone out of the way: they are together become unprofitable: there is none that doeth good; no not one." Secondly the passages he cites next, are to prove that not only are all corrupt, but each one wholly corrupt, as it were all over unclean, from the crown of his head, to the soles of his feet; and therefore several particular parts of the body are mentioned, as the throat, the tongue, the lips, the mouth, the feet. *Romans 3:13–15*, "Their throat is an open sepulcher, with their tongues they have used deceit, the poison of asps is under their lips; whose mouth is full of cursing and bitterness, their feet are swift to shed blood." And, thirdly, he quotes other passages to show, that each one is not only all over corrupt, but corrupt to a desperate degree, in the *Romans 3:16–18*; in which the exceeding degree of their corruption is shown, both by affirming and denying: by affirmatively expressing the most pernicious nature and tendency of their wickedness, in the *Romans 3:16*, "Destruction and misery are in their ways." And then by denying all good, or godliness, in them, in the *Romans 3:17–18*, "And the way of peace have they not known: there is no fear of God before their eyes." And then, lest the Jews should think these passages of their law don't concern them, and that only the Gentiles are intended in them, the Apostle shows in the verse of the text, not only that they are not exempt, but that they especially must be understood, "Now we know, that whatsoever things the law saith, it saith to them that are under the law." By those that are "under the law," is meant the Jews, and the Gentiles by those that are without law; as appears by the *Romans 2:12*. There is special reason to understand the law, as speaking to and of them, to whom it was immediately given. And therefore the Jews would be unreasonable in exempting themselves. And if we examine the places of the Old Testament, whence these passages are taken, we shall see plainly that special respect is had to the wickedness of the people of that nation, in every one of them. So that the law shuts all up in universal and desperate wickedness, "that every mouth may be stopped." The mouths of the Jews, as well as of the Gentiles; notwithstanding all those privileges by which they were distinguished from the Gentiles.

The things that the law says, are sufficient to stop the mouths of all mankind, in two respects.

1. To stop them from boasting of their righteousness, as Jews were wont to do; as the Apostle observes in the *Romans 2:23*. That the Apostle has respect to stopping their mouths in this respect, appears by the *Romans 2:27* of the context, "Where is boasting then? It is excluded." The law stops our mouths from making any plea for life, the favor of God, or any positive good, from our own righteousness.

2. To stop them from making any excuse for ourselves, or objection against the execution or the sentence of the law, or the infliction of the punishment that it threatens. That it is intended, appears by the words immediately following, that "all the world may become guilty before God." That is that they may appear to be guilty, and stand convicted before God, and justly liable to the condemnation of his law, as "guilty of death," according to the Jewish way of speaking.

And thus the Apostle proves that no flesh can be justified in God's sight, by the deeds of the law; as he draws the conclusion in the following verse; and so prepares the way for the establishing of the great doctrine of justification by faith alone, which he proceeds to do, in the next verse to that, and in the following part of the chapter, and of the epistle.

Sermon Explication on Romans 5:6. (Preached 1735)

OUR WEAKNESS, CHRIST'S STRENGTH
"For when we were yet without strength, in due time Christ died for the ungodly." *Romans 5:6.*

The Apostle, in the foregoing chapters, having insisted on the doctrine of justification by faith alone, he here, in the beginning of this chapter, takes notice of these happy fruits of this justification by faith. He mentions some fruits of it, viz. "peace [with] God [through our Lord] Jesus Christ," and access to God and righteousness, ["and rejoicing in hope of the] glory of God," and glorying "in tribulations [also]."

And having mentioned glory [in tribulations as the] fruit of our justification [by faith], he is [making a further] point, probably [that in] tribulation one [learns patience; and he proceeds to] explain [the triumph of hope over the] evil of [the world] . . . ; i.e. experience of God's past goodness and faithfulness, will beget hope in his promises for the future, and of more complete salvation, when tribulation shall be at an end. "And hope maketh not ashamed," because a true Christian's hope is attended with love, a hope of salvation; and glory is attended with love to that being that [had] purchased [our] salvation; and love will make [us not] ashamed of suffering, and bearing [tribulations for the] person beloved.

[In the words of] the text is declared the [death of Christ for the ungodly, because] Christian hope works love. Hope, or the salvation [of the ungodly, was purchased by] the wonderful love [of the Lord Jesus Christ, who died to purchase] it. . . . [It is upon the first part of the verse] only that I would insist on now, viz. our being without strength.

And the doctrine I would draw from the words may be this, viz.

Sermon Explication on Romans 3:11–12. (Preached 1736)

ALL THAT NATURAL MEN DO IS WRONG
"There is none that understandeth, there is none that seeketh after God. They are all gone out of the way, they are together become unprofitable; there is none that doth good, no, not one." *Romans 3:11–12.*

The drift of the Apostle in all the former part of this epistle is to establish the doctrine of justification by faith in Jesus Christ alone, and to prove that no man can be justified by his own works. And to this end, from the beginning of the epistle to this place, he insists wholly on it to show that all that world are under sin, and for that reason can't be justified by their works, or by anything, but faith in a Savior. In the *Romans 1*, he showed how the Gentiles were under sin; in the *Romans 2*, he shows how the Jews are under sin; in the beginning of this chapter, he answers an objection; and in the *Romans 2:9*, he sums up the matter: "What then? are we better than they? No, in no wise: for we have before proved both Jews and Gentiles, that they are all under sin"; and then proves what he had insisted on out of the Old Testament: "As it is written, There is none righteous, no, not one: there is none that understandeth, there is none that seeketh after God. They are all gone out of the way, they are together become unprofitable; there is none that doth good, no, not one."

The passages here quoted out of the Old Testament are to prove three things. First, that mankind are universally sinful, and that all of them are corrupt. This is chiefly aimed at in the *Romans 3:10–12*: "As it is written, There is none righteous, no, not one: there is none that understandeth, there is none that seeketh after God. They are all gone out of the way, they are together become unprofitable; there is none that doth good, no, not one." Second, that [they] are not only all corrupt, but that everyone is totally corrupt in every part. This is aimed at in the quotations in the *Romans 3:13–15*, where the several parts of the body are mentioned: the throat is an open sepulcher; the tongue is used for deceit; under the lips is the poison of asps; the mouth is full of cursing and bitterness; and the feet are swift to shed blood. Third, that everyone is not only corrupt in every part, but that in an exceeding degree, so as to have no goodness and only badness, and that to the most dreadful degree. And this is what is aimed at in the *Romans 3:16–18*: "Destruction and misery are in their ways: and the way of peace have they not known: there is no fear of God before their eyes." In the text there are five things predicated of natural men.

1. That they don't understand, i.e. they neither know God nor know how to seek or serve him. Natural men, many of them, are taught concerning God and his ways, but they are without understanding. They neither know nor will they learn.

2. That they don't seek after God. Many of them seem to seek after God: they attend on the ordinances of religion; yea, and some of them have their minds very much engaged in it. But yet they don't seek after God. They may pray to God earnestly, and beg mercy of him; but yet they don't seek after God. They seek themselves, and not God.

3. That they are all gone out of the way. Natural men may, to outward appearance, be in the way of their duty. They may be very conscientious,

and none that see them may be able to say but that they go in the way they should do. But yet in reality they are not in the right way, but are out of the way. Even in those very duties of religion that seem right to outward appearance, they are going on in wrong ways.

4. They are together become unprofitable. All natural men are unprofitable; they are unprofitable servants. Though some of them may seem to be religious, yet they don't serve God; but in all that they do, they serve other masters, yea, they serve God's enemies.

5. There is none that doth good, no, not one. Many natural men seem to do many things that are good: they attend in the matter of their duty strictly. Many do very much in religion. Some natural men do a great deal that is to the benefit of their fellow creatures: some natural men may be men of great good to the public. But yet there is none of them that doth good, no, not so much as one.

Sermon Explication on Romans 11:22 (Preached 1735)

+ April.1752. 11 Octob. 1735

Rom 11:22. "Behold therefore the goodness and severity of God": on them which fall severity

The apostle is here speaking of rejection of the Jews from being his people and his calling the Gentiles in their room, which is the subject that this and the two foregoing chapters of this Epistle are taken up about.

The apostle is here in this place cautioning the believing Gentiles against a twofold misimprovement of their dispensation of God. In breaking of the natural branches the Jews grafting them in in their viz insulting and self-confidence.

They are warned against proudly boasting against or insulting over the unbelieving Jews in the 17th, 18th and 19th verses. They are warned against self-confidence in the 20th and 21st verses.

What the apostle says in the verse of the text is to make them sensible that they have cause rather humbly to admire the free and sovereign grace of God towards them, who had so distinguished them from the Jews. Then to boast themselves against them to that end knows then to consider the exceeding different dealing of God towards them and towards the Jews. The wonderful, free and rich grace and goodness which God had exercised in his dealings with them and his severity is his dealing with the Jews. Behold the goodness and severity of God in them that fell severity but—towards thee goodness.

God dealing with the Gentiles in receiving them into his Church was a dispensation of wonderful grace. It was a mercy they were most unworthy of for until then they were heathens and worshipped idols and devils, and were given up to all the abominable wickedness of the heathen world. It was the wonderful, just grace of God to take such a people out of the midst of their heathened sin and to make them his own people to translate them out of the knowledge of darkness to bring them into the Church under so glorious a dispensation as that of the Gospel wherein God's people had so much greater privileges than the Church of the Jews of old had. It was wonderful goodness that they that were so far off should be made so nigh. On the other hand, God's dealings with the Jews were very awful and terrible. They who for many ages had been God's only people of all the nations of the world were now rejected. They were broken off from their own given up to blindness of mind and hardness of heart so that they resisted the greatest light and the most glorious mercies. They continued obstinately under all means that could be used to reject God, Christ and their own salvation and so were brought into miserable circumstances.

They became subject to the most awful spiritual judgment viz judicial blindness and hardness and also were subjected to the most terrible outward judgments. Their country and city were miserably destroyed and they were dispersed and sent forth to be, as it were, vagabonds on the earth, and so continue under the awful tokens of God's anger for many ages.

Explication on Romans 2:8–9 (Preached November 1735)

Rom 2:8–9, "But unto them that are contentious, and do not obey the truth, but obey unrighteousness, indignation and wrath, tribulation and anguish, upon every soul of man that doeth evil . . ."

'Tis the drift of the apostle in those three first chapters of this epistle to show that all, both Jews and Gentiles, are under sin, and thereof are in necessity of a savior and can't be justified by the works of the law but it must be only by faith in [Christ].

In the first chapter he had shown that the Gentiles were under sin. In this chapter he comes to the Jews and shows that they also are under sin . . . they themselves did the same things for which the apostle very much blames them. And [he] warns them [v. 1] not to go on in such a way by forewarning them of the misery they will expose them[selves] to by it, and giving them to understand that instead of their miseries being less than that of the Gentiles it would be the greater, for God [had] distinguish[ed] goodness to them above the Gentiles [v. 2]. The Jews had a notion that they could be exempt from the future wrath of God because [of this]. And then come in the verses wherein is the text.

The Jews thought that they should be exempt from future wrath because they were the nation that God had chosen to be his peculiar people, but the apostle informs them that there should be indignation and wrath and tribulation to every soul not only to the Gentiles but to every soul yea and to the Jews first chiefly to them when they did evil because their sins were more aggravated a description of wicked men.

1. Those qualifications here spoken of that have the nature of a cause and not obeying the truth but obeying unrighteousness. By their being contentious it meant their being contentious against the truth. Their quarreling with the gospel finds fault with the declarations and offers that are made to them in it.

Unbelievers find many things in the ways of God to stumble at and be offended at they are always quarreling and finding fault with one thing or other whereby they are kept from believing the truth yielding to it. Christ is to them a stone of stumbling and rock of offense so that they do not obey the truth, that is, they don't yield to it. They don't receive it with faith that yielding to the truth and embracing of it that there is in saving faith is called obeying in ss. *Rom. 6:17* obeyed that form of doctrine *Heb. 5:9.* became the author of eternal salvation. *Rom. 1:5.* Received grace and apostleship for the obedience of faith among all nations through his name, but they obey unrighteousness instead of yielding to the gospel. They are under the power and domination of sin and are slaves to their lusts and corruption.

2. The effect: they do evil. This is the first of their opposition against the gospel and their slavish subjection to their lusts

'Tis in those qualifications of wicked men that their wickedness does radically consist their unbelief and opposition to the truth and their slavish subjection to lust is the foundation of all wickedness. Those wicked principles are the foundation and their wicked practice is the superstructure. Those were the reasons and this is the fruit.

Secondly we may observe the principles not of wicked men in which we may observe the cause and effect. 1 Therefore things mentioned in their punishment that have the nature of cause, viz. indignation and wrath, is the indignation and wrath of God. 'Tis the anger of God that will render wicked men miserable. They will be the subjects of divine wrath, and hence will arise their whole punishment. The form of that punishment radically consists in this: that they are the subjects of divine wrath.

2. Those things in their punishment that have the nature of an effort, tribulation and anguish, [and] indignation and wrath in God, will work extreme trouble and anguish of heart in them.

Explication on Romans 2:10 (Preached December 1735)

Romans 2:10. "But glory, honor, and peace, to every man that worketh good."

The Apostle having in the two preceding verses declared what is the portion that the judge of all shall assign to wicked men viz. tribulation and wrath, he in this verse declares what is the portion assigned to good men, and we may observe in the words:

1. The description of a Godly man viz. the man that worketh good, they are here described by the fruit that they bring forth. Christ has taught us that the tree is known by its fruit the apostle describes them here by that which is not distinguishing of them. He don't describe them by any external privilege they enjoy as the light they live under, but the fruits they bring forth. For as the apostle says in the next verse but two not the hearers of the law are just before God, but the doers of the law shall be justified. That which distinguishes good from bad is not that they hear good, or that they profess good, [or] that they intend good, but that they do good. They are workers of Good.

2. The Reward of such viz. glory, honor and peace in which there are mentioned three sorts of good. That they have assigned their portion. 1. Their name expressed by that word glory. "Glory shall be given them," that is, they shall be made excellent and glorious. They shall be adorned with these excellent qualifications that shall render them glorious creatures. They shall have the image of God and be partakers of God's holiness and of the divine nature. Thus the word glory is used *2 Cor 3:18* we are changed from glory to glory.

2. Their relative good honor. They shall be in most honorable circumstances. They shall be advanced to great dignity in a relation to God and Christ and the heavenly inhabitants and God shall put honor upon them.

3. Their natural Good Peace which as is used in ss. signifies happiness and includes all comfort joy and pleasure.

Having already lastly shown what is the portion that God has assigned to wicked men from the two foregoing verses, I would now show what is the portion he has assigned to the saints from the words now read, the foundation of what I say upon this subject on this doctrine.

Sermon Explication on Romans 5:10 (Preached 1736)

Aug 1736.
Rom 5:10. "For if when we were enemies we were reconciled to God by the death of his son."

The apostle hitherto from the beginning of the epistle to the beginning of this chapter had insisted on the doctrine of justification by faith alone and having particularly spoken to that. In this chapter he goes on to consider the benefits that are consequent on justification.

There are hence benefits that flow from justification that are here spoken of viz peace with God and hope of Glory. Peace with God is mentioned in the first verse: "therefore being justified." In the following verses he speaks of hope of glory as a benefit accompanying justification. By whom also we have access into this grace wherein we stand and rejoice in hope of the glory of God.

Concerning this benefit of the hope of glory the apostle does particularly take notice of was this viz the blessed nature of this hope and the sure good of it.

1. He insists on the blessed nature of this hope that it enables us to glory in tribulations. Reward enables us patiently to bear tribulation and so this excellent nature of true Christian hope is described in the third, fourth and fifth verses. Through hope of a blessed reward that will abundantly more than make up for all tribulation we are enabled to bear tribulation with patience. We then bear tribulation with patient waiting for the reward. This brings experience of the earnest of the reward viz the earnest of the Spirit in our seeking the Love of God shed abroad on our hearts by the Holy Ghost so that our hope don't make us ashamed though we do bear tribulation. Our hope is not disappointed for in the midst of our tribulations we experience those blessed benefits of the Spirit into our souls that make even a time of tribulation sweet to us and is such an earnest as abundantly confirms our hope, and so experience works hope.

2. The apostle takes notice of the sure and abundant friend there is for this hope or the abundant evidence we have that we shall obtain that glory that is hoped for in that peace that we have with God in our

justification through Christ's blood. Because that which we were yet without strength in due time Christ died for us while we were ungodly and sinners enemies to God. The apostle's argument is exceeding clear and strong that if God has done already so great a thing for us as to give us Christ to die and shed his Precious blood which was the greatest thing. We need not doubt but that he will bestow life upon us after all this is already done. The giving of Christ to purchase it was natural. It included the whole grace of salvation. When Christ had purchased salvation at such a dear rate all the difficulty was got though all was truly over and done. 'Tis a small thing in comparison for God to bestow salvation after it has been thus purchased at a full price.

Sinners that are justified by the death of Christ are already truly saved. What remains is no more than the necessary consequence of what is done. Christ when he died made an end of sin, and when he rose from the dead he did vertually rise with the elect. He brought them up from death with him and ascended into heaven with them. Therefore when this is already done and we are thus reconciled to God through the death of his Son we need not fear. But then we shall be saved by his life. The love of God appears much more in giving his Son to die for sinners than in giving eternal life after Christ's death.

The Giving Christ to die for us is here spoken of as much as a much greater thing than the actual bestowment of life on two accounts.

1. That this is all that has any difficulty in it.

2. Then God did this for us he did it for us as sinners and enemies. But in actually bestowing salvation on us after we are justified we are not looked upon as sinners, for after we are justified God don't look on us any longer as sinners but as perfectly righteous persons. We are no more enemies for then we are reconciled. When God gave Christ to die for sinners he looked on them as they are in themselves; but actually bestowing eternal life he don't look on them as they are in themselves but as they are in Christ.

There are three epithets that are mentioned as in the text and context as appertaining to sinners as they are in themselves.

1. They are without strength. They can't help themselves. Verse 6: for while we were without sin . . .

2. That they are ungodly or sinners. Verses 6, 7, 8.

3. That they are enemies as in the text.

Sermon Explication on Romans 3:11–12 (Preached 1736)

ALL THAT NATURAL MEN DO IS WRONG

"There is none that understandeth, there is none that seeketh after God. They are all gone out of the way, they are together become unprofitable; there is none that doth good, no, not one." *Romans 3:11–12.*

The drift of the Apostle in all the former part of this epistle is to establish the doctrine of justification by faith in Jesus Christ alone, and to prove that no man can be justified by his own works. And to this end, from the beginning of the epistle to this place, he insists wholly on it to show that all that world are under sin, and for that reason can't be justified by their works, or by anything, but faith in a Savior. In the *Romans 1*, he showed how the Gentiles were under sin; in the *Romans 2*, he shows how the Jews are under sin; in the beginning of this chapter, he answers an objection; and in the *Romans 2:9*, he sums up the matter: "What then? are we better than they? No, in no wise: for we have before proved both Jews and Gentiles, that they are all under sin"; and then proves what he had insisted on out of the Old Testament: "As it is written, There is none righteous, no, not one: there is none that understandeth, there is none that seeketh after God. They are all gone out of the way, they are together become unprofitable; there is none that doth good, no, not one."4

The passages here quoted out of the Old Testament are to prove three things. First, that mankind are universally sinful, and that all of them are corrupt. This is chiefly aimed at in the *Romans 3:10–12*: "As it is written, There is none righteous, no, not one: there is none that understandeth, there is none that seeketh after God. They are all gone out of the way, they are together become unprofitable; there is none that doth good, no, not one." Second, that [they] are not only all corrupt, but that everyone is totally corrupt in every part. This is aimed at in the quotations in the *Romans 3:13–15*, where the several parts of the body are mentioned: the throat is an open sepulcher; the tongue is used for deceit; under the lips is the poison of asps; the mouth is full of cursing and bitterness; and the feet are swift to shed blood. Third, that everyone is not only corrupt in every part, but that in an exceeding degree, so as to have no goodness and only badness, and that to the most dreadful degree. And this is what is aimed at in the *Romans 3:16–18*: "Destruction and misery are in their ways: and the way of peace have they not known: there is no fear of God before their eyes." In the text there are five things predicated of natural men.

1. That they don't understand, i.e. they neither know God nor know how to seek or serve him. Natural men, many of them, are taught

concerning God and his ways, but they are without understanding. They neither know nor will they learn.

2. That they don't seek after God. Many of them seem to seek after God: they attend on the ordinances of religion; yea, and some of them have their minds very much engaged in it. But yet they don't seek after God. They may pray to God earnestly, and beg mercy of him; but yet they don't seek after God. They seek themselves, and not God.

3. That they are all gone out of the way. Natural men may, to outward appearance, be in the way of their duty. They may be very conscientious, and none that see them may be able to say but that they go in the way they should do. But yet in reality they are not in the right way, but are out of the way. Even in those very duties of religion that seem right to outward appearance, they are going on in wrong ways.

4. They are together become unprofitable. All natural men are unprofitable; they are unprofitable servants. Though some of them may seem to be religious, yet they don't serve God; but in all that they do, they serve other masters, yea, they serve God's enemies.

5. There is none that doth good, no, not one. Many natural men seem to do many things that are good: they attend in the matter of their duty strictly. Many do very much in religion. Some natural men do a great deal that is to the benefit of their fellow creatures: some natural men may be men of great good to the public. But yet there is none of them that doth good, no, not so much as one.

Sermon Explication on Romans 12:4–8 (Preached 1739)

DEACONS APPOINTED TO CARE FOR THE BODIES OF MEN ("On Occasion of the Ordination of the Deacons, Aug. 19, 1739")

Romans 12:4–8. "For as we have many members in one body, and all members have not the same office: so we, being many, are one body in Christ, and every one members one of another. Having then gifts differing according to the grace that is given to us, whether prophecy, let us prophesy according to the proportion of faith; or ministry, let us wait on our ministering: or he that teacheth, on teaching; or he that exhorteth, on exhortation: he that giveth, let him do it with simplicity; he that ruleth, with diligence; he that sheweth mercy, with cheerfulness."

In the words we may observe three things:

1. We observe what is the theme of the Apostle's discourse in these verses, namely, the different offices there are in the church of Christ, as in

the first of these verses: "For as we have many members in one body, and all members have not the same office." So in the sixth verse, he speaks of the different gifts that are exercised in the church in those different.

2. Here is an account of the business belonging to these several offices rehearsed in a variety of expressions: prophesying, teaching, exhorting, ruling, ministering, giving, showing mercy.

Concerning these businesses that the Apostle speaks of in this place as belonging to the different offices that are in the church, we may observe two things:

(1) That they all concern the welfare of the church, as it is in that to which the Apostle compares it, namely, the natural body. Different members of the body have different offices, but the office of every member is some way to subserve to the benefit of the body. So it is in the body of Christ: the different offices that are in it respect the benefit of the body, or of the church. The business that belongs to each officer in the society is to do good to the society, though the business of one office is to do good to the society in one respect, and another in another.

Thus, to prophecy, to teach, to exhort, and to rule is to do good to those that are taught, exhorted, and ruled. So to minister, give, and show mercy is still another way to do good to the members of the body. And

(2) It may be observed that all those businesses of officers in the church that are here mentioned are of two sorts. Some of them respect the souls of men and some their bodies. They all are to do good to the members of the society in which they are officers, but there are two ways of doing good to the society. One is to do good to their souls, and another is to do good to their bodies.

And 'tis observable that all the businesses here mentioned are one or the other of these. Prophesying, teaching, exhorting, and ruling all respect the souls of men. They are so many different ways of officers doing good to the souls of the society. But the other things mentioned—ministering, giving, and showing mercy—especially respect the good of their bodies.

So that there are two sorts of work of a distinct kind that the Apostle mentions when he reckons up the kinds of work that belong to the different offices in the church. One is to do good to the souls, and the other is to do good to the bodies of men.

And 'tis observable that all these businesses here mentioned that concern men's souls belong to the office of elders or bishops—prophesying, teaching, and exhorting, and ruling. The other therefore, namely, ministering, giving, showing mercy, that concerns the bodies of men, belongs to some other office Christ has appointed in his church. All three expressions—ministering, giving, and showing mercy—are only a diverse expressing the same thing. By ministering, as the word used in the New Testament is most commonly meant, [is] meant giving or communicating of our goods to others. So the apostle Paul, when he was going to Jerusalem to carry the contributions of other churches to the poor saints there, he says, *Romans 15:25*, "But now I go to Jerusalem to minister to the saints." So in *II Corinthians 8:4*, speaking of the same contribution, he says, "Praying us with much entreaty that we would receive the gift, and take upon us the fellowship of ministering to the saints." So when he exhorts the Corinthians to the same contribution, he says, ch. 9:1, "For as touching the ministering to the saints, it is needless that I write unto you." So when the Apostle commends the Christian Hebrews for their charity to the saints, he says, *Hebrews 6:10*, "For God is not unrighteous to forget your work and labor of love, which ye have showed towards his name, in that ye have ministered to the saints, and do minister." And so in innumerable other places that might be mentioned.

And therefore Mr. [Matthew] Henry, in his Annotations, says that when the Apostle says in the text, "or ministry, let us wait on our ministering," that he has respect to the office of deacons, as that is the general opinion of expositors and divines.

The word that is translated "deacons" is, in the original, *diakonoi*. The signification of the word is "they that minister." The name is taken from their business, which is to minister to the saints. This is the business spoken of here: "or ministry, let us wait in our ministering." The word ministry in the text in the original is *diakonia* or deaconship. Whence Mr. Henry argues that the office of a deacon is meant in the text. What this ministering is, is plainly signified in the following expression of "giving and showing mercy."

3. [The third] thing that is observable in the words is the counsel the Apostle gives to the different officers of the church well to execute the business of their offices, and to the church well to perform the business performed by their offices. Bishops or elders were to wait on their teaching, exhorting, and ruling, and the deacons on their ministering, giving, and showing mercy.

"Or ministry, let us wait on our ministering: [. . .] he that giveth, let him do it with simplicity; he that ruleth, with diligence; he that sheweth mercy, with cheerfulness." Which may be looked upon as an exhortation both to those officers of the church whose business it was to take care and minister to the saints, that should take the care and burden of their office and serve cheerfully as a work of mercy and charity, and do it with simplicity and faithfulness; and also to the church with respect to the work that they did by these offices, their showing mercy by them, that they should do it cheerfully.

Sermon explication on Romans 9:22 (Preached Nov 1741)

In these words we see what compellation the Spirit of God gives to some of the children. They are called "Vessels of Wrath." Concerning which, I would observe two things:

1. What is implied in the name or compellation by which some are called.

(1) It implies that they are of some use. By their being called vessels it appears that God has some use for them. Vessels are utensils; they are made for the use of the householder. The apostle observes that in a great house are various kinds of vessels: some precious and others mean, some for noble uses, others for very mean uses. *2 Tim 2:20*, "In a great house there are not only vessels of gold." The vessels of wood and earth, and vessels to dishonor, yet have their use as well as vessels of gold and silver.

(2) The use of vessels is to hold or contain something. If it don't answer its end this way, it is useless. That which contains nothing, don't answer its end as a vessel.

(3) Therefore, the use of vessels of wrath is to contain wrath, to be the subjects of wrath, and to be filled up with wrath, as if they answer their end no other way than by containing wrath. A vessel of wrath is fitted for that use, as 'tis said in the next words, "fitted to destruction"; and if a vessel of wrath is for no other use but that, it is otherwise of no use at all.

2. We may observe who they are who are thus called. And they are all those sinners [that] shall finally continue in impenitence and unbelief. There is respect in the verse to their great obstinacy in spirit and their final impenitency under all the means that are used with them; as is evident, because the apostle speaks of God's enduring them with much long suffering, i.e. long waiting upon them till they prove themselves desperately hardened and obstinate, and so till by their obstinacy under such merciful dealings, they are fitted for destruction.

Sermon Explication of Romans 5:21 (Preached Feb 1742)

One special design of the Apostle in these 7 last verses of this chapter is to show the grace of God in Christ and the blessed fruits of it, are exalted above men's sin and misery that come by Adam.

That the grace and the happiness that is the fruit of it is far beyond "[the offense of one]," v. 15.

Condemnation was of one offense, but "[the free gift is of many offenses unto justification]," v.16.

[The] reign of the saints in life by Jesus Christ shall far exceed the reign of death, v.17.

Then, in the 18th and 19th vss. The apostle shows wherein the manner of imputation is parallel in the two Adams.

But then, in these two last verses, he again shows wherein grace is exalted above men's guilt and misery.

[their] sin and misery is great, but the grace [of God] is greater.

The former is in such power as it might be said "to reign." And the latter reigns over that and over all.

Sermon Explication of Romans 8:29–30 (Preached 1739)

N Contribution Lecture December of 1739

Rom 8:29–30. "For whom he did foreknow he also did predestinate to be Conformed to the Image of his son that he might be the firstborn among many brethren moreover whom he did predestinate them he also called and whom he Called them he also Justified & whom he Justified them he also glorified."

In the Preceding verse the apostle says that all things work together for good to them that love God, to them that are the called according to his purpose. And there is an argument couched in these words to prove that it is so his mentioning that being called according to God's purpose carries in it an argument that all things that work together for them.

For without doubt everything shall conspire to the bringing about God's purposes for he that purposed has the ordering of all things and government of the world and therefore will order and govern all things so as shall tend to bring about his own designs and if that be God's purpose to make any a certain number of persons happy, everything shall be ordained agreeable to that purpose.

But this argument is more enlarged upon in the words that next follow, viz. the words of the text how God's gracious purposes with respect to his elect shall infallibly be accomplished, [and] how that eternal purpose is as it were a string and immoveable foundation on which their happiness is built, and how that in God's dispensations towards them one thing shall come to pass after another as in a chain that can't be broken in pursuance of that gracious purpose till the purpose has reached its highest—in the eternal glory of the elect for whom he did foreknow.

This is the argument that the apostle brings and that he come to the conclusion in the next verse what shall we say to these things if God be for us who can be against us? I.e. if God be for us after this manner in an eternal immutable purpose of making us happy and be answerably for us in his providence who or what can be against all things must be for us. And all things must work together for our Good which was the thing to be proved.

In the Text I would observe 1. The things that God hath done for the elect before their conversion he foreknew them and predestinated them to be conformed to the image of his son.

2. What he does for them at their conversion he calls them and justifies them and,

3. what he does for them afterward to eternity he glorifies them.

Sermon Explication of Romans 8:22 (Preached 1737)

April 1756 September 1737
Rom 8:22. "For we know that the whole creation groaneth and travaileth in pain together until now."

The apostle in the verses speaks of a twofold state that the church of Christ [are] in viz. a suffering state and a glorified state. If so be that we suffer with him that we may also be glorified together. The suffering state of the church is its present state the Christian Romans that the apostle wrote to were more than under suffering. Though Christians are, as the apostle says in the beginning of this verse, the sons of God and therefore heirs of God and joint heirs with Christ and so heirs of glory, yet at present they are not the possessors of this glory, but their present state is a suffering state and their state of Glory is reserved for hereafter.

The Reason why the state of the church in this world is a state of suffering is because this world is a sinful world. It is a world that is subject to the sins and corruptions of mankind.

The apostle encourages the Christian Romans under their sufferings with two considerations that the sufferings of their present suffering state are not worthy to be compared the Glory of their future glorified state v. 18.

And the other consideration that he encourages them with is the certainty of their glorified state that though now they were under sufferings yet their glory would come.

And there are several arguments that he makes use to show the certainty of it from this place to the end of the chapter, but the first is that the whole creation is as it were earnestly waiting for that time. [Vv.] 19, 20, 21, 22.

The passage of SS contained in these verses to be a difficult and obscure passage but yet if we diligently consider it taking notice of the scope and drift of the apostle and comparing it with the context the apostle's meaning in it seems to be very clear and plain. By the Creatures being made subject to vanity and brought into the bondage is meant the world in its present state being subject to the sin and corruption of mankind. This is the cause that the present state of the church is a suffering state and this is mentioned as the cause of it here. 'Tis because the world is its present state subjected to men's sins that the godly suffer reproach and persecution. By vanity in SS is very commonly meant sin as *Deut 32:21*, "They provoked me to anger with their vanities," and *Job 31:5*, "If I have walked with vanity," [and] *Psalm 10:7*, "Under his tongue is mischief and vanity and so in many other places."

So when the apostle speaks of the bondage of corruption he means the sinful corruptions of mankind. So the sin of man is often called in SS *1 Tim 6:5*, "Perverse disputings of men of corrupt minds," *Matthew 7:17*, "a Corrupt tree cannot bring forth good fruit," *2 Peter 1:4* "Have escaped the corruption that is in the world through lust," and so in many other places. The creatures are subjected to the sin and corruption of mankind and made, as it were, servants to it through the abusive use that man puts them to. Thus the sun is a sort of a servant to all manner of wickedness as its light and other beneficial influences are abused by men and made subservient to their lusts and sinful purposes, so of the rain and the fruits of the earth and the brute animals and all other parts of this visible creation. They are abused by sin and all from men's corruptions and God doth in a sort subject them to it, for he leaves them thus to be abused. He causes his sun to shine on the unjust and wicked world that improve its light only to serve sin by and causes the rain earth to bring forth ———[1] the ———. But that it is so is a kind of a force of the nature of the creature for the things of the world are good and not designed as servants to men's corruptions and therefore it is figuratively represented by the apostle as though the creature was subject to this bondage not willingly as though the sun did not shine to give men light to improve to serve their sins willingly as though the earth did not yield ———.

But by reason of him who hath subjected them in hope that it so is confusion and a sure sign that the present state of things is not lasting but shall come to an end God would not suffer it to be so but that he designs an alteration wherein he will put an end to this state wherein the creature shall be subject to men's sins no more seeing this to be but a little while. God chooses rather to subject the creature to men's corruptions than to disturb or interrupt the course of nature. But the creature would not be subject but that it as it were hopes for an alteration, i.e., God the author of nature would not subject were it not that he designed an alteration and therefore by a beautiful figure the creature is represented as burdened with its present bondage and earnestly the alteration or manifestation of the sons of God at the death of Jesus when this world shall be in subjection to men's corrupt wills no longer. In the text 'tis represented by two things

1. That the creation groans. It is a grievous bondage to it. It groans by reason of this hard bondage of serving men's lusts.

2 It travails in pain as though it were laboring to bring forth a better state of things. Though the world is now subject to the corruptions of men yet all things by the providence of God that orders them are working to bring about that glorious alteration wherein sin shall be spewed out and the sons of God shall be manifested and things shall come to rights when the creature shall no longer serve sins but shall be subservient to the holiness and happiness of God's church, that it will serve with delight. It is waiting and wishing as it were for this and laboring for it. Laboring to bring forth this blessed state as in travail. Labors to bring forth the fruit of the womb, 'tis said ——— until now for the creature was partly delivered from this bondage when Christ came and set up his kingdom by the preaching of the Gospel in the world and will be more fully delivered when the glorious times we are expecting shall commence and perfectly at the Last Judgment.

1. The dashes are in the original ms.

Sermon Explication on Romans 14:8 (Preached 1738)

Romans 14:8. "For whether we live we live unto the Lord and whether we die we die unto the Lord whether we live therefore or die we are the Lord's."

The occasion of what the apostle in this chapter writes to the Christian Romans seems to be certain differences and strifes that had risen among them concerning some of the observances of the ceremonial law, particularly concerning those sorts of food that were forbidden by that law and concerning those festival days that were therein appointed. There were many Jews that lived at Rome as appears by the last chapter of the Acts of the Apostles and some of the Christians that dwelt there that the apostle sends this epistle to had before been Jews and many of the Christian Jews that were in those days in all parts of the world after their conversion to Christianity were still very zealous of the observances of the ceremonial law and urged the same upon the Gentile converts. Hence arose a great difficulty in the church that was at Rome for held that it was now under the gospel lawful to eat those things that had been forbidden in the law of Moses and another held it unlawful. One held that the Jewish festivals were now abolished but another held that it was necessary to observe 'em still. Hence arose hot disputation among them to the wounding of their charity one towards another. Those that held it to be necessary to keep the Jewish festival days and to abstain from meats ceremonially unclean were ready to condemn others that used their liberty and freely made use of legally unclean meats and did not observe the Jewish festivals and look upon them impious and doing transgressions of God's commands and on the other hand the others that were sensible that in these gospel days there was no obligation lay upon Christians to observe these things were ready to despise those that were zealous of them for their weakness ignorance and superstition and therefore the apostle begins the chapter[—]1[st,] 2[nd, and] 3[r]d verses[—]and then the apostle proceeds to speak of their observation of festival days in verses 5 and 6. The apostle condemns their censuring one another and shews that there is room for charity on both sides notwithstanding such a difference of opinion with respect to things that were ceremonial and circumstantial. Because though their opinions and practice in these things was different yet both sides might be truly conscientious in what they did and might act from a religious regard to God's authority and glory. The one side was mistaken as to what God's commands were and therefore the apostle says v. 6. He that regardeth that day . . .

And then the apostle proceeds in verses 7 and 8. The apostle expresses his charity towards both these contending parties both they that abstained from legally unclean meats and observed legal festival days and those that did not both of them did out of a sincere regard to the will and glory of Christ because no man so far as a true Christian either lives or dies to himself. But is wholly Christ's for Christ he has denied and renounced himself as it were and he is now no more his own. His life is not his own he lives to Christ and so when Christ's time came and he sees it to be to for his glory to live no longer but to die and so he dies unto the Lord. So that he acts as one that is wholly Christ's whether living or dying by the Lord is here is meant Christ 'tis the second person of the trinity that is almost universally understood by that appellation of the Lord in the New Testament. So the discipline used to call Christ *Matt 21*. The Lord hath need of them. *Luke 24.34*. The Lord is risen. *John 20..2* They have taken away the Lord and we know not. Where v. 25. the other disciples said unto him we have seen the Lord and it may be observed through the New Testament.

Sermon Explication on Romans 11:7a (Preached August 1753)

Aug 1753
Romans 11:7. "What then? Israel hath not obtained that which he seeketh for . . ."

The subject that the apostle insists upon in this and the two foregoing chapters is the sovereignty of Divine Grace manifested in calling the gentiles and rejecting the greater part of the Jews. And also on the great difference that God made some of the Jews and others calling a small part of them while most of them remnant while most were rejected. Here in this context he is showing what made the difference namely sovereign Grace. Verses 5–6 say, "Even so then at this present time also there is a remnant according to the election of grace. And if by grace, then is it no more of works: otherwise grace is no more grace. But if it be of works, then it is no more grace: otherwise work is no more work."

In the verse wherein is the text, he sums up the matter in these words, "What then? Israel hath not obtained that which he seeketh for; but the election hath obtained it, and the rest were blinded." Tis the former part of the verse, that in which the subject spoken of is Israel by which is meant the bigger part of the nation that had been for so many ages the peculiar people of God and what is predicated of them is unsuccessfulness in their behavior or practice there is a certain endeavor or pursuit of theirs mentioned. There was something they sought after: before it was justification and salvation in the last chapter, but in [*Romans*] *9:31*, the apostle speaks of Israel's following after the Law of Righteousness. There we are told what they was that Israel sought after and what they sought after may be further learned by what the apostle desired and prayed they might obtain, [He says in *Romans*] *9:1*, "I say the truth in Christ, I lie not, my conscience also bearing me witness in the Holy Ghost . . ." and that which they sought after is the same the apostle in *Romans 11:6*, "And if by grace, then is it no more of works: otherwise grace is no more grace. But if it be of works, then it is no more grace: otherwise work is no more work."

3. Observe their unsuccessfulness in this pursuit though, that people in general sought after acceptance with God and eternal salvation. Yet the bigger part of them did not obtain what they sought for.

Sermon explication on Romans 11:7b

Rom 11:7. "But the election hath obtained and the rest were blinded."

I have already in speaking to the former part of the verse what that is that is spoken of as not being obtained by some namely acceptance with God and eternal salvation here spoken of namely the People Israel had alone been favored with means of Grace for a Great may ages and were a People that in the days of Christ and his Apostles were the first that were favored with the means of Grace and were strove with for some times the Apostles turned to the Gentiles Christ said he was not sent but to the Lost sheep of the House of Israel, *Matthew 15:24*, and the Apostles at first preached to the Jews only, *Acts 11:19*.

And even after the calling of the Gentiles was begun yet the Apostles wherever they came if there were any Jews there they made the first offer to the Jews in every city. They in the first place went into the synagogues of the Jews before they preached to the Heathen as we read from time to time of the apostle Paul.

In this latter part of the verse which I am now to insist upon we have an account of a very remarkable distinction that was made among this people with respect to the success of the Gospel among them and their obtaining that salvation that was offered. Though they were all the posterity of the same holy ancestors Abraham, Isaac, and Jacob, and though they were all favored alike with external privileges, and means of grace, and also all words we may observe:

1. The different not elected there is a great difference but originally there is no inherent difference. They are in themselves alike they have the same nature alike in their pedigree they descended of the same ancestors and were of the same nation and their advantages were the same they all had the same Gospel preached to 'em. Those that God of his sovereign good pleasure has been pleased to set his love upon from eternity and ordain 'em to eternal life, others he has left.

2. We may observe their different success in what they sought for. The election obtained those among that people that from eternity had been chosen of God to eternal life they obtained their justification and salvation. But the rest were blinded. Blind men wander in the dark and can't find what they seek for but weary themselves as the men of Sodom did when they were struck with blindness to find the door: they never find it and so never enter in.

Though there were many thousands of the Jews that in the Apostles' times were enlightened and brought home to Christ yet they were but few in comparison of the whole nation agreeable to the Prophecy of Isaiah which is cited by the Apostle in *Romans 9:27*, Though the number of the children of Israel be as the sand of the sea, a remnant shall be saved. All the rest but only that remnant were blinded and a little while suffered a terrible national destruction, and their posterity this very day.

Sermon Explication on Romans 11:10

Rom 11:10. "and bow down their back always."

The Apostle observes that the election had obtained mercy v. 7 and then it described the exceeding miserable state of the rest of them that were not elected the awful curse that they are under. The Curse that those among the Jews that were not elected were laid under we have in verses 8, 9, and 10.

This description is taken out of the Old Testament as is intimated by the words with which it is introduced in verse 8. The Curse here described consists of two parts:

1. A being given over of God to blindness.

2. A being given over of God to earthly and carnal mindedness.

The former part of their curse viz. their being given over to blindness and stupidity is described in verse 8 and in the former part of verse 10. (According as it is written, God hath given them the spirit of slumber, eyes that they should not see, and ears that they should not hear; unto this day).

Which words are of Isaiah. The latter part of their curse viz their being given over to a sensual earthly mind is described in verse 9.

And David saith, Let their table be made a snare, and a trap, and a stumblingblock, and a recompence unto them:

Psalm 69:22, Their table becomes a snare and a trap i.e their earthly enjoyments become a snare to them by possessing their hearts and by enslaving their affections. Thus these two parts of their curse are described in the two foregoing verses from different passages of the Old Testament. But then the verse of the text they are both described from one and the same passage of the Old Testament.

Let their eyes be darkened, that they may not see, and bow down their back alway. In the former part of the verse "Let their Eyes be darkened" is described as the former part of the curse viz their being given up to blindness and stupidity. In the latter part "bow down their back alway" is described the Latter part of their curse viz their being given over to a carnal and earthly mind. Their backs are bowed down always and their faces are forever set towards the earth to signify that their hearts are forever set upon men.

Psalm 69:23, Let their eyes be darkened, that they see not; and make their loins continually to shake. They shake & totter under the weight of the body as being unable to support it . The words in the text describe the weakness of their loins as backs unable to support the body in an erect posture. They are bowed down to the earth and have no strength to lift up themselves.

Their disease of soul that is here spoken of was represented by that disease of body that Christ cured in the woman that we read of in *Luke 13*, "And, behold, there was a woman which had a spirit of infirmity eighteen years, and was bowed together, and could in no wise lift up herself. And when Jesus saw her, he called her to him, and said unto her, Woman, thou art loosed from thine infirmity."

As I have often observed to you the diseases and calamities that Christ by his miracles healed persons of were all of them figures and representations of those spiritual diseases that he came into the world to heal men's souls of. And so doubtless this disease of the woman was a representation of that spiritual calamity spoken of in the text and that 'tis their hearts being bowed down and bent on the things of the earth. For which way do men's sensual and earthly enjoyments become a snare to them but by their setting their hearts upon them?

Sermon Explication on Romans 14:7–9 (preached 1740)

Rom 14:7–9. "For none of us liveth to himself and no man dieth to himself, for whether we live we live unto the Lord."

In these words may be observed:

1. Who they are that are here spoken of and they are Christians or the followers and disciples of Christ. None of us says the apostles liveth to himself, i.e., of us Christians those of us that are truly so as we profess to be.

2. We may observe with respect to what it is that Christians are here and that is two things viz their living and their dying.

[3] Declared both negatively and affirmatively 1) negatively none of us liveth to himself. 2) affirmatively for whether we live we live [unto the Lord].

4. We may observe the great privilege or benefit that Christians obtain by such a manner of living and dying and that is that whether they live or die they are the Lord's.

5. How such a privilege even by the death and resurrection of Christ for to this end Christ both died and rose and revived.

INDEX